INFLAMED

ABANDONMENT, HEROISM, AND OUTRAGE IN WINE COUNTRY'S DEADLIEST FIRESTORM

ANNE E. BELDEN
PAUL GULLIXSON

PERMUTED
PRESS

A PERMUTED PRESS BOOK
ISBN: 978-1-64293-936-1
ISBN (eBook): 978-1-64293-937-8

Inflamed: Abandonment, Heroism, and Outrage in Wine Country's Deadliest Firestorm
© 2023 by Anne E. Belden and Paul Gullixson
All Rights Reserved

Cover design by Tiffani Shea
Cover photo: A wheelchair rests amid the rubble of Villa Capri by John Burgess / *The Press Democrat*, published online October 17, 2017.

PERMUTED
PRESS

Permuted Press, LLC
New York • Nashville
permutedpress.com

Published in the United States of America
1 2 3 4 5 6 7 8 9 10

To our parents—Robert S. Chappell and Joanne Chappell, and Dorothy Gullixson and Conrad F. Gullixson—for modeling love, strength, and persistence throughout their lives and for reminding us of the blessings, hardships, and vulnerability in aging. Rest in peace, "poor old Robert."

CONTENTS

PART III: FALLOUT

MAPS AND DRONE PHOTOS

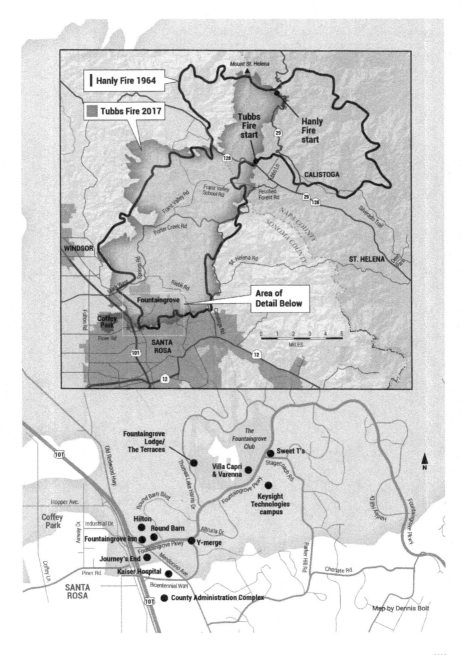

Varenna at Fountaingrove in 2017

Varenna and Villa Capri in May 2017, five months before the
Tubbs Fire and before Santa Rosa recorded its hottest summer
on record. The 29-acre hilltop complex includes 33 buildings
scattered across the ridge. Varenna residents lived in the
four-story Main Building, the three-level North and South
buildings, and 27 casitas. At Villa Capri, memory care residents
lived on the first floor while most assisted living residents
resided on the second floor.

500 feet

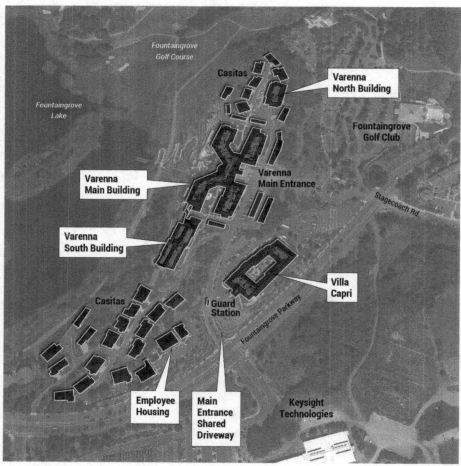

Source: Google Earth

Map by Dennis Bolt

An overview of the Varenna complex with Villa Capri
on the front right. *Photo by Donald Laird.*

Varenna overlooks Fountaingrove Lake. *Photo by Donald Laird.*

KEY INDIVIDUALS

Ages given are at time of fire.

Residents and Family Members

Villa Capri

Helen Allen—89, assisted living resident, second floor
  Mark Allen—66, son
  Kathy Allen—61, daughter-in-law
Bess Budow—92, assisted living resident, second floor, bedridden
  Sherry Minson—daughter
  Sarah Minson—granddaughter
Ruth Callen—92, assisted living resident, second floor
  Ruthie Kurpinsky—daughter
  Liz Schopfer—youngest daughter
Mary Lou Delaney—91, assisted living resident, second floor
  Tim Delaney—son
Alice Eurotas—84, assisted living resident, second floor
  Beth Eurotas-Steffy—daughter
  Gloria Eurotas—daughter
Inez Glynn—91, memory care resident, first floor
  Joey Horsman—grandson, Sonoma County sheriff's deputy, married
  to expectant wife Stacie
Virginia Gunn—81, assisted living resident, second floor
  Melissa Langhals—50, daughter, partner to Roxanne
Henrietta Hillman—90, Villa Capri's longest-term assisted living resident,
  second floor
  Corky Cramer—son

Margie Cramer—daughter

Arlyn Jacob—77, assisted living resident, second floor
Gena Jacob—52, daughter, former Fountaingrove Lodge marketing director, married to Sheri

Louise Johnson—87, memory care resident, first floor
Eric Johnson—son
Craig Johnson—son
Jonell Jel'enedra—daughter

Len Kulwiec—92, assisted living resident, second floor, president of the Residents Council
Michael Kulwiec—son

Bill and Wanda Lee—90 and 76, memory care residents
Dawn Ross—daughter

Noella "Nell" and John Magnuson—92 and 95, assisted living residents, second floor

Susie Pritchett—89, assisted living resident, second floor, lived with her parrot, Tiffany

Viola Sodini—82, memory care resident, first floor
Vivian Flowers—60, daughter

Varenna

Edel Burton—92, South Building third-floor resident, owner of dog, Abigail

John Hurford—91, Main Building first-floor resident
R.J. Kisling—42, grandson, married to Betty
Steffany Kisling—38, granddaughter

Katheryn Mann—86, Main Building third-floor resident

Bob Mitton and Mimi Vandermolen—73 and 71, North Building second-floor residents, owner of dog, Cocoa

Frank Perez—89, North Building first-floor resident

Sally Tilbury—89, South Building first-floor resident

Carole and Richard Williams—72 and 78, North Building second-floor residents

Oakmont Employees
Villa Capri
Deborah "Debie" Smith—48, executive director
Jane Torres—health and wellness director and registered nurse

Janice Wilson—Traditions Memory Care director

Tony Moreno—maintenance director

Barbara Lawler—concierge

Marie So—32, night shift med tech

Cynthia Arroyo—21, night shift caregiver

Elizabeth Lopez—30, night shift caregiver, at the time dating Juan Carlos Gonzalez

Anett Rivas—22, night shift caregiver

Elizabeth Bruno—long-term former activities director

Varenna

Nathan Condie—33, executive director

Andre Blakely—57, maintenance technician

Michael Rodriguez—26, maintenance technician

Chris DeMott—20, maintenance technician

Mika Alcasabas—21, dining hall server

Maria Joffely Cervantes—caregiver

Ma Teresa Martinez—caregiver

Alma Dichoso—caregiver

Oakmont Senior Living (OSL)

William "Bill" Gallaher—66, cofounder of Oakmont Senior Living and part owner of Oakmont Management Group, cofounded Aegis Assisted Living, chairman of Poppy Bank, general contractor, developer

Cynthia "Cindy" Gallaher—65, cofounder of Oakmont Senior Living, oversees interior/exterior design

Molly Gallaher Flater—daughter of Bill and Cindy, CEO of Gallaher Homes Management Group, COO of Gallaher Companies, Poppy Bank board of directors

Oakmont Management Group (OMG)

Chris Kasulka—president and CEO of Oakmont Management Group through summer 2018

Christian Holland—in-house counsel

Courtney Siegel—VP of operations, took over as president and CEO summer 2018

Ken Garnett—VP of operations

Tammy Moratto—regional sales marketer, former Villa Capri executive director

Joel Ruiz—senior regional maintenance specialist

Pouya Ansari—regional director of maintenance

Tony Ruiz—maintenance director

First Responders

Officer Andrew Adams—Santa Rosa Police Department

Firefighter Tony Albright—Mountain Volunteer Fire Department, married to Caroline Upton

Gary Basile—CityBus driver

Officer Orlando Macias—Santa Rosa Police Department

Sgt. Daniel Marincik—Santa Rosa Police Department

Officer Dave Pedersen—Santa Rosa Police Department

Sgt. Steven Pehlke—Santa Rosa Police Department

Capt. Tony Riedell—Mountain Volunteer Fire Department

Officer Eric St. Germain—Santa Rosa Police Department

Capt. Mike Stornetta—Windsor Fire Protection District

Firefighter Caroline Upton—Mountain Volunteer Fire Department, married to Tony Albright

Others

Monique Dixon—senior living industry expert, former executive director and operations specialist at Brookdale Senior Living, former director of senior living at Avalon Senior Living

Michael Fiumara—founding partner of Fiumara Law, personal injury attorney who sued Oakmont on behalf of several employees

Alex Giovanniello—Giovanniello Law Group, Oakmont attorney

Jill Ravitch—Sonoma County district attorney

Kathryn Stebner—Stebner and Associates founding attorney who filed three fire-related lawsuits against Oakmont and one class action suit about billing and staffing practices

NOTE TO THE READER

This book documents events leading up to, during, and following the October 2017 Wine Country Fires with an emphasis on the devastating impacts of the Tubbs Fire that swept through and around the area encompassing Varenna and Villa Capri, two senior living complexes in Santa Rosa, California. We began investigating this story in August 2018 after interviewing Melissa Langhals, a family member who rushed to Villa Capri to check on her mother, and seeing how her version of events contradicted the story Oakmont Senior Living was telling on a new website dedicated to defending the company's fire response.

During the course of researching and writing *Inflamed*, we interviewed more than 100 sources, from senior residents and their family members to present and former Oakmont employees and managers, as well as police and firefighters, and city, county, and state officials. We also talked to experts in emergency planning, assisted living, fire, weather, and climate science. Key sources were interviewed multiple times in person, over Zoom, and by phone, email, and text messages. We pored over thousands of pages of police and fire reports, city and county documents, newspaper and television reports, and social media feeds. We studied maps, photos, and body camera video and listened to hours of police and fire dispatch calls. Sources' trauma, post-traumatic stress disorder (PTSD), and fading memories resulted in some conflicts, and in these cases, we relied more heavily on statements made in the immediate aftermath of the disaster.

As part of our reporting, we were able to gain access to more than three dozen depositions that, before now, have not been made public and, after our acquisition of them, were subsequently sealed under the terms of court settlements identified within this book.

Not everyone present the night of October 8, 2017, or involved in the aftermath agreed to speak with us. Some lived with PTSD and did not want to relive events. Some feared losing their jobs, while others simply chose not to participate. And, as is the case when powerful people are involved, some feared retribution or legal action if they told their stories or shared their opinions and observations. In a few cases involving critical elements of the book, we agreed to give former employees or family members anonymity to obtain their stories.

We made multiple attempts—including texts, emails, phone calls, and certified mail—to reach certain current employees and corporate officials from Oakmont Senior Living and Oakmont Management Group for an on-the-record response to the facts and opinions expressed by former employees and residents. These attempts were unsuccessful. On December 16, 2021, two Oakmont Senior Living officials agreed to an off-the-record meeting, but only with co-author Anne E. Belden. After a two-hour meeting at OSL's Windsor, California, headquarters, Komron Shahhosseini, director of site acquisition and development for Oakmont Senior Living, and Brandon Cho, site acquisition specialist, told Belden that neither the corporation nor its employees would participate in the book project. OSL would not grant access to employees for interviews or comment on the record. Some former employees who had insight into the events that unfolded also declined to talk while others agreed to be interviewed.

Police dispatch transcripts and Nixle and SoCo alerts retain native errors to indicate the speed with which authorities operated. Dialogue is based on sources' recollections in interviews and depositions as to how events transpired. We attempted to verify whenever possible important conversations with others who were present. The endnotes elaborate on our sources and the reference material we used to compile this book.

Telling this story was like assembling a 10,000-piece puzzle with no clear image for guidance; no one person's narrative could tell all aspects of the story. While details of what occurred on the night of the fire remained fresh in the minds of most, for many sources their sense of timing was off, as is often the case with trauma, further complicating our efforts to put the pieces together. Whenever we could, we relied on timestamps from photos, videos, electric company records, and police transcripts to support our chronology of events.

To the best of our ability, we have recreated as narrative journalism the events before, during, and after the Tubbs Fire. We have tried to tell the stories of dozens of people whose lives intersected that terrifying night, with special attention given to those individuals—family members, frontline staff, and first responders—whose stories of courage and selflessness in the face of catastrophe have yet to be fully told or officially acknowledged. This is also a story about those whose persistence and quest for accountability in the fire's aftermath resulted in changes to laws, routines, and emergency practices in ways that still touch Sonoma County residents whenever the air is hot, dry, and windy. It is our hope these lessons will be shared and heeded far beyond the boundaries of Northern California and adapted for natural disasters apart from devastating wildfires to ensure, in particular, the protection of those most vulnerable.

"As long as no one is standing in its way, a wild-fire is a natural event. Put people in front of it, and it becomes the stuff of tragedy."
—John Maclean, *Fire and Ashes: On the Front Lines of American Wildfire*

PROLOGUE

October 9, 2017, 3:46 a.m.

Flaming embers, some the size of fists, whipped through the air as two women yanked at the handles of the heavy wooden doors. They wouldn't budge. The women shouted and pounded on the windows. They motioned to the elderly residents inside, pleading with them to open the doors, their fingers jabbing toward the brass handles. A propane tank exploded in the distance, punctuating the near-hurricane-force winds that blunted their cries for help. The power was out inside the building save for dim emergency lights illuminating the halls and casting a faint glow on the faces of the senior citizens lining the lobby. Most were in shock, having just been rousted from bed by strangers holding flashlights or glowing cell phones. Some wore robes or slippers while others arrived in the lobby barefoot, with only sheets covering their near-naked bodies. No one in the hazy lobby moved to let the women inside.

Kathy Allen and Melissa Langhals were locked out, and some two dozen elderly men and women—half in wheelchairs, half sitting on walkers—were trapped inside, incapable of helping themselves. Their home, a luxury assisted living and memory care facility in California's fabled Wine Country, was in the path of a titanic, fast-approaching firestorm, one that would prove to be among the most destructive and deadliest in state history. At that moment, flames were already eating away at the northeast side of the rectangular building.

The women had no key or pass card to the facility. Those who did, or those who could have buzzed visitors into the opulent complex of stucco walls and red-tiled roofs, had long since fled in vans or personal cars packed with other residents—or had never shown up at all. Kathy and Melissa, who'd only just met, were neither employees nor first responders. Besides having a family member who lived at Villa Capri Assisted Living and Memory Care, the only thing they had in common was the paralyzing conviction that no one was coming to help. They were on their own.

Kathy and Melissa peered inside at the elderly faces. Fourteen were residents of the memory care unit, having been admitted with varying degrees of Alzheimer's disease or some other form of dementia. One set of eyes staring back belonged to outspoken 91-year-old Henrietta Hillman, the self-described queen of Villa Capri for much of the past decade. Sitting near Henrietta was Alice Eurotas, a former legal secretary who resided in one of the few low-income rooms in Villa Capri, a place she navigated by walker and fondly called "my castle." Nearby in a wheelchair sat Louise Johnson, a former musician and local landscape artist, and a lifelong asthmatic. Diagnosed with advanced dementia, the mother of four lived behind secured doors in Villa Capri's Traditions Memory Care center.

Kathy and Melissa knew these people were not the only ones locked inside. Upstairs, still positioned on the second-floor landing overlooking the lobby, was the blind and nearly deaf Bess Budow, who had wailed when strangers carried her out of her room. Near Bess was Virginia Gunn, Melissa's mother, paralyzed on her left side, unable to roll over in bed without help, who was now seated in her wheelchair. Melissa had wanted to get her mother out right away when she arrived an hour and a half earlier, but Virginia insisted her daughter take care of others first. "I'll be all right," Virginia assured her.

Four additional residents waited in wheelchairs on the landing beside Virginia and Bess as the temperature rose and emergency lights could no longer cut through the heavy gray haze. But without electricity or backup power, Villa Capri's elevator was out of commission, leaving the six elderly residents with no way down unless they were carried. Given Kathy's recent back surgery and Melissa's recent hip replacement, that was nearly impossible. Outside, the smoke thickened and embers grew more frequent, flung into the air as if by bellows pumping 70-mile-per-hour winds. In desperation, Kathy flipped over her flashlight and used its butt end to strike a heavy blow at the windowpane. Nothing happened. Again she rammed it into the glass, this time with greater force. Nothing, not even a crack.

Even if Kathy and Melissa could get back inside, they had but a single car between them. A bus large enough to carry all the remaining residents sat locked in the parking lot, but no one, not even the frightened Villa Capri employees they encountered earlier in the evening, knew where to find its keys. Kathy and Melissa were running out of options—and time. The firestorm would soon surround them on three sides. Even the driveway marking their exit to Fountaingrove Parkway appeared to be on fire. The blaze was so intense that the slivers of grass in the median and the trees and shrubbery on each side of the road were aflame.

Villa Capri had promised around-the-clock care for as much as $12,000 a month, but in the darkness foisted upon them by the power outage, its residents were trapped, and their "castle," known for its fine china, chandeliers, and elegant furnishings, had transformed from a palatial complex that pledged to care for them to one threatening to entomb them.

In the past six hours, the Tubbs Fire had already claimed more than a dozen lives and consumed thousands of homes, shops, offices, hotels, and historic structures within a nine-mile radius of Villa Capri and its sister complex, Varenna. The bulk of the residents from the surrounding tony Fountaingrove neighborhood had already fled their multimillion-dollar homes. Villa Capri's table-top perch, a broad shelf of land cut into the hillside above Fountaingrove Parkway, typically afforded views across the Santa Rosa basin. But smoke shrouded the expanse, so Kathy and Melissa could see little of the devastation smoldering beyond the burning shrubs and hillside grapevines abutting the complex. And there was no sign of emergency vehicles coming to help.

As Kathy and Melissa stood stymied, a brown GMC Sierra pickup pulled into the narrow, shared driveway and raced past Villa Capri toward the entrance of the larger but equally opulent Varenna, located just a few hundred feet to the northwest. Behind the wheel was Petaluma welder R.J. Kisling, who, encouraged by his sister, had come to check on their grandfather. Varenna was dark, with just a few vehicles in the lot, and R.J. was relieved. It bolstered the assurance he offered his sister an hour earlier, a conviction shared that night by many family members and friends of Varenna and Villa Capri residents: "Certainly they would have found a way to get everybody out by now."

R.J. called his sister back to tell her he'd arrived and the place looked empty. "Are you sure?" she challenged him. "Go check [Papa's] apartment." R.J. did as she pleaded, exiting his truck, pulling on his headlamp, and stepping into Varenna's sweeping foyer. Normally during his arrival, R.J. was struck by a sense of opulence thanks to the lavish decor. The building's Romantic Italian aesthetic was not one he favored, but he knew Papa and the other residents appreciated it.

This time, however, it wasn't the grand setting that grabbed R.J.'s attention. It was the faces. Beyond the double doors, Varenna's dark and smoke-filled lobby was packed with residents, some sitting on chairs or benches, others perched on couches and walkers. It was just about a quarter to four in the morning when one gentleman rose from a chair near the café and approached R.J.

"Are you the firefighters?" he asked calmly. "Are you here to rescue us?"

PART I
FOOTPRINTS

1

Hanly

Fifty-three years before

Early on the morning of September 19, 1964, a deer hunter walking on a wooded slope in upper Napa Valley flicked a smoldering cigarette into the brush. Aided by a breeze and brittle-dry conditions, the discarded butt soon ignited the grass and surrounding vegetation. The fire grew with ferocious intensity. By 10:15 that Saturday morning, flames could be seen from nearby "Hanly's-on-the-Mountain," a popular local tavern located along Highway 29 toward Mt. St. Helena. The fire "was not thought to be too serious at the time," according to local newspaper columnist Harriett Madsen. "The Calistoga Fire Department responded and held the situation until the [California Department of Forestry] units began arriving. The fire, during that day, was contained in about 40 acres of timber and rocks."

But what soon was dubbed the Hanly Fire refused to be quelled. Fanned by ever-increasing winds, it swelled and moved south toward the town of Calistoga, picking up speed as it devoured the oak woodland in its path. Help from additional fire departments was hard to come by because Northern California's fire season was in full swing thanks to a foreboding series of environmental conditions. As any Boy Scout will tell you, starting a fire requires three key components: fuel, heat, and oxygen, and conditions that Saturday in Napa and Sonoma counties presented the trifecta.

The combination of fierce wind, high temperatures, low humidity, and dry vegetation created the potential for explosive fires everywhere. And explode they did. During the last two weeks of September 1964, some 94 forest fires burned through Mendocino, Lake, Napa, and Sonoma counties and through the mountainous areas of Solano County to the east. But the most ominous of those was the Hanly Fire, one that capitalized on the dry air, high winds, and brittle shrubs and trees of the Mayacamas Mountains— all thanks to an abandoned cigarette.

As Saturday wore on, 70-mile-an-hour wind gusts threatened to scatter the Hanly Fire in multiple directions. One structure immediately at risk was the Tubbs mansion that, for the better part of the twentieth century, welcomed westbound travelers dropping into Napa County along the sinuous two-lane highway from Lake County. The sprawling, gabled residence stood in a grove of redwood and eucalyptus trees and was a symbol of the emerging elegance of an area called the Redwood Empire, named for the rich timber industry fed by the region's enormous, ancient trees.

Alfred Lovering Tubbs built the Tubbs mansion in 1888 for $100,000, a considerable sum given that land in Napa and Sonoma counties could be had at the time for roughly $25 an acre. As with many well-to-do entrepreneurs before and since, Tubbs accrued his fortune in San Francisco, where he established a rope-manufacturing company following the Gold Rush but sought refuge on holidays and summers in the natural splendor of the Redwood Empire. In 1882, he purchased 254 acres in Calistoga at the base of Mt. St. Helena, where he built the regal hideaway for himself and his family. "The house was a beautiful three-storied country manor, whose mellow charm reflected all that was elegant and plush in the America" of the time, one local reporter recalled years later.

Tubbs also built a wood-frame winery with a reported capacity of 150,000 gallons and then traveled to France to learn winemaking. The winery, christened Chateau Montelena, was said to be the seventh largest in Napa Valley and, endowed with tens of thousands of grapevine cuttings from a few of France's most esteemed wineries, produced wines that were said to rival any in Europe. Ultimately, Chateau Montelena would prove that point to the world in 1976, when its chardonnay—mixed with a blend of grapes grown in Napa and Sonoma—beat multiple French wines in a blind tasting now referred to as the Judgment of Paris. The competition put Napa Valley on the winemaking map. But the Tubbs family's association with the winery had long since dissolved, the family having sold its final interest in the property in 1958, six years before the Hanly Fire.

For two days, firefighters and volunteers armed with garden hoses, buckets, and wet gunny sacks waged war against the Hanly Fire, and by Monday, the blaze had ebbed. California Governor Edmund G. Brown toured the footprint by plane and quickly declared it a disaster area. Calistoga residents thought it was over, but professional firefighters didn't trust the fire, and for good reason. It soon ignited again with a fury. "This is the craziest fire I've ever seen," Grant King, chief of the Guerneville Fire Department, told a *San Francisco Chronicle* correspondent. "The wind just hangs back, then fire comes in a rush with the wind, and you're dead."

Locals tried to help where they could, according to newspaper accounts. Among them was teenager Edd Vinci of Sonoma County's Rincon Valley, who, along with two friends, headed south Monday afternoon from their Santa Rosa neighborhood to the Forestry Station in Glen Ellen. They believed Glen Ellen, a tiny town nestled in the densely wooded hills flanking Sonoma Valley, to be in more danger than their homes. "You the boys from Rincon?" a fire captain asked the teens as they arrived. They confirmed they were. "You better get your butts back home," he ordered. "The Calistoga Fire is heading to Santa Rosa fast." Edd and his friends had been wrong in their assumption, so they hopped on a northbound engine headed for Sonoma County's largest city and county seat.

Later that Monday night, after Edd and his buddies made the drive back to Santa Rosa, the winds picked up again, driving the fire southwest from Calistoga over the Mayacamas Mountains that separate Napa and Sonoma counties. According to local historian Jeff Elliot, "Before that day was over, the 16-year-old Edd Vinci would face a wall of flames rushing towards him faster than he could possibly run, and in that moment felt certain he was about to die."

Witnesses claimed the flames created their own wind as the fire moved west, traveling at roughly 40 miles per hour through the wooded mountains. Along the way, the firestorm destroyed clusters of homes along Mark West Springs and Riebli roads and tore through the small community of Wikiup. With terrific speed, the Hanly Fire was suddenly on the ridgelines overlooking Santa Rosa.

As it made its way toward the city, the fire approached the Sonoma County Hospital located on a former working farm amid a pastoral landscape of hills and knobby oaks on Chanate Road. It was here that Santa Rosa Fire Department Fire Marshal Mike Turnick decided to draw the line in the battle against the flames. Either the fire would sweep through the hospital campus and down into the heart of the city, or it would be stopped right there. It was all or nothing.

Turnick commandeered a bulldozer, cut down a swath of trees north of the hospital to create a break in the forest, stationed fire engines along its length, then turned his dozer uphill to cut another break, depriving the fire of fuel. As Turnick finished the job, trees exploded from the fire's heat and pressure, and deer, rabbits, and coyotes ran down Chanate Road to escape the flames. But he had succeeded in halting the fire's fierce progression toward downtown Santa Rosa. More importantly, he stopped the blaze just 100 yards shy of the hospital. Turnick was celebrated as a hero.

The Hanly Fire had been deprived of its southeast momentum but not its destructive capability. It pivoted west, burning downhill and along open fields and sloped grasslands. It left unscathed the Fountaingrove Round Barn, a burgundy circular icon that had survived the 1906 earthquake and stood as a landmark at the city's north entrance. The fire churned toward Mendocino Avenue and Highway 101, which at the time cut through downtown, two lanes in each direction. Once there, at the edge of the asphalt, the fire stopped in its tracks, just across the street from a trailer park called Journey's End.

Miraculously, no one was killed, but the Hanly Fire was the most destructive the North Coast had ever recorded, destroying 53,000 acres, 84 homes, 24 summer cabins, and untold outbuildings on farms and ranches. Calistoga residents returned to their evacuated town to find 80 buildings reduced to ash, among them the majestic Tubbs mansion. The estate would not be rebuilt, but many of those homes and cabins would be, and by spring 1965, the charred hills and craggy ridgelines were once again green after a typical chilly, wet, North Coast winter.

The flames were out, but debate over lessons from the Hanly Fire raged across Sonoma County, and never was it more intense than in the 1970s and '80s when developers sought to push the urban limits of Santa Rosa and build homes inside the Hanly burn scar. One target was the hillside where the Hanly crested, the hillside just before the Sonoma County Hospital and above the city center, in an area called Fountaingrove, an alluring expanse of natural wonder with rambling woodlands, hidden lakes and ponds, and breathtaking vistas. Mother Nature had already left her fiery mark here, and now developers wanted to stake their claim to the ridge.

2

Utopia

The building of Varenna and Villa Capri: 2004, 13 years before

The northern ridgeline overlooking Santa Rosa had for decades been seen in idyllic terms. The hills had once belonged to enigmatic spiritual leader and vintner Thomas Lake Harris, who boasted more than 1,000 followers on two continents but chose this particular hilltop setting to build one of the more successful 19th-century American utopian communities. When the settlement's residents put down roots in 1875, they called the area "the Eden of the West," boasting of grounds "planted with exotic shrubs and trees which flourished on the hillside," wrote founding member Arthur A. Cuthbert. They christened the area Fountain Grove "because high among the hills was an exceptionally abundant spring of flowing water."

The first homes built in this bucolic setting were majestic and memorable. The *Sonoma Democrat* noted in November 1875, "Mr. Harris came from New York about seven months ago and commenced immediately to erect…a residence, which surpassed anything in Sonoma County for its architectural beauty and magnificent design. If Mr. Harris carries out the designs he has now in contemplation, he will have one of the most picturesque and beautiful places north of the [San Francisco] Bay." According to Sonoma County historians Gaye LeBaron and Bart Casey, Harris named the majestic house Aestivossa, which he said meant "high country of divine joy" in a language only he could understand. Harris left his leadership role and departed for England a year later. Yet, the historians wrote, "Fountain Grove remained important as a destination for famous visitors and a gathering place for Santa Rosa's elite, including politicians and townspeople such as Luther Burbank," the famed botanist.

Harris' successor, Kanaye Nagasawa, continued operating a vineyard and winery in the hills. Despite the winery becoming one of the top 10 in the state and the first to sell California wine on the East Coast and in Europe, a subsequent owner uprooted the vineyards and used the land to raise cattle. Eventually, the property fell into the hands of a polo player and horse breeder named Robert Walter, who saw something far more profitable than grapes or cattle for those rolling hills—housing development.

Environmentalists immediately objected to his plans. Many wanted to see the land, known for panoramic views of the Santa Rosa plains, preserved for residents' enjoyment. But development began anyway, starting with a project proposed by two engineers named Bill Hewlett and David Packard. They came to town in 1972 seeking to use 200 acres on the hill to expand their Palo Alto-based operations. Given the promise of the lucrative jobs on a state-of-the-art campus, county leaders quickly approved the plans.

The seminal shift in the neighborhood's future, however, came in the 1980s and '90s with proposals for hundreds of luxury homes to be constructed in the southern portion of the former commune-turned-cattle ranch. One project called for a 2.4-mile highway spur over the ridgeline to connect the bedroom communities of the east, such as Rincon Valley, with the growing job centers of north Santa Rosa. Planners spelled out how this would be the first leg of a proposed "beltway" circling the city and improving traffic flow around the community.

Opponents not only feared the new thoroughfare would encourage and accelerate growth—like a trellis nurturing a grapevine—they also worried the roadway and buildings would mar the unspoiled views from the valley below. Nonetheless, the widened thoroughfare, originally named "Fountain Grove Parkway" in honor of the commune's winery, was approved and opened in 1997 at a cost of $23 million. As expected, it ignited a new enthusiasm for the area.

"Through a series of owners, each with their own plans—some more grandiose than others—Fountaingrove emerged in the new century [with] a high-end golf course around the lake, two hotels, and high-end homes, dubbed McMansions by the flatlanders, growing more expansive and expensive as they moved upward and north and east into open land beyond the ranch boundaries, ultimately going all the way to Mark West Springs

Road," LeBaron and Casey wrote. And despite promises from city planners and elected officials that the development would not be seen from below, it was clearly visible.

In 2001, community outrage over Santa Rosa's ridgetop development reached its apex. A cascade of criticism triggered a city analysis of hillside developments that found Santa Rosa city planners had indeed erred in their interpretation of building policies when approving construction. As a result, planners had inappropriately allowed developers to build homes along more than a dozen prominent ridgelines. But there was nothing to be done, other than promise it wouldn't happen again. The City Council adopted new get-tough policies, restrictions that prohibited ridgeline development, and it forbade construction on any slope with more than a 25 percent grade. For the most part, the new rules shut down new projects—with at least one major exception.

A prominent local developer went before Santa Rosa city planners in 2004 with the goal of creating a special type of residence, a retreat of sorts, on the ridge. The project would be the area's largest and most opulent housing project since the construction of Aestivossa 130 years earlier. Like Thomas Lake Harris, this new developer sought to create a utopia for his residents, a luxurious retirement complex on 29 acres of the same land Harris's disciples once called the Eden of the West. The plan and its later addition called for more than 170 housing units to include 28 freestanding houses, 126 apartments, 20 employee housing units, a 63-unit assisted living facility with a memory care center, and a 7,500-square-foot common area all situated in a place still regarded as paradise.

He looked to Italy for inspiration, naming the complex Varenna and its assisted living and memory care center Villa Capri, after a small town on Lake Como and an island in the Bay of Naples, respectively, signaling that he would imbue the design and ethos with a Mediterranean air. The developer was William "Bill" Gallaher.

***

When Bill Gallaher unveiled blueprints in 2004 for Varenna and Villa Capri, he was not just planning. He was surfing, riding a massive wave known as the "Silver Tsunami." A 2002 study by the U.S. Department of Health and Human Services concluded that by 2030, America's senior population, defined as anyone 65 or older, would more than double to 70 million people. At the time, the older population represented one in every eight Americans. By 2030, thanks to aging Baby Boomers, that ratio would become one in five. California was at the forefront of these shifts. By 2040, the Golden State's over-65 population is expected to nearly double and will include high percentages of childless and single adults who will need support services in lieu of younger family members or partners caring for them. Few counties in the state will be more impacted by this demographic tidal wave than Sonoma County. By 2030, the number of county residents over 65 was expected to rise by more than 40,000, with single women over 70 as the largest subgroup.

Like many other business leaders and investors, Gallaher recognized these shifts presented scores of business opportunities. No opportunity was more potentially lucrative than housing, and no demographic had more accumulated wealth than those embodying the Silver Tsunami. Despite the 2007 economic downturn, seniors born between 1925 and 1947 entered their golden years in strong financial shape. Between 2013 and 2016, the Silent Generation saw a 60 percent increase in mean net worth. *Forbes* magazine reported: "The Silent Generation holds roughly 1.3 times the amount of wealth as Boomers, more than twice that of Xers, and 23 times that of Millennials." Many of the seniors moving to the North Bay wanted to retire in luxury for one simple reason: they could.

Seeing what was coming, Gallaher had partnered with a friend in 1997 to form a company that would develop and operate assisted living and dementia care facilities. The company, Aegis Assisted Living, had two primary divisions, one that built the complexes and another that managed caring for the residents, with each partner responsible for the side of the business he knew best. The company grew rapidly, and for several years in the early 2000s, *Washington CEO Magazine* listed Aegis Assisted Living the winner or a finalist in its "Best Company to Work For" category. In 2003, INC Magazine rated Aegis the third fastest-growing private company in America.

By the time Gallaher proposed Varenna, he and his Aegis partner Dwayne Clark had already built 30 senior housing complexes, but none was as large or as elaborate as the project they planned for the lot that stood just above the Fountaingrove Golf and Athletic Club. "If you're a senior who wants to live on your own, this is probably not the place," Gallaher told the *Press Democrat* in 2004. "Residents will be eating in the main dining room together.... It promotes socializing and companionship."

This kind of socializing was intended only for a discriminating clientele, one looking for a lifestyle akin to passage on a five-star ocean liner. When completed, the community would include a library, movie theater, fitness center, indoor and outdoor pools, bank, beauty salon, and—in keeping with its Wine Country location—an ornate wine cave used for storing private reserves and hosting intimate dinner parties. To the west, the complex came with an expansive view overlooking Fountaingrove Lake, with a funicular-style cable car that transported residents down to a dock jutting into the lake. Residents could employ staff to walk their dogs, do their laundry, and chauffeur them into town.

When Varenna first accepted applications, one-time buy-in fees ranged from $300,000 to more than $1 million, in addition to monthly fees starting at $2,500 and rising to $4,900 depending on the Italian-named floor plan chosen. The Livorno apartment was the smallest model at 536 square feet, and the Portofino the largest at 2,750 square feet, with 19 layouts of various sizes in between. For those who wanted a bit of distance, Varenna also offered 2,540-square-foot Umbria "casitas," or stand-alone houses. The prices were not off-putting. On the day Varenna executives began accepting deposits in August 2004—four years before the complex would open—a line had already formed outside the door of a temporary office. The first gentleman to enter, a Bodega Bay resident, said he had waited for 29 hours.

City planners acknowledged the complex exceeded the new slope restrictions, but they were divided over whether it would be visible from the flatlands. Of course it would be, opponents argued. After all, the buildings would be more than 40 feet high in places and would be positioned on a prominent ridge overlooking Fountaingrove Lake and houses on the city's west side. "I'm ecstatic about 70 percent of the project, but 30 percent of it does not meet our hillside guidelines," Planning Commissioner Shaun Faber said at the time.

Yet commissioners approved both projects on April 29, 2005. Afterward, Chairman Scott Bartley said it came down to weighing competing objectives: "[housing for] seniors and the preservation of hillsides." As he laid it out to reporters, "Sometimes you have to pick between the two." But no sooner had construction begun than the blowback came rolling in. "Is the city of Santa Rosa expecting an invasion, thereby granting the building of the Varenna fortress on Fountain Grove Parkway across from Agilent?" wrote a Santa Rosa resident in the *Press Democrat*. "It has the castle walls; what's next, the moat?"

Many locals would later look back and wonder how Varenna and Villa Capri were given the green light during an era of such magnified controversy about Fountaingrove development. As to how this imposing project was approved, many credit—or blame—the political acumen and persistence of Gallaher and Aegis Assisted Living. The company had brilliantly built public support by taking out a series of newspaper advertisements pushing the merits of the project and sending mailers to local senior citizens extolling the project's virtues, all to build anticipation and encourage sign-ups before the plans were even approved. The campaign underscored the growing need for senior housing in the region. This kind of housing was not just wanted, the mailers claimed, it was needed.

The Gallaher team worked hard in other ways as well to ensure their plans came to fruition. Along with family members and business associates, Gallaher donated to City Council members who were receptive to the project and some who were up for reelection that year. Combined, the group donated $22,500 to four council candidates. Three of the four won. In hindsight, one point everyone seems to agree on is that in all the discussion about the Varenna and Villa Capri projects—about slopes, traffic, and impacts on views—little to nothing was said about the threat of wildfire, despite the fact the site sat squarely in the path of the most destructive fire in North Coast history, one that had visited just 40 years earlier. The focus in 2005 was on the impact the senior complex would have on the natural environment, not on what impact the natural environment might have on the complex—or its residents.

3

Halcyon Days

Ten years before

In May 2007, Elizabeth Bruno watched as her grand opening festivities came together and the handful of seniors who moved into Villa Capri on opening day enjoyed balloons, catered food, and an old-time blues band she had arranged to greet them. Though only a few residents occupied the Mediterranean villa–style rooms at the time, Elizabeth lined up a regular schedule of activities and classes for them, including yoga, Tai Chi, painting, crafts, and pet classes for those with dogs or cats. Within months, she was planning events for 20 residents, and by the end of the first year, all 63 units were occupied. Varenna would not open for another year, so Villa Capri anchored the complex despite being the smaller of the two facilities.

As activities director, Elizabeth worked alongside Bill Gallaher and his wife, Cindy, to build a vibrant assisted living community. Cindy—whose own mother would move into Villa Capri—pulled weeds from the planters, and once a year, Bill personally handed out Christmas bonuses. "It was like a family," Elizabeth said, and the newly opened facility was her second home. "I took care of that building like my own," she said.

The family feel permeated both the community and its parent company, Aegis Assisted Living, a partnership formed by two friends who leveraged each other's strengths. According to a former high-ranking marketing employee, "Dwayne [Clark] handled the care side, and Bill handled the construction. Bill would build the buildings and hand the keys to Dwayne to do day-to-day operations."

The focus of those operations during Villa Capri's first years seemed to be on residents' quality of life, and Elizabeth Bruno was the heart of it all, the source of joy who not only kept them busy and engaged but got to know them personally. Such was the case with Henrietta Hillman, who, along with her second husband, initially plunked down a deposit on Varenna. But Joel's health declined, so they opted for Villa Capri and eventually moved Joel into its memory care unit until his death two years later.

Henrietta considered herself above the daily activities and was selective in her friend making. But everyone knew her, and some called her "Spike," a reference to Snoopy's desert-living brother in the *Peanuts* cartoons. Henrietta wasn't a *Peanuts* fan, but she did project a tough-guy image. An Ivy League–educated world traveler, she fit the classic New Yorker stereotype: outspoken, sarcastic, and liberal-minded. She was once married to music-business royalty, the former president of music publishing giant BMI.

Henrietta's first husband, Edward Cramer, represented Irving Berlin, Rodgers and Hammerstein, Aretha Franklin, Dolly Parton, Whitney Houston, the Bee Gees, The Beatles, and other Broadway and Hollywood greats. Family photos captured him with Michael Jackson, and Henrietta with Paul Simon. They counted Dizzy Gillespie as a friend. Henrietta was not so easily impressed with most of the movie stars and musicians, although she did like John Lennon. "He was more than nice," she said. "He was a human being."

In the early 1970s, Henrietta crossed paths with a college flame and soon after asked her husband for a divorce. She had dated both Edward Cramer and Joel Hillman at Cornell but had chosen the handsome, top-of-his-class lawyer-to-be Edward over the worldly and fun-loving Joel. In 1974, after having married and borne two children with Edward, Henrietta married Joel, "a true gentleman with a fabulous sense of humor," Henrietta's son Corky Cramer said. Joel spoiled her with jewelry, flowers, and candy. "My mom got really fat when she was married to Joel," her daughter Margie Cramer said. Perhaps it's no wonder why, as her daughter explained, Henrietta "thinks she's the queen."

When Henrietta ate meals in the Villa Capri dining room, she would purposely arrive late to make an entrance. Henrietta reminded Elizabeth Bruno of her Italian grandmother, "very strong and staunch and no BS," and because she never hesitated to offer her opinion to anyone and everyone. Even the waitstaff and chefs frequently heard Henrietta's culinary reviews.

Though she skipped Villa Capri's art and exercise classes in favor of doing the *New York Times* crossword puzzle on her own, Henrietta did strut the catwalk for one of Elizabeth's fashion shows, adorned in a stylish new outfit with her hair slicked back. She also followed the activities director on a few field trips, most notably the one arranged just for her, a night at the San Francisco Opera. Henrietta "dressed to the nines" and was in her element, relishing an evening that included a posh dinner out with a handful of other residents.

It was the kind of personalized special event that Elizabeth Bruno repeated over and over again for the residents: discover what they love, then create an event or party with that theme. So when an Oakmont regional activities director announced "Bucket List Week," a corporate challenge encouraging staff to make dreams come true for residents, it was Elizabeth Bruno's moment to shine.

When a couple with dementia desired to return to Hawaii, Elizabeth set up a canopy and lounge chairs at a Bodega Bay beach, adorned everyone with leis, and served Mai Tais. Dorothea Collins wished to be a princess for a day, so Elizabeth Bruno took her to a farm, crowned her, and had her driven in a horse-drawn carriage. Mary Lou Delaney had always wanted to ride in a biplane, so the overachieving activities director arranged a flight in an open-cockpit red biplane and bedecked the 89-year-old with a leather bomber jacket, aviator hat, goggles, and a beige scarf. A bus full of residents drank champagne and cheered Mary Lou as her two sons pushed her onto the wing so she could climb into the front of the cockpit. After landing, Mary Lou, who had earned her pilot's license some 45 years earlier, beamed as she posed for photos in her aviator gear.

There was also the dying wish of a resident who wanted one last boat ride despite her physician saying an open water trip was out of the question. Elizabeth Bruno roped the executive director into helping her take the woman out in a dinghy on Fountaingrove Lake. The two women brought the resident down to the hillside funicular that delivered her to the dock where Elizabeth set her into a rowboat. The woman ran her hand through the water as she skimmed around the lake with her daughters. She died three days later.

Elizabeth Bruno also checked off a bucket list item for Len Kulwiec, a man raised in a Russian-Polish family on the south side of Chicago who dreamed of being a cowboy. She borrowed a horse, his son brought boots and dungarees, and they took Len to cowboy coffee and donuts over a campfire at Cloverleaf Farm, where, at 92, Len got to ride a horse again. In Len's case, Elizabeth did more than bring him joy. The activities she planned "brought him back to life," she said.

Len had moved into Villa Capri in 2015 after losing his wife of 70 years, a woman he fell for at his brother's wedding. After serving in the South Pacific with the U.S. Navy in World War II, Len planned to become a Roman Catholic priest—until he saw Lavern Rybacki on the dance floor. The couple married and raised three children. Recognizing Len's deep bereavement, Elizabeth took him under her wing and spent hours talking to him. She said goodnight to him every evening before she headed home. Len grew attached to Elizabeth as well. He attended every field trip she led and admired the way she helped his fellow residents on the bus; he said he could tell she genuinely cared about them. "She got me to paint again," he said.

After spending the beginning of his stay at Villa Capri without much zest for life, he memorized the vistas from Elizabeth's field trips and recreated on canvas the rural landscapes of Napa and Sonoma wineries and the sweeping ocean views of Bodega Bay beaches. In thanks, Len gave the activities director several of his paintings, including one he dedicated "To Elizabeth, with all my love." His outlook changed so drastically that he dove into research again—on topics like genetics, enzymes, amino acids, rheumatoid arthritis, healthy healing, longevity diets, vitamin C, and apple cider vinegar—and completed a manuscript on how to live to 105.

While Elizabeth Bruno was Villa Capri's activities director, her effect on the residents was profound. "She did more than that," Henrietta's son Corky Cramer said. "She was really the heart and soul of what was going on up there."

In 2007, just as Elizabeth Bruno was getting into full swing, Aegis Assisted Living cofounder Dwayne Clark bought out partner Bill Gallaher. Gallaher retained the properties in his hometown, including Villa Capri and Varenna, as well as a handful of other California senior communities, and he rebranded them under Oakmont Senior Living, a limited liability company he incorporated in 2000 as a "family owned and operated continuing care provider."

The rumor was that the longtime partners had a falling out, and, according to one former employee, the split wasn't amicable. Regardless, Aegis Assisted Living continued to manage day-to-day operations until 2011 when Clark and Gallaher's management agreement dissolved and Gallaher contracted with Integral Senior Living of Carlsbad, California, to handle daily management. The move, former employees say, was costly and took a chunk out of the bottom line. Gallaher opted to bring the care operation in-house and recruited the CEO away from Integral Senior Living to create Oakmont Management Group in 2012. Oakmont Senior Living would continue to build and own the communities while Oakmont Management Group took over the day-to-day operations.

4

Lifeguard

Sunday, May 14, 2017, five months before

Spending Mother's Day on the banks of the Russian River had been Betty Kisling's second choice. Her first was to have a family day at the coast, but their plans changed abruptly when she, her husband, R.J., and their two sons, ages 8 and 13, encountered heavy fog and strong winds in Bodega Bay. So they turned inland, landing at a spot below the Monte Rio bridge, where Bohemian Highway intersects Highway 116, a two-lane artery that ushers travelers through the many hamlets lining the lower Russian River. Monte Rio Beach was known for its amenities, including a concession stand and a kayak rental shop, and its tranquility. Children in particular enjoyed the gentle, shallow raft flume formed by the rush of water compressed between the shore and a sandbar in the middle. This reputation coupled with the sparkling weather meant a large crowd had gathered that Sunday. And due to the record rainfall all winter and spring, the river was flowing more briskly than usual for May.

Betty rested on the sand while R.J., a welder by trade and reveler of adventure sports such as surfing, mountain biking, and snowboarding, floated along the shore on his boogie board. The day's calm was suddenly broken by a horrific cry from down the beach. It was "a scream of terror," R.J. later said, the kind only a parent can make. Down the bank, he saw a woman pointing toward a bend in the river, shouting something he couldn't quite make out.

R.J. dove off the board, swam in the direction the woman was pointing, and began scanning the dark green water. Everything seemed so natural. There was no disturbance. No splashing. R.J. wasn't even sure what he was looking for. Then, in the depths, he spotted a pair of orange goggles. They were visible just past a shelf in the river where the water's depth suddenly dropped from about 2 feet to 5 or 6. R.J. took a breath and plunged in, throwing himself toward the bottom. There he found a boy, staring up at him through the colored frames. He was very calm. "He was looking straight up at me like nothing was wrong," R.J. later recalled. He swiftly pulled the lad to the surface, but when they broke through, the boy began to struggle, which made it difficult for R.J. to get them both to shore. By the time he fought through the water and walked them to the bank, both R.J. and the boy were exhausted. The boy's mother was effusive in her show of gratitude, but R.J. was too winded to respond. As R.J. and Betty learned later, the boy didn't know how to swim and was on the autism spectrum, which, as his mom explained, contributed to her son's lashing out when R.J. pulled him to the surface. Between bouts of hugging and thanking, the boy's mom swore she had only turned her back for a minute.

R.J. hadn't fully caught his breath before he heard another cry for help. This one came from a girl who appeared to be grabbing for somebody or something slipping below the surface. Without thinking, R.J. grabbed his boogie board and kicked and paddled furiously in the girl's direction, but before he could reach her, she also disappeared below the surface. As soon as R.J. reached what he believed was the spot, he pushed off from the board and dove down. This too was near that shelf drop, a "sneaker spot in the river" he called it. Fortune would have it that R.J. was able to grab her hand quickly. Even more fortunate, she was still holding on to the object she had been reaching for—her little brother. Despite their combined weight, R.J. managed to pull both siblings to the surface and push them onto his boogie board. As he gasped for air, he felt a wash of relief. The girl, however, was still frantic. "My brother, my brother!" she shouted, pointing into the darkness. R.J. looked around. "That's when I saw just the top of the head of another boy," he said. There was a third child down below.

His relief receded into despair; he was physically spent. Fortunately, another bystander who'd heard the girl's pleas had also raced into the river and managed to pull the third child to the surface. The two men dragged all three children ashore. Once there, the other man, pushed to extreme exhaustion, let go of the child and wretched on the sand. "It was horrible,"

Betty later recalled. And unlike the first mother who was on the beach for the rescue, the second was nowhere to be found. She had gone to her car and left her three kids unattended. As others cared for the rescued children, Betty and R.J. didn't wait around to talk. They packed up their gear and left.

On the way home, they considered stopping to visit R.J.'s grandfather who, just a few years earlier, had moved into the Santa Rosa retirement complex known as Varenna. "Papa," as his grandchildren called him, had recently lost his wife, and the Kislings made a point to visit him as often as possible to take him out to dinner. But a dinner date would have to wait. "I had too much excitement for one day," R.J. said.

In all, he had his hand in saving four children that Mother's Day, but none of this was surprising to Betty. "He has a knack for being in the right place at the right time," she said.

5

Castle

Three weeks before

Louise Johnson was languishing in a rehabilitation facility when her daughter received a call from Villa Capri's Traditions Memory Care center that a room had become available. Seven months earlier, the widowed Louise had fallen in a grocery store and broken her hip, adding a significant complication to her already troubled existence with Lewy body dementia, a cruel disease that causes delusions and vivid hallucinations. In her case, Louise believed she lived with 15 children and fussed over their daily care. "I came home one day, and she'd set out six bowls of cereal. She was furious with me because I wasn't making the kids eat their food," said her daughter Jonell Jel'enedra, who had moved into a tiny home on her mother's property to become her primary caregiver.

After Louise's fall and move into rehab, Jonell visited daily, although Louise was so disoriented that she often mistook her daughter for her deceased mother or sister. A petite woman with a white pixie cut and blue eyes that matched her favorite color, Louise would ask when her father was coming to take her home—to her childhood home. The 88-year-old mother of four remained stoic, but it was hard for Jonell to see Louise in the hospital-like setting. "I was the one who cried every day in the parking lot," Jonell said.

Finally, after six months sharing with three others a room so cramped she couldn't maneuver her wheelchair inside, Louise moved into Villa Capri. Its website promised "luxury around every corner" and touted its "2017 Best of Senior Living" award, one of 176 senior care facilities within California given that distinction from SeniorAdvisor.com. All four of

Louise's children jumped into action. Eric Johnson drove across California to meet his brother Craig, who flew in from Arizona. The pair rented a U-Haul to transport their mother's furniture, artwork, bedspreads, and family photos to Villa Capri.

The next day, Louise's third son made his mother's room feel like home. Clinton arranged her heirloom furniture and hung 15 of her oil paintings, including landscapes of redwoods, vineyards, and Sierra Nevada mountain scenes. Louise had been a respected local artist who told the *Cloverdale Reveille* in 2015 her paintings came from "a fierce love of nature and the God who created all things beautiful." When Clinton was finished, Jonell delivered Louise to her new room, a space larger than Jonell's entire house and classy like a private suite in a luxury hotel. Her three brothers showed up the next morning to take Louise on a tour.

All 25 Traditions Memory Care residents lived with various stages of Alzheimer's disease or other forms of dementia and could not be trusted to walk around the facility or operate a stovetop or oven unsupervised, so their rooms—named after Italian cities of Sorrento, Ravello, and Rossana— were situated on a locked corridor and had only bedrooms and bathrooms without kitchens or patios. Memory care residents were unable to leave the designated space without an escort, but since her sons were present, Louise was allowed to walk the premises.

After marveling at her new room, they stopped into an art class, where Louise painted a daisy with watercolors. Her attention span wasn't strong, so she lasted only 15 minutes, but the former painter's work was meticulous. Then the group wandered into the portions of Villa Capri accessible to its 37 assisted living residents, those who didn't need the same level of care and keeping. As the foursome entered the lobby to check out the Bistro, a coffee and tea bar stocked with fresh cookies, a staff member approached. "The concierge, she knew all our names. She was really good and asked if we needed anything. It was kind of surreal," Eric said. The lobby's fanciness amazed Craig. The polished tables, floral bouquets, chandeliers, cozy chairs, baby grand piano, and sofas surrounding a fireplace reminded him of a five-star hotel. "I didn't expect it to be as nice as it seemed. It looked like where you'd go on vacation."

Outside in the courtyard, they admired the winding paths, tiered fountain, and rose bushes. The dining hall was an elegant room with Tuscan columns and white linen tablecloths where a staff "hand-selected from some of the finest culinary schools and fine dining facilities" served "Gourmet. Every Day," per the promotional materials. "I got the flavor of Italy when we were there," Eric said.

Up a short elevator ride, the group saw where the assisted living residents lived in plush apartments with kitchens and private patios, and views of the Fountaingrove hills or the Santa Rosa valley. They peeked into the movie theater with its Golden Era movie star posters and old-fashioned popcorn cart and into the Ivy League–styled library with crown molding, reading chairs, and a fireplace. And they were sure to take in the artwork on the walls, the paintings of California's golden hills and dramatic beaches, the landscapes Louise loved and attributed to the Almighty.

As they returned to memory care, they passed the piano in the common area, but her sons knew better than to encourage Louise. She had played the organ and piano constantly before she took ill, during 40 years of Sundays on her Baptist church's organ and during a lifetime of weekdays when she played the same hymns on her home piano. The boys equated her constant playing to someone else's mother leaving the radio on. But this time, Louise didn't pull up the piano bench. "Maybe she was embarrassed that she couldn't play anymore or read the music. She had lost that ability," Eric said. Yet somehow, she seemed to gain a new one. Louise had never been an affectionate mother, but dementia changed her. She hugged Eric more since her diagnosis than she had his entire life, and she hugged him again as the boys said goodbye.

Louise's sons left feeling relieved their mother was finally in a better situation. "She was thrilled," Eric said, likening her reaction to a kid at Disneyland. "She didn't have a care in the world. She seemed content. She seemed to feel safe there."

It was only in the parking lot when the brothers realized that because Louise was in the memory care unit, she would remain behind locked doors all day every day unless someone came to visit and escorted her around. She wouldn't have use of the full courtyard, the lobby, or the Bistro; she wouldn't use the movie theater or the reading room either, all for her own safety, of course, but saddening nonetheless. "The facility as a whole was luxurious. But if you narrowed it down to that L-shaped memory care hallway," the place where Louise would actually live her life, Eric said, "it wasn't that impressive."

Six days before

Helen Allen's day was planned out. Her daughter-in-law, Kathy Allen, would pick her up from Villa Capri, take her to the doctor and for mani-pedis, then they'd round out the afternoon with a bowl of French onion soup. But they never made it past the doctor's visit.

Helen had a painful diaper rash and winced when the doctor approached to apply medication under her medical gown. "Don't touch me!" she cried. The gynecologist diagnosed yet another urinary tract infection, one she said Helen contracted from being left too long in wet incontinence briefs.

A former Pan Am Airlines executive secretary, Helen was known for being tidy and fastidious as she raised and doted on her three sons, which is why the infection and subsequent exam resulted not only in physical pain, but shame. "She was embarrassed and uncomfortable," Kathy said of the woman she'd loved like her own mother since she was 15, when she'd started dating Helen's son, Mark. Helen was still crying when they left the doctor's office. Kathy canceled the rest of their plans and returned Helen to her second-floor apartment at Villa Capri.

Five years earlier, Kathy and Mark moved Mark's parents into the Oakmont Senior Living community from their Belmont home of 55 years. Mark's father didn't want anything to do with the new place. "Dad wanted to die with his boots on in his TV room," Mark said. "Mom was ready to move." Because Helen and Victor Allen moved into the assisted living portion of Villa Capri—not Traditions Memory Care like Louise Johnson— they were free to roam the grounds on their own, attend bingo night, and visit classic car shows in the parking lot.

Helen and Victor had traded domestic drudgery for luxury and simplicity, for a place where they could enjoy a social life and pay others to take care of all their needs. Helen loved the frills, but Victor wanted to go home. Mark's father's dementia ultimately became an unexpected blessing because Victor came to believe he was staying in the same hotel he frequented when visiting Kathy and Mark, even thanking them for consistently booking him the same room. "He just couldn't figure out where the [gift shop] was downstairs," Mark said. Helen, whose poofy shoulder-length brown hair curved around her neckline, blossomed at Villa Capri thanks to activities like flower arranging and lunching daily with friends. She was happy, but her son and daughter-in-law weren't always pleased. They lived only 12 miles away and visited several times a week. What they saw didn't always impress.

They were concerned about the high turnover rate of caregivers, whom Mark and Kathy would get to know by name only for them to leave shortly thereafter. "They'd say they had earned a certificate from Santa Rosa Junior College and could now earn two dollars more per hour down the street," Mark said. "That's kind of sad. I don't know what they got paid, but it wasn't enough to keep them there. A lot of them were nice and wonderful, but they were the ones who would leave." Villa Capri's assisted living fees were based on monthly apartment rent plus the cost of care. Staff calculated the cost using a points system tallied in categories like grooming, bathing, dressing, eating, toileting, medications, and fall prevention—any area where a resident might need staff support. Staff evaluated residents twice a year, unless their condition changed, and provided a chart of the categories assessed. Higher point totals meant the resident needed more care, and management adjusted fees accordingly.

According to Mark, his parents' evaluations inevitably raised the rate without increasing the intensity of staff interaction. In one instance, after Kathy slept overnight at her in-laws' unit, a caregiver entered the apartment with a message: "Vic, don't forget to comb your hair and brush your teeth today." Kathy was dismayed. That simple message was their version of "grooming care," which cost extra. What started as $6,000 per month increased each year as managers added points for the number of daily prescription pills Helen required, for her transition from walker to wheelchair, and for the "grooming care" Kathy witnessed.

After Victor died in June 2016, Helen downsized from a two-room apartment to a studio without a kitchenette. In the summer of 2017, her monthly costs jumped by almost $2,000. Mark approached the executive director. "How can you do this to us?" he asked her. The math didn't make sense to Mark. When the price went up, he didn't see the level of care go up.

"At the price they were going to increase us, I could hire someone to sit with her for eight hours a day."

Mark started looking for a less expensive option, and he found a spot at another facility, but the director told him moving Helen would be too disruptive to her dementia. So Mark negotiated a few hundred dollars off Villa Capri's monthly rate, bringing it down to just over $9,000, to keep his mom in familiar surroundings. And he kept taking notes, just like his fastidious former-secretary mother would have done. For the five years Helen lived at Villa Capri, Mark meticulously documented every visit, problem, phone call, or meeting with staff or managers. His concerns and complaints filled three steno pads.

It was unusual among residents' children to record every visit and complaint over the years, but it wasn't uncommon for a family member to be dissatisfied with their relation's care. Such complaints are common in the assisted living industry. According to industry estimates, the U.S. is home to between 30,000 and 40,000 assisted living facilities such as Villa Capri and about 2,500 continuing care retirement communities, including luxury complexes like Varenna. Yet despite their ubiquity, few people have a grasp of the level of care and security they actually provide. Misconceptions abound.

For one, there is no federal oversight for assisted living facilities; instead, they abide only by a state-by-state patchwork of laws and regulations. Because assisted living facilities market to society's frail and vulnerable elderly, family members and residents often assume a doctor works on the premises. Not so. Most don't even have a registered nurse on-site; the only medical-adjacent role is that of a "med tech" or medical technician who doles out medication under the supervision of a nursing manager or contract physician. As Eric Carlson, an attorney with Justice in Aging, a national non-profit legal advocacy organization that fights senior poverty via the law, put it, when one looks below deck at assisted living facilities, "There's not much health care there."

***

Two days before

Ruth Callen was thrilled to open her door late Friday morning to find daughter Liz Schopfer and her husband, Urs, standing there. Liz wanted to return to Ruth a yellow jade necklace she'd borrowed, one of the beautiful exceptions to her mother's vast QVC jewelry collection. When she still lived in her Santa Rosa home, Ruth was a QVC shopping network "freak" who ordered so much jewelry—often gaudy and ugly in her daughter's opinion— that she'd have boxes arriving five days a week. Her husband's discontent finally tempered the orders, but it didn't dampen her lifelong attraction to shiny things. Ruth's sister Mary Lou nicknamed her Sparkle Plenty for her love of bling, real or fake. Ruth loved anything that gave off a monied air.

Ruth was not wealthy, but she admired rich people, their designer clothes, authentic diamonds, and fancy cars, and she regretted being unable to live their lifestyle. Instead, she'd tried gambling her way into luxury. Ruth studied tip sheets to bet on racehorses at the annual county fair, and in off-track betting, Ruth put money on the Triple Crown. She usually wagered on her favorite jockeys, though an Irish-named horse or one carrying her kids' names might draw her bet. And she couldn't pass a slot machine that didn't tug at her purse strings. Ruth had spent two of her last three birth-days at the local casino, including one night when she stationed herself at a leprechaun-themed slot until 3 a.m. before Liz finally managed to drag her away. Ruth's claim to fame was winning a couple thousand dollars in Vegas once, but that sum wasn't enough to make her wealthy. Moving into Villa Capri, however, was the ticket to her desired lifestyle. "This is a classy joint," she said upon entering its marbled lobby during a tour in 2016. Her husband's pension from decades as a police officer made it attainable. Ruth was thrilled to land the lucky-sounding Room 222, even though it was the smallest unit available, a 395-square-foot Rossana studio with a tiny kitchenette. Liz purchased a beautiful Italian leather chair and loveseat set for the sitting area along with a seven-drawer oak leaf nightstand for her mother's bedside.

The highlight of the apartment sat perched atop that nightstand. Lydia, a four-foot-tall bronze lamp sculpted like a dancer with one leg and one arm outstretched, wore the flowing apron dress of a peasant girl. But thanks to her pride of place on the nightstand, Lydia commanded the room like a noblewoman. She almost reached the ceiling, and her bronze form was weighty and substantial. "If Lydia falls over, don't be next to her because she'll kill you," daughter Ruthie used to joke. Lydia was more than just a lamp; she was a remnant from the family's San Francisco days. Ruth purchased her from a wealthy woman in the Marina District, then gave her a nickname—like she did most things she loved. And Ruth loved Lydia.

Ruth also loved to eat. So when her daughter and son-in-law showed up on October 6 to return her yellow jade necklace, they decided to take her to lunch downstairs. An uneven hip replacement and Paget's disease left Ruth a slow traveler down the long hallways, despite the use of a bright red walker she nicknamed Ferrari and adorned with the luxury car maker's logo. Urs liked to tease his mother-in-law. "Oh, your Ferrari's going slow today," he'd say. "Maybe it needs a tune-up." The trio eventually reached the elevator and rode it to the lobby, then Liz and Urs walked slowly while Ruth inched to the dining room.

It was difficult to have a quiet lunch with Ruth. She preferred to dine near the entrance, which meant every resident passed her as they came and went. "Hey, kid!" she'd call out to her friend Margaret, a worldly, well-traveled woman. "Here comes my friend JoMary," she would quip, poking fun at Joellen Mack's uncommon mash-up of a name. Or she'd find a space for Susie Pritchett, a stylish woman with an elegant apartment and a tropical bird she would wheel around in a cage on her deceased husband's wheelchair. Ruth held court for at least an hour at every meal and was often the last one to leave the dining room, after which she and Ferrari slow-hauled through the lobby, up the elevator, and back down the long hallway to her apartment.

On this unseasonably hot Friday, Ruth hobbled back to her room and said goodbye to Liz and Urs. She was always glum when her youngest child left, but her other daughter was visiting tomorrow, and had her two local sons not been on vacation, she likely would have seen them in a surprise visit Sunday night. Their presence would have been especially welcome; all three sons were retired firefighters.

***

On the same day Ruth dined with Liz, a different resident's daughter fired off an email to Villa Capri management about her parents' care. Bill and Wanda Lee's daughter was ticked off. Once again, for the nth time in the past 12 months, local attorney Dawn Ross was fed up with Villa Capri's Traditions Memory Care center.

Dawn's dad, Bill, a former accountant, already had five children and was 14 years older than Wanda when he got the former high school valedictorian pregnant at 19. The couple had two daughters, after which Wanda earned a bachelor's and master's degree and rose in the ranks of corporate human resources. She retired as vice president of HR for a large health care company, then started her own consulting firm.

The Lees, married for 40 years, lived in Southern California until they grew older and moved north near Dawn, settling in a house in Fountaingrove across the golf course from Villa Capri. Bill smoked a pipe, drank scotch, and never exercised; Wanda, on the other hand, kept herself in great shape. So it came as a surprise in 2012 when airline personnel called Dawn because Wanda was at the Oakland airport but didn't know where she was. "Overnight—it was that sudden—she had dementia," Dawn said.

Dawn's high-functioning mother spiraled from a woman who was never seen without her lipstick into a 72-year-old hospice patient who had forgotten how to chew and swallow. Doctors suspected the dementia was a side effect from a drug Wanda took for restless leg syndrome. A speech pathologist worked with Wanda and eventually got her to eat lemon-lime yogurt, the only food she would swallow for months. She slowly regained weight and seemed to fully recover. Wanda petitioned the DMV to reinstate her driver's license and had her health insurance company expunge dementia from her medical records.

But a year and a half later, it happened again. A neighbor called Dawn to report that her parents' garage door had opened and closed all night. "Your mom was sitting in the car and she couldn't figure out how to get into the house," the neighbor told Dawn. "Then we woke up this morning and the car had rolled into the street." Dawn rushed over.

"Oh, Dawn, I'm so glad you're here. Your dad is dead, and the cat is dead," Wanda told her daughter.

Dawn steeled herself. *Oh my God*, she thought, *she killed my dad, and she killed the cat*. Neither was true, but Dawn took Wanda to the hospital for evaluation.

Dawn was also concerned about her father. Bill had started stuffing his pockets with granola bars because Wanda wouldn't let him eat. "We thought, this isn't safe. Dad's going to starve to death." Then one day, Dawn opened the cupboards to find everything gone. "I think if it bothered her or felt complicated, she'd just throw it away." Eventually, Dawn and her son would visit the night before garbage pickup to lay a tarp on Bill and Wanda's law, dump the contents of their trash cans, and sift. There, in the pile of refuse, Dawn and her teenager found everything from cutlery to discarded computers.

A room in Traditions Memory Care opened up in August 2016, so Dawn and her brothers "tricked" Bill and Wanda into relocating to the other side of the golf course. One weekend, Dawn's brother and his wife took Bill and Wanda on an outing to keep them busy just long enough for movers to relocate their bedroom furniture, a table, chairs, clothes, and favorite artwork to Villa Capri. Dawn met her parents out front. "This is strange," Bill said, marveling at the homey familiarity of an unfamiliar place. Wanda asked what was going on. "I told my dad he's there for my mom and my mom she's there for him. So we convinced them to try it for a week," Dawn said.

At first, Villa Capri seemed like home. Bill was eating regularly, and Wanda liked having her blonde hair done weekly in the salon. But Dawn soon found herself disappointed in the care they received for $14,000 a month. "Sometimes I'd show up and my dad would be lying in his own urine-soaked diapers," she said. Frustrated, Dawn fired off emails to the memory care director and Executive Director Deborah "Debie" Smith about various complaints, including that her mother hadn't had a shower or shampoo in two weeks. Wanda's hair was matted, and she had body odor. Then she fell near the dining hall and broke her hip, necessitating the use of a wheelchair. Dawn considered relocating her parents but abandoned the idea, hiring a personal caregiver for an additional $8,000 a month to ensure her parents stayed clean, fed, and healthy. That brought their monthly care cost to $22,000, paid for by a long-term care policy.

A few months later, during spring 2017, the memory care director with whom Dawn corresponded resigned. She told Dawn she couldn't provide the level of care Oakmont promised. "She looked like a wreck all the time. Dark circles," Dawn remembered. "When she left, she said, 'I can't work here anymore. They are understaffed. I keep complaining. They won't get me proper staffing.'"

Shane McCallum, a former med tech at a sister facility, replaced her, and, according to a former manager, on his first day, three of the four scheduled caregivers didn't show up because they were angry about the previous director's departure and working conditions. No one prepared notes for or trained McCallum, and he lasted only four months before he quit for reasons similar to those of the woman he replaced. Other employees said he was working 16-hour days and begging Debie Smith for more staff.

Dawn wanted staffing increased too, and she was upset about the high turnover, which she attributed not only to workload but also low pay. In 2017, she wrote a series of emails to Smith and that year's three different memory care directors, including one on May 17 when Dawn asked, "I am concerned that so many good employees, like Rene, are leaving to make more money elsewhere. Who can I talk to at the corporate office about raising [pay] rates to decrease turnover?" In another email, Dawn said it was "devastating" to lose yet another caregiver, and she closed by saying, "I hope you can figure out what the problems are and get them fixed. So far, it just seems like lots of empty promises."

Two months later, on October 6, 2017, Dawn emailed Smith and memory care director Janice Wilson, who had been in the role for less than eight weeks. Dawn relayed an upsetting episode when her parents' personal caregiver arrived to find Bill lying in bed with feces leaking out of his briefs. She hit the call button for a Villa Capri caregiver, waited 15 minutes, then hit the button again. No one came. The Lees' personal caregiver then located and confronted the Villa Capri caregiver, who simply asked where Bill was, then turned around and walked away. Dawn's email was pointed, both in tone and in structure.

It took three days for Smith to respond to Dawn, and when she did, it had nothing to do with Bill and Wanda's daily care. Sent the morning after the fire, Debie Smith's single-line email was Dawn's first indication as to whether her parents had made it out of Villa Capri alive.

Eleven hours before

Just before Sunday's temperatures began their precipitous rise from the morning's low 50s to the afternoon's high 80s, and about the time residents headed to Sunday circuit training classes, Len Kulwiec accidentally accomplished his long-sought-after-goal—to bring Communion to Villa Capri.

If Henrietta Hillman was its queen, Len had undoubtedly become the facility's king. The mobile widower with a full head of hair and a mischievous crooked smile that exposed deep laugh lines—his only wrinkles—didn't look a day over 75. These features put him in high demand in the woman-dominated care home. "He's got the ladies going after him, asking him up to their room. And then you've got the men who are jealous because the women are looking for a good time with Lenny," his son Michael said with a laugh.

In his two and a half years at Villa Capri, Len made a name for himself with his involvement in, well, everything. Besides partaking in field trips and exercise and craft classes, he presided over a resident council to give voice to their complaints and concerns. But while the veteran enjoyed staying active to keep his body fit and his mind sharp, he didn't have an option to nourish his soul.

Though Villa Capri did arrange Christian religious services, including twice monthly church services and monthly "religious films," Catholic Mass wasn't offered. So Len called St. Rose of Lima Roman Catholic Church to inquire about bringing Communion to Villa Capri but was told the bishop would not allow Communion outside the church in a corporate setting. For the two years Len lived at the community, he had not received Communion on-site.

So it was unusual on the morning of October 8 that Len spotted in the parking lot a couple he knew who happened to be Eucharistic ministers. He asked them if they would give residents Communion, and the couple agreed, playing music, praying, and administering the sacrament to approximately 15 Villa Capri residents. "It was just by pure coincidence that we all received Communion that morning," Len said. "I think they brought a couple of angels."

***

That same day, Alice Eurotas received a gift of her own. When her daughters, Gloria Eurotas and Beth Eurotas-Steffy, moved Alice into Villa Capri, they'd withheld a gallon Ziploc bag full of jewelry: jade, onyx, and lapis pendants, 24-karat gold omega chains, and antique opals that were heirlooms and collectibles from Alice's mother's world travels. Gloria worried the pieces could get stolen, so she took them from her mother and hid the bag at her house. Alice begged for months to have her precious belongings returned. "We finally said, 'Hell, just give it to her,'" Gloria recalled. Problem was, Gloria couldn't find the bag. She finally fessed up to her mom. "Shit happens," Alice responded.

Alice, a former legal secretary on a tight budget, spent money both frivolously and to show her love. One time she invited eight friends to San Francisco to see a Broadway show and footed the bill for everyone's tickets and an expensive dinner, despite Beth's pleadings that she couldn't afford such extravagances. The one good financial decision she made was buying a long-term care policy when she was only 35. There were years she didn't want to pay the premium, and Beth would remind her she'd paid for the past 25 years. "She'd say, 'Put me in a horrible place,'" Beth said. "But [my mom would] secretly tell her friends, 'Beth will take care of me when I'm older.'" Alice expected to inherit far more money from her mother than came to pass, so she wound up in a mobile home park in Calistoga until Beth and Gloria chipped in to buy Alice a triplex in a senior housing development in Santa Rosa, where Alice lived, dined, socialized, and shopped for 17 years.

She loved perusing the stores in Montgomery Village until the day she was en route to the shopping center and hit a motorcyclist. Since it was her faulty left turn, Alice gave up her license. Homebound, she grew sedentary and depressed, frequently complaining she didn't feel well. She overmedicated with painkillers for abdominal issues, and her daughters felt she could no longer care for herself.

It took Beth a year to convince Alice to get on waiting lists for low-income assisted living housing. Beth could only find two facilities in Sonoma County that offered low-cost rooms as conditions of their building permits. Nearly a year later, in March 2017, a Villa Capri employee called to say a low-income room had opened. The space would cost $2,950 a month and include meals, TV service, transportation, a "nurse" to oversee her medications, and med techs to dispense them. Alice would pay extra for help showering.

Beth lived less than two miles away and took Alice to lunch at Villa Capri before moving in. Alice thought she was walking into a palace. A sign reading "Welcome to Villa Capri, Alice Eurotas" sat on a round table in the foyer decorated with a fresh flower arrangement. "When my mom first walked in, it was so opulent and fancy with chandeliers and lovely fixtures. She called it 'her castle,'" Beth said. "My mother loves movies, and when she saw [the movie theater], she thought she'd died and gone to heaven."

Once moved in, Alice decided she missed her house and her routine and was angry with Beth for initiating the move. She especially resented the fact that someone else handled her medication, both the dosage and the dispensation. "The nurse held all the power, and Alice did not like that," Beth said, referring to her mom by her first name, which she and her sister Gloria initiated as teenagers when calling Alice "Mom" didn't seem to fit. And the nurse seemed stretched thin. "I called and emailed and could never connect with her, because there was one nurse for all of the residents." Alice grew surly and refused to partake in the daily activities.

That changed, however, when she met 92-year-old Norma Porter in the dining room and the two women hit it off, long before Alice learned of Norma's status at Villa Capri. Norma had attended Alice's 84th birthday party at Sweet T's, a popular Fountaingrove restaurant serving Southern cuisine; her friendship was just what Alice needed to embrace her new life.

And her daughters were reliable supports, alternating weekend-day visits with their mother. Saturday, October 7, was Beth's day to visit, and the women had lunch on the patio despite temperatures in the upper 80s. The heat was oppressive, but Alice's mood was light, and she asked Beth to snap a photo of her standing in front of "her castle's" four-tiered Italian-style fountain. Beth returned home feeling relieved. "Alice is finally content. I think she's going to be OK at Villa Capri. She finally feels like it's her home."

That night, Gloria was primping for her fortieth high school reunion, rummaging through drawers in search of a strapless bra when she happened upon the Ziploc bag containing her mother's misplaced jewelry. On Sunday, Gloria brought the bag of treasures to Villa Capri and presented them to Alice. "Lasted about 15 hours before they burned," Gloria said.

Nine hours before

By the time the sun rose at 7:13 a.m., Robert "Bob" Mitton had already been up for more than an hour. The 73-year-old retired deputy minister from Ontario, Canada, was eager to squeeze in a morning walk before the sun grew too intense to bear. The days had been unseasonably hot in recent weeks—hitting 109 degrees during two consecutive days in September—and Bob's hilly three-mile loop was already strenuous enough. He had just returned from a trip north with his wife, Mimi Vandermolen, and they were still adjusting to the California weather.

Mimi had been a designer for Ford Motor Co. in Michigan, so between her time in Detroit and Bob's in the Great White North, both were ready for California's temperate climate and famed sunshine upon retirement. They thought they had found it in a coastal hamlet midway between Los Angeles and San Francisco, but they didn't love Cambria's intense coastal storms, often accompanied by prolonged power outages. The experience left them feeling isolated and open to moving to a more urbanized setting with a gentler climate.

But uprooting was not a decision they made overnight. While helping a friend move to Healdsburg, they toured Sonoma County for the first time and came upon Varenna. They took a brochure and held onto it for four years. "It was marketed as a place for active seniors," Bob said. "We thought relieving ourselves of yard work...and being closer to an urban service center was a logical choice." In July 2014, after another volatile winter on the central coast, Bob and Mimi secured a two-bedroom apartment in Varenna's North Building. Now, three years later, Bob and Mimi were grateful to be back in their Sonoma County home after a visit north, and Bob was glad to shove off on his walk.

After taking the elevator downstairs, Bob strode past Varenna's South Building and the stand-alone casitas, past the Main Building and Villa Capri, and through the tiered parking lots to a sidewalk on the north side of Fountaingrove Parkway. From there, he proceeded downhill past the entrance to the 33-acre Nagasawa Community Park, and turned right onto Thomas Lake Harris Drive, a gently rolling road that fronted two other Oakmont properties: Fountaingrove Lodge, billed as the nation's first senior living community for lesbian, gay, bisexual, and transgender people and their allies; and Oakmont of the Terraces, a dedicated memory care complex. He walked past 11 holes of the exclusive Fountaingrove Club golf course, past enclaves of three- and four-bedroom single-family homes, most of which featured 12-foot ceilings, open floor plans, master suites larger than some two-bedroom apartments, and eligibility to join the members-only Fountaingrove Club. Bob then made a right back onto Fountaingrove Parkway, past the T intersection with Stagecoach Road, and returned to Varenna. Given Bill Gallaher's ownership of the Lodge and the Terraces, and his controlling interest in the Fountaingrove Club, Bob's three-mile loop essentially traced the boundaries of the developer-investor-banker's Fountaingrove empire.

Although the heat was on Bob's mind that morning, it wasn't much of a news story. Neither was the fact that the National Weather Service was issuing fire-weather warnings throughout much of Northern California. These red flag warnings indicate when an inbound weather pattern may contribute to extreme fires within the next 24 hours. Conditions that trigger red flag warnings include low relative humidity, strong winds, dry fuels, and the possibility of dry-lightning strikes.

The forecast projected winds from the north gusting between 25 and 35 miles an hour and temperatures reaching 88 degrees with a relative humidity of 12 percent. An average October day's humidity in Northern California is 53 percent. The landscape was a tinderbox. On the morning of October 8, Santa Rosa checked almost all the warning's boxes, and meteorologists made a stark projection: "Any fires that develop will spread rapidly."

Red flag warnings and weather watches had become almost routine for this part of the state, and as usual, the story was buried in the news coverage of the day. The primary weather news was Hurricane Nate, which had made its way along the Mississippi coastline and landed outside Biloxi that morning. It was the first hurricane to make landfall in Mississippi since Hurricane Katrina in 2005. If there was any place in the nation that was vulnerable to natural disasters, it was the Gulf, not Wine Country.

After his three-mile stroll, Bob and Mimi dined on Varenna's veranda, overlooking Fountaingrove Lake, Nagasawa Park, the country club, the golf course, and the swanky neighborhoods nestled around Varenna. As they took in the view under the brilliant California sunshine, Bob appreciated it all. "I was back in my routine that day," he thought, having no clue as to the events ahead. By the time the sun rose the following morning, almost all that Bob had seen Sunday—and everything he and Mimi took in from the patio where they dined—would be gone.

PART II
FIRE

6

Spark

The Firestorm: 10 p.m.

Fire distance from Villa Capri and Varenna: About 10 miles

Pinpointing who and what was to blame for igniting the Tubbs Fire has been the focus of lawsuits, state investigations, and robust public debate, but there is no dispute as to where it started. Although referred to for its proximity to the road named for the Tubbs mansion, ground zero proved to be a slope of private property on nearby Bennett Lane, a remote crease of pavement where Napa Valley's famed vineyards give way to Northern California's oak-studded hills.

The source was an aged power pole that distributed electricity to a hillside residence. Eight months before the fire, according to an investigation by the California Department of Forestry and Fire Protection, better known by its abbreviated title Cal Fire, a caretaker of the 10.5-acre property noticed the pole had broken and was left suspended by the power lines about 3.5 feet off the ground along a narrow tree-lined driveway. The pole had been "wood-peckered so damn bad" that it broke, the caretaker said. A week later, with the help of a company with an excavator, the worker replaced the pole. But neither the caretaker nor the company he hired were licensed electricians, and no one had examined the integrity of the power lines. Investigators believe it was atop this power pole that the fire began.

By 9 p.m. Sunday night, winds were blowing from the north/northeast at around 25 miles per hour with sustained gusts of 60 miles per hour while relative humidity in Santa Rosa was dangerously low at about 11 percent. The lower the humidity, the more easily a fire will start; there isn't enough moisture in the air to serve as a damper. Perhaps the most alarming measurement of the region's fire risk, however, was the fuel moisture level, which determines how

41

much vegetation is available to burn. When the level drops below 30 percent, the vegetation is considered essentially dead. The fuel moisture level in Santa Rosa that night was 4.5 percent. In Napa Valley, it was 3.7 percent. Climate scientist Daniel Swain of the UCLA Institute of the Environment and Sustainability said he was nervous that night "because it was pretty obvious the conditions were going to be bad. The National Weather Service put out a statement that vegetation is literally the driest it's ever been, historically."

The first recorded 911 call came in at 9:41 p.m. from a woman saying, "There's a fire, there's a fire," as she ushered family members out of the house near Highway 128 and Bennett Lane in Calistoga. Three minutes later, at 9:44 p.m., a caller standing at Highway 128 and Tubbs Lane, reported a "big huge" fire, one that was already "raging" just north at Bennett Lane. "All the trees are on fire—and the wind is blowing it," the caller said. Calistoga Police Officer Dale Hoskins was the first to respond at 9:48 p.m. The winds were "very intense" and "basically fast enough that you could hear it…[making] almost like a roaring sound," he said. Within minutes of his arrival, the fire crossed Highway 128 with flames up to 20 feet high, and he began evacuating homes in harm's way.

Napa Valley residents Caroline Upton and Tony Albright, members of the Mountain Volunteer Fire Department formed in the wake of the 1964 Hanly Fire, were at home when they heard the first call. The husband-and-wife team didn't have to go far to confirm the report. Despite the darkness, they could see from their front porch the billowing cloud off Highway 128, only a half mile away. But the odd thing was they couldn't smell any smoke. As Upton later noted, the fire "was basically like a torch" pointed away from them. The wind was so strong that anyone upwind by even 50 feet could be oblivious to what was happening if they had their back turned. If you were downwind, however, heaven help you.

After a quick stop at the fire station for their wildland gear—including fire-resistant pants and shirts, helmets, eye protection, gloves, and leather boots—Upton and Albright headed up Mountain Home Ranch Road. They hadn't gone far before they reached a Y intersection where they saw a vehicle parked on the roadside, its occupants frantically flagging them down. One of the car doors was open with a passenger's leg extended awkwardly outside. Nearby was another car with a driver who appeared to be slumped over the wheel. As Upton and Albright jumped out to assess the situation, a third car pulled over.

Each vehicle carried fire victims with various injuries. Two were elderly sisters who had avoided the rapidly moving flames by jumping in their unheated pool. Upton quickly diagnosed the two as mildly to moderately hypothermic. Another individual had a fractured ankle. Two others had extensive burns on their bare feet and elsewhere. They were forced to flee their residence so quickly they didn't have time to put on socks and shoes.

Upton and Albright could do little, having only a small cylinder of oxygen at their disposal and the most basic of first aid supplies. So they did what they could, giving the oxygen to the one patient with inhalation burns. Upton was worried about possible "airway swelling and edema." The two burn victims, a man and a woman, had ducked the flames by hiding in a large walk-in freezer, but as the blaze washed over them, the freezer filled with smoke, so they opened the door and made a run for it. They ended up dashing across a burning field, and the woman fell on the hot coals, adding to her injuries. Upton estimated their burns covered 35 to 40 percent of their bodies.

Soon, other residents joined them, and the intersection of narrow, potholed roads became an assembly point for stunned Mountain Home Ranch Road residents. Upton and Albright treated the burn victims with the help of a small burn kit they got from a lone Cal Fire responder who pulled up in his utility truck. They put the two hypothermic women in their own truck, cranked up the heat, and continued trying to call for support. "No matter how much I radioed to give an update, and no matter how much the Cal Fire guy radioed both to the [Napa County] side or the Sonoma County side, we could not get through," Upton said.

Finally, one of Upton and Albright's calls connected, and an ambulance from Napa Valley showed up. Medical technicians provided aid to the injured, while Upton and Albright drove to a Napa Valley hospital to drop off the elderly sisters. From there, the firefighters headed back up the mountain and connected with their engine company, headed by Capt. Tony Riedell, to join the swelling ranks of regional fire crews responding to pleas for mutual aid support.

By then fires were erupting in multiple locations in Sonoma and Napa counties, most due to toppling power lines or the failure of other electrical equipment. At 10:51 p.m., Sonoma County issued its first advisory via the Nixle alert system:

> Multiple fires reported around Sonoma County…. Local
> fire departments are on scene, and we will notify you if any

evacuations are called for. The strong winds are making these fires difficult. Dispatchers are being overwhelmed by 911 calls on reports of smoke smell. Please only call 911 if you see actual unattended flames.

***

Villa Capri, 1397 Fountaingrove Parkway

As the Tubbs Fire sprung to life some 10 miles away, Elizabeth Lopez was already on duty at Villa Capri doing residents' laundry. Unlike the rest of the night shift employees who started at 10 p.m., Elizabeth started an hour before, which allowed her to leave earlier to meet the demands of being a single parent with four jobs. Every day, Elizabeth commuted 45 minutes to Villa Capri, worked her night shift, then drove home to take her daughter to elementary school and then her boyfriend to his job, 30 minutes southeast of where they lived. Then Elizabeth checked in at an elderly day care center for her second job, followed by an afternoon that included two one-on-one caregiving stints. She returned from her fourth gig between 5 and 6 p.m., slept for a few hours, and then headed back to Villa Capri for the night shift, where Elizabeth—her dark hair pulled back into a bun, her black rectangular glasses adjusted on her face—always started with the residents' laundry.

Somehow, Elizabeth survived on two to three hours of sleep. She had to; she had a little one to care for. Such a feat would make most caregivers irritable and snappy, but coworkers described Elizabeth as friendly, hardworking, and big-hearted, someone who never slept on the job and loved the residents.

The youngest daughter of a vineyard worker and a homemaker, Elizabeth held her high school diploma and attended Solano Community College for two plus years, where she took criminology classes in hopes of becoming a parole or probation officer. She dropped out, though, because her financial aid package was only enough to cover books or classes. Not both. So Elizabeth worked temp jobs before becoming a caregiver and a medical technician—a med tech—and ultimately determining she liked working in an assisted living setting. "You help them get dressed, you help them take a shower, you change them. They see you as family, not a stranger," she said.

Elizabeth was sad when her charges moved to another facility or died. "You get really attached to them."

In the summer of 2017, Elizabeth dropped off an application at Villa Capri. "When I walked in, I thought it was a very nice, beautiful place," she said. "I thought everybody was on top of business, like it was well-run." Management at Villa Capri hired Elizabeth at $17.50 an hour, and ever since, she'd been enjoying the increase in pay over her previous jobs and counting down the 90 days until this particular night shift. As of tomorrow—October 9, 2017—Elizabeth would be eligible for health care benefits and a 401(k).

At 10 p.m., three other employees pressed their fingers to a screen to clock in alongside Elizabeth. Anett Rivas was eight months pregnant and had worked at Villa Capri for nearly a year. Though she didn't have the high school diploma the company normally required for her role, she had worked a few prior caregiving jobs. Anett made $15 an hour, an amount she considered decent, and was now full-time and earning benefits, but still preferred the night shift because it meant she could work a second job during the day. With dark brown eyes featuring long lashes and blackish-brown hair parted slightly off-center and pulled back into a ponytail, the 22-year-old worked nights sans makeup and jewelry, except for a small pair of diamond stud earrings. As she drove to work, her uniform of green scrubs and black pants fit snugly over her egg-shaped baby bump. A warm wind swayed her car on the freeway, and she smelled smoke in the air when she parked.

Cynthia Arroyo, a 21-year-old with dimpled full cheeks and long black hair, also ponytailed, had earned her diploma from a Santa Rosa high school but didn't have any CPR or caregiving certificates when she started working for Villa Capri five months earlier. Cynthia had sustained a sprained wrist when helping a resident out of bed, and it hindered her ability to lift and move residents, though she had spent the last few weeks doing physical therapy.

Of Villa Capri's 62 residents, 47 were considered "nonambulatory," meaning they couldn't walk without assistance due to physical or mental impairment. Some required either wheelchairs or walkers; others were among the 25 who lived behind locked doors in the Traditions Memory Care wing and, while capable of walking, required an escort because their cognitive impairments could lead them to wander or hurt themselves. Two other memory care residents were bedridden.

The night shift—or "NOC" for nocturnal shift—often operated with only two caregivers, but managers had added another for this Sunday because Cynthia's wrist and Anett's pregnancy categorized them as "light duty." Neither woman could lift more than 10 pounds. That meant only one caregiver, Elizabeth Lopez, could maneuver residents from bed to wheelchair and back.

On October 8, 61 residents were at Villa Capri—one woman was spending the night with family—and it was Elizabeth, Anett, and Cynthia's responsibility to care for them, checking on the elderly residents every two hours, repositioning in bed those who couldn't roll over on their own, and changing residents' briefs and incontinence pads. Some residents were "heavy wetters" who required more frequent changes of their briefs and sometimes their sheets. Each caregiver had a dozen residents to manage Sunday night, with six or seven in assisted living and the remainder in memory care. When they weren't tending to the seniors on their watch lists, Elizabeth, Anett, and Cynthia did laundry, delivered clean clothes to residents' rooms, swept and mopped the floors, and took out the trash. Toward the end of their shift, they set out breakfast china, cutlery, and glassware in the dining room.

Unlike dayshift caregivers who had the opportunity to befriend residents, take them on field trips, and greet their children and grandchildren, the NOC shifters were invisible, fulfilling nightly routines amid sleeping or groggy seniors. Still, they forged bonds when they could and all loved the residents. Cynthia's current favorite was Louise Johnson, who asked about Cynthia's day and offered pleasantries, including "please" and "thank you" when Cynthia woke her for a middle-of-the-night changing. Elizabeth enjoyed Bill and Wanda Lee in memory care. Bill was more independent than his wife and could walk to the restroom himself but still required changes overnight. Wanda selected her pajamas each night and instructed Elizabeth how to fix her pillow and blankets. Both treated Elizabeth with kindness.

The caregivers also got earfuls from residents. Many complained that the food, advertised as gourmet, was "gross" or "cold" or that their clothes went missing from the laundry. Some of the neediest residents could not articulate their preferences or circumstances, which meant the caregivers sometimes found them in uncomfortable situations, like soiled underwear. "We had that a lot. The previous shift was too lazy to do their last round and change them," Elizabeth said, knowing full well that sitting in wet briefs could lead to urinary tract infections, like Helen Allen repeatedly suffered.

Cynthia felt the work required at least three caregivers. Elizabeth felt the job called for four, but most nights, only two caregivers were scheduled in addition to the med tech on duty, the person responsible for dispensing prescribed medication. On Sunday night, that was 32-year-old Marie So, a cosmetology school dropout and former Walmart employee who held no licenses but had been hired at Villa Capri as a caregiver in December 2016 and promoted to med tech the following spring. She'd held the role for five months, was a workaholic according to Anett, and was supportive of the younger caregivers. "We communicated, we joked around, we laughed, we helped each other out," Elizabeth said of the group. Cynthia said they "got pretty close." Sometimes that meant cranking up tunes in the laundry room and doing silly dances for Snapchat. Off duty, Cynthia and Elizabeth went to a party on one occasion, and Marie joined them once to go clubbing in San Francisco. Another time, Cynthia and Marie got manicures together.

After clocking in on October 8, the four women exchanged notes with the previous shift. Virginia Gunn, who had been diagnosed with colon cancer, had been declining the past few days, so the caregivers were instructed to keep a close eye on her and turn her from side to side every two hours because she wasn't moving enough on her own. Then the swing shift went home, and the NOC crew got to work, with Anett and Cynthia—the two on light duty—paired together. Elizabeth and Marie were on their own.

At 11:10 p.m., up in the craggy Mayacamas Mountains straddling the Sonoma-Napa border, the Tubbs Fire was spreading with violent force. Back at Villa Capri, six miles southwest, Anett and Cynthia were in the dining room, and Elizabeth was standing near Marie's office when the power suddenly cut out.

Varenna, 1401 Fountaingrove Parkway

Andre Blakely grew uneasy as he accelerated to the top of the hill where Oakmont of Varenna rested like the center jewel on a crown facing western Santa Rosa. The winds were strong, shaking loose every leaf that hinted of fall colors and sending branches big and small crashing to the ground. No doubt the groundskeeping crew would have its hands full tomorrow. But there was something else unsettling. As Andre pulled into a parking space, the deer—or rather, the lack of them—stood out. The usual collection of California blacktails eating around the oaks and shrubs on the side of the driveway was missing.

"You got to stay close to me tonight," Andre said to his friend and coworker, Michael Rodriguez, as the two exited Andre's blue Mazda 3. "I've got a feeling that something is going to happen." The night wind blew warm and steady against their faces. Michael was spooked as well. "Damn, Dre," he replied. "Whenever you say something like that, it always happens." Once when Andre had "that feeling," an alarm went off in the middle of the night, rattling tenants and sending workers scrambling to discover a security door had not properly closed. Another time, a resident was injured falling out of bed, requiring Andre and Michael to notify management. The two men worked together to open the medical office, get the resident's paperwork, and make sure paramedics had what they needed.

Although both were relatively new to working at Varenna, Michael knew enough to follow Andre's advice out of respect for his age and experience. The 26-year-old Michael trusted the 57-year-old Andre. He always had. The two had known each other since Michael was a teenager, and "Dre," as he was known to friends, had mentored him through a program that helped children and young adults, some with disabilities, in learning basic life skills such as how to apply for jobs, pay bills, and take care of themselves. Andre's stay at the Skills for Life organization was short, however. He told them he needed something full-time. But in truth, Andre thought many of his fellow staff members weren't supportive and didn't put as much effort into their jobs as those in the program deserved. But by then he and Michael had become friends, and when Andre left the program, he promised Michael they would stay in touch.

Good as his word, when Andre landed a job at Varenna in June 2017, Michael got a call. The complex needed more maintenance help, and Michael applied. He started work that same day. Michael's only concern was how he would get to work, especially for a night shift, but on his first night, Andre pulled up in front of Michael's apartment complex without even a call from Michael. From that day forward, Andre gave him a ride. Even on days when they weren't on the same shift, Andre would take Michael uphill. He was always the mentor, and although Andre was a good 6 inches shorter, Michael looked up to him. "Dre's the best," Michael told friends. "I've never met anyone in my life that's as genuine as that man."

Andre and Michael checked into work, Andre in his company-issued green shirt with the Oakmont label and sweatpants, and Michael, once again, in something he'd pulled together. He had asked several times since he started for the uniform shirt that Andre wore, but none had been provided despite promises to the contrary. So Michael came up with one of his own, borrowing a black shirt from a friend, a black pair of pants, and black shoes. Michael wanted to appear professional and steady, but tonight, he felt anything but. Something was in the air. "It was very, very ominous. I'll never forget the feeling."

During the NOC shift, Varenna's caregivers were responsible for the residents while Michael and Andre took care of the buildings. In all, there were approximately 230 residents that night, including 150 to 160 in the Main Building. The caregivers took care of cleaning the second and third floors of the complex, while maintenance staff took care of the lobby level and lower floor. Michael and Andre's tasks were basic: vacuum, clean bathrooms, take out the trash, and be available if problems arose. More often than not, nothing noteworthy happened during their 11 p.m. to 7 a.m. shift. Most residents were asleep while the two of them did their chores, and they rarely encountered anyone else. That included the other maintenance staff, who, according to Andre, sometimes slept in their cars after dispatching their cleaning duties. They weren't lazy, necessarily, although there were some of those. Rather, it was the price of making a living in expensive Sonoma County. Many had day jobs too, so they caught sleep whenever they could.

It was different for Andre, who was "always awake." Sometimes, out of boredom, he would clean the South Building or the North Building because it was needed, not because he was asked. When there was no more work to be done, he would sit in the activities room or in his car, facing the front entrance so he could keep an eye on things. In those moments, he often thought about his days as a boxer.

Standing 5 feet, 3 inches tall, Andre had always been a fighter. Having grown up in North Carolina, he moved to California in the fourth grade and was raised by his aunt and uncle. Making new friends was hard. So was everything else growing up in the Petaluma area, except martial arts. First it was karate. Then, for 11 years, Keiko martial arts. Then Taekwondo. But it was in boxing where Andre had found his greatest success and passion. He taught himself during high school, then joined a gym and began entering tournaments. In doing so, he quickly earned a name and reputation for himself. He became a Golden Glove champion in high school and, soon after graduation, was rated the No. 2 bantamweight in the Western region. A neck injury—one that happened playing football in high school and still nags him today—brought that dream to an end. After 115 boxing matches, his career was over.

From then on, Andre focused on caring for the elderly. One of the first people who hired him as a part-time caregiver turned out to be one of his eighth-grade teachers. Their reunion proved beneficial for both of them. Andre found he was at his best when he was helping older residents, something he had little opportunity to do given his current shifts and responsibilities. Working with seniors "is the ultimate job," he said. "You don't get paid a lot of money, but it really humbles you. And it feels good to bring a smile to someone's face."

After punching in early for their 11 p.m. shift, Andre and Michael went down to the supply room. "I'll start cleaning the bathrooms, and you dump the garbage," Andre told Michael. "And then we'll start vacuuming." Michael nodded, and they went their separate ways.

At Varenna, most of the residents were settled in for the night. Among them were Bob Mitton and Mimi Vandermolen, who lived in the North Building overlooking the Fountaingrove Club's tennis courts. Bob turned in early in anticipation of an early departure for a business trip. Down the hall, Richard and Carole Williams were also in bed, which was never an easy process for them. Richard had familial cerebellar ataxia, a debilitating brain disorder often characterized by abnormal speech and difficulty moving. To Carole, being at Varenna was an "answer to prayer," as she knew someone was always nearby to help Richard if he should fall or need assistance when he was alone. "They have nurses available, and if you haven't opened your door by a certain time, by 1 p.m., they would come check on you," Carole said. "There are lots of ways I feel safer being here—and freer."

Another resident turning in was Sally Tilbury, a Minneapolis native but long-time Californian who lived alone on the first floor of the South Building. As Sally would admit, she lived a charmed life. After marrying Charles Tilbury in 1950, they opened a travel agency in the Beverly Hills Hotel, from where "Chuck" booked business travel for large corporations and became best friends with the doorman, who kept the Tilburys in the loop about the resident celebrities and their scandalous bedfellows. After retirement, the couple moved to west Sonoma County to become gentleman farmers tending grapevines until Chuck's death in 2006.

Sally moved into Varenna shortly after it opened in 2008 and "flourished" thanks to the friendships she formed with a group of widows who would dine around at one another's apartments. Sally had always lived a regimented lifestyle; her proclivity toward organization meant she even labeled her towels with their purchase date. Every morning, Sally read the *Press Democrat* and the *Wall Street Journal* cover to cover. On October 8, to ready herself for bed, Sally locked her doors. Then she put on a long-sleeved cotton button-up nightdress, applied her trusty Lancôme night cream to her face and a different lotion to her hands, after which she slid-on gloves to seal in the moisture. She pulled her dark hair back with a headband, took out her hearing aids, positioned a neck pillow on her shoulders, and strapped on her CPAP mouthpiece. She had become used to wearing the apparatus to help manage her sleep apnea, and, thanks to its cool stream of forced filtered air, Sally often slept straight through the night.

7

Smoke

The Firestorm: 11 p.m.

Tubbs Fire distance from Villa Capri and Varenna: About six miles

Most of those in harm's way in the early hours of the fire lived in the Mayacamas Mountains, a 52-mile-long range of rolling hills and peaks from Cobb Mountain in Lake County to Mt. St. Helena in Napa County to Hood Mountain just above Sonoma Valley.

Composed of multiple ecosystems and natural features, these lands hosted fire for thousands of years—and they needed it. Many native trees, shrubs, and wildflowers in the area require the heat, smoke, or chemical leftovers from fire to regrow after the first spring rain; water and sunlight are not enough to spur germination. The Indigenous peoples of Sonoma County—the Pomo, Wappo, and Miwok—have long understood the value of fire. In addition to letting lightning-sparked fires burn, they also started their own fires long ago to shape the landscape. Their efforts regenerated the soil with rich ash, decreased pest populations like ticks, created habitat for deer, elk, and bison, and made it easier to hunt large game by eliminating underbrush. Cultivating fire was a means to cultivating life, and fire was considered sacred.

But as European colonizers settled in the West, they brought with them a far different approach. In some instances, ranchers and shepherds would start fires at the end of the grazing season and let them run free, a far cry from how native people monitored each burn. In most others, colonizers forbade prescribed burns and worked swiftly to extinguish any and all fires. In 1935, the U.S. Forest Service codified this approach when it enacted its so-called "10 a.m. policy," an aggressive fire suppression rule that required all fires be controlled by 10 a.m. the day after discovery. All-out war was waged against forest fires as the chief of the U.S. Forest Service called for "fast, energetic, and thorough suppression of all fires in all locations."

Due largely to such tactics, as well as the expansion of housing in fire zones, which made fire prevention in forested areas urgent, by October 2017, the foothills and valleys of the Mayacamas served as a prime example of the pitfalls of fire suppression and residential planning. In the 53 years since the Hanly Fire torched the landscape, native brambles and thickets had grown tall underneath the 100- to 200-foot canopy provided by Douglas fir and foothill pine at higher elevations and by California live oak in the lower. Invasive species thrived without natural fire to kill them off. Decades' worth of detritus—dead twigs and branches, and decomposing plants and animals—had accumulated. When the Tubbs Fire reached these stands of dense forest, there was basically kindling for miles. One resident of heavily forested Franz Valley School Road said when the fire came through at around 10:30 p.m., "It sounded like a freight train."

At 11:03 p.m. the Sonoma County Sheriff's Office released a mandatory evacuation notice for everyone within a roughly 4-mile radius downwind of the fire's epicenter. "911 lines are inundated," the alert added. "Please only call for immediate emergencies." Eleven minutes later, another advisory alerted subscribers that evacuation areas had been expanded to include Franz Valley and Mountain Home Ranch Road, the area around Caroline Upton and Tony Albright's stationhouse.

The notification went only to targeted residents who had subscribed to the Nixle emergency notification system. Data would later show the alert—or Nixle, in local shorthand—went out in 21,246 text messages and 16,344 emails in a county of half a million people. Sonoma County emergency officials also used a second system, the SoCo Alert system, to send automated calls and texts directly to cell phones, landlines, and telecommunication devices for the deaf and hard of hearing. Both the Nixle and SoCo Alert systems allowed Sonoma County emergency officials to geotarget subscribers, meaning they could send messages to specific neighborhoods or regions with details of the threat, exit routes, or other area-specific instructions. SoCo Alert also required residents to sign up in advance, and less than 3 percent of the county had done so. Both services were free, but users were few.

Further complicating communications was that those who registered for Nixle had to choose the local agencies from which they wanted to receive *notifications. Subscribers may have selected the Sonoma County Fire District and the Santa Rosa Police Department, for example, but not the Sonoma County Sheriff's Office, from where the balance of the night's alerts originated. And even for the relatively few residents who had subscribed and chosen every public safety agency, receiving calls, text messages, and/or emails was not guaranteed. It required those on the receiving end to have power and cell service, both of which were spotty. Power outages were widespread as strong winds knocked out electrical systems countywide. Fires in the mountainous regions also were impairing key infrastructure, including cell phone towers and the state's emergency services.*

County emergency officials had one other communication option at their disposal, a reverse-911 alert system that would allow them to simultaneously send a mass-communications blast to all cell phones within a certain geographic area, no subscription necessary, vacationing wine tasters included. This system— the Wireless Emergency Alert system—would cause phones that were powered on to vibrate and make a noise akin to the deep buzz televisions make during a test of the emergency broadcast system. In fact, the Wireless Emergency Alert system is the contemporary sister of the original Emergency Alert System for TV and radio.

But Sonoma County's Department of Emergency Management officials were hesitant to use the WEA system, as they believed it did not yet allow targeted outreach, meaning if one area of the county was notified, all areas were notified. "If I had notified half a million people, many wouldn't have read the whole message and would have thought it was an order for them to evacuate," Sonoma County Emergency Coordinator Zachary Hamill said four days later. "People from Cloverdale to Petaluma would have started leaving," Hamill added, naming a 50-mile corridor packed with residents who could have impeded first responders' access to the fire.

As a result, county emergency managers chose not to use the WEA system, deciding instead to send only targeted messages via multi-step opt-in programs. It would be a decision many county leaders would come to regret.

Villa Capri

Villa Capri caregiver Cynthia Arroyo had always been afraid of the dark, so much so that she often slept with her TV on. Anett knew Cynthia was easily frightened, so to tease her, Anett would sometimes pipe in scary music to Cynthia's walkie-talkie when she was alone. But now, at 11:10 p.m., Villa

Capri was dark, save for circular emergency lights near the ceiling that cast a dim glow in the hallways. This time, Anett did not joke around.

The two caregivers flicked on their phones' flashlights and met Elizabeth and Marie in the lobby, where Marie called the local utility company to report the outage. She received an automated message saying the company, Pacific Gas & Electric Co. (PG&E), would send a technician. Elizabeth, Anett, and Cynthia agreed they needed to find flashlights, but they didn't know where to look in the 58,000-square-foot building.

Cynthia, Marie, and Anett had attended some of the monthly training meetings where they had learned CPR skills, how to use the Hoyer lift machine for the heavier residents, and most recently, how to use a fire extinguisher. The trainings were held during the day, so Elizabeth couldn't attend them. None of the caregivers could recall what to do in a power outage. They discussed possible flashlight storage locations as they huddled in the lobby waiting for the PG&E technician, still using their phones for light—a battery-draining move they would later regret.

Just before 11:30 p.m. Marie called Debie Smith, Villa Capri's executive director, to report the power outage. This was the first outage in Smith's 20 months on the job, during which time she had hired each of the four women. According to Elizabeth, who was standing a few feet away, Marie said Debie suggested they check the laundry rooms for flashlights. Cynthia and Anett found six or seven flashlights there, but half were dead or lacked batteries, and the women couldn't find new batteries anywhere. They did, however, locate four or five old-fashioned battery-operated glass lanterns that worked. Cynthia and Anett recalled that Debie offered to bring batteries, but Marie told her boss they would make do with what they had. Cynthia and Anett both had a similar thought in response: *We kind of need batteries.*

Smith determined she didn't need to drive to Villa Capri since it was only a power outage, and then instructed the four women to keep their radios on, split up, and stand guard by the three electromagnetic locking doors to memory care. With the power out, the locks were disabled, meaning residents with dementia could theoretically wander outside. One of those residents, a woman named Jane, rolled her wheelchair into the memory care center's all-purpose room that served as a lobby, dining room, and hangout area. Cynthia tried to convince Jane to return to her room, but she refused. Cynthia left a lantern nearby but was afraid to leave her.

The caregivers ignored Debie's instructions. "We stick together," Elizabeth said, and the four women continued their search inside residents' rooms, borrowing what flashlights and batteries they could find. They set up flashlights to better light the hallways and placed lanterns in the rooms of residents who needed changing or who needed light in case they got up on their own. All the while, they worried an elderly resident might become disoriented and fall in the dark. Inez Glynn, for example, was among the more independent memory care residents who might try to use the restroom on her own. She was also a known fall risk, so Cynthia left a lantern in Inez's room just in case.

Five dozen additional residents needed checking on, and it was clear PG&E wasn't coming anytime soon. The caregivers paired up—one light duty with one regular—and started their rounds. Cynthia, favoring her injured wrist, headed upstairs with Elizabeth to the assisted living floors, while Anett, due to give birth in six weeks, joined Marie to change incontinence briefs and bedding for residents downstairs in memory care.

All four were unaware that as midnight approached, fire authorities were expanding the evacuation area between Calistoga and Santa Rosa, an area home to thousands of residents in remote getaways either nestled in jagged canyons or on sprawling hillside ranches and estates, all less than five miles from Villa Capri and Varenna's Fountaingrove neighborhood.

Palo Alto, 90 Miles South of Santa Rosa

Cancer, not wildfire, was foremost on the mind of Mike Stornetta, a Windsor Fire Protection District captain, as he and his parents settled in for the night at the Sheraton Palo Alto Hotel. Mike's 69-year-old father, Mike Sr., was scheduled to begin a trial treatment the following morning at Stanford Medical Center, something of a last-ditch effort to defeat his non-Hodgkin's lymphoma. Mike was deep in thought about the long day and the long odds ahead of them when, around 11:30 p.m., his cell phone rang.

It was his wife, Stacie, a nurse in the intensive care unit at Kaiser Permanente's Santa Rosa Medical Center. "There's a fire up in the Mark West Springs Road area," she said. "We're hearing reports."

Mike's instinctive calm kicked in. "It's OK," he told her. "That's pretty far away." He said he would monitor the situation and asked her to keep him posted as well.

After Mike hung up, his mother's phone rang. A neighbor was calling to say she thought there was a fire up behind their neighborhood somewhere. "There's a glow," she said. She smelled smoke and heard sirens. The calls added to the family's already frayed nerves. Mike continued to remain calm, lest he worry his mother further. To the best of his knowledge, he assured them, the fire was still far to the east of their home on the southern slope of Fountaingrove. But soon more calls came in from friends and neighbors.

Mike logged into a radio scanner app that provided access to public safety channels, including the Redwood Empire Dispatch Communication Authority, better known as REDCOM, which handles medical and fire dispatch services for more than two dozen Sonoma County agencies. Calls were streaming in from all over. Help was needed for an evacuation in one location; someone was trapped in another. Roads were impassable in multiple directions. Appeals for assistance were pervasive. Stornetta's concern heightened as the radio traffic shifted to increasingly strained pleas and orders. Among the escalating back-and-forth, Mike heard someone say, "This thing is making a hard run," a hard run toward Santa Rosa.

Mike turned to his parents. "I need to head back up," he said. "I'm not sure what's happening, but this is not good." He arranged for his parents to Uber to Stanford Medical Center the following morning and packed up his Chevy truck. He also packed up his partner, Rocket, his perpetually restless half Belgian Malinois, half border collie rescued from a Sacramento shelter where he had been deemed unadoptable because of his rambunctious nature. But in the three years since his adoption, Rocket and Mike had trained and tested to become the only urban search and rescue K-9 team between northern Marin County and the Washington state line. This accreditation made them eligible for dispatch to any incident in the country as part of the Federal Emergency Management Agency's 35-member Rescue Task Force-4 based out of Oakland, a unit that included doctors and paramedics as well as hazardous materials and search and rescue specialists. So specialized were Mike and Rocket's skills that they earned assignments of heroic proportions in destinations far from their home in Windsor.

Just two months earlier, FEMA had deployed Mike and Rocket as part of a 72-member, 15-vehicle convoy of rigs and 18-wheelers from the West Coast to assist victims of Hurricane Harvey, the first Category 4 hurricane to make landfall along coastal Texas since 1970. After seven days of work there, they were on the way back when they were stopped in New Mexico and redeployed to Florida for Hurricane Irma, a Category 5 storm that reached landfall just two weeks after Harvey. During that assignment, Mike and Rocket had played a central role in searching through the debris of Marathon Island homes and businesses flattened by the storm's winds of 132 miles per hour and storm surge up to eight feet. In all, their deployment for the two storms had lasted 26 days. By the time they returned home to Sonoma County in late September, they were exhausted.

Mike listened to REDCOM as he drove north on I-280 toward San Francisco. Some of the descriptions he heard in the dispatches reflected the menacing conditions around him, with trees bending like seagrass and branches, leaves, and other debris scattered across the six-lane inter-state. As they followed 19th Avenue through Golden Gate Park toward the bridge, Mike grew increasingly worried. The fire was running, crews were stretched thin, and the flames were aiming right for his family's home in Fountaingrove.

Varenna

The piercing shrill of a fire alarm permeated the 75,000-square-foot Main Building. "It's a scary noise to hear in the middle of the night," Michael would later recall. Andre had just started cleaning the elevator when he stepped out at the sound. *What now?* he thought. An electrical problem? Perhaps another safety door wasn't closed properly.

Either way, the procedure in cases like this was defined. Tony Ruiz, Andre's supervisor, had told him to proceed to the alarm panel to check the source of the problem. If something was wrong, they were to call 911. If they couldn't identify the issue, they were to silence the alarm and go back to their duties. It never made any sense to Andre or to Michael—they didn't like it at all—but those were their instructions.

When Andre arrived at the panel inside Varenna's foyer, a light indicated a problem in the main boiler room, a locked space off the underground garage. Michael joined him, and the pair took the elevator down to check it out. When the doors opened, they were greeted by a whiff of smoke. They speculated about the source as they walked the final 40 yards to the boiler room, checked the gauges, studied the equipment, and looked around. There was nothing to indicate anything was wrong. So they did what they were instructed to do if there was no threat. They silenced the alarm. "I really didn't think anything of it," Andre said. "There was no smoke smell in the boiler room, but I did feel it was weird that there was a smell of smoke in the garage itself. But I didn't really pay too much attention to it. We just went back upstairs and went back to work."

At 11:10 p.m. the power went out. This time, Andre and Michael met caregiver Ma Teresa Martinez at the front desk. First the alarm, then the smell of smoke. Now the power outage. "Andre, what are we going to do?" Teresa asked. "We have people on oxygen and the power is out." After a brief discussion, Teresa said she would call Nathan Condie, Varenna's executive director, while Andre dialed 911. "Sir, I cannot send you any help," the dispatcher told Andre. "We have all of our resources fighting the fire. If I were you, I would call PG&E," she said. Andre wanted to ask what fire she was referring to, but the call ended before he got the chance. A moment later, Teresa was handing him a landline receiver. It was their executive director. "You have Teresa count how many people we have on oxygen," Nathan told Andre. "I'm on my way in."

Andre passed the instructions on to Teresa and then called Tony Ruiz, his supervisor, to tell him what was happening. "Go into the boiler room," Ruiz told Andre. "There are three or four portable generators in there. Get those out and stage them for those who need oxygen." It was an odd request. Andre was already familiar with every closet and storage area in the complex and had never seen any generators. "I don't know what he is talking about," Andre told Michael after he hung up. "There are no generators down there." But they did as instructed.

With the power out, he and Michael took the stairs, which were illuminated only by yellowish emergency lights. This time, when they came out into the garage, the smoke was heavier and was now obscuring dumpsters a mere 20 feet away. Wherever it was coming from, the smoke was pouring into the Main Building garage unhindered. The retractable garage door was broken due to an electronics issue, leaving the entrance wide open. Andre and Michael covered their noses and mouths with their shirts as they made their way back to the boiler room and storage area. They looked around. No generators.

Throughout this period, Michael was impressed with how Andre was "really smooth" and calm the whole time, while he, an asthmatic, was starting to panic because of the smoke. Michael was not alone. "Everybody was really stressed out because it wasn't just our lives that we're accountable for," he said. "It was the lives of others."

8

Fireball

The Firestorm: Midnight

Tubbs Fire distance from Villa Capri and Varenna: Approximately five miles

For all the debate about PG&E failures, fire-suppression policy, and land-use planning that enabled widespread residential expansion into fire zones, the single biggest contributor to the Sonoma County fires' devastation, scientists agree, was climate change.

Traditionally, Sonoma County's Mediterranean climate has been marked by hot, dry summers with limited or zero rainfall from the end of May to October. Then, just as harvest season is winding down, the rainfall begins and then ramps up through the holidays to its peak in February, when it tapers off until May. Historically, an average of 34 inches of rain descends on the county over roughly four months, enough to sustain drought-tolerant native vegetation through the arid summer months. During this seasonal wet-dry cycle, a second climate pattern plays out over Wine Country. While light rain falls over picturesque vineyards and cool temperatures usher in the fog, a pressure differential between coastal and inland air causes hot, dry bursts of wind to gust from the northeast. The winds are called Diablos, named for Mount Diablo, a landmark peak in the East Bay. These "devil" winds represent all northeasterly offshore winds that arrive each fall over Northern California's Coast Ranges, including the Mayacamas.

These patterns, however, were changing dramatically. In 2017, Sonoma County residents were emerging from California's longest drought, which extended back to December 2011. Not only did the county see less rainfall during the drought years, but its rainy season had compressed, starting later and ending earlier. Rather than rain falling in October, it started weeks later. Then, 2017 broke climate records in all directions. Santa Rosa experienced its wettest January, its wettest winter, and its wettest overall rainy season since 1902 with more than 57 inches of ground-saturating moisture that spurred massive vegetation growth. The rain was followed by oppressive heat, with Santa Rosa enduring its hottest summer on record, drying out all the new growth. As UCLA climate scientist Daniel Swain noted, Northern Californians were left even more vulnerable thanks to these seasonal shifts. "The vegetation in September, October, and November is as dry as it would be during the summer," Swain said. "But then we have the winds added in." When the Diablos arrived in October 2017, rather than their 40- or 50-mile-an-hour gusts rushing over damp, spongy forest, they whipped down mountains as dry as sandpaper.

The result of these climate change-induced shifts—in seasonal wet-dry wind cycles, with an acceleration of winds and a menacing escalation of dry conditions in summer and fall—was a perfect storm of deadly conditions in the North Bay on October 8.

As firefighters battled the spreading flames, the rolling mountainous terrain made the attack a challenge, and in many cases, it meant residents couldn't see the fire until it was almost upon them. Such was the case for 18-year-old Robert Lee and his 57-year-old uncle Michael Dornbach. The burly Dornbach, known for a gruff exterior but heart of gold, lived east in the Sierra Nevada foothills and was looking to buy property in the county. Sometime before midnight, Lee saw flames racing up the mountainside, and he pleaded with his uncle to leave with him. Dornbach said he would, just as soon as he found the keys to his pickup. He promised Lee he'd be right behind him. Dornbach never made it. The retired longshoreman was the Tubbs Fire's first fatality.

At 12:32 a.m., the Press Democrat, *the largest newspaper between San Francisco and the Oregon border, posted its first fire story on its website.*

> "Wind-whipped fires broke out across Sonoma County late Sunday night and early Monday morning, forcing the evacuation of rural neighborhoods northeast of Santa Rosa as firefighters attacked the blazes...."

The story was authored by managing editor Ted Appel, who, still in his pajamas, was fielding reports from his longtime photographer Kent Porter. Porter had been tracking the fire since it jumped Highway 128 in Calistoga. At one point, Porter had pulled over at Camp Newman, a 485-acre wooded summer haven for Jewish youth located on Porter Creek Road. As he drove, "I could see the fire in my rearview mirror," he said. "This thing is going all the way to Santa Rosa," he told Appel. Within the hour, the fire would wash over where Porter was parked, incinerating 81 of Camp Newman's 90 structures.

Blue Gate Road: The Gallaher Residence, About Three Miles Northeast of Villa Capri

According to his sworn deposition taken nine months after the fire, Bill Gallaher, founder of Oakmont Senior Living, and his wife, Cindy, were getting ready to turn in for the night when they smelled smoke. It was around 10 p.m. As with so many others in the region, the high winds contributed to their general sense of anxiety. Cindy did an online search to discover "there was a small fire close to Calistoga," Gallaher said. But the skies were clear over their expansive house on Blue Gate Road in the hills northeast of Santa Rosa, and the stars were visible. Plus, "the fire wasn't close to us," he said. So they tried to get some sleep.

At around 11 p.m., Bill got up and looked out the window in the direction of Fountaingrove where he could see that about half of the sky was black. "When I first looked at it, I thought they were clouds and realized that no, it wasn't clouds. It was smoke, and it was extremely thick," he said in his deposition. He quickly moved to the front of the house, which faced northeast toward Mt. St. Helena and Calistoga. From there he could see what was coming: flames approaching over the hills and through the trees, just a half mile away, maybe less.

"I screamed at my wife to get up," he said. He put on shoes and a pair of pants and called his daughter, Molly Gallaher Flater, who lived in a home on their property about a quarter mile away. Luckily, she had her phone on. More than a family member, Molly, 34, was a key part of his businesses. She was a part owner of several Oakmont Senior Living holdings and, for the previous 10 years, held management positions at both Gallaher Homes and Gallaher Companies, where she oversaw the senior living portfolio. When Molly answered, Gallaher didn't mince words. He told her "to pack up and get out as quickly as she could," he said. He then called his next-door neighbor only to find he was in San Francisco, where he lived part-time. "But he had a caretaker on the property, and so [my neighbor] was able to warn his caretaker," Gallaher said.

He then turned to his wife, Cindy Gallaher, another critical Oakmont Senior Living executive who was in charge of project design for each Oakmont property. "You have one minute," Gallaher told her and then rushed to load the four family dogs while Cindy "threw a few documents in a box and headed out for the car." The power was out, making their work even more challenging.

Once he secured the dogs, Gallaher raced to warn a tenant living above their detached garage. Luckily the front door was open, so he ran upstairs to call for her. "It was extremely difficult," he said. "The winds up there were probably 60 or 70 miles an hour, and the noise was tremendous."

When the tenant came downstairs, she said she could only find one of her two cats. Gallaher ran back up to her apartment to help her look. When they found her pet, Bill gave her the keys to a spare car so her two cats and their four dogs were not all in the same vehicle. Then they left in tandem. "The [front] gate was not powered so we had to drive out a back road on dirt roads to get out," he said. They headed for the stables about a quarter of a mile down the road. "At this point, you could see the fire coming closer, and it was pretty terrifying," he said.

Once there, the Gallahers had to quickly decide what to do with their eight horses. After a quick discussion, they opted to remove them from the stables and put them in different pastures. "Horses have their buddies, so we had to make sure each horse went with horses that they got along with," he said. But leaving them behind was a difficult decision. "I advised my wife that this would be the best thing to do." Their other option was to leave the horses in a covered, mostly steel-built arena near the stables. But the arena had a wooden fence, which, if burned, would let the horses roam. "I told [Cindy] that the vinyl fences in the pastures wouldn't burn," he said. So, together, with the help of their ranch manager, whom Cindy had called, they grouped the horses, found a spot for their four goats, and closed the pasture gates. It was after midnight as Bill and Cindy Gallaher and their dogs, followed by their tenant and her two cats, drove off their 200-acre property. It was the last time they would see their home in one piece.

Once they reached the valley floor, the Gallahers turned onto Riebli Road and then west onto Mark West Springs Road, which by then had become a river of headlights and taillights from vehicles packed with evacuees. Ten minutes later, they turned north onto Highway 101 to seek refuge at the Windsor home of Bill's brother. Once there, they watched TV for about an hour and went to sleep.

Gallaher said in his deposition that he did not call anyone else during that time, aside from his brother. Did he consider going by Villa Capri on their way out? Gallaher's answer under oath during his deposition was succinct. "I had no reason in the world to think to drive by Villa Capri."

Skyhawk Neighborhood, About Four Miles West of Villa Capri

Around midnight, Elizabeth Bruno, standing outside her front door, watched a ball of fire crest the hills to the northeast and churn like a tornado toward her eastern Santa Rosa neighborhood. She sprinted up and down her street, banging on doors to wake her neighbors, including an 86-year-old woman who lived alone. Then Elizabeth, her wife, and their teenaged son scrambled to pack their three cars. When they were ready to leave, she stepped outside to track the fireball, but it wasn't there.

The wind had continued to push the Tubbs Fire toward Fountaingrove, and while she couldn't see the flames, she could hear backyard propane tanks exploding in the distance. Elizabeth's first thought was of Villa Capri and the seniors inside. *How are [the night staff] going to get them out of there?* she worried. She thought of her friends Helen Allen and Bess Budow, as well as Villa Capri's queen Henrietta Hillman and its king Len Kulwiec. Instinct told the former activities director to rush to their aid, as she had done before.

In 2014, when a 6.0 earthquake centered in Napa rattled Villa Capri at 3:20 a.m., Elizabeth and the management team had raced to the building to assist the residents. It was typical of the group's synergy, a group that included Tammy Moratto as Villa Capri's marketing director, then later its executive director. The team worked well together, according to Elizabeth. The group of seven directors and managers from the business, marketing, activities, maintenance, dining, health, and memory care offices met regularly to discuss emergency procedures and hold fire drills with the help of a consultant who delivered safety training to multiple shifts. The group forged friendships with one another and maintained consistency for the residents, a source of pride for the team.

But tonight, Elizabeth Bruno was no longer an employee. And the core team of long-term employees she envisioned rushing to execute an emergency plan no longer existed. Now, Villa Capri's executive director was Debie Smith, who had run the business department at rival assisted living complex Brookdale Chanate, and in the opinion of some former employees, put too much of an emphasis on the bottom line. She came with no elder caregiving experience or health care training, and she lacked the mandatory two years of college and at least three years of experience providing residential care to the elderly that California required for administrators of assisted living buildings with more than 50 people. Smith had to petition the California Department of Social Services for an exception waiver to get the job.

"I had a year of business school, and then some community college, just shy of two years," she said later. "But my—I think my experience made up for that." Before Brookdale, Smith worked as a receptionist in a real estate office, as a quality assurance auditor at Medtronic, and as a customer service representative who dispatched drivers to deliver oxygen and medical equipment for Apria Healthcare. She had also owned and operated her own small family daycare and an automobile detail shop.

Smith started in February 2016, and though employees say the first month or two went smoothly, shortly thereafter Elizabeth and other managers watched as one by one, core employees either quit or were fired. One of the first to go was the long-time maintenance manager, fired for what managers said was a minor infraction. Another long-term manager said Smith wrote her up for not saying goodbye to her before leaving for the day. "It seemed like she was cleaning house to get rid of the long-term employees," Elizabeth said. "You have this great-working machine. All of us had at least six years' experience."

After 10 years at Villa Capri, Elizabeth decided it was her time to leave. She gave a month's notice. "I was one of the best activity directors in Northern California," she said. "[Oakmont] corporate didn't want me to go anywhere." Elizabeth's departure was especially devastating for Henrietta. Among the tearful testimonials offered during Elizabeth's going-away party in April 2016, Henrietta stood up and told everyone Elizabeth Bruno was the rock of Villa Capri. "Without you, we wouldn't have what we've had here," Henrietta said. "I appreciate you, and I'll miss you. Your dedication will be missed by all." The "party" was like a wake, Elizabeth recalled. "I was leaving them. That was the hardest day of my life, walking through those doors."

Although she no longer collected a paycheck, Elizabeth continued to visit her Villa Capri friends, a move that ultimately contributed to the departure of long-term Health Services Director Lynda Tillman. It was customary for former staff to visit residents, especially if they left on good terms as Elizabeth had. One Saturday, after visiting Len, Henrietta, and others, Elizabeth popped by Tillman's office to say hello and to let her know she was there. The following Monday Tillman mentioned the visit to Smith, who wrote Tillman up for allowing an ex-employee to visit, former employees said. Disturbed by the reprimand, Tillman gave 30 days' notice and offered to train her replacement after a planned vacation. On the day Tillman was to depart for her trip, Smith told her not to return. As health services director, Tillman felt she needed to report each resident's history and care needs to the new hire, but Smith reportedly told her not to worry about it. According to former managers, Tillman felt awful about leaving without properly passing the baton.

Not all Villa Capri community members were critical of Smith. Resident Noella "Nell" Magnuson had only kind words for the new executive director. "We loved Debie. She was so nice. Anything I asked for, I got it," she said. "If I wanted special things done for dinner, she made it happen. She was wonderful." But Henrietta, an ex-wife and a widow to two successful executives, summed it up differently, and in her classic blunt-yet-decorous way. "Anybody who's going to be the boss is going to get a lot of criticism, but Debie didn't know what she was doing," Henrietta said. "She was a very nice young woman, but she didn't know her *blank* from her *blank*."

Villa Capri

During the first hour after midnight, Fountaingrove residents who weren't already awake were rousted by phone alerts, neighbors banging on their doors, police cars with sirens screaming, and officers shouting through PA systems for residents to flee immediately. But no patrol cars or fire engines had yet entered the gates to Villa Capri and Varenna, and no one had yet banged on the doors at Villa Capri, where med tech Marie and caregivers Cynthia, Anett, and Elizabeth were still working their first rounds in what they thought was an isolated and temporary power outage.

In the darkness, Elizabeth and Cynthia started with the highest room numbers and worked their way down. Since the two women had started at least an hour later than usual thanks to the power outage and subsequent flashlight search, some residents had soaked through their briefs, and so the duo needed to change sheets as well. Everything took longer than usual because Cynthia's injured wrist was in a brace and because they had to use flashlights for the first several apartments.

During a short break, Cynthia opened Snapchat on her phone. A friend had posted a view of a fire from somewhere in Santa Rosa. "I had a sucky signal because we weren't connecting to Wi-Fi, so I couldn't ask any questions to the girl who posted it," she said. Cynthia told Anett about the post, but neither was too concerned. They couldn't tell exactly where the fire was located, nor that it was a wildfire.

The room next to the second-floor landing belonged to Bess Budow who was frail, blind, and hard of hearing—and a functional quadriplegic because she had stopped using her arms and legs over the past year. Bess was a tough cookie who grew up in poverty in New York City during the Great Depression, then taught second grade in Chicago city schools and took her own children to anti-Vietnam War and Ban the Bomb protests in the 1960s. Once staunchly independent, Bess now needed help from caregivers for all daily functions, including two caregivers to turn her over in bed.

After logging dozens of complaints about Bess' $12,000-a-month care at Villa Capri, her family hired a personal caregiver for an additional $8,000 a month to tend to her for 12 hours a day. Occasionally, Maritza, who didn't want her last name used, stayed overnight. "Sometimes I was coming in [in the morning] and finding half of her body on the floor," Maritza said. "She was unable to help herself."

Bess' daughter, Sherry Minson, and granddaughter, Sarah Minson, insist Bess was active when she moved into Villa Capri in 2013. "But they kept banning her from doing activities because she was blind and needed attention. Finally the stick that broke the camel's back was [when] they said she couldn't eat in the dining room with her friends," because Bess would call out if she needed help while dining, Sarah said.

"The director decided that was too disturbing for the other residents," said Sherry, an employment attorney. Villa Capri was required to accommodate her mother's blindness, she said, but didn't have enough staff or functionality to deliver the care Bess needed. "They were not equipped to take care of disabled people, which is the whole reason people go into assisted living. They just acted like it was a camp or a resort."

The Minsons considered moving Bess into an apartment and hiring round-the-clock caregivers, but Sarah didn't like that idea for one very specific reason. "What if a caregiver doesn't show up, and there's a fire?" Sarah said. "The reason you put them in a facility is because if there's a fire, there's other staff there."

9

Chaos

The Firestorm: 1 a.m.

Tubbs Fire distance from Villa Capri and Varenna: Approximately 1.5 miles

As hundreds of vehicles fled west along Mark West Springs Road, Armando and Carmen Berriz of Southern California slept in the hills to the south, in the Crystal Court home they were renting with their daughter and son-in-law. The foursome was among the thousands of tourists who, each fall, chose Sonoma County for wine tasting, hiking, and bathing in mud baths and hot springs. At 12:54 a.m., the fire was at their doorstep. Armando and Carmen's son-in-law Luis Ocon woke up and looked out the window to see a glowing red ember explode when it hit the ground. He quickly woke everyone, and they all fled from the house in their pajamas.

According to press accounts, the family piled into their three cars and began an intense drive down Riebli Road. Flames burned all around them, and the smoke was so thick Luis said he had to navigate "by the feel of the tires on the reflectors that bumped like Braille down the middle of the road." What he didn't realize is that soon after they pulled out of the driveway, a tree fell, trapping his in-laws behind them. Knowing they couldn't get out, Armando and Carmen, married for 55 years, returned to the house—and jumped in the pool.

Overnight, as flames flashed 30 feet high around the pool deck and the winds tossed lawn furniture over their heads, 76-year-old Armando gripped the pool's brick sides while 75-year-old Carmen clung to him. When the heat was at its fiercest, they dipped underwater, leaving only their mouths and noses exposed. It was just before dawn, when the worst of the firestorm had passed, when Armando noticed that Carmen had stopped breathing. He held her for *hours in the water, not letting go until the smoke cleared. Then he carried her out, laid her on the pool deck, and walked 2 miles down the hill wearing the only two shoes he could find: one of his and one of hers. Carmen Berriz was one of 11 people who perished between midnight and 2 a.m.*

At 1:12 a.m. firefighters warned over REDCOM channels the fire "will be within Santa Rosa city limits within the hour."

Ten minutes later, the Sheriff's Office sent an advisory via Nixle.

> Santa Rosa fire spreading quickly: The fire from Porter Creek road has spread very quickly and has moved down Mark West Rd to Riebli, Thomas Lake Harris towards Fountaingrove...If in this area, you need to move out.

Tens of thousands of residents from the neighborhoods adjacent to Villa Capri and Varenna began fleeing their homes, residences prized for precisely what made them vulnerable—their proximity to the wild.

Northbound Highway 101

As Windsor Fire Capt. Mike Stornetta crossed the Golden Gate Bridge and traveled the remaining 50 miles to Santa Rosa, he listened intently to the constant stream of radio chatter over REDCOM where dispatchers typically handled roughly 25 calls an hour for daily emergencies. On October 8 and 9, they received in excess of 300 calls an hour—more than they typically received in a day—and processing them all was overwhelming. Some voices on the radio came from individuals Mike knew personally, people who, by their nature, didn't rattle easily. Mike could tell from the tenor of their voices that they were spooked. There were now more than a dozen wind-fueled fires, in addition to the Tubbs Fire, scattered throughout the North Bay including the Nuns Fire in Sonoma Valley and the Atlas Fire north of the city of Napa.

On the road, now about 20 minutes south of Santa Rosa, Mike could see the fire spanning the hills to the northeast. Fearing he wasn't going to make it to his childhood home in time, he called his wife, who was still on shift at the hospital. Activity had picked up there, she told him. Things were getting worse. He could hear the anxiety in her voice. "I need you to do me a favor," Mike told Stacie. "I need you to go over to Mom and Dad's house and get Grandma. I'm concerned that the fire is heading that way."

Stacie understood the urgency of the situation, and so did the charge nurse who cleared her to check out early. Stacie sped to her in-laws' house on Clear Ridge Road, just a mile west of Villa Capri. But she didn't have a key to the house, and the power was out. To make matters worse, Mike's 85-year-old grandmother, Mary Peterson, had taken sleeping pills before turning in for the night. Mike's mother tried calling from Palo Alto multiple times while Stacie banged on the front door. Eventually, Mike's mother was able to get through and convinced a still-groggy Mary to carefully descend the home's long staircase leading to the front door. Once there, Mary, still wearing her nightgown and carrying the family's Lhasa Apso, climbed into Stacie's Chevy Camaro and headed out. Stacie called Mike to report they were safe. "But where should we go?" she asked. It was a question many were asking at that hour.

Mike didn't know what to say. *Where is there a location in Sonoma County that's not at risk?* he thought. "Then we're going to the beach," Stacie responded. At least the beach was flat, the vegetation limited, and it was west—as far west as they could go. When they reached Bodega Bay, they found they weren't the only ones with that idea. Hundreds had flocked to the seashore, filling up campgrounds and parks to wait for the crisis to pass. For many, it would be a long wait.

Villa Capri

At 1 a.m., the power flipped back on. Caregiver Elizabeth Lopez hop-scotched up and down the stairs catching up on her rounds, oblivious to the growing wildfire risk outside. It was during a downstairs trip that Elizabeth first smelled smoke. She followed her nose to the building's northeast corner, in the memory care unit. The hallway looked foggy. She entered the closest room. The blinds were open, and through the window, Elizabeth saw a PG&E truck holding a worker aloft to the top of a utility pole. The lineman's presence would have been reassuring but for the scene that surrounded him. Bright red ashes blew in the wind. It was, in Elizabeth's words, "raining fire."

Elizabeth radioed Marie, but there was no response, so Elizabeth set off to find her. When she couldn't find Marie downstairs, she headed back to the second floor where Cynthia needed help in room 218, the room belonging to Virginia Gunn, 81, who needed turning because of partial paralysis and a decline due to colon cancer. When Elizabeth and Marie entered, tree branches were smacking Virginia's window, and outside, what should have been a clear, dark sky was illuminated by a flickering red glow.

Howarth Park Neighborhood, About Three Miles Southeast of Villa Capri

Melissa Langhals looked outside and knew the bloodshot sky meant a fire was burning in the hills northeast of her home. She watched as it grew, and soon she smelled smoke. An unemployed electrician, Melissa lived with her partner, Roxanne Campbell, near 138-acre Howarth Park, a beloved community treasure that, at times like this, presented a massive fire risk. Melissa told her partner she wanted to check it out, a prospect Roxanne shot down. "You don't do that," she said. "That's like chasing an ambulance." But Roxanne knew Melissa; it was her adventurous spirit that had drawn Roxanne to her some 20 years earlier. Before going to sleep, Roxanne instructed Melissa, "Don't you go anywhere without waking me up."

Not going anywhere included not going to Villa Capri, where several times a week Melissa made the 10-minute drive to visit her mother, Virginia Gunn. Virginia aspired to be an archeologist, so Melissa brought her *Smithsonian* and *Archeology Digest* magazines. Virginia once met an archeologist who offered to take her to Egypt to uncover reliefs, but she declined because of her four kids. Instead, Virginia became an artist and later worked as a career counselor for tough clients like members of the Hells Angels. According to Melissa, Virginia was nice to everyone, the kind of person who would take in anyone in need, including neighborhood kids whose parents had locked them out.

Melissa cared for both her parents after they suffered strokes, and then helped oversee their move to assisted living when it became overwhelming to have them in her home. After Melissa's father died in 2016, Melissa and her siblings moved Virginia into a single unit at Villa Capri. It seemed like a nice place for her, quite fancy for the girl who had grown up skinning rabbits for a living as a farm girl in Fort Bragg, California, but a good fit for the 24-hour care she needed after a stroke had left her left side paralyzed.

Virginia retained full mental function, but she couldn't cook, get to the restroom, or bathe independently.

Surrounded by strangers at Villa Capri, Virginia became reclusive and usually took meals in her room. Roxanne blamed management, not her mother-in-law. "I felt they isolated her," she said. "They didn't include her in any of the functions. They never had anyone take her down to the events. They pretty much wanted her to stay in her room." Virginia began to have bouts of dementia and continuous urinary tract infections that Roxanne thought affected her memory and coherence. "It was so bad; the doctor was, at one point, pursuing filing something [as evidence]" in the event neglect or abuse charges were warranted.

Melissa tried to make up for Virginia's isolation with frequent visits. Her sister swung by on days Melissa couldn't make it, and on Tuesdays, a neighbor stopped in. Another friend dropped by a couple times a week to help Virginia make collages with her one good hand. With four children and several grandchildren and cousins, someone was always checking on Virginia. But in the Tubbs Fire's early hours, only one family member lived close enough to ensure Virginia's safety, the one who shared Virginia's toughness and resourcefulness, the one who shared her instinct to put others first: Melissa.

At 1:15 a.m. Melissa called Villa Capri but couldn't get through. The power had gone out at home, so she lit a couple candles and set one on Roxanne's nightstand, then got into her car and sped toward the glow. When she came to a barricade at Brush Creek Road and Montecito Boulevard, about a mile from Villa Capri, she knew something was seriously wrong. She called her sister to let her know she was en route to check on their mom, and then Melissa, who inherited her mother's blonde hair, blue eyes, strong jawline, and signature selflessness, found a detour through the smoke.

Varenna, 1:15 a.m.

Outside Varenna, headlights cut through the hazy darkness as cars descended its long driveway toward Fountaingrove Parkway. Residents who had access to their cars were starting to leave. One of the first included Dick Lemmerding and his wife Nancy, who had woken to the sound of ferocious wind rattling their casita's windows. "The wind was unbelievable. It was up to almost hurricane force," Dick said. "We could see the flames outside our window, in the distance," toward the northeast. They woke their overnight guests, grabbed their dog, Charlie, jumped in their car, and drove away from their casita, the last unit at the complex's north end.

Inside the Main Building, Andre and Michael returned to the foyer from their second trip to the boiler room, this time looking for generators. Caregiver Teresa had started helping downstairs any residents on oxygen, those most vulnerable during the power outage. By then, Varenna Executive Director Nathan Condie arrived, and he was not happy. "Why are you bringing people out of their rooms?" Nathan asked her.

Nathan's position was based on company policy and practice. Should an alarm go off, residents were to remain in their rooms until instructed otherwise. It was a clear shelter-in-place policy, one printed in residents' instruction materials. "When the fire alarm goes off, we tell residents to stay inside and somebody will come tell you what to do," Nathan said. "We rely heavily on first responders telling us [what to do]. We don't evacuate unless we're told to because it's hard on the residents. That's when falls happen."

Nathan acknowledged, though, that the balance of the residents in the lobby were those whose portable oxygen concentrators couldn't run in their rooms during the power outage. He told the residents generators were on the way, and he directed those residents to wait for them in the activities room. At one point, Nathan told Andre to return a resident in a wheelchair to her apartment, but Andre was frustrated. He explained to Nathan that he and Michael had carried her down from her second-floor unit, step-by-step. They couldn't possibly be expected to carry her back up again. Nathan instructed them to put her in a vacant first-floor room.

Andre was still unsettled. "We need to start telling people that we may need to evacuate," he told Michael.

Larkfield Estates Neighborhood, About Three Miles Northwest of Villa Capri

Gena Jacob had stayed up later than usual watching the ten o'clock news because she had the next day off for Columbus Day. A report of the fire in Calistoga caught her ear because Gena and her wife, Sheri, had spent Sunday down the street from Tubbs Lane celebrating their friends' fiftieth wedding anniversary. Now, fire engines, sirens blaring, were racing down Mark West Springs Road, which ran alongside her development and wound through the mountains to Calistoga. It was the route they'd taken home after the party. That's crazy, she thought. We were just there.

Just before 11 p.m., Gena had received a confusing Nixle alert announcing fires at Mark West Springs and Riebli roads. *This must be a miscommunication*, she thought. That intersection was only three miles away, and they had friends who lived there. Gena didn't know it, but her night as town crier was just getting started. She rang their friends, who hadn't received the alert, although while Gena and her friend spoke on their cell phones, a robocall rang her friend's landline. They needed to leave immediately and decided to bug out to Gena and Sheri's home. After packing their dog and two cars, the couple said they were on their way. The drive usually took only a few minutes, but 10 minutes went by, then 15. As Gena and Sheri stood on their porch watching for their friends, the wind blew so hard their trees bowed and touched the lawn. Then a sheriff's deputy flipped a U-turn in the street. He told them the fire was just up the road. They, too, needed to leave. Right now.

Sheri jogged up and down the street to wake their neighbors, pairing up a couple of widowers with families, while Gena loaded her mother and their cat and dog into Sheri's car. Sheri left voicemails for neighbors who didn't open their doors. One man finally woke up and listened to her message, which prompted him to look through the glass in his front door. He was confronted by a solid wall of fire. He escaped through his back fence gate and jogged down Old Redwood Highway, eventually hitching a ride to an emergency shelter. He later told Gena and Sheri, "You saved my life. If you hadn't left that message on the phone...."

At 1:23 a.m., Gena snapped a photo of the huge red mass practically hovering over their home. For another six minutes, she fumbled in the dark to find something to house a rabbit and two guinea pigs because their cages were too big to fit in her car. The couple's original plan was to meet in the Coddingtown Center parking lot, but in the nine minutes since Sheri pulled out of the driveway, Gena called Sheri twice. "Don't be upset, but seeing what I'm seeing, I think I need to go get my dad," Gena told her.

She knew the drive to Fountaingrove well. Not only did Gena's father live at Villa Capri, Gena used to work for Oakmont Senior Living. Molly Gallaher Flater hired her as senior marketing director in 2010 for the Fountaingrove Lodge, the first retirement community in the nation to be marketed to lesbian, gay, bisexual, transgender, and queer seniors. "I was really excited to work there," Gena said. "It was very professional. It seemed caring." While waiting for final permits on Fountaingrove Lodge, Gena spent six months selling residents into both the Lodge and Varenna. Prospective residents were eager to hear about the location, amenities, and care options. They and their families rarely asked about emergency plans, she said.

The topic wasn't on Gena's mind either when she moved Arlyn Jacob, a former Pentecostal pastor and property manager, into Villa Capri in 2012. At that time, he could no longer live by himself, especially after he tried to hang a Christian flag on a rotting telephone pole that gave way, resulting in a broken hip and knee. He couldn't bend his leg afterward and needed regular support from caregivers. At 77, Arlyn was among the younger residents and still largely independent. He was allowed to sign himself out and drive his own car to Gena's house 10 minutes away.

When Gena worked for Oakmont Senior Living, the company owned at least four senior or assisted living communities like Villa Capri and five "Signature Living" properties like Varenna. Over the next four years, the company expanded rapidly. "They were buying land, getting projects approved, and then building them," Gena said. But Oakmont was not running daily caregiving, housekeeping, maintenance, and food service operations; those fell under the purview of another company.

In 2012, Oakmont Management Group took over those operations at Villa Capri and eventually at other Oakmont Senior Living-built complexes. Former employees said something changed when Villa Capri went from being the Gallahers' first care home after the Aegis split to one of a dozen, then two dozen, facilities in the rapidly expanding Oakmont Senior Living empire. "Nobody was willing to listen. Nobody was willing to follow up," said a former Villa Capri manager who requested anonymity for fear of retaliation. "It was corporate. It no longer felt like family. It no longer felt like what you said or did made a difference. The quality of food went downhill. And so did the quality of [employees]." Other former managers also said they felt pressure from those above them to fill rooms more quickly—within two to three days of a resident leaving or dying. They thought the company had become strictly "profit driven."

Gena left Oakmont employment in 2014. She was tired of working evenings and weekends and dismayed by the staff turnover she had witnessed over the previous two years. "They built their corporate army, and that's when the whole culture changed," Gena said. Residents noticed a change too. "The suits came in, the MBAs," resident Len Kulwiec said. "They had only one option and that was to bring the bottom line down. They started to squeeze the company."

But Gena's dad remained at Villa Capri, where she was pleased with the care Arlyn received from Activities Director Elizabeth Bruno and her team of long-term colleagues, including Gena's close friend, Tammy Moratto, who was then the executive director. In Gena's mind, both women took residents' safety and well-being seriously.

101 Southbound

It had already been a long day for Vivian Flowers by the time she left the Healdsburg restaurant she owned and saw fire on the ridgelines. It was well after midnight, and she immediately worried about her mother, Viola Sodini, 82, a resident of Villa Capri's Traditions Memory Care center for the past nine months. As Vivian drove, she dialed Villa Capri and asked the woman who answered, Marie So, if everything was OK. Her response—"We're fine"—eased Vivian's fears in the moment. "Later on I found out they'd already lost power [once], and everything wasn't fine," she said.

For four years, Vivian had taken care of her mother in her own home in Sonoma after Viola was diagnosed with Alzheimer's. The turning point came when Vivian found her mother trying to open a walnut with a chef's knife. "I wasn't out of the room for two minutes. She would have cut her fingers off," Vivian said. "That's when I realized 'I can't keep her safe.'" It was a difficult decision for Vivian, who felt guilty, as if she was choosing her own life over her mother's. Viola, whom Vivian described as a cross between 1970s television icons Edith Bunker of *All in the Family* and Marion Cunningham of *Happy Days*, had always been her daughter's "base camp," the person who never turned her away, even when Vivian ran away or endured stints with drugs and alcohol. "I was the 'shit kid,' as she puts it, who gave her all of her gray hair," Vivian said.

Viola married in high school and had three children, each one a year apart, and settled just south of Santa Rosa in Kenwood with her truck-driving husband. When she sought work outside the home, she found a job that allowed her to be present when her children returned from school. She spent 32 years as head chef at a Santa Rosa elementary school. Once her kids were grown, Viola continued to be their rock; Vivian moved back in with her mother when she was 47 and going through a divorce.

Eventually, Vivian repaid her mother's lifelong devotion by becoming base camp for Viola. But after four years of managing rotating and live-in caregivers while she and her husband worked at their restaurant, Vivian realized she couldn't keep doing it once they retired. "I love being with my mom and doing stuff with her, but 24 hours a day, seven days a week—I'm just not that person," she said.

They chose Villa Capri largely because of its beauty, quickly submitted a $10,000 deposit, and began paying $6,700 a month in fees. But complaints about her mother's care mounted. The laundry would misplace Viola's clothes, so Vivian would find her mother wearing shoes without socks, or someone else's pants two sizes too small. Occasionally, she would find her mother in soiled incontinence briefs. Viola's medication would get mixed up. Her belongings, and her glasses and dentures, kept going missing. Vivian asked about security cameras hoping they could catch the thief, but there weren't any. It turned out Viola's next-door neighbor had dementia that manifested as kleptomania.

More serious were the five urinary tract infections Viola suffered. "It seemed like she was on antibiotics all the time," Vivian said. And then Viola developed rashes that she would scratch until they bled. Her doctor diagnosed an allergic reaction to the sun, so Vivian asked staff to keep her mother in the shade or inside, but when employees were distracted, Viola would wander outdoors. Vivian took this and other complaints to Executive Director Debie Smith. According to Vivian, Smith replied, "We'll see if we can do better," but Vivian didn't see any progress. A month before the fire, one former Villa Capri employee stopped by Vivian's Healdsburg restaurant and told her employees "were quitting right and left" and Villa Capri was "not rehiring," so remaining employees had to juggle multiple jobs.

This all led her to a dreadful conclusion: "Villa Capri was like a beautifully painted egg, but the inside was rotten."

As she continued on Highway 101, Vivian took a call from her nephew who worked for PG&E and told her Fountaingrove neighborhoods were being evacuated. Vivian tried dialing Villa Capri again, but no one answered, so she and her husband, Howard, turned around and headed north, but they only made it to the bottom of Fountaingrove Parkway at Mendocino Avenue. "The police already had the road blocked off," she said. Vivian was told seniors from assisted living complexes were getting bused to the Finley Community Center. "From then on, it was absolute chaos."

Villa Capri, 1:30 a.m.

Gena Jacob pulled out of her driveway and headed south toward Fountaingrove. The first person she thought to call was Tammy Moratto because hers was the only Oakmont-related cell number Gena still had programmed into her phone. Tammy was no longer the executive director after Oakmont transferred her to a corporate regional marketing role, but Gena thought it made sense to alert her anyway. Gena said she was frantic when Tammy answered at 1:30 a.m., according to phone records. Gena asked if the Villa Capri team was removing her father from the building. Tammy responded, "What are you talking about?" She had been asleep; Gena was hyped up and scared. "There's a huge fire, and it's going to move with the wind, and I'm assuming it's going to hit Fountaingrove," Gena said. "You need to call the fire department to check what I'm telling you."

At 1:36 a.m. the Sonoma County Sheriff's Office issued via Nixle an evacuation advisory for Gena's neighborhood at the base of the Mayacamas' slopes, just over a mile north of Villa Capri. Two minutes later, the Santa Rosa Fire Department tweeted, "Due to a large wildfire, all residents north of Fountaingrove Parkway at the city limits are urged to evacuate." This included Villa Capri and Varenna.

By that point, Gena had reached the base of Fountaingrove Parkway. A police officer at the intersection motioned the four or five cars ahead of hers to turn around. He approached Gena's window, but before he could finish giving her the same order, she said her father lived at Villa Capri, "and nobody is evacuating him." She was still on the phone with Tammy. Gena held the handset out to the officer. "She can validate my father is in the building," Gena said. The officer waved her uphill.

Within minutes Gena pulled up to the Villa Capri and Varenna gates. They were locked. Typically only residents and employees had the code, and visitors had to use the call box for a staff member to remotely open the gate. Gena called, but no one answered. She tried all the codes she could remember but was unsuccessful until a man she believed was an employee dressed in black came walking down the driveway. He opened the gate manually, and Gena drove through, turned right toward Villa Capri, and pulled her car under the portico by the front doors.

After her conversation with Tammy Moratto, Gena anticipated what she would see as she walked into the building at 1:40 a.m. "I'm thinking I had called someone from the executive management team, and they are busting up there, executing the emergency evacuation plan, and they are going to get people out of there," she said. "That's what I thought was going to happen." But when she entered the lobby, Gena found nothing of the sort. Two employees were hanging out in the living room area. "What's going on out there?" one of them asked.

"I'm here to get my dad. There's a fire," Gena told them. "I called Tammy. She should be contacting you about what to do."

Gena's wife had already called Arlyn to tell him to get dressed and packed, so he was ready except for collecting his wallet and medications. On their way to the elevator, Arlyn saw his friend Henrietta out for her typical midnight stroll and told her there was a fire and that she should return to her room and call her son to pick her up.

"Yes, go call your son," Gena told her with urgency in her voice.

Though the lights were on upstairs, they flickered and dimmed as Gena held the elevator door for her slow-moving father on his walker. She shouted for him to hurry while she waited for him to get there. She worried that if the power went out, they would get stuck between floors. But the alternative was also problematic. *How could she possibly get her disabled father down two flights of stairs?* As Arlyn stepped inside the elevator, Gena told herself they would be OK because surely Villa Capri's backup generators would kick in. After all, when she had sold residents into Varenna, prospective families would sometimes ask if they had generators, and she always confirmed they did. "We were told there were requirements to have backup generators," she said.

Fortunately, they made it downstairs in the elevator, and Gena led her father into the lobby where Arlyn insisted on signing himself out like usual. As she helped her father into her car, it struck Gena as odd that the two employees hanging out in the living room weren't in evacuation mode. "They were very nonchalant," she said. She reasoned management must have been in the midst of an emergency meeting and was about to give direction.

At 1:49 a.m., Gena turned her green Ford Fusion onto Fountaingrove Parkway, just as Tammy called. Gena told Tammy that all 400-plus residents of Oakmont's four Fountaingrove communities—Villa Capri, Varenna, Fountaingrove Lodge, and The Terraces—needed to leave. Now.

As Gena drove down the hill, she asked her father whether he had ever participated in a fire drill. "Not in the five years I've lived at Villa Capri," Arlyn replied. Gena thought that was impossible, but her dad insisted. When Gena had briefly worked for Varenna five years earlier, she recalled participating in a fire drill that involved all the residents and staff. "I assumed Villa Capri would have the same protocol."

Gena was later haunted by the fact that she didn't take additional residents with her as she left that night. She assumed the cavalry would soon arrive to usher Arlyn's neighbors to safety, and she worried about liability if she took residents, like Henrietta, out of the building. "I had no idea they didn't have a plan, and they were flying by the seat of their pants," she said. "I thought I was doing the right thing by blowing the horn."

Villa Capri, 1:53 a.m.

Cynthia had finished caring for Helen Allen in room 206 and was on her way to get help changing Mary Fitzpatrick in room 204 when she crossed paths with Gena Jacob, who had come to get her father. Cynthia wondered how Gena got inside, considering Villa Capri's doors were locked at night, as was the gate at the bottom of the hill. Cynthia watched bewildered as Gena asked her father if he had packed his medications, then Cynthia asked

Gena what was going on. "There's a fire two miles up. I'm taking my dad," Gena said, an act that reduced the number of residents to an even 60.

Cynthia hadn't discounted the glow she and Elizabeth saw from Virginia's room, but they didn't know a fire was so close. "That's when I freaked out," Cynthia said. Instead of waiting for help, Cynthia put Mary in a new nightgown, swapped her fitted sheet, and told her to lie back down; Cynthia would be right back. She hurried downstairs to find the others.

While Cynthia looked for her coworkers, Elizabeth looked for Marie and also came upon Gena, who she said was walking like "Speedy Gonzalez" and coaching her father to "Come on, Dad! Hurry up, Dad!" Marie still wasn't answering her radio, so Elizabeth stepped outside for a cell signal, a hit-or-miss proposition on a regular day in Fountaingrove. She needed to hear her daughter's voice, to make sure she was safe, but Elizabeth couldn't get service. The wind spun ashes all around her.

Out of nowhere, a man approached. It was her then-boyfriend, Juan Carlos Gonzalez. He'd heard about the fire moving toward Fountaingrove and tried to call Elizabeth, but she hadn't picked up. She checked her phone but didn't have any messages. Unbeknownst to Elizabeth, wind and flames had knocked out 70 local cell towers in those first few hours. When Juan couldn't reach her, he begged a friend to give him a ride to Villa Capri. He was glad to see her, but she was worried she might get in trouble for having her boyfriend at work, so she made him wait in her minivan while she went back inside.

Finally, Elizabeth, Anett, Marie, and Cynthia converged in the lobby. Marie's radio was broken. Cynthia relayed Gena's message about a fire headed their way. They checked their phones to verify Gena's report, but they were cut off from any news. The four women were scared. To make matters worse, the person in charge, med tech Marie So, appeared panicked. Elizabeth could see it in her face. "She didn't know what to do," Elizabeth said.

In all the training Elizabeth, Anett, Marie, and Cynthia attended at Villa Capri, from their initial onboarding to the monthly in-person training sessions, no one had broached what to do in a wildfire. There had been no fire drills. They were shown how to use a fire extinguisher, but even an army of professional firefighters with tactical gear would be no match for the firestorm approaching their backyard. "We didn't know what the plan was. We were never trained for that," Cynthia said. "At least, I wasn't."

Needing direction, Marie called Debie Smith to relay the news that this wasn't a simple power outage. Smith asked her to walk outside to see if the fire was visible. Marie admitted she smelled smoke and noticed the wind, but when she returned to the phone she told her boss, "There's no fire near us yet." After she hung up, Marie told her coworkers Debie wanted them to stay calm and do their routine resident checks every hour instead of every two.

Though Elizabeth was the newest Villa Capri employee, the 30-year-old had more caregiving and med tech experience than the other three combined. She considered Debie's orders. "My understanding was 'Stay in the building, check on [the residents] every hour, it's going to be fine,'" Elizabeth said. But she felt differently. *It's not going to be fine*, she thought.

And then she seized the moment. "We are not doing this, because I'm trying to go home tonight," she told the others.

Marie later swore she called 911 because Debie told her to, but Elizabeth said Marie called for a different reason. "I refused to do what Debie said to do," Elizabeth recalled. She said she was the one who told Marie, "You need to call 911 and ask if we need to evacuate. Are we going to be safe?"

On a night when dispatchers received more than a thousand calls in six hours, Marie managed to get a live operator when she dialed 911. She gave the dispatcher their address, 1397 Fountaingrove Parkway, and asked whether there was a fire nearby. The dispatcher confirmed there was, and after Marie asked, "Should we evacuate?" the dispatcher didn't hesitate to say yes. Marie then called Debie Smith, who said she was on her way and again instructed them to keep residents in their rooms and guard the exits until she arrived.

Elizabeth took charge again. "No," she said firmly, and she pitched her own plan. "What we're going to do is we're going to start getting the residents out, and we're going to start [on the] first floor from the back to the front."

It made sense to the rest of the women to start with memory care, but after that, then what? How would they move them off the property? The obvious answer was to load residents into the two vehicles the activities director used for field trips. The larger bus could seat at least 26 passengers while the smaller shuttle carried as many as 15, depending on whether passengers were in wheelchairs. Both buses were equipped with wheelchair lifts. The four women knew both buses were in the rear parking lot, but none of them knew where to find the keys. In the midst of their phone calls and strategizing, the power cut out at 1:53 a.m.—this time for good.

Using flashlights and cell phones, the employees paused on moving the residents in favor of hunting for bus keys. Cynthia checked Smith's office, which was locked. She also checked the activities room and the scheduler's office where the caregivers picked up their shift keys. Anett searched the front desk and a supervisor's office. She watched Marie pace, distraught. *Surely*, Anett thought, *when the executive director arrives, she will be able to find them.*

Without success in their key-finding mission, and feeling time was of the essence, the four women shifted to moving memory care residents from their first-floor rooms to the lobby. The caregivers awakened, changed, and escorted to the lobby those who could walk. Elizabeth and Cynthia devised a system for those who couldn't. Elizabeth maneuvered the residents from bed to chair on her own while Cynthia and her injured wrist held the wheelchair steady. Then Cynthia pushed the resident to the lobby while Elizabeth prepared the next resident. "What's your location?" Cynthia would call over the radio, then meet Elizabeth in the next room. For help transporting the heaviest residents, Elizabeth retrieved her boyfriend from her minivan outside. A quick study, Juan assumed the role of her evacuation partner in moving memory care residents into wheelchairs and then pushing them to the lobby.

It was dark in the halls, and the air was dingy with smoke. The going was slow, and the residents sometimes complicated the women's efforts. Louise Johnson, for example, wanted Cynthia to take her to the restroom before wheeling her to the lobby. Seniors with dementia can be disagreeable when taken out of their routine and living quarters, and some residents fought the prospect of dressing and leaving their rooms in the middle of the night. In the midst of all this, Cynthia managed to reach Health Services Director Jane Torres and told her they were evacuating because of a fire. "She thought I meant a fire inside the building," Cynthia said, shocked that Smith hadn't called Torres. "Debie hasn't called you?" Cynthia asked. "There's a huge wildfire."

At one point, Elizabeth, Marie, Cynthia, and Anett convened in a hallway. Elizabeth told Anett to go home; she didn't want her pregnant colleague breathing the smoke. Anett refused, so Elizabeth sent her to the front of the building where the smoke seemed thinner. Someone needed to care for the residents accumulating in the lobby, especially with three or four wanderers who kept trying to return to the comfort of their room. It became Anett's job to corral them so they didn't return to the memory care unit or walk straight out the front door.

Sebastopol, About 10 Miles Southeast of Villa Capri

A Nixle alert at 1:22 a.m. woke Kathy and Mark Allen, but they ignored it. Whatever the hell was going on at that hour wasn't going to get Mark out of bed. But when another Nixle sounded minutes later, it piqued Kathy's interest. She looked at her phone and told Mark there was "a grass fire at Mark West and Riebli Road." Mark couldn't believe it.

"How close is that to Mom?" Kathy asked of her mother-in-law at Villa Capri.

"About three miles," Mark assessed.

Mark called Villa Capri, and Marie answered. He asked if they were aware a "grass fire" was headed their way, and Marie said yes. They were planning to get residents out of bed. Mark also asked if they needed help, and Marie said they did.

The couple jumped up and got dressed. Mark put on his black-rimmed glasses and, figuring he might be put to work, the retired high school shop teacher dressed appropriately. He put on old blue jeans, a wool shirt, and worn work boots. Kathy threw on jeans too, along with running shoes. Mark grabbed batteries and two flashlights, and they left home to traverse their familiar northeast route from upscale-hippie Sebastopol to well-to-do Fountaingrove. The air was warm and smoky and ashes were falling as Mark pulled their Suburban out of the garage. "We had no clue how this was going to develop," he said.

Varenna, Main Building, 1:53 a.m.

According to Varenna staff members, Executive Director Nathan Condie spent most of the night near the front lobby, sometimes directing residents, sometimes talking on his phone. Michael thought he looked nervous and uncertain.

Nathan was frustrated. He didn't understand why residents kept leaving their rooms despite orders to the contrary. "Every time a resident came down to the Main Building from a casita or from another building or from their room, people were opening doors, letting smoke in," he said. "If they had stayed where they were, the building would have been more sealed up." The fire alarms would have kept quiet too.

Then, sometime around 1:45 a.m., two men bounded through the front door. One was Hector Hernandez, an Oakmont employee who lived on the property. The second was a relative who had arrived to pick up a resident. "Did you guys see the fire?" the family member asked Nathan and others nearby.

Andre said Nathan "looked like a deer in the headlights." Nathan would later say he had no idea there was a fire because when he drove to Varenna around midnight, he took a back route, one that obstructed his view to the north and the east. His cell phone worked, but every attempt he made to call 911 was met with a busy signal. Nathan said he didn't know there was a fire that close until that moment.

The second man to enter motioned toward the back of the building, and the group flocked through the sitting area, past the grand piano, and through the wood-framed arched glass doors onto the terrace where they stood at the top of the steps that descended beside a Varenna landmark, the circular water feature that towered above the patio and pool area like a giant compass. At its center sat an illuminated golden chalice-shaped fountain designed to spill unbroken veils of water as if in perpetual homage to the biblical sentiment so steeped in the Varenna ethos: "My cup runneth over." But now, the stiff wind had turned the elegant fountain into something of a sprinkler, casting water onto the steps and terrace deck. Nathan, Andre, Michael, Hector, and the resident's relative stared into the distance across Fountaingrove Lake and the golf course. "All you could see was the glow of orange," Andre said. "And you could see the lights of first responders rushing out there." What they saw was the glow of the fire burning in the Larkfield and Mark West Springs area, and it was moving south toward them. Ash was starting to fall like snowflakes. Michael used his cell phone to record the scene, while Andre looked at Nathan.

"What's the fire evacuation program?" Andre asked his executive director. Nathan didn't answer. Andre asked twice more, both times reiterating the importance of getting residents off the hill. "Each time, Nathan looked at me and didn't answer," Andre said.

Michael recalled the same thing. "Dre asked, 'What's the fire evacuation process like? What's our plan?' He asked [Nathan], like, three times, four times, and I was there next to him. And [Nathan] never answered once. Not once." Nathan's silence rattled them all, according to Michael. "He was quiet as a mouse…And we were just kind of disoriented by that because he's supposed to be the captain of our ship. But yet, he looked on the edge of the plank like he was ready to jump."

Even when Nathan had seen the fire so close, he didn't think Varenna was in immediate danger. "I figured it was, you know, not [coming] toward us," but moving west. He tried warning Robert May, the executive director of Fountaingrove Lodge, located to Varenna's west on Thomas Lake Harris Drive. Nathan said he thought "that's where it was headed, on that side of the hill," but his call didn't go through.

As the others hurried inside from the terrace, Nathan turned to Michael. "When you get a chance, can you fix that umbrella over there?" he asked and pointed to a large canvas umbrella that lay twisted and half submerged in the half-moon-shaped illuminated pool below them. Although he thought it an odd request, coming in the middle of a crisis, Michael did as Nathan requested, pulling the umbrella from the pool. Moments later, at 1:53 p.m. the power went out again.

By then, the five who had been on the veranda were back inside. The relative who had come for his family member asked Andre if residents were able to exit through the main gate now that the power was out. The man gave Andre a ride down to the gates, while Hector followed in his car. Once there, Andre showed Hector how to open the gate manually and how to secure it to ensure it remained open. Then Hector did the same for the entrance gate. While they worked, a steady stream of cars passed by on Fountaingrove Parkway's two westbound lanes.

When Andre returned to the Main Building, he found Nathan on the phone, talking as he walked. Andre assumed he'd gotten through to the fire department or the city but soon realized that Nathan was speaking to the alarm company. "So you're going to come tomorrow and reset the alarms?" Nathan asked. "That's great."

Andre was fighting frustration. He didn't understand why Nathan was so focused on resetting the alarms when they could now clearly see that a wildfire was just beyond the crest of the hill. "That's when he should have really been getting people out of their rooms, in my opinion," Andre said. "He should have known in his own mind that the fire was going to be on that property before long."

10

Velocity

The Firestorm: 2 a.m.

Tubbs Fire distance from Villa Capri and Varenna: Less than one mile

At 2:02 a.m. a firefighting crew radioed that the fire had jumped six-lane Highway 101 just north of the Kohl's department store in Santa Rosa. "When you find anybody available, we need assistance," the firefighter pleaded. The fire would soon begin its deadly assault on a neighborhood of single-family, ranch-style homes known as Coffey Park.

Seven minutes later, Sonoma County sent another Nixle advisory warning that the fire had reached Larkfield, Gena's neighborhood three miles northwest of Villa Capri and Varenna. The alert also said northbound 101 was closed near Bicentennial Way. The fire front had torn through the narrow canyons threaded by Porter Creek Road and was burning through the residential areas of Mark West Springs and Larkfield just off Highway 101 north of Santa Rosa. As flames moved toward neighborhoods deeper into northwest Santa Rosa, another front was burning through the Sky Farm subdivision above Fountaingrove, consuming blocks of multimillion-dollar homes like kindling.

Sometime after 2 a.m. the fire reached the top of Fountaingrove at Newgate Court, where Santa Rosa's newly constructed Fire Station No. 5 sat perched near a water tank. Built in 2015 as a model for future stations, the 5,500-square-foot building featured a gym, a large kitchen, and a day room constructed on a small piece of city-owned property. Before the station's approval, Planning Commissioner Scott Bartley, an architect who would go on to be mayor, noted the location would help protect Fountaingrove from future disasters like the Hanly Fire. "History will repeat itself," he said. But the fire station proved no match for the Tubbs Fire. The structure was consumed in a matter of hours, *rendering the city's $4.6 million investment not only short-lived but inoperable during the firefight.*

Meanwhile, Janice Laskoski, 66, lived alone in a house on nearby Skyfarm Drive on the other side of the golf course from Villa Capri; she had grown up in San Francisco with the children of Villa Capri residents Ruth Callen and Mary Lou Delaney. Janice woke after the wind slammed an outdoor heating tower against her house, and she opened the drapes to see homes and trees lining the Fountaingrove Club golf course on fire. Janice put on her pink cotton robe and fluffy slippers, ran downstairs, grabbed her purse and cell phone, and entered her garage. As she struggled to open the door without power, friends down the hill called to pick her up. She ran inside for a flashlight, then back out to meet them in the street. "I couldn't see three inches from my face. It was so smoky, and it was as quiet as could be, and frightening," she said. "Fire was just spinning all over, like a hurricane of fire."

Janice, whose driveway was less than three-quarters of a mile from Villa Capri and Varenna, realized no one could reach her, so she walked uphill to a house with a recessed entry, thinking the concrete nook would provide decent shelter. But through the home's picture windows, she saw flames at the back of the house. She crouched underneath the front windows, but the fire breached the building and blew out the glass, causing shards to fall around her. She crawled along the garage wall to escape and came upon a garden hose, which she used to cool herself and drench the ground around her.

Then she lay down, unsure what would come next. After an indeterminable period, Janice saw a shadow retreat in the distance. "I wasn't sure what it was. It was just a big form moving," she said, thinking perhaps it was a vehicle. "And I was just praying it would turn around."

Rather than get up and race toward possible salvation, Janice first behaved like a good Californian. "I turned the water off, like it made a difference," she said. "We were in a drought." She waited in the street, and mercifully, the shadow reappeared. Rancho Adobe Volunteer Fire Department engine 9161 had gone up to her home at 3812 Skyfarm Drive looking for Janice because her friends said a woman was in desperate need of rescue. It was only after the crew U-turned to head back that they spotted Janice's flashlight beam through the smoke.

They scooped her up—her clothes, skin, and hair coated with soot—handed her a bottle of water and asked her for directions to the Kaiser hospital. But the whole way down Skyfarm Drive, Thomas Lake Harris Drive, and Fountaingrove Parkway, Janice questioned whether the hospital would be a safe haven. "It was so, so smoky, and the fire was right there," she said.

Janice was treated in the Kaiser emergency room for eye irritation and shoulder burns. Although the soles of her pink slippers had melted, they were still on her feet as she shuffled to a chair and sat near a woman around 90 years old and her 30-something caregiver. The pair had come from Varenna, they said, where the young woman told Janice she "basically dragged [her elderly charge] out of the building into her own car and drove to the hospital." The Varenna resident was vibrant but not strong enough for the stairs, and her delicate skin now had the bruises and bleeding to prove it.

As the three women sat chatting, the waiting room filled with people needing treatment, and each time the doors opened, smoke drifted inside. Before long, the hospital would need to be evacuated, and Janice and her new friends from Varenna would be triaged, loaded on a bus, and taken to a county shelter.

Despite her harrowing experience, Janice was one of the fortunate ones that evening. Five of the people who perished in the North Bay fires died because they were unable to raise a garage door during the power outage, leaving them no way out.

Skyhawk Neighborhood, 2 a.m.

As Elizabeth Bruno, her wife, and their teenaged son left their neighborhood in a caravan of three cars, Elizabeth had Villa Capri's residents on her mind. By all accounts, the facility was a very different place since her departure the year before. In the previous 14 months, Villa Capri onboarded new directors for the health services, business, activities, and maintenance departments. The year 2017 also brought three different memory care directors, with Registered Nurse Janice Wilson having been on the job for less than two months.

During the halcyon days of Aegis ownership, Elizabeth, Tammy Moratto, Lynda Tillman, and Javier Mendez had worked closely to address residents' needs, and the group became skilled at evacuations. In one instance, after Tillman smelled gas on the patio and a PG&E representative instructed her to evacuate the building, the staff had all residents and their wheelchairs and walkers outside in the parking lot within 20 minutes. Firefighters found a leaky propane tank in the barbecue area, so the episode served as more of an unannounced drill. But it proved insightful. Evacuating the building in broad daylight with a building chock full of staff was feasible. However, managers worried about overnight emergencies, when the facility would be staffed by a handful of employees who were likely to be new to the industry or to Villa Capri.

Former managers raised these concerns with corporate management and advocated for a night shift manager. "We used to tell [Oakmont to] put more staff up there in the evening. They need management in the evening. It's not a nine-to-five job in this industry anymore. You need management there around the clock. At least one," a longtime manager said.

Family members were also upset by the night staffing ratios. In one instance, Henrietta's son Corky Cramer returned his mother to Villa Capri at 8:30 p.m. and rang the bell to the locked entry but got no response for more than 10 minutes. He called the front desk, and a young woman who spoke limited English picked up. She indicated she was one of only two caregivers on staff that night for the 62 residents. She was the only employee for the 25 residents in memory care. Corky was incredulous and took his complaint to Debie Smith, who he said checked the logs and seemed satisfied because there were not two but three employees on duty. "But one is just a pill person," Corky countered. "I do not understand how someone is not required to be at the front desk 24/7." He suggested Smith post a sign with instructions for what to do if no one answered the door, but "there was no change," he said.

Concerns came from residents too. Henrietta was the staff's eyes and ears after hours, a notorious night owl who would roam the building and inform managers about the nocturnal goings-on. Her reports ranged from the personal—"Dorothea's been up all night"—to the procedural—"You know, this place isn't safe at night because these kids don't know what they're doing."

And then, thanks to Elizabeth Bruno's buoying his spirits, Len Kulwiec got involved. Len had served on an assisted living resident council in Southern California and knew assisted living residents had legal rights to organize and have their complaints taken seriously about everything from food to care to price increases. Through the establishment of resident councils, California gives residents the right to recommend to administrators changes to improve daily life and promote residents' rights. Administrators are required to respond within 14 days. Elizabeth had started Villa Capri's three-member resident council when the building opened; Len was elected president in early 2015.

Len did his homework on California law and came prepared for the monthly meetings, attended by a dozen or so residents who voiced a range of complaints. Residents hated losing their favorite caregivers, which Len thought was due to low pay. The emotional component of caregiver consistency was highly valued by residents, but safety was at the heart of their staffing concerns. In case of fire, residents were instructed to stay in their rooms. The fire marshal told managers the fire doors would close and sprinklers would engage.

Len reiterated the process at a council meeting. "I told everyone that this was the safest place in the world," he said, "that those blue dots, [the retracted sprinkler heads], would pop out and the room would be sprinkled in case of a fire." That might suffice for a room or two, or a wing, but Elizabeth had bigger concerns. "What if the whole place was on fire? How do you get them out of there? How do you get them from upstairs to downstairs?" she wondered.

Other former managers who spoke on the condition of anonymity said they questioned all five of Villa Capri's former executive directors and the admissions office staff about the merits of placing on the second floor any residents in wheelchairs or those who couldn't navigate the stairs independently. From as early as 2009, former staff members recalled asking about on-site generators, units strong enough to power an elevator or HVAC system and capable of automatically engaging when the power cut out. Staff members were told Oakmont's assisted living license didn't require generators of any type.

One former manager recalled the topic of generators coming up at a morning staff meeting when an employee discussed the 2014 Napa earthquake. "Why didn't Villa Capri have generators?" the employee asked. Tammy Moratto, who was executive director at the time, took the issue to

Oakmont and reported back. "Corporate didn't think we needed it," the employee recalled Moratto telling them. Len ultimately left the resident council in 2016 because he felt he couldn't make a difference.

By October 8, 2017, Villa Capri's long-standing management team—and its institutional knowledge—was gone. "It's sad to say, they set themselves up for disaster," said one former manager. "If anyone looks at all the [changes among] department heads and looks at every single person who left within a few months of Debie taking over, they would think, 'What happened?'"

Had Elizabeth continued in her role as activities director, she knows what she would have done when she first saw puffs of black smoke billowing in the direction of Villa Capri. "I would have called Debie or Tammy and said, 'I'm on my way' and told them how to help the staff," she said. She would have told the NOC shift crew the whereabouts of everything: the bus keys, the red emergency binder, the medication cart, the residents' medical data, and the emergency supplies. "I would have gone to help those kids," Elizabeth Bruno said. "That's what managers do. They flock to help."

Coddingtown Center, Two Miles Southwest of Villa Capri

As planned, Gena and Sheri Jacob reunited in the smoky Coddingtown Center parking lot just on the east side of Highway 101. It was a little past 2 a.m., and they sat in separate cars trying to figure out where to go and what to do. The fire was reported burning through their neighborhood. Then Gena's phone rang. It was Tammy Moratto, now in regional sales marketing for Oakmont Management Group, asking where Gena had taken her father. Gena told Tammy they were parked at Coddingtown Mall, and Tammy asked if there was room for Villa Capri buses. "It's smoky and hazy," Gena said, "but there's plenty of room."

Villa Capri, Second Floor

Near the end of Mark and Kathy Allen's 15-minute drive from Sebastopol, a man in an orange vest stopped them at the triangular merge of Fountaingrove Parkway and Bicentennial Way. It was too dangerous to continue, he told them. They should turn around. After the Allens explained that they were going to help residents at a senior care home, the man let them pass. From that point on, Mark and Kathy felt they had landed on a movie set. To Kathy, it felt like the tornado scene from *The Wizard of Oz*. The wind blew crosswise so fiercely that sticks and other debris hit their windshield and limited their visibility. Mark described it as something out of *Star Wars*. As their headlights reflected off the smoke, the whirling, ash-pocked air combined with the angle of their ascent to give the impression they were careening at hyperspeed through a galaxy far, far away. Theirs was the only car headed uphill.

They swerved around a tree that had blown over, and then Mark almost missed the left into Villa Capri and Varenna's shared driveway, a turn they had made hundreds of times. Their familiar guidepost, the entrance to the Keysight Technologies corporate complex, was dark. The strange, gaping blackness threw them off. Mark parked in one of Villa Capri's disabled parking spaces, worrying at first that he might get a ticket.

It was a little after 2 a.m. when they hopped out and felt the hot wind on their faces. The front doors were locked, as expected, but when they peered inside, they saw 10 residents sitting in wheelchairs or on the seats of their walkers. It took a bit of pounding before someone heard them and opened the door. Three employees came to the entrance. One identified herself as Marie. They presumed she was in charge.

"Do you have an evacuation plan?" Kathy asked.

Kathy recalled Marie telling them, "No. We've called our director, and we talked to her, but it's been 45 minutes, and we haven't heard from her again." The employees had started bringing residents to the foyer but didn't have a plan past that.

Mark and Kathy asked about keys to the vans or buses in the back. The employees didn't know where they were. Nor did they know where to find keys to the locked front doors. The Allens asked if there was a backup generator to power the elevators. The employees didn't know anything about it.

It was clear to Kathy and Mark that the employees and residents didn't realize the gravity of the situation; without power, cell service, or a landline, "no one had communication with the outside world," Kathy said. She tried to call 911 but couldn't get through. Mark still had Tammy Moratto's number from her days as executive director, so he stepped outside, called her, and got through—briefly. "What are we going to do?" he asked. She told him to bring people to the tire store at Coddingtown Mall, but then the line went dead. The Allens thought it odd to deliver Helen to a tire store, never mind the fact there were three such stores around the 60-acre shopping complex and Tammy hadn't indicated which one. But there wasn't time to ponder the odd instructions.

The three employees in the lobby appeared frantic to Kathy, as if they didn't know what to do. The Allens were convinced Villa Capri needed to be evacuated. Flames weren't visible from the entrance, but the smoke was so heavy they knew the situation was serious. They also realized that if there was to be an evacuation, they would have to execute one on the spot.

Improvising was something that came naturally to both Mark and Kathy, as was responding to a crisis. Between them they had 60 years of middle and high school teaching experience, where pivoting, helping, and addressing problems on the fly were part of the job. Kathy had taught physical education at Santa Rosa Middle School for 32 years until her retirement in 2016, while Mark had taught shop class and drafting at Healdsburg High for 34 years until 2009.

Kathy and Mark's two adult children described their parents as so calm and collected that neither could recall a moment from their childhood when they felt afraid. "I'm not sure if it was all the years of teaching and being in school, from earthquake drills to breaking up fights on campus, [but] both are so accustomed to assessing a situation and orchestrating what needs to happen without a second thought," their son Michael said. As a teenager, Michael and several friends were on a boating trip with Mark when the weather shifted and the waves turned rough. The boat took on too much water, but Mark quickly devised a plan, calmly instructing everyone to put on life jackets and sit on the floorboards. He assigned one teen to flip the bilge switch as he guided the boat back to shore. Despite the rough journey, Michael never worried because he knew, he said, "Dad's got this."

Their daughter, Julie Allen, vouched for Kathy's steady nature with a story about the aftermath of a middle school fight. Kathy got word her young teaching assistant was in the principal's office, a highly unlikely occurrence for this particular student. She went to check on him, kneeling down to look him in the eyes. That's when he told her another student had stabbed him. Without raising her voice, Kathy had someone call 911 while she applied pressure to his wound. "She's very calm. She knows how to see the whole situation and break it down without any panic," Julie said. "She just handles it."

With an understanding of the disaster outside their doors, Mark and Kathy kicked into gear. "Let's get everyone out of their rooms," Kathy said. Cynthia gave the Allens radios and master keys, and Kathy headed to the second floor while Mark started in memory care. They got to work helping the night shift staff continue waking, lifting, and either wheeling or slow-walking to the lobby the remaining 50 or so residents who had not yet been assisted. Mark soon joined her upstairs to deploy a system similar to what Elizabeth and Cynthia had used in the previous half hour. Kathy worked with those who used walkers, rousing and guiding them to the landing. Mark and one of the caregivers helped those with wheelchairs, staging them alongside Kathy's group. Eventually, the team started guiding residents down to the lobby.

Alice Eurotas, 84, was asleep in her room when Mark barged in. "Top of his male lungs he said, 'There's a fire, and we have to evacuate right now,'" she recalled. He helped her put on a robe and her Birkenstocks, but in her panicked rush to get out, she didn't think to grab anything else. Mark walked her to the landing. When it was Alice's turn to descend, Kathy steadied her and her walker. Alice hadn't used stairs in years but gripped the railing with both hands and stepped down gingerly in the dark.

Unlike her sleeping peers, Henrietta Hillman had stayed awake that night thanks to Arlyn Jacob's warning. When Mark showed up to escort her from her three-bedroom apartment, Henrietta wasn't groggy or confused. She knew something was awry, and she was already dressed in her favorite pants and a blue-and-white–striped blazer. She grabbed her purse and some cash and ordered Mark to find her a pair of shoes. The selection wasn't easy, though, given that Mark was confronted in the dark with what he described as an "Imelda Marcos" closet. He chose a pair of tennis shoes, but Henrietta was still not pleased. "Mark, what? Were you born in a barn?" she scolded. "Close the closet door. You're as bad as my kids."

Nearby, Ruth Callen had been awake in her bed listening to sirens for nearly an hour. It seemed as if the whole world was on fire. She had spent her life around firefighters, and she knew something serious was happening outside. Ruth was the oldest of nine children in a Catholic family; her father and uncles were San Francisco firefighters. After the former Russell Stover candy salesgirl married Thomas Callen, who became a police officer, they had five children, three of whom became firefighters.

Suddenly, an unfamiliar man—not in a uniform of any kind—entered Ruth's room and "shook" her out of bed. There wasn't time for her to pack her prized QVC jewelry collection or bubble wrap Lydia, her treasured 4-foot-high bronze peasant-girl lamp. The man could only help her don a robe over her favorite floral and leopard-print night dress, put on her specially formulated orthopedic shoes, and collect her walker, "Ferrari," before leading her out the door.

Being unable to move freely was a sad twist in Ruth's otherwise happy story. She was frequently the life of the party, grabbing the microphone at weddings to belt out Benny Goodman's "Dancing in the Dark" or Francis Langford's "I'm in the Mood for Love." She loved to dance too, until 2002, a month before her 60th wedding anniversary, when she suddenly couldn't stand up. She underwent hip replacement surgery to fix the problem, but it didn't go as planned. The doctor used the wrong size implant. Her left leg was now one-and-a-quarter inches longer than her right, but Ruth didn't want to undergo another corrective surgery. Even after adjusting her right shoe, she retained a major limp. Still, Ruth managed to walk half a mile a day around Villa Capri, albeit slowly, relying on Ferrari and the elevator to move between floors.

But the elevator was out of commission now, so Ruth sat as instructed on the landing near her friends Joellen Mack and Susie Pritchett, waiting and wondering if they would make it out. Ruth didn't know if she could walk down the stairs, and if she couldn't, she knew she might not survive.

Villa Capri, Second Floor

After encountering a police barricade, Melissa Langhals took back roads to Villa Capri, winding her way via Stagecoach Road, which intersected Fountaingrove Parkway about 1,000 feet from Villa Capri's driveway. From her route, Melissa could see the fire heading rapidly toward the assisted living home. No one was out front when she pulled into the driveway around 2:15 a.m. She had expected to see buses and vans lined up, but the front plaza was empty. Inside, three employees were clustered together talking, and about 15 residents sat in chairs, on walkers, and in wheelchairs. Melissa approached the employees to ask if they had been given an evacuation order. One answered yes. "Well, what's your plan?" Melissa asked.

"We don't have a plan," one of them said.

Shaking her head in disbelief, Melissa walked upstairs to check on her mother, who lived at the rear of the second floor, closest to the fire's path. Virginia was sound asleep, so Melissa went back to the foyer. "Shouldn't we get these people out of their rooms and down into the lobby," she asked, "so they can be ready for rescue and they won't suffocate upstairs?" The building was filling with smoke, yet most residents were still asleep, and the smoke alarms, for some reason, weren't blaring.

Cynthia told Melissa that their executive director was on her way from Windsor, but based on the time of night and the direction from which Debie Smith was traveling—she only lived 15 to 20 minutes away by car— Melissa knew Smith should have already arrived. Unaware that Mark and Kathy had shown up minutes earlier or that the employees themselves had begun bringing residents out of their rooms, Melissa assumed it would be up to her to figure out how to rescue the five dozen residents. She asked for keys to the buses, but Cynthia told her they didn't have them. "They're under lock and key, and only the manager knows how to get them," she said.

Melissa, like Kathy and Mark, seemed clearly frustrated with the situation, and Cynthia said the employees felt interrogated by all their questions. "We answered with the best of our knowledge. No one else came to help us," she said. "We were trying our best. We were just doing what we could." What Cynthia didn't tell the family members was that she, too, was upset that no Villa Capri managers or staff had come to help. And she, too, was scared for herself and her own family in Santa Rosa because she didn't know where the fire was or where it was headed. *Was her boyfriend awake? Was anyone home to rescue her four dogs? Did her own family have to flee?* she wondered.

Melissa tried to call 911 but couldn't get a signal on her cell. An employee handed Melissa a set of master keys, a walkie-talkie, and a flashlight, and she walked upstairs through the smoke to begin evacuating the building's eastern side where her mother lived. Melissa started with the rooms closest to the stairwell, farthest from her mom's, and pounded on each door before using the master keys to open them. The residents were confused. They asked if they could get dressed or grab their clothes. "No," Melissa said, "there's no time for that. This is not a drill. This building is going to burn down. We need to get out of here."

If residents could walk, Melissa sent them to the landing while she moved to the next unit. She repeated this pattern over and over, just as Mark and Kathy were doing in the western wing. Most of the residents were cooperative, but then Melissa encountered Henrietta Hillman sitting in the hallway. Mark Allen had helped her out of her room, but she had stayed upstairs. "Why are we even going to bother going downstairs?" she asked Melissa. Melissa told her explicitly it was for rescue. "How do you know help will come?" Henrietta challenged her. "It's going to come," Melissa replied. "I have faith I'm getting out of here. So is everybody else. We're all getting out of here together." Henrietta didn't budge, so Melissa got tough. "I've seen you walk," she asserted. "Now get the hell up, and get down those stairs." Henrietta complied.

Although Melissa tried to manifest authority and even bravado for the residents, the thoughts racing through her mind were anything but. *We're all going to die here*, she feared. Nevertheless, she pushed ahead, periodically checking on her mother, who stayed in her room and encouraged her daughter to keep going. "You're doing great, Missy. Keep it up," Virginia told her. "Don't worry about me. I'm fine."

At some point in the flurry of waking and escorting, Melissa saw a couple talking in the lobby. She overheard the woman tell the man to get his mother out of the building, which is how Melissa knew they weren't staff. She walked up to Kathy, and they exchanged first names, both grateful that someone else had shown up and understood the need for a swift evacuation. Then they separated and set off toward different wings on the second floor.

Santa Rosa Police Dispatch

At 2:24 a.m., nearly three hours after receiving her first call from Marie So about problems at Villa Capri, Debie Smith dialed 911 and reported a fire at 1397 Fountaingrove Parkway. "Do you see any flames?" the dispatcher asked. "I'm trying to get there," she said. "I'm the executive director. It's assisted living and memory care. I've been redirected. I know we've been told to evacuate. I'm trying to get in contact with somebody at the fire department or something to help evacuate those residents. I—I can't get there."

Smith later testified the dispatcher told her "there were 25 fires burning in the area, and there were no resources" available to help.

At the exact same time, an unidentified police officer reported to dispatch that the fire had jumped to the south side of Thomas Lake Harris Drive, the road on the other side of the golf course. Only half a mile of manicured greens and sand traps stood between the Tubbs Fire's front line and those who remained of Villa Capri and Varenna's combined 290 residents.

Varenna, 2:30 a.m.

It was only as the smoke thickened and Nathan Condie saw cinders, some as large as his palm, darting through the air that he conceded to staff it was time to get all residents from their rooms, something Andre and Michael had already been doing.

"I made the decision at one point we were going to evacuate," Nathan said. "Nobody told me to. Nobody told me what was going on. All I saw was embers and a lot of smoke, and I figured, 'You know what, it's time to at least start getting people out of here just in case, because I don't know what's going on.' Nobody was telling me anything."

Evacuating Varenna would be no small task. The complex covered 29 acres with a four-level Main Building, stand-alone three-story and two-story apartment buildings, and 27 casitas with two-car garages. In total, there were 33 buildings scattered across the ridge, including Villa Capri and another apartment building used for employee housing.

Varenna's Main Building was constructed in an elongated X shape, which allowed apartments in each wing to offer views either of the hills or Fountaingrove Lake, or of the gardens and sculptures in an interior courtyard. The North and South buildings and the casitas were linked to the Main Building by long, concrete paths for pedestrians and golf carts, and by a driveway that snaked along the ridge. But aside from a gated and locked driveway access point, to which only the fire department had a key, the entire complex had one way in and out, through an electromagnetic gate and gatehouse just off Fountaingrove Parkway.

Sometime between 2:30 a.m. and 3 a.m., Michael and Teresa set out to clear apartments in the Main Building while Andre headed to the South Building. The idea of entering apartments was deeply unsettling to Michael, who had been firmly instructed—warned, even—never to enter the units. Given that he worked nights, his interactions with residents had been rare. He was entirely unprepared for the task at hand. In fact, beyond occasionally assisting paramedics with calls involving residents, Michael had little experience with and had received no training for emergencies. He didn't even have a flashlight, so he and Teresa used their phones to light their way down the wide halls.

They stepped off the stairway onto the third floor and knocked on the first door to the right. Teresa pulled out a set of keys and opened the door as they announced themselves inside the dark apartment. "Oh my God!" a woman cried as she bolted upright in bed, startled at the two silhouettes illuminated by the glow of their cell phones. They apologized but said the complex was being evacuated. "A fire?" the 90-year-old woman asked. "Where?" The woman refused to leave and reminded Michael and Teresa that residents had been told to stay in their rooms and await instruction in the event of a fire. "You go on ahead," she said. "Just leave me here." They pleaded with her to get up, but she dug in her heels. Michael shook his head. "Here this lady was saying that she wanted us to leave her. And we weren't going to do that," he said. He brought the woman's wheelchair to her bedside while Teresa found her robe. Partly by encouragement, partly by force, the two of them helped the resident into her chair and pushed her to the landing—with her protesting all the way.

It was helpful to work in pairs, but Teresa and Michael had been moving residents for nearly 20 minutes, and so far they had only managed to collect one resident. Teresa suggested they split up. She would take the Main Building's south end; Michael was to take the west. She tossed him a ring of master keys, and Michael was on his own.

Most residents were cooperative, respectful, and compliant. Some of the younger and more independent residents headed straight for their cars. Others asked if they could pack first, but Michael encouraged them as politely as possible to just grab shoes and come as they were. Many fled in nightgowns or pajamas. One lady insisted on changing into street clothes, so Michael agreed to come back. The pace was maddening. "It was dark. One woman had actually borrowed my phone [to use the light] for at least 15 minutes," Michael said. He had to wait in the hall until she was ready. Trying not to be cross, he reminded the woman that there were others to notify, and he urged her to hurry.

Another woman told him she needed to use the restroom before they left. "I'm not going to tell an 80-year-old woman not to go," Michael said. While he waited, he walked to her window and pulled back the blinds. The ridge below them, southwest of the complex, was awash in flames. "I'll never forget it," Michael said. "I remember telling her, 'Ma'am, we really need to go. The whole mountain is on fire.'" When she emerged and looked outside, her pace accelerated.

To make matters worse, some residents had opened their windows or patio doors to determine where the smoke was coming from, which only worsened visibility inside. "I came into some rooms, and they were foggy," Michael said. It didn't help that he didn't have a mask. As the minutes ticked by and the smoke built up, he wet a cloth and held it over his face as he worked.

There were about 20 apartments on each floor of the Main Building's four wings. After working through the units in the north half, Michael circled back to the landing where he and Teresa staged those who typically required use of the elevator but now needed to be brought down the stairs. There were about 10 in all at this point, including the 90-year-old woman who had resisted leaving. "We had no choice," Michael said, recalling the indignity of the situation. "We had to carry them down by hand." Michael transferred some in his arms with the crook of their legs over his forearm, and others mounted on his back, their arms wrapped around his neck. Sometimes Teresa would take one side of the wheelchair and Michael would man the other while they lifted and dragged it down the stairs, resident included. In other instances, Michael held the wheelchair handles and walked down backward, with Teresa guiding the front down each step.

The two expected that once the residents arrived in the lobby, someone, perhaps Nathan, would load them into one of Varenna's large buses to drive them to safety, but as Michael and Teresa began delivering residents to the first floor, they found that wasn't happening. At first, Nathan sent residents into the living room. Then he moved them to the dining room. Then he moved them to the activities room. "I don't know what he was thinking," Michael said. "We were sending them all downstairs, and he was moving them like cattle to this side and to that side."

Nathan would later say he was trying to gather residents in first-floor areas where there was the least amount of smoke as he pondered their next move. Other Oakmont employees had begun arriving to lend a hand. Among them was Chris DeMott, a 20-year-old maintenance technician whose shift ended at 10:45 p.m. He pulled up at Varenna around 2:40 a.m. with his then-girlfriend, Mika Alcasabas, a 21-year-old server in Varenna's dining room, where she had worked for two years as she earned her sociology degree at Sonoma State University. They had been following the police scanner on their phones and had heard the fire was entering Fountaingrove. They decided to see if they could help. On their way to Varenna, they passed an unmanned roadblock at the foot of Fountaingrove Parkway at Mendocino Avenue with enough room to drive around the barrier. Further up, at Bicentennial Way, a police officer was blocking the road and directing traffic back downhill. They called him over to their car and Chris said, "We work at a retirement home in Fountaingrove, and we want to make sure the residents are evacuated safely." The officer told them he "would highly advise you don't do that." According to Chris, the officer "didn't seem happy, but he moved his car for us."

Mika was horrified by the scene ahead of them. The streetlights were out, and trees and other debris had fallen in the road. "The wind was super strong, and we were just driving into darkness and the orange glow," she said. When they pulled up outside the Main Building, "it was a confusing clusterfuck," Chris said. "We walked in through the front door, and Nathan Condie was trying to talk to five different people at once." Nathan was glad to see them. "We can use the help," he told them.

Adjacent to where Nathan was standing was the concierge desk that held a binder with Oakmont's emergency response policies and procedures, as well as the roster of residents and their contact information. Behind the concierge desk was a small office with a series of three or four lockboxes containing keys accessible via three-digit codes. One lockbox held the maintenance keys, another the vehicles' keys. Chris said he saw Nathan looking for the codes to the van and bus keys. He didn't know them offhand. Chris knew the code to the maintenance lockbox, which he opened and then distributed the master keys inside. He didn't know the codes for the other boxes. "Apparently only the concierge has the key to open the cabinet with all the codes in it," Chris said. "But the lockboxes were pretty flimsy, so I broke it open for [Nathan]. Then they had access to the vehicles." Chris felt awkward "breaking company stuff in front of the executive director," but he felt the situation called for it. "We were very, very unprepared."

At the same time, one of the caregivers asked Mika to call residents via the front desk landline to direct them downstairs. She handed Mika a booklet of residents' numbers, one that hadn't been updated. After her first call went unanswered, she stopped. *This is not the most effective way to be doing this,* she thought. Mika persuaded the others that continuing going door to door was their best option. So they joined the others in clearing rooms. "It was still a little bit chaotic on what sections everyone was doing," Mika said.

She and Chris separated, each taking different floors on the Main Building's north end. She took the hall with the wine cave. "As I knocked on doors, my heart raced faster," she said. "The hallways were pitch black, and at the end was a window that was glowing red and orange. The air was hard to breathe. I pulled down my turtleneck from my mouth and nose to get more air, but it wasn't working." She encouraged some residents to drive their own cars off the property if they could. "Obviously, they were terrified," she said. "We were all terrified. They kept asking, 'What's going on?'"

Mixed signals abounded. Some residents were told to go to the lobby, others the dining room. "It was just stressful," Mika said. "People didn't know what we were supposed to do." She said the staff wondered aloud, "What is the protocol for this kind of situation?" but she said "There wasn't one. We never got trained." Any drills they did have consisted of the staff convening in the lobby where a fire marshal led a talk and a Q&A. Residents were never involved, as she recalled.

After helping six or seven leave their apartments, Mika retreated to the dining room where she tried to calm residents. Chris came in around a quarter after three to tell her the fire was at the golf course. "We have to go," he said. She asked what would happen to the 30 or 40 residents in the dining hall. There was an equal number in the lobby. "They are going to get a shuttle bus," Chris said.

Before they departed, Mika told two residents she had space in her car. But Chris had already offered rides to three others. Rather than back out of their promises, they loaded all five residents into her Jeep Renegade, including one who sat with Mika in the rear cargo space. None of their walkers would fit so they left them behind. "I feared for my life along with the residents' and employees' as we left," Mika said.

Flames flashed just 15 feet from their car as the seven of them drove downhill around fallen branches. Mika was struck by a sudden worry. *Nobody had checked the casitas.* Staff members had discussed it earlier, but no one had followed through. She acknowledged she hadn't because she "was terrified. There were already embers falling, and there was no protocol. It still makes me feel really bad, to this day, that we didn't check [them]. But when you're in that situation, it was just chaotic."

Villa Capri, Lobby, 2:30 a.m.

By all accounts, the scene at Villa Capri was pandemonium as the Diablo winds blew the Tubbs Fire ever closer. Three family members and four employees were bringing residents to the lobbies when the front doors opened and two men from Oakmont corporate arrived, one with a company logo on his shirt.

One was Joel Ruiz, the brother of Andre and Michael's supervisor, Tony Ruiz. Joel had previously worked as Varenna's maintenance director before becoming a senior regional maintenance specialist for Oakmont Management Group. Joel said Debie called and woke him to ask for his help at Villa Capri. He left his home near Petaluma and drove 100 miles per hour on Highway 101 before exiting at Bicentennial Way, where he hit a roadblock at Fountaingrove Parkway. A police car blocked his path, and an officer said he couldn't go up the hill. Joel said he told the officer to get out of the way because he needed to get the residents out. "If you don't, I'm going to move you with my truck," he said. The officer responded, "It's your life," and backed up.

As Joel wound uphill, the glow was striking. "This whole side was lit up, like the sun was on the ground," he said. As he exited his truck, he saw his boss, Pouya Ansari, whom Joel had woken on his way to Villa Capri. Pouya had been regional maintenance director for only a month and lived in Oakmont's employee housing close to Varenna. Pouya said he had also taken a call from his boss, Ken Garnett, who sent Pouya directly to Villa Capri and told him other employees couldn't get through roadblocks. A staff member let Pouya into the lobby where he said he saw 15 to 20 residents waiting. At that point, Pouya left Villa Capri and walked uphill to Varenna, where he talked with Nathan about bus keys. Nathan pointed him to the busted-open lockbox. Pouya grabbed keys to Varenna's Sprinter van, which he drove a mile down the hill to Oakmont's Fountaingrove Lodge property, but he couldn't get through because a fire engine was blocking the street while firefighters worked a vegetation fire.

Pouya returned to Villa Capri and parked the Sprinter out front. That's when he and Joel teamed up and decided to tackle the problem that already vexed Elizabeth, Cynthia, Anett, Marie, Kathy, Mark, and Melissa: how to transport 60 seniors and their walkers and wheelchairs off the hill. Their initial plan was to first find the bus keys, but once inside, they opted to support the ongoing effort of gathering residents first.

Joel said he sent Anett to find extra sheets to make slings for carrying residents down the stairs, and he told Cynthia to station herself at the top of the stairs to help residents down. One by one, Cynthia held each resident's free hand while they held the railing with the other as they descended. When they reached the bottom, she would run up to retrieve their walkers.

Pouya said he took the second floor and Joel took the first, checking each room to ensure it was empty. Pouya didn't have a master key, and though most doors were unlocked, he said he had to break down two so he could escort a man and a woman downstairs to the lobby, where at least half of the residents now waited. Joel also said he opened rooms and ushered residents downstairs while checking other apartments to make sure they were clear. Upstairs, Joel ran into Mark Allen, who told him, "I already evacuated that side of the building."

During this frenetic time, one more Villa Capri employee entered the scene, albeit briefly. Barbara Lawler, Villa Capri's part-time concierge, lived a half mile away. Only moments earlier, she had woken to the sound of a deep voice over a bullhorn urging Fountaingrove residents to leave immediately because the fire was rapidly approaching. She called out to her husband, threw clothes over her pajamas, gathered some of her daughter's clothes, and fled. On Barbara's way out, she passed Villa Capri and felt compelled to make sure they knew to get out.

She pulled her Honda Accord in front of the portico and left her door open and the engine running as she darted inside. She ran upstairs and joined Kathy, Mark, and Melissa's operation in progress, knocking on doors, bringing two residents out, and passing a third to Mark. Seeing Melissa working farther down the hall gave Barbara confidence all the units were being vacated.

In what she thought was only 10 minutes at Villa Capri, Barbara had two exchanges with Joel. She had just helped one woman put a collar and leash on her dog and assisted her out of her room when Barbara saw Joel heading down the hallway. As they passed, "He told me we didn't need to take pets," Barbara said. The second exchange happened when she headed downstairs, unlocked a drawer, and set on her concierge desk a binder with a resident roster. She saw Joel and told him about the binder's contents. He told her to move her car as it was blocking the driveway where they would be bringing shuttles around.

What they didn't talk about was the 26-seater parked out back and the fact that Barbara knew where its keys were kept. So at Joel's urging to clear the driveway, Barbara closed and locked her desk drawer, returned the key to the corkboard behind the front desk, climbed into her still-open driver's side door, and left.

Upstairs, Len Kulwiec woke to find a strange man with a flashlight offering to help him with his robe and slippers. Outside his window Len saw a red horizon with flashing explosions. It seemed to him the blaze was shooting fireballs, and a long-dormant sense of terror washed over him. "Reminded me of being back in the South Pacific," the 92-year-old World War II veteran said. But one thought gave him solace; he had received Holy Communion that morning. "That was the thing that ran through my mind," he said. "Don't be afraid. Everything's going to be fine. The Lord came down and visited you."

Len walked with his cane outside his apartment where he grasped the banister that ran the length of the hallway. As he passed his neighbor's apartment, he could hear her screaming, "My cat is under the bed!" It shook him. When he reached the landing, he said a man told him to go downstairs, instructing him to sit on the top step and drop his shoulder and roll. The man promised he'd be at the bottom to catch him. As Len attempted to execute the maneuver, he caught his leg on the edge of the third step. A sharp pain pierced his knee, as though his kneecap ripped off. When he reached the bottom, only his friend Norma was there. She pointed to a wheelchair and told him to get in, but Len couldn't manage it himself. "Someone picked me up and put me in the wheelchair," Len said. He could feel his knee starting to swell.

The friend seated next to him, Norma Porter, had lived in Villa Capri for two years, her first stay in an assisted living home. Although many of the residents were more advanced in what she called their "mental illness," the 92-year-old Norma had befriended Alice Eurotas, Len, and Henrietta Hillman. Norma liked Henrietta's "upfront business." A caregiver had awoken Norma to tell her to get out but didn't tell her why. She heard the wind gusting and thought she saw fire from her room. She took her purse, glasses, hearing aids, a flashlight, and her slippers and added a robe over her nightgown. Norma didn't recall how she managed to descend the stairs, but her walker was waiting for her at the bottom. "Nobody really knew what was going on," she said.

One by one, the residents were brought downstairs, where they joined a group of memory care residents from the first floor. That group included Bill and Wanda Lee, whose private caregiver had left nine hours earlier; Viola Sodini, clad only in a light blue nightgown; and Louise Johnson, a new resident and lifelong asthmatic who sat with no protection from the unhealthy air beyond a flimsy blue surgical mask. Viola was missing her dentures and glasses. Len had nothing with him, not his oil paintings nor his extensive research and writings on how to live to be 105. Norma didn't have her dentures either, but assured Len everything would be OK. A bus was coming for them, she told him. Alice Eurotas watched "her castle" fill with smoke while she sat without her hearing aids, glasses, and phone, and without her treasured photo of her mother and the bag of heirloom jewelry her daughter had returned mere hours earlier. Alice felt numb and wondered how she would make it out. Henrietta hadn't grabbed any valuables from her jewelry or pewter collection, but she did retain her moxie. Even if she had been scared, Henrietta—the queen—would never show it.

The tenuous nature of their situation was becoming more apparent. Through the living room's wide windows, the residents could see bushes and trees on fire. "Where the hell are the fire engines?" someone asked.

As employees came in and out, the front doors opened and closed, filling the lobby with even thicker smoke that burned Anett's eyes. A gust of embers landed on the floor inside. When Joel had sent her to get sheets, she had also found blue surgical masks in the laundry room and placed them over residents' noses and mouths. They were confused and questioned why they were in the lobby and why they needed masks. Anett tried to keep them in one place, both to calm them and to maintain a headcount. Her job grew even more difficult as caregivers and family members delivered additional groggy residents in their nightclothes—or sometimes just incontinence briefs and wrapped in a sheet—to the lobby. Aside from worrying about the residents, Anett had no way to get information about her young son, who was home with his father, and she worried the smoke she was inhaling could harm her unborn child.

No matter how smoky it was, none of the employees or family members recalled hearing Villa Capri's commercial smoke detectors or fire alarms trip inside all night, although Elizabeth said she heard a loud smoke detector beeping in the memory care wing. Why the alarm system wasn't sounding throughout the building was unclear.

At around 2:45 a.m., an off-duty sheriff's deputy showed up to collect his grandmother from memory care. Joey Horsman and his wife, Stacie, were expecting a child and lived less than a mile from Villa Capri. After driving to the top of the ridge to see the fire for themselves, they had loaded their dogs and a smattering of belongings into separate cars and fled. Stacie took their Ford truck and turned onto Stagecoach Road while Joey, driving his Sheriff's Office gray Dodge Charger, stayed on Fountaingrove Parkway and drove to Villa Capri. According to his sworn deposition, Joey said an employee let him into the lobby, where he saw about 50 residents gathered. His grandmother, Inez Glynn, was sitting in a wheelchair to his right. He greeted her with a simple "Hi, Grandma" and kissed her. He told her she'd be fine, that he was there for her.

Just as every new arrival had done, Joey asked who was in charge. Kathy, who was in the foyer when he arrived, gave him the straight answer: nobody. Joey told a caregiver he was taking Inez, but the caregiver replied there were residents still in their apartments. She pointed him to the rear of memory care, a unit he knew because his grandmother lived in room 120. Instead of leaving as planned, Joey left Inez in the lobby and began helping with the evacuation, starting with waking an elderly woman in the building's northeast corner. She was confused, but he helped her into her wheelchair, pushed her to the lobby, then returned to the next room. The smoke had become intense. He felt the fire's arrival was imminent. "We were all in danger," he said.

Joey returned to the lobby to tell employees the situation was dire, and they needed to get as many people out as fast as possible. Two men, Joel and Pouya, said they had a Sprinter van ready to go; one asked if Joey would drive it down the hill. He agreed, and they gave him the keys.

As Joey pulled the Sprinter van under the portico, Joel and Pouya turned their attention back to finding the shuttle bus keys. Cynthia told them the keys were nowhere to be found. So, the two men headed back to Varenna to look for a spare set. Between the two properties, Villa Capri had a 15-seat shuttle with a wheelchair lift and a large Lincoln while Varenna had the 26-seat bus, two Lincoln Town Cars and the van that Pouya had already brought to Villa Capri.

Once at Varenna, Joel grabbed two keys labeled "bus" from the lockbox and ran down to the Villa Capri lot, testing each key in each vehicle. None worked on the 26-seater bus, which could have fit nearly half Villa Capri's residents. But one key worked for the 15-seater van, a high-ceilinged Ford Econoline 350. It started right up, so he pulled it behind the Sprinter van.

At that moment, Kathy and Mark and a couple employees were busy loading the van with residents. Norma Porter was not surprised when an employee called her by name, and she was the first to be loaded. "Because I was the mother of one of the owners of the building," Norma said. Her oldest daughter, Cindy, was Bill Gallaher's wife. "I questioned it at the time because there were others who really needed help," the 92-year-old said. The lady next to her, for example, continued to frantically call out. *It wasn't fair*, Norma thought, but she stood anyway when called.

Norma had brought her flashlight and used it to help her friend Len step into the Sprinter van. His injured knee was making it difficult to walk, let alone climb stairs. Len remembered that Norma "butt-pushed" him up the steps, after which a woman named Heidi climbed onto his lap.

Between loading residents, Kathy grabbed Joey's arm. "Oh my God, look!" she said as she pointed to the side of the building facing Fountaingrove Parkway. The hillside had exploded in flames, and embers cascaded into the parking lot and over the dumpsters. Kathy had never seen anything like it, and for the first time that night, she was frightened. The pair returned to the van where both Elizabeth and Cynthia insisted Anett climb aboard to escape the smoke. "I was scared I might go into labor," she said. She agreed to go.

A few minutes later, Joey took the Sprinter van and left the Villa Capri parking lot with the first group of residents. He left his Dodge Charger, loaded with his wife's wedding dress, a rifle, two pistols, golf clubs, and his bowling balls, in the parking lot. Just before 3 a.m., Joey drove away with his grandmother Inez, Anett, Len, Norma, and five other residents. He told one of the three remaining women employees that he would be right back.

Finley Community Center, About Four Miles Southeast of Villa Capri

As they sat in a grocery store parking lot, Dawn Ross, her partner Jim McLaughlin, and their teenage son contemplated their next move, having just fled their Riebli Road neighborhood. Two hours earlier, Jim had woken Dawn, an attorney whose parents lived in Villa Capri's memory care unit, to show her fire coming over the ridge from Calistoga. It seemed far away, and, as Dawn pointed out, wildfire usually travels uphill faster than downhill, and they lived downhill. She went back to sleep. Half an hour later, Jim woke her again because the fire was doing exactly what she thought it wouldn't do—speed downhill directly toward them.

"Should we wake up the neighbors?" Jim asked, referring to the nine other houses on their cul-de-sac. Dawn initially didn't think it worth waking them for a fire that would never reach their homes, but Jim protested, so house by house, they banged on front doors. The wind felled a tree across an elderly couple's driveway, so Jim used his chainsaw to section it while Dawn and their son Joshua moved the logs to the side. Then Dawn, Jim, and Joshua piled into two cars and met in the Oliver's grocery store lot in a

113

northeast Santa Rosa shopping center. The couple texted their immediate neighbors who were vacationing in Paris. They begged Jim to return for their cat, Goofy, so he drove back toward home. But another tree had come down and was blocking access to their street. Unable to pass, Jim was forced to turn around.

They thought about Dawn's parents but didn't think it possible the fire could make it the mile and a half from their street to Villa Capri. It would first have to "blow all through" their neighborhood to get there, and Dawn couldn't fathom that happening. Just in case, she thought, they had better check on her parents. So the family convoyed to Fountaingrove, where a police officer stopped them at a roadblock. The officer told them the senior complexes were being evacuated to Finley Community Center, so they rerouted to the shelter.

"It was like chaos," Dawn said. "The streets were middle-of-the-day traffic jams everywhere." Everyone was fleeing. Still in her pajamas, Dawn pulled up to the community center and double parked, leaving Joshua with the keys. She searched inside but could not find her parents. Outside, she asked arriving ambulance drivers if they were coming from Villa Capri. Not a single one had.

Dawn and her family then headed to a friend's house where Dawn set up headquarters for a singular operation: to find Bill and Wanda Lee. She never imagined they could still be up on the hill in Fountaingrove.

11

Samaritans

The Firestorm, 3 a.m.

Tubbs Fire distance from Villa Capri and Varenna: On the property

Across the county, emergency crews tried to open shelters as fast as they could to provide a haven for thousands of evacuated residents. The first to open, Finley Community Center west of Highway 101, quickly filled to capacity. Then county workers opened the Santa Rosa Veterans Memorial Building across from the Sonoma County Fairgrounds, followed by the Elsie Allen High School gymnasium on the southwest side of town, and soon the Petaluma Community Center to the south and Analy High School to the west. Countless places of worship also opened their doors. Some accepted dogs and cats, but in a million-acre county that's mostly rural, residents kept all manner of pets and livestock, including horses, goats, llamas, alpacas, sheep, pigs, and chickens. County workers soon announced that the Sonoma County Fairgrounds was accepting large animals. Nevertheless, hundreds of owners had no way or no time to collect and transport their creatures and companions. Many were left behind.

At the same time, a mile west of Varenna and Villa Capri, Santa Rosa's famous Round Barn, which had survived earthquakes, torrential storms, vandalism, and even the Hanly Fire, had caught fire. Situated on a flat shelf overlooking the highway, the red landmark had been commissioned 117 years earlier by Kanaye Nagasawa, a Japanese samurai and a disciple of Fountaingrove founder Thomas Lake Harris. As caretaker of this utopian colony, Nagasawa also became a winemaker credited with introducing California wines to Europe and Japan. For years, the barn stood as a symbol of a community that famed horticulturist and author Luther Burbank had once declared as "the chosen spot

115

*of all this earth, as far as nature is concerned." Now, it served as little more than
a symbol of the flaming devastation befalling the region.*

*Press Democrat photographer Kent Porter recalled the weight of the
moment as he shot the landmark burning at around 3 a.m. "It felt like a part of
history was disappearing," he said. Within the hour, a number of other nearby
structures would be ablaze as well, including the Hilton Sonoma Wine Country
Hotel and the Fountaingrove Inn Hotel & Conference Center at the major intersection of Mendocino Avenue and Fountaingrove Parkway. The fire then leapt
across Mendocino Avenue and devoured most of Journey's End mobile home
park, destroying 117 homes and claiming two lives.*

*With the destruction of the Round Barn, the fire had reached one of the city's
most heavily traveled intersections, only a half mile from the Sonoma County
Superior Court, Sheriff's Office, and other county offices, and within 100 yards
of stores, businesses, and Kaiser Medical Center. The Tubbs Fire was now at
the point where the Hanly Fire had been stopped 53 years earlier. Back then, it
had taken four days for the flames to reach this line. This time it had made the
journey in four hours.*

*The residents of Varenna and Villa Capri were now essentially surrounded
by fire, and the eye of the firestorm was shrinking.*

***

Villa Capri, Room 206, 3 a.m.

As the oldest of three boys in his self-described *Leave it to Beaver* family
that spent time together playing cards and football, Mark Allen was the
stereotypical responsible eldest. Growing up, his father referred to him as
"Straight Arrow," while his middle brother was "Sneaky Pete." Decades later,
Mark assumed much of the responsibility of caring for his aging parents.
"You need to get some distance between you and Mom," his brothers told
him. "You're doing too much." But on this night, there was no such thing
as too much.

By now, Mark thought all the Villa Capri residents were out of their
rooms, all of them except for one, his mother. Helen was still asleep in
her bed. As Mark walked to her room, he passed the residents collected
on the landing, some sparsely clad, and he decided it was worth the time

to get his mother dressed. But first, he had to wake her. He walked inside her studio, gently rubbed her shoulder, and in a deliberately calm voice said, "Good morning, Mom. Time to wake up." Helen opened her eyes and asked Mark what he was doing there. "We've got to go, Mom. We'll go to my house," he said.

Using his cell phone for light, Mark helped Helen add white sweatpants and a white sweater over her nightgown and slide her feet into white tennis shoes. Shining the light around the room, he looked for anything else to grab, but in that moment everything seemed expendable. Even though his gut told him they might never see her room again, Mark took nothing. Once Helen was dressed and in her wheelchair, Mark parked her with her peers on the second-floor landing, then jogged the entirety of Villa Capri. He entered each apartment, checked bedrooms, bathrooms, and closets to make sure no residents had returned to their rooms and left the main doors open to indicate the apartments were empty.

In the very last room he checked, Mark found a frail, blind, and nearly deaf woman still in bed. It was Bess Budow, and he quickly realized he couldn't move her alone. "Every time you'd touch her, she'd scream," Mark said. Mark found Elizabeth Lopez in the lobby, and she sent her boyfriend to assist. Juan had already helped Elizabeth transfer three seniors into wheelchairs, and he had repeatedly retrieved one memory care resident who kept returning to her room. "Every time we lost her, [Juan] was the one getting her and bringing her back to the lobby," Elizabeth said. But this task, moving Bess, seemed more daunting, especially with Juan and Mark's language barrier. Elizabeth offered instruction in Spanish as she gave Juan a pair of disposable gloves. "He needs help with a transfer. That's all," she told him. Together, despite Bess' cries, Mark and Juan figured out how to pick Bess up, put her in her wheelchair, and roll her safely to the landing.

Downstairs, eight residents had left in the Sprinter van, but 52 still needed transport. Joel pulled the Ford shuttle under the portico, and he, Cynthia, Marie, and the Allens packed it with residents. There was no formal selection process for deciding who went in which vehicle. Kathy simply chose the residents in the nearest chairs, although she did give priority to those who appeared most anxious. Joel carried onto the shuttle the residents who couldn't climb the stairs, and he was concerned he wouldn't be able to manage the needs of the memory care residents. He asked for someone who knew the residents to ride with him. With that, Marie walked up the steps to board.

Marie's decision did not sit well with Kathy, who didn't hear Joel's request, nor did she know Anett had left with Joey. "Those seats are for the residents. You are not to be sitting on this bus," Kathy told Marie in an admittedly "snippy" tone. Marie disembarked, and Kathy ushered a resident to her seat. Kathy didn't see Marie again, nor did she notice Marie re-board moments later.

No one is sure how many residents filled the shuttle. Marie said it held 12, but others said 15. Kathy suggested the caregivers keep track of which residents were leaving by recording names and room numbers before they left the lobby to board. According to Elizabeth, "Some helpers were just grabbing residents and putting them in cars, so we didn't know who was [with] who." And one caregiver thought another family member might have come at some point and taken their parent and additional residents.

But the lobby was filling with thick, dark smoke now, creating an environment so opaque flashlights couldn't slice through. "It got to the point the mask wasn't helping us at all. We had residents coughing really bad," Elizabeth said. Conditions had deteriorated so much that employees gave up trying to record who went in which vehicle. They would take roll at Coddingtown, they figured.

The visibility was so poor that when Mark backed his Chevy Suburban out of the disabled space up front, he dinged a car parked behind him. He pulled around behind the Ford shuttle and hopped out. Near the bottom of the lobby stairs, he found Kathy. "It's time to get your mom out of here," she said. Mark scanned the foyer, taking in all the others waiting for rescue. Kathy read his mind. "Mark," she said. "We didn't come here to *not* save your mom."

When Mark arrived on the second-floor landing to retrieve Helen, he saw the other residents alongside her. He knew them, some very well. He had dined with them and chaperoned them on field trips. Mark didn't want them to see him escort his mother downstairs, leaving them behind. So he said aloud, "Mom, we're going to go back to your room."

As they turned, he looked over his shoulder and visualized the sinking of the *Titanic*. He thought of the film scene where lifeboats departed with mostly women and children who didn't know if they would ever again see their loved ones still standing on the deck. "That's kind of the feeling that flashed through my head because I looked at these residents that I was abandoning to save my mom, which any son would do." Still, he was wracked with guilt.

Mark maneuvered his mom's chair past her room and into a stairwell that led to an exterior exit. It was one long, straight shot of stairs to the first floor, with no landings in between. Mark spun Helen to face upstairs, so as she descended, he could lean the weight of her chair against his body. But this arrangement meant he would need to take the stairs backward. "Mom, this is going to be a real hard ride. I need you to hold on," he told her. Normally, the frail and sensitive Helen squealed every time he hit even a teeny bump in the road. Not this time. "My mom grasped the seriousness of the situation, and she clutched the wheelchair with her arms and was silent all the way down," he said.

As Mark stepped down one riser at a time, the wheelchair gained momentum and Mark started to lose control. He tightened his grip and moved his feet faster—hot-stepping backward to keep from getting run over. At the bottom, the momentum slammed Mark's back against the wall, but Helen remained unharmed and silent. Mark caught his breath, and they exited the dimly lit stairwell into total darkness, howling wind, and suffocating smoke. Embers whizzed by. "I could not see where the sidewalk ended and the roadway started, and I went off and almost dumped her," Mark said.

They rounded the front of the building as a wall of fire erupted 15 to 20 feet high, filling his field of vision. "Flash poof!" Mark said, mimicking the sound of the vineyard Oakmont had planted on the hill as it exploded in flames. An ember landed in Helen's hair. "I squeezed it in my fingers, pinched it out," he said. Mark rushed Helen to his Suburban and asked her to hold on tight as he picked her up, "kind of like a sack of potatoes, [and] plopped her in the back seat."

Kathy, Mark, and Cynthia added six more residents in the Suburban's three rows. They loaded wheelchairs and walkers in the cargo area. The fire wasn't just close anymore; it was here. And there was no time to wait for the Sprinter van or the Ford shuttle to return, so Kathy told Cynthia they needed to load residents in the caregivers' cars, and Cynthia relayed the message to Elizabeth.

Cynthia pulled her white Chevy Equinox up behind Mark, who was talking to Kathy, discussing which Allen should stay and who should drive the residents to the tire store at Coddingtown. The family always joked that Kathy—at 5 feet, 4 inches tall—was abnormally strong. But the former PE teacher had endured back surgery for spinal stenosis a year earlier and they reasoned Mark could lift the residents in and out of the Suburban better than Kathy. So they decided he would shuttle the residents and she would stay to usher more residents to the foyer.

Logically, the plan made sense. But for Mark, saving his mother meant leaving behind his wife of 43 years, the woman he met while performing in a Catholic folk band. Mark had learned to play guitar just so he could meet Kathy, and they had started dating when they were teenagers. They had raised two children together, spending summers and vacations camping, hiking, and boating. For the past five years, Kathy and Mark cared for his ailing parents, taking turns visiting Helen every other day after Victor died. But there was no time for a heartfelt goodbye, just a hurried "Go, go, go!" from Kathy. "I'll be all right," she said. "Just make sure you come back."

Mark promised he would, then got behind the wheel of the SUV, said goodbye, and headed out the gate. "That was probably the most heart-wrenching part," he said, "leaving Kathy."

Varenna, North Building

Carole and Richard Williams awakened to the sound of Carole's cell phone. "We're getting out of here," some friends in one of the casitas said, giving a quick update on the approaching fire. "You should really leave as well." Even before she hung up, Carole was torn. The Williamses, as with other residents, had been schooled to shelter in place when there was a fire. "We had been told, 'Do not leave your apartment,' so it was really difficult to think independently and assess that maybe that wasn't the best thing to do." Sparks flew sideways past their windows, but they didn't see fire from their apartment. "So we really didn't know how much danger we were in."

Carole convinced Richard he needed to get up. "Getting Richard dressed is very difficult because he has no balance at all" due to his brain disorder, Carole said. "He can't stand as he gets dressed. And he can't do anything quickly." They managed to get his clothes on in the dark, and Carole pulled together important documents, jewelry, and keepsakes before helping Richard down the stairs. "He could stand if he had something to hold onto, but he's very unsure of his feet. So getting him down the two flights of stairs was not easy," the 75-year-old Carole said. "So I had a bag on my back, a walker under my arm, which is really heavy, and Richard on my other arm."

A rush of adrenaline helped her navigate the stairs to the North Building's garage and, somehow, load Richard into the car. As Carole pulled out of their parking space, however, she realized that, with the power out, the electronic garage door opener wouldn't work. She got out and yanked on the chain to manually raise the doors. "I pulled and pulled and pulled and got it up about 10 inches, and that took, like, 10 minutes," she said. "Smoke was just pouring under the door." To her horror, embers swept through the gap as well. "I was terrified I was going to be setting the whole building on fire by having the door open," Carole said. So she repeated the whole process in reverse, closing the door, returning to their car, backing it into a stall, and then helping Richard out and up the stairs. Not knowing where else to go, they headed back to their apartment, where they had no choice but to heed Oakmont's guidance—wait until someone told them what to do.

Around that same time, Andre was about to start knocking on apartment doors in the South Building when he realized the building's garage door was inoperable as well. The staff had been so concerned with residents who couldn't help themselves that they had forgotten about residents who could. Andre ran to the garage's entrance. The smoke was heavy, and his lungs burned. He yanked the chain to raise the door manually, but it wouldn't budge. "It just spun and spun but wouldn't open," he said. "So I thought to myself, 'I can't even see the exit.' I didn't want to die in that garage." Andre gave up and pressed against the concrete wall, following it until he reached a way out.

Varenna, Main Building

Equipped with the keys Chris DeMott freed from the lockbox, Nathan Condie said he tried to reach the large bus stored in the parking lot behind Villa Capri. "But on my way down the path, the flames were already coming across," he said. "Embers were blowing across the pathway, and it was so smoky I couldn't breathe." In addition to combatting the worsening conditions, Nathan was wary because he'd never driven the bus before. It required a Class B commercial license to operate, something Nathan didn't have. "It would have been an interesting experience in all of that smoke trying to drive this big old bus up [to Varenna from Villa Capri]...but I would have given it a shot if I had gotten there," he said. But he couldn't. The heat and smoke were too intense, he said, so he turned back.

When he returned to the Main Building, Nathan said he returned the keys to the lockbox. By all accounts, it was the last time they would be seen that night.

Petaluma, 20 Miles South of Varenna, 3:15 a.m.

R.J. Kisling, the 42-year-old welder from Petaluma, was asleep when his sister called from her home in Marin County to alert him to the horror sweeping through Santa Rosa. Steffany's primary concern was for their grandfather, John Hurford, who lived at Varenna.

"He's going to be fine," R.J. assured her, assuming the complex had an evacuation plan. But uncertainty grew as Steffany relayed the devastation she was seeing on TV. As she spoke, R.J. caught a whiff of smoke inside his own home, some 20 miles from Santa Rosa. Going back to bed was no longer an option as he, too, was now worried for Papa.

A Southern California native, John Hurford had taught mechanical engineering at UCLA and worked as a general contractor and inventor, obtaining several patents. But he was best known for his residential construction projects, including some 400 high-end single-family homes in Hidden Hills and Malibu Canyon Park. John knew a thing or two about working with people and about luxury living and had won hard-earned government approval and neighborhood support by agreeing to preserve the scenic hillsides along the Ventura Freeway's famed Calabasas Grade as part of the project.

John had moved to Varenna from Thousand Oaks with his wife several years earlier. Because of her poor health, she moved into Villa Capri while he stayed at Varenna, where he could visit frequently. After she died in 2016, John stayed at Varenna. According to Steffany, John enjoyed explaining to his friends there how the ownership structure worked. "He would tell them, 'Look, you know that you actually don't own your place. We put down the deposit, but they're the ones who actually make it work, and you don't have a pink slip on your unit.'" Steffany said he was just trying to help them recognize the dollars-and-cents side of their living arrangements.

Steffany often made the trip to visit Papa for breakfasts and the occasional dinner. As the founder of a private flight attendant training and placement company, Steffany, a devoted Christian, cherished the advice and wisdom of her business-savvy grandfather. But more than anything, she admired his dedication to helping others. "His mission in life was to bring a smile to anybody's face, especially if he saw somebody sitting by themselves," she said. "He has a loving heart."

Steffany knew R.J. was the savior type, the kind of guy who didn't hesitate when the situation demanded, like when he had rescued the three kids at the Russian River six months earlier. Or the time in Los Angeles when R.J. saved a surfer whose surfboard leash held him underwater after getting stuck near a pier. And then there was the time in Monterey when R.J. swam through heavy surf with a diving knife to free a scuba diver caught in a kelp bed. "I definitely feel like God gave him the skills to be the first to respond to things like that," his wife Betty said. "He doesn't freeze. And it's never occurred to him to not do something."

Steffany didn't really think it would come to any of that tonight. She just wanted someone to check on Papa at Varenna, and R.J. happened to live closer. R.J. threw on his usual white T-shirt and jeans and raced out the door. *Worst case*, he figured, *I lose an hour of sleep.*

Coddingtown Center

Gena Jacob watched as Villa Capri's former executive director, Tammy Moratto, parked near them, then exited her car and stood nearby on the phone, gesturing with her hands. "You could see she was very stressed," Gena said. "It was pretty chaotic. Nothing was going smoothly." At one point, Moratto let Gena in on her conversation: Villa Capri staff couldn't find keys to the large bus. "That is the dumbest thing ever," Gena would later remark. "They were trying to scramble to get more transportation for more people. They were talking like they still had other people, family, workers, or employees, that needed transportation out of there."

A hodgepodge of vehicles showed up over time, including a Fountaingrove Lodge van, Varenna residents in their own cars, and Joel Ruiz in the Ford Econoline shuttle full of Villa Capri residents. Joey Horsman and the Villa Capri Sprinter van had yet to materialize. Outside of Oakmont residents, Coddingtown's parking lot was filling with streams of evacuees from all over Sonoma County, so Moratto began looking for an alternative gathering spot. A church pastor agreed to let Oakmont Senior Living staff set up camp at New Vintage Church, situated in the heart of Santa Rosa. It would be their new rendezvous point.

Mark Allen was surprised to see that his Suburban was the only vehicle descending Fountaingrove Parkway and that he didn't encounter any roadblocks or police cars on his way down the hill. He took in another novel sight as he crossed Highway 101; the major artery was devoid of cars. Mark took back roads to Coddingtown and pulled into the closest of the three tire store lots. Tammy Moratto was standing outside.

"Do you want me to unload the passengers I have here?" he asked. Mark planned to drop off the seven residents and race back to Villa Capri. He figured he could make it back in 10 minutes to load another group. Moratto told him no, they had transportation covered for those still at Villa Capri. "But Kathy needs me to go back and take more people," Mark told her. She insisted his return trip was unnecessary. "Tammy assured me that they had school buses arranged to come and pick these people up," he said.

Since the tire store had become nothing more than a meeting point, Moratto gave Mark directions to New Vintage Church. As he left Coddingtown, some of the memory care residents in the back of his Suburban began to fuss and wail. One woman swore profusely, according to 89-year-old Susie Pritchett who rode shotgun. Although Susie sat in silence, she was anything but calm. Her heart was aching for what she'd left behind in her apartment.

Susie had one line for the man who burst into her room at around 2:30 a.m.: "I need to bring my bird." Though she had an apartment full of cherished belongings, including a coffee table and Chinese bowls from the historic Tubbs mansion, Susie's most precious treasure was Tiffany, a tropical parrot who had kept her company for 15 years. Susie housed the sun conure in a large bird cage, one she placed in her deceased husband's wheelchair to take Tiffany for walks around the complex. Tiffany loved their outings, and everybody loved to see her. "Tiffany and my mom had a special language," Susie's daughter said.

In the darkness and disorder, Susie had pleaded with her rescuer to save Tiffany. The problem was Susie didn't have a small cage to transport her. When Susie sat at the top of the stairs, she had asked the other strangers about her parrot, but they were all too busy saving her fellow residents. "I need to get my bird," she repeated to anyone within earshot. But there was no opportunity. Susie was ushered off the landing, into the lobby, and then into Mark Allen's SUV. Behind her sat some people from memory care whom she did not know. Assisted living residents rarely saw anyone from memory care. The passengers had been quiet for a while, but after the Coddingtown stop, the middle-of-the-night evacuation from all things familiar set in.

"Because we were driving in silence for a while, I guess they were processing what was going on, and the emotions started to overwhelm them," Mark said. They insisted Mark turn the Suburban around so they could retrieve shoes or other items.

Mark didn't have time to deal with their demands. He turned on a country western station and headed southeast toward New Vintage Church, farther from Villa Capri, but fully expecting he would soon reunite with his wife.

Varenna, Around 3:30 a.m.

As Nathan Condie would later explain, he always intended to come back. It was never his plan to leave for good. After he began asking anyone with a car—staff and residents alike—to bring it around front, he instructed them to take residents to the tire shop. "Every vehicle that pulled through, we just shoved as many residents as we could in their cars and told them to go," Nathan said. "At that point, we had not seen a single fireman or policeman or anybody…I think that was the most frustrating part. I know [emergency crews] were busy with the imminent threat and stuff like that, but it would have been really nice if they had given us a warning ahead of time," he said. However, most of those who fled the flames that evening were notified by emergency alerts, social media, news bulletins on radio, TV, or the internet or by neighbors, family, or friends calling to wake them or pounding on their doors. Few received individual warnings from emergency crews.

After filling 10 or 12 cars, Nathan said he was running out of vehicles and employees. Finally, at around 3:30 a.m., Nathan pulled around his four-door Kia, which, according to Nathan "was the only car left." "I'm going to go down and get reinforcements, figure out if we can get a bus or something else up here," Nathan recalled telling some of the staff including Teresa, Alma Dichoso, and Michael.

Nathan would later say that when he pulled away about 3:45 a.m., he left a med tech in charge, possibly Teresa or Alma. He couldn't recall which. But other staff refuted his claim. According to Michael, Nathan left no instructions and left no one in charge. He just remembered seeing Nathan load four residents in his car underneath Varenna's porte-cochère and drive away. Frightened, Michael ran up to Nathan's driver-side window to plead for a ride. But Nathan told him his car was full. "And so I panicked," Michael said. He ran toward a resident who invited Michael into his car. "That guy was on oxygen…and he was driving down the hill, and the trees were falling in front of us. It was just crazy," Michael said.

As he watched in terror as they drove down the hill, Michael grew worried about Andre. He called Nathan to ask if he had seen him. But Nathan said he hadn't. "Andre is still up there," Michael told him. There was a pause on the other end, before Nathan responded. "Well, just worry about yourself," Michael heard Nathan say.

Varenna, South Building

After escaping the smoky garage, Andre returned to clearing the third floor of the South Building. He knocked on the door of apartment 302, but no one answered. One unit away, in apartment 301, Andre caught an elderly couple off guard with the news, even after hours of evacuations and smoke infiltrating the building and despite the intermittent squawking of fire alarms. But Andre realized he shouldn't be surprised some residents were still unaware of what was happening. Elderly people tended to remove their hearing aids at night, and others took sleep-aid medication with no need for an alarm to wake them in the morning.

Andre moved down to apartment 300 and knocked, but there was no answer. He started to head downstairs with the couple from 301, but "something inside told me to go back to 302," he said. Why that particular room when there were others that also did not generate a response, he's not sure. But he went back and knocked, louder this time. He knocked again. It was then, from deep within the apartment, Andre heard a small, weak voice. "Just a minute," someone said. "I'll be right there."

When the door opened, there stood Edel Burton, a 92-year-old woman leaning on her walker. Andre recognized her from her slow strolls around the Varenna grounds during which she greeted people cheerfully and walked with as much grace as she could muster given her uneven gait. Tonight, she looked scared, having awoken to the smell of smoke, no power, and a stranger pounding on her door. That stranger knew he was about to be tested. Andre and Edel were both about 5 feet, 3 inches tall, but Andre—at only 140 pounds—said Edel outweighed him. Getting her downstairs was going to be difficult.

Andre prompted her to leave immediately. "Sorry," Edel said, "but I need to get my things." Among the items she needed to collect was her German Shepherd, Abigail. Old and blind, Abigail was Edel's trusted companion, and Edel was going nowhere without her. Knowing he couldn't get Edel and Abigail down the stairs by himself, Andre told her he needed to go for help, so he sprinted back downstairs and through the hot smoke to the Main Building.

When he entered the lobby, Andre found only a smattering of residents. No Nathan Condie. No caregiver Ma Teresa Martinez. And no Michael either. He checked the dining room, then the activities room. No staff. He ran back toward the South Building, flames visible in the trees around him. Once inside, Andre searched a third-floor storage closet, where he found a wheelchair. He pushed it back to 302, locked the wheels, and assisted Edel as she sat down. Then he put Abigail on her lap. "You'll have to hold her," he said.

Edel nodded and hugged Abigail tightly as they rolled down the wide carpeted hall, past the alcove with black leather chairs and a coffee table and backed through the door into the stairwell. Just getting down this stretch was a challenge, and Andre didn't want to risk injuring her as he guided the unwieldy chair down one long flight of stairs. He told Edel he was going to find help, again. Andre locked her wheels and left the South Building. Outside, he saw a handful of Varenna residents lined up perpendicular to the service road that ran between the South and the Main Building, about 40 yards away. Somebody clearly was staging them for departure. Whether it was by car or shuttle bus, Andre couldn't tell, but he was encouraged by the only attempt at organization he had seen all night. Regardless, Andre felt a great sense of urgency to get Edel down the stairs so she could leave with the rest of them.

Andre paused for a moment, his shirt pulled over his mouth, when he spotted a caregiver emerging from the Varenna Main Building. He asked her to help him bring Edel down from the third floor, but as soon as the words came out of his mouth, he could tell his appeal was going to go unheeded. "Save yourself, Andre," she said. And then she ran.

Andre watched as the caregiver raced toward the parking lot. The people lined up at the side of the Main Building watched as well, and they looked toward Andre with eyes that asked, *What are you going to do?* He shook his head and put his hands on his knees. "Fuck it!" he exclaimed. His eyes were burning, and his limbs ached. He looked down at the asphalt under his feet. "Lord, just give me the strength," he asked. "Give me the strength to help this lady."

Varenna, North Building

Cocoa was not acting like herself. The chocolate Labrador was usually a calm companion who slept serenely on the bed of Bob Mitton and Mimi Vandermolen, but tonight she was pacing their second-floor corner apartment, whining and upset and breathing heavily. "I knew this was not normal for her," Mimi said. Mimi's main concern was that Cocoa would wake Bob, who had turned in early in preparation for a trip Monday morning. Finally, around 3:30 a.m., Mimi got up to see what was agitating Cocoa.

"I opened our little blinds," she said. "All of these sparks were running up and over the building. I ran into the bedroom and shouted to Bob, 'There's fire everywhere!'" Bob bolted out of bed to see for himself. What he witnessed astounded him. The rose bushes and their pots on the deck were burning. He looked at Mimi. "We've got to get out of here," he said. They swiftly leashed Cocoa and headed for the North Building's underground garage but soon realized exiting by car was wishful thinking. Bob pressed the button to raise the garage door, but it didn't go up. He disconnected the automatic opener and tried to raise it manually. "I got it up about two inches, and it was like I just opened the floodgates," he said. Burning embers and sparks came pouring into the garage. "I realized that if I didn't get that thing closed, I was going to set the whole place on fire."

They returned upstairs and decided to join other residents fleeing to the Main Building. As they passed between buildings outside, low-flying embers covered the driveway. "The ground looked like lava," Mimi said. "It reminded me of the flow of a volcano with the red and the black."

The group decided to run. "There was so much fire around us, and everything was burning," Bob said. "We got junk in our eyes, but we didn't get burned." They raced past Varenna's dog park and into the Main Building, where they found a dozen residents huddled together in the lobby.

One floor below Bob and Mimi, Frank Perez, 89, had been awakened a few hours earlier by his across-the-hall neighbor, Ruth, who smelled smoke. She had called Varenna's concierge and left a message but hadn't heard back, so she knocked on Frank's door. Frank advised her to go back to her room, saying, "I'll keep an eye on things."

He then opened the blinds to his first-floor rear window, which overlooked a steep hill dotted with oaks. At the bottom of the slope, the Fountaingrove Country Club's five tennis courts were lined end to end like boxcars. Through the trees, he could see the flickering of a fire in the distance.

Frank knew the lay of the land outside Varenna well. The former San Francisco English teacher was a competitive distance runner who ran well into his 80s, often at just over a 6-minute-mile pace and had once been photographed for *Runner's World Magazine*. He and his late wife, Ginny, had been drawn to the rolling terrain around Varenna when they put down $700,000 for their ground-level apartment some 10 years earlier. They appreciated the outdoor patio where their border collie could roam, and they were grateful Varenna allowed them to punch a hole in the wall for a doggy door. But a year after they moved in, Ginny died suddenly. To deal with his grief, Frank kept running, often with his border collie. "I used to run eight miles a day, but the dog could run 10 miles longer," he said. Eventually, Frank lost his running partner too, and at 87, he decided his body could no longer take the pounding.

But he didn't hang up his running shoes entirely. In fact, he had put on his gray and blue Nikes when Ruth had knocked at his door, and he was wearing them as he looked out his window and saw the fire through the hillside oaks' knobby, knotted limbs, and small brown leaves. Knowing there was a fire station down the block on Stagecoach Road, he wasn't too concerned. Plus, the fire was so small he could measure it between his fingers.

Nonetheless, as the North Building's first-floor fire captain, Frank donned his Varenna-issued neon yellow safety vest, as well as goggles and a whistle, and performed his assigned duties in checking on his neighbors. There were 12 units in his building, six on each floor, housing about 20 people total. He started with Ruth.

"I think I found where we are getting that smoke from," he told her. He then knocked on other doors in his hall, where he found a number of his neighbors already awake and increasingly worried. Some had difficulty moving and were concerned about how they would escape if the time came for that. Most of their cell phones were without a signal. Frank told them to stay in their apartments until they heard otherwise. He was unsure what else to say. "We got no message about what to do," he said. "We didn't know what was going on."

When Frank returned to his apartment, he discovered the small fire in the distance was no longer just one house ablaze as he previously thought. To Frank's amazement and horror, the fire had jumped Fountaingrove Parkway and the tennis courts below him and was rolling up the hillside toward the oaks off his patio. *If the trees go, this whole place will go*, he thought. "The fire was quite fierce," he said. "The sky was just on fire." In an instant, the flames were suddenly at his deck, swirling counterclockwise and forming what looked like a small funnel cloud that swept over his patio, burning his plants to a crisp and slamming against his patio door. The heat was so intense it burned the gasket around the doorframe and sent embers cascading inside onto a large hand-woven rug. "The wind just forced [the fire] right in. It was coming in two, three, four, five [embers] at a time," he said.

Frank began stomping out the flaming ashes as quickly as he could, doing a two-step on the rug for several minutes in his Nikes. "Finally I was getting tired, so I went to the sink and filled up a pail of water and poured it all over the area," he said. The fire was out. At least in Frank's apartment.

Varenna, South Building

As Andre ran back to the South Building, he could see grass and trees burning on the southwest side of the building and embers the size of his work gloves landing in the landscaping near the entry. As he entered the front door, the interior of the building was quiet save for a thin faint voice emanating from the top floor.

"Is anybody going to help me?" the voice cried through the darkness. Andre called back up as he climbed the stairs, telling Edel he was on his way up. "You couldn't find anyone to help?" she asked as he reached the top floor.

"It will be all right," he said, trying to convince both of them it was true. Andre tried not to think about their size difference, or about the challenges of handling her dog, Abigail, or the cumbersome wheelchair, or the fact they were in near-total-darkness, or his new hip joint, replaced five months earlier. What he did think about were numbers. Andre had a knack for them. While doing his job, he liked to count steps as he cleaned, and he knew from experience there were 18 steps between floors in the South Building.

He set Abigail, along with Edel's medication bag, on her lap again, and the three of them began the slow, steep descent. Andre turned the wheelchair around and walked backward, slowly bumping down one step at a time, bracing his legs and counting each step as he completed it. He could feel the strain in his knees and arms—and in his hip. He moved his right leg down another step and planted it, then rolled the chair down with a bump. Two. He stepped his left leg down and planted it and reversed the chair again. Another bump. Three. Another, four. All three of them shook with each abrupt landing.

Andre thought about the line of residents outside the Main Building. He wanted to get there as quickly as he could, to get Edel in line for the shuttle he assumed was coming, but he didn't dare go any faster. Bump. Bump. Bump. Slowly and steadily, they took each step. But about halfway down, Andre had to stop. He was exhausted. His knees couldn't take it.

After locking the wheels of the chair, he lifted Abigail to the steps, helped Edel out of the wheelchair, and asked her to grip the railing with one hand and hold him with the other while they worked down the remaining nine steps. Andre counted as they walked. Two. Three. Four. "That's good," he coached her. Each step was a challenge, but when they reached the number 18, Andre knew they had reached the bottom.

"Hold onto the wall, and don't move," he said, then he raced back up to carry down Abigail and then made a second trip for the wheelchair.

The only light was from a single exit sign, but the small green glow was a comfort. He was exhausted, but somehow, by the grace of God, Andre had gotten Edel and Abigail downstairs without injuring any of them. He settled Edel and Abigail back into their chair and pushed them through the door into the main hall and then out the front entrance. He immediately looked to the left toward the service road where the residents had been lined up earlier. Andre was devastated. Everyone was gone.

Not wanting Edel to see his disappointment, he pressed ahead as quickly as possible, pushing the chair through the smoke and toward the street with all the power he could summon, but the wheelchair lurched to a halt. One of the wheels had wedged between a decorative paver and the curb. Andre pushed and lifted with his weary arms, but there was no moving her. His eyes burned from the smoke. He looked down and was about to say another prayer, when suddenly a man appeared. "Do you need a hand?" the gentleman asked. Andre assumed he was a resident who lived in one of the casitas, but he wasn't sure. At the moment, he didn't care. Yes, Andre said, and between the two of them, they lifted the chair out of the crack and set it back onto the road. Before Andre could say a word, the man was gone.

Andre hunched over and put his hands on his knees, breathing heavily, and prayed. He tried calling Michael, but his call wouldn't go through. He wondered whether the shuttle bus had left and whether it would come back. When they reached the bend in the driveway where he could look toward the main entrance and his car, he could see nothing but smoke. No light. No movement. Going back up was not an option. He had to get Edel to lower ground.

He turned away from Varenna and began pushing her down the steep driveway. Below them, flames shot up from the back of Villa Capri. The trees just below Varenna's South Building were ablaze, and the smoke was thick. Andre and Edel covered their faces as best they could. *Lower ground,* Andre thought. *That would allow us to at least get out of the smoke.* And if they could get to Fountaingrove Parkway, maybe there was a chance someone would pass and give them a lift. Andre gripped the wheelchair handles as he navigated the right side of the road, but the combination of the soreness in his arms, the pitch of the pavement, and the welling anxiety that they had been left behind was taking its toll.

The chair began to pick up speed. Then, with a jolt, they both went sprawling through the air. Ejected from the wheelchair, Edel hit the pavement with a mighty force and Abigail spilled to the side. Andre noticed a mound in the street. It was a speed bump he failed to see amid the darkness and smoke. "Ma'am!" he cried as he knelt beside her. Edel lay twisted, splayed on the asphalt. She had struck the ground face first, and as she rolled toward him, Andre could see her glasses pooling with blood. Her dog, blind and disoriented, walked in circles.

Andre knew he couldn't heave Edel back in the chair alone, so he dialed 911. Busy. He looked around for a sign of help. Nothing. His only option was to walk back uphill to his car, the Mazda 3 he parked with Michael hours earlier. "Ma'am," he told her. "I'll be right back."

He ran back up the hill to his car, the only vehicle remaining in the long row of parking spaces. Andre eased it slowly down the hill in the left lane, deathly afraid of running over Edel or Abigail who he knew were on the right side. He stopped about 10 feet shy of the speed bump and ran to Edel's side. She was frantic at this point, calling and striking out in fear. She thought she had been left in the road. Andre tried to lift her into the car but couldn't. He could barely move her at all. He stepped behind her and tucked his arms under hers and tried dragging her uphill toward the car, but she resisted, twisting her body side to side and hitting his arms.

Andre didn't realize it, but at some point during the struggle, he had accidentally dialed Michael—and the call went through. When his phone rang, Michael was at a shopping center where the resident with the oxygen tank had dropped him off. Michael was relieved to get the call, but all he could hear were the sounds of Andre's struggles.

"Andre!" he shouted into the phone. Andre didn't respond.

Then Michael heard Andre's voice clearly. "Ma'am," Andre said, "If you don't give me your hands, we're going to die here."

Michael listened but was powerless to help. Then the phone went dead. On his end, Andre said another silent prayer. There was no way he was going to leave Edel. Either she was going with him, or the two were going to remain on that pavement together.

Just then, she stopped fighting him. "She gave me her hands," Andre said, "and God gave me the strength." He tugged and dragged and somehow managed to load Edel into the back seat of his hatchback with just enough space to close the door. Then he found Abigail and put her in the front passenger seat. Andre climbed into the driver's seat and started downhill, bouncing off the curb in the dense smoke. When they reached Fountaingrove Parkway, he turned right but couldn't see the road through the smoke and flames, so he straddled the double yellow lines as he drove. If his tires hit the rumble strips, he knew he had steered too far off center.

A mile down, Andre saw a police officer and pulled over. "Sir, I have a lady in the back. She's bleeding from the head, and I just got her from [Varenna]," Andre said. "I think there are more people up there." The officer immediately made a call to dispatch, then instructed Andre to take Edel to the Kaiser hospital only a thousand feet away, not realizing that the hospital would soon be evacuated as well.

Coddingtown Center

After Nathan dropped off the four residents at the mall parking lot, he said he met up with his boss, Ken Garnett, and, soon after, the pair began the three-mile journey back to Varenna. They encountered a barricade at the intersection of Bicentennial Way and Mendocino Avenue. "A volunteer police officer was there and told us we couldn't go up," Nathan said. The man was wearing a big yellow vest that read "Volunteer." "I told him that we needed to go back up there and let us through. And he said, 'Nope. Can't let you guys up. We've got emergency personnel that are handling it from here.'"

Nathan turned the car around and tried another route to the south off Chanate Road, the route he usually took to work and the route he had taken earlier in the night. But as they made their way up Stagecoach Road, "the fire was on both sides of the road. And it was bad," Nathan said. "We couldn't see anything." To the right, "Sweet T's restaurant was on fire. The trees across the road were on fire, and the flames were jumping across the road into the center median…right in front of our car." Thinking about it "still scares the crap out of me," he later said in sworn testimony.

It was too dangerous to continue, he decided, so they turned around and went back to Coddingtown Center where Nathan dropped Ken at his car. "I was sweating bullets," Nathan said. "Part of me really wanted to drive through the barricade and force my way up Fountaingrove to make sure everything was being taken care of." Instead, he headed to New Vintage Church.

Finley Community Center

Two miles from Coddingtown Center, Vivian Flowers and her husband unloaded busloads of seniors at the Finley shelter. They had been there since 2:30 a.m. on the advice of her nephew, who heard from a police officer that Finley was the destination for all assisted living residents in Fountaingrove. But so far, there was no sign of Vivian's mother.

As each bus pulled to the entrance, Vivian scanned the seniors aboard. She helped each resident descend the stairs while an employee traveling with each bus reunited the passenger with a walker or wheelchair at the bottom. Over the next three hours, 10 to 12 buses, a mixture of school buses, CityBuses, and retirement community shuttles, arrived from Fountaingrove, none of which carried Viola. "With each empty passing vehicle my mom was not in, the more scared I got," Vivian said, until she got the update she feared. "Last bus," the staff told her. "There's no more coming in." Then Vivian received news that sent her into a tailspin. Viola wasn't at the Veterans Memorial Building shelter either. "I gotta tell you, I was a mess," Vivian said. She worried her mother's selflessness would be to her detriment.

"She would be worried about the lady two doors down from her, to make sure her dog was safe. I could see my mom being one of the last people to ask for help."

Vivian called every phone number she had for Villa Capri managers, leaving messages for Debie Smith, Jane Torres, and Roberta Murray. Getting no answer, Vivian called again and again and left multiple messages. No one called her back. "Five hours. It was horrible," Vivian said. "Your vision is your mom's up there, that she's going to die up there, that they are going to leave her there."

Villa Capri, Second Floor, Rear, Room 218

Melissa Langhals was so busy clearing her half of Villa Capri's second floor—comprising about 16 or 17 residents—that she didn't see the concierge or the men from corporate come and go, nor did she know vehicles had already left with the first 33 residents, Mark Allen, Joey, Anett, and Marie. Melissa was alone on the second floor's eastern side armed only with a radio, flashlight, and a set of master keys.

When she reached the room next to her mom's, she realized she needed help to move a heavier resident from her bed into a wheelchair. She called on her radio, and a stranger wearing gloves but not a uniform arrived a few minutes later. It was Juan Carlos Gonzalez, Elizabeth Lopez's boyfriend. He lifted the woman out of bed while Melissa held the wheelchair and then pushed her to the second-floor landing. Melissa parked the woman, turned, and ran down the hall.

It was now time to make her final rescue: her mother.

Melissa had told herself Virginia would be the last person she saved. Her mom had insisted on it, and Melissa knew she might have been tempted to leave if she had taken her mother first. She arrived at Virginia's room not a moment too soon. Flames were consuming the bushes outside her window, and smoke was seeping inside while flying debris smacked the side of the building. "It was getting difficult to breathe, but my adrenaline was so high at that point, I didn't care," she said.

Melissa needed to move Virginia into a wheelchair, so she radioed for help as she had moments earlier, but now her pleas were met with silence. She called again and again. No one came. She tried other channels, hoping to find anyone, maybe even a police officer or fire engine crew in the vicinity. She was met with only silence. Melissa felt she was on her own.

Partially paralyzed and suffering from cancer, Virginia couldn't roll over in bed or use her right arm. A couple months earlier, Virginia had slipped out of her wheelchair and fallen to the floor, twice, so Villa Capri staff decided to keep her in bed. The decision had devastating results. Virginia atrophied. She had been left lying in bed so long she could barely bend to sit in a chair.

At a compact 5 feet, 7 inches tall, Melissa, then 50 years old, had always been strong, fit, and active. As a certified electrician, she was used to climbing ladders and hauling conduit up and down stairs. But 10 months before the fire, Melissa had hip replacement surgery and was still in recovery. She knew how to lift her mother into a wheelchair but, flustered from seeing flames gnaw at the building, she forgot to lock the chair's brakes. When she slid her arms underneath her mother's then lifted her out of bed, the wheelchair slipped out from underneath them. Virginia's arm struck the bed frame, leaving a gash on her forearm. They tumbled to the floor in a heap. Melissa scooped Virginia under her arms and wrangled her from the floor back into the chair. Melissa swore out loud at the exertion, and Virginia admonished her. "Missy! Missy! Quit dropping the F-bomb," she said. Melissa, exasperated, was unbowed. "Mom, shut the fuck up," she said. "I'm trying to do a job here."

Once she had secured her mother in the wheelchair, Melissa pushed Virginia to the landing where she joined nine other residents—five in wheelchairs, three with walkers, and one on her feet—waiting to be taken down the two flights of stairs. Melissa went to find help, but the lobby was quiet, with 14 residents sitting in the dark near the front door. Melissa found only one other person in the building who didn't require a walker or wheelchair, the only other person staying behind to lend a hand: Kathy Allen.

Villa Capri, Second-Floor Landing, 3:30 a.m.

Kathy and Melissa met in the lobby and formulated a plan. If they could somehow get everyone on the second-floor landing down the stairs, Kathy reasoned, they could hustle outside as many as possible should flames sweep through the building. *If worse comes to worst, maybe I could sit everyone in the middle of the parking lot and place wet sheets over their backs*, she thought. *By then, Mark will be back.*

They headed upstairs where roughly 10 residents waited. Kathy first assisted John Magnuson, approaching him with a friendly, "Come on, we're going to get you out of here." John's wife, Nell, watched as Kathy took her husband, who was hard of hearing and legally blind, and his walker and practically carried both down the stairs. All of this was becoming too overwhelming to believe. Nell had awoken to the smell of smoke, then saw tall flames outside the kitchen window of their $8,500-a-month, two-bedroom apartment. She was shocked not to find an employee ready to assist them. Usually, Villa Capri was "five-star," but "nobody said anything" on this night, Nell said. "There was never a wisp that anything was wrong," until the situation was so bad that she didn't even have time to change out of her pajamas. "I was wearing a stupid bathrobe. It wasn't a nice one either," Nell said. Neither were the "very ratty" gold sandals she wore because she couldn't find her slippers.

So many other things, so many other valuables, were left behind as well. She and John had traveled the world, and Nell collected gold and silver jewelry from each country they visited. There was the 6-inch-long solid gold Nefertiti pendant from Egypt, the large jade figurine pendant from China, and the black pearl necklace and diamond-and-black-pearl earrings from Japan. And, of course, there was the metal container with the silver and gold U.S. Mint proof sets for coins they had collected for every year since 1955, the year their son was born. Nell packed none of it. With only the clothes on their backs and a purse in Nell's arms, she followed Kathy and John into the lobby clouded with smoke.

As Kathy led John toward the front doors, Nell looked around, uncertain. There were still so many residents seated and waiting, yet here she was, walking out. "I thought, 'Gosh, I hate to leave them,'" she said. "It was scenery from hell." Another resident noticed Nell's reluctance and encouraged her to go with her husband. Nell nodded and continued outside where Kathy helped the Magnusons into the back of Cynthia's white Chevy Equinox with one other resident.

Kathy then sent them on their way before racing back upstairs where she met Ruth Callen, who had waited on the landing for what she felt were

three hours, listening to sirens wailing in the distance and residents coughing around her. Between her hip replacement limp and Paget's disease, a
condition that left her with porous, cement-like bones, Ruth had avoided
stairs for decades. She knew there was no way she could get down on her
own. As she sat in the dark with her friends, Ruth assumed the worst. How
ironic, she thought, that her dad, multiple uncles, and three sons were all
firefighters, and here she was, about to perish in a fire.

Then Kathy and Melissa, the "good Samaritans," as Ruth described
them, appeared through the haze and shouted instructions to those on the
landing who could walk. "Everybody get up and go down the stairs as best
you can," the two women said. Kathy propped up Ruth and guided her,
hand over hand on the railing, one careful step at a time. "This is a woman
who [essentially] couldn't walk with her walker down the hall," Ruth's
daughter Liz Schopfer would later observe in awe. "How she got down the
stairs—it was pure adrenaline."

Had there been an opportunity to compare family histories, Kathy and
Ruth would have learned they were both daughters of San Francisco firefighters, and that Kathy's dad, George Payne, had worked with Ruth's son
Tim at San Francisco Fire Station 36, where George was Tim's chief for five
years. Tim fought countless fires with George and described him as calm
and even-tempered in emergencies. His daughter Kathy evidently inherited
the same mettle.

Kathy then helped a heavyset man whom she gently pressed against the
banister to keep his weight shifted toward the wall as they stepped down.
When he reached the landing, he fell, and Kathy couldn't lift him. So she
had him sit on his rear and scoot down the rest of the flight like a toddler.
His wife, upset watching her husband in such distress, tried to stay with him
and held his hand.

Once the more ambulatory residents reached the bottom of the stairs,
Kathy suggested Melissa bring around her Jeep. Both women exited the
building, and as Melissa headed toward her car, Elizabeth Lopez pulled her
Toyota Sienna minivan under the portico. Kathy suggested Elizabeth take
residents to Coddingtown and supervise them there while Mark and others
completed the back-and-forth trips to get more people to safety. Elizabeth's
boyfriend, Juan, lifted three memory care residents—Bill and Wanda Lee

and Viola Sodini—into the Sienna's middle row. More residents could have fit, but Elizabeth feared it would have been too difficult to put residents in the van's far back row, so those seats were left unfilled. But that wasn't their biggest problem at the moment. Somehow, as they loaded the minivan, the chair that had been propping open the front door was moved and, without anyone noticing, Villa Capri's front door slammed shut—and locked.

Fountaingrove Parkway, 3:30 a.m.

Cynthia Arroyo didn't know the three passengers in her car as she drove down Fountaingrove Parkway. Before she left, she had written their names on a list of departing residents; they weren't among the residents she usually cared for. She planned to drop her charges at Coddingtown and then return in the shuttle to load more residents. However, in the smoke-induced blackness with trees burning around her, on a road she had driven to and from her night shift for five months, Cynthia suddenly didn't have a clue where she was.

"I blacked out," she said. "[It was] so smoky. It was hot. I couldn't even roll down my window to check [my location]. I thought the road was so hot my tires might melt off, and we would just be stuck there." In the back seat with her husband John, Nell Magnuson was also shocked at the conditions. "It looked like a ring of fire. We could see the actual fire. It was red all around us," she said.

"Oh God, oh God, oh God," Cynthia cried over and over again as she drove.

"We're going back the way we came," Nell told Cynthia at one point.

Nell knew their driver was terrified and couldn't find a way out because "she kept going around and around in a circle. There was no exit," Nell said. The woman who had been placed in the front passenger seat was too frightened to speak. Nell and John assumed this was the end. *What an awful way to go*, she thought. "I don't think we're going to get out of this," she said to her husband. John put his arm around her and held his wife close. She didn't see the point in panicking and making it rougher on Cynthia. "It was a horrible situation all around," Nell said.

Cynthia's mind had gone blank. She couldn't remember how to get to Coddingtown Center, a mall she had visited more than a hundred times.

Eventually, she found herself on an overpass where a couple was walking. She rolled down her window to ask them for directions, but the heat was too oppressive, so she kept driving. It felt like the street itself was ablaze.

In tears, the 21-year-old called her mother as she struggled to find her way off the hill. Her mom answered and tried to help her focus and get her bearings. Confused, Cynthia headed down a freeway ramp. Somehow, she wound up on Highway 101 northbound toward Windsor, not the road nor the direction she wanted to go. So, without thinking, Cynthia made an abrupt U-turn in the highway's northbound lanes and drove the wrong way up the on-ramp she had just come down. From there, she turned right, crossed over the overpass, and finally registered where she was. She had made it to the Bicentennial overpass, heading west.

It was close to 4 a.m. when she arrived at her destination, finding the Coddingtown tire shop parking lot empty. She drove around looking for Oakmont buses and vans, but none was to be found. Given that she hadn't yet saved her coworkers' numbers on her new phone, she wasn't sure whom she could contact. So she called Health Services Director Jane Torres, who told her she was sitting in a car in a nearby department store parking lot with Janice Wilson, the new memory care director. When Cynthia arrived to meet them, she tried to hold it together as she relayed the desperate situation at Villa Capri, where they were still loading residents and waiting for Joel to return with the shuttle bus, and what they went through getting to Coddingtown.

To her relief, Jane offered to take Cynthia's three passengers to New Vintage Church while Cynthia went home to check on her boyfriend and dogs and to see if they needed to evacuate their home. But as she sped away, her brain fog lifted, and a single thought took shape. *If Jane and Janice had a car, why couldn't they go up to Villa Capri to help? Why were they sitting in the parking lot outside a Nordstrom Rack?*

***

Back at Villa Capri, Elizabeth Lopez knew they needed to leave as soon as possible, but as she saw Kathy struggling to open Villa Capri's front door, she got out of her minivan to help. Kathy stopped her.

"No, I have to stay here and help you," Elizabeth protested. "At least I'll try to open the door."

"No, just leave," Kathy said. "Leave. You have residents in your car. I'll figure it out."

Elizabeth suggested one option. "Just grab a chair and break the window."

Kathy motioned for Elizabeth to pull away from the building. "I told her I will be back," Elizabeth said. She planned to drop the three residents at the tire shop and return to take more. As the caregiver made her way down Fountaingrove Parkway, she scanned for the police roadblocks Debie Smith cited as the reason she was unable to make it to Villa Capri. She didn't see any police or fire crews. "My question was," Elizabeth later asked, "if it was blocked, how did the family members get up there?"

As Elizabeth drove, Juan recorded a video of their journey. In the background, Dawn Ross' father, Bill Lee, can be heard saying, "Buildings are burning like mad over there." Minutes later, Elizabeth arrived at the parking lot outside the tire store, but she, like Cynthia, found it empty. She texted Marie. "Where do I go? Nobody is here." She couldn't return to Villa Capri as she had planned, and she didn't know if the two Oakmont corporate men were still there or were on their way back up to help.

In fact, neither were at the facility, and they wouldn't be returning. After spending less than an hour at Villa Capri, Joel Ruiz had driven away with more than a dozen residents packed in the Ford shuttle to Coddingtown and was rerouted from there to the church. Pouya Ansari would later explain in sworn testimony that he had left alone in his SUV in search of help. At the base of Fountaingrove Parkway, he said he asked a police officer for help, but the officer said, "You need to leave." Pouya claimed he told the officer he came from Villa Capri and more residents still needed rescue. According to Pouya, the officer told him, "We have help," and said Pouya couldn't return up the hill. "I'm going anyways," Pouya said he told the officer and did a U-turn onto the sidewalk in defiance of the officer's orders. But as he looked up Fountaingrove Parkway, Pouya discovered the whole road was on fire and impassable. He claimed he then headed down a side road, got lost, and ended up five miles north of town, where he ran out of gas and sat parked for the next few hours.

***

Although theirs was the first vehicle to leave Villa Capri, Sonoma County Sheriff's Deputy Joey Horsman and Anett Rivas never made it to the impromptu meeting point at Coddingtown. Joey had steered the white Sprinter van down the shared driveway and onto Fountaingrove Parkway, where he passed through a gauntlet of blinding ash and smoke and downed trees without a clear destination in mind. "The Round Barn was completely up in flames," Joey later described. "The Hilton was already up in flames. And I could just see [the fire] was, at that point, bigger than I could have ever imagined."

Anett Rivas, in the front passenger seat, said Joey had to brake often because the van's lights couldn't cut through the thick, dark smoke. Anett felt heat penetrate the vehicle from the flames. She was terrified the road and the van would combust. "Joey was in shock," she said, "and I was too."

An even more chilling scene unfolded as they approached the intersection of Fountaingrove Parkway and Mendocino Avenue, where emergency vehicles filled the intersection and people milled about in gusting winds as the fire tore through Journey's End mobile home park at the southwest corner. Joey turned left onto Mendocino Avenue and passed Kaiser, where staff were preparing to load patients into cars in anticipation of evacuating the hospital.

Anett suggested taking their passengers to the emergency shelter near the Sonoma County Fairgrounds, but Joey said he wanted a closer drop-off point so he could return to Villa Capri. He considered the Sonoma County Sheriff's Office, but the fire was fast approaching Kaiser and the buildings were separated by only a couple blocks. Instead, he drove deeper into the county government complex and chose the permit department building, surrounded by a parking lot. He and Anett unloaded the eight residents, then Joey took off for Villa Capri alone, this time using a different route to avoid the busy intersection near Journey's End. When he reached Fountaingrove Parkway, Joey maneuvered around a set of cones laid out to block eastbound traffic and headed up the hill, where his rescue mission took a perilous turn.

On his right, fire ate away at structures on the Keysight Technologies campus. Across from Keysight was the entrance to Villa Capri and Varenna, but Joey only made it 10 to 15 yards up the driveway before flames extending the length of Villa Capri's hillside stopped his progress. He was too late. Joey assumed everything was on fire, and there was nothing he could do except try to save himself. He turned the van around and started west on Fountaingrove Parkway, the shortest distance to safety. But there was no going back the way he came; he was trapped by another wall of flames. Joey drove over the center divider and turned east in hopes of finding a new escape route. It wasn't only buildings and trees that were ablaze. The air itself seemed to have ignited. The deputy could see no way out. There was no point in calling 911, he thought, because anyone at Villa Capri must be dead by now. And he, too, was likely going to die. If that was the case, he needed to talk to one specific person.

His pregnant wife, Stacie, answered. All he could offer were two words. "Sorry," he said, and "goodbye."

She screamed, and the line went dead.

Sonoma County Permit Department Parking Lot, About Two Miles South of Villa Capri

As she waited for the sheriff's deputy to return with the Sprinter van, Anett Rivas paced in the unfamiliar parking lot under a bright red sky. It looked almost like dawn, she thought. It wasn't. It was the fire itself, casting light as it incinerated Journey's End mobile home park only a half mile away. She kept an eye on the eight residents, some of whom had dementia, and she wondered, *How am I going to get all of these residents somewhere with no car? And I'm pregnant.*

Anett had Joey's grandmother, Inez, sit on the pavement because she was unsteady on her feet. Len Kulwiec sat on the concrete steps, shivering in his pajama bottoms and robe. He was afraid to move because of his throbbing, swollen knee. Norma Porter sat on a low wall with the others, some of whom were barefoot. It seemed to her that her driver didn't know where he was going because he had stopped and turned around a few times on Mendocino Avenue before dropping them in this random lot.

Norma was no stranger to challenging times. When her parents moved the family to California during the Great Depression and Dust Bowl, they had arrived with no money or jobs and five kids to feed. For a time, they lived in a tent in the San Fernando Valley. Her father had only five dollars to his name when a slab of cement meant for their house's foundation was laid on the wrong lot. "That was a blow," she said.

Now, Norma sat in the middle of the night amid another crisis, waiting with seven other vulnerable assisted living residents. At least she knew the area well. In 1954 she and her husband had moved into a home only 1,800 feet north of where she now sat, and they were raising four children in that Russell Avenue house when the Hanly Fire swept over the hills to Santa Rosa in 1964. "I do remember looking up and seeing fire was coming," she said of the Hanly.

Despite the hardships, Norma had learned to focus on the positives in life, and that trait was coming in handy now as she watched the Tubbs Fire cut a similar path through her adopted hometown. As others vocalized their fears, Norma remained calm. "I thought we were in good hands," she said.

Anett, however, felt exposed and vulnerable. All nine of them were. Her phone was dead, and she had no way to recharge it. Len was injured, Inez was a fall risk, and one woman needed to relieve herself, which she did around the side of the locked building. When she and another female resident came back around the corner, Anett noticed one of them had a phone and a signal. She borrowed it and called her sister for help. It was a moment of relief, on multiple levels, but it didn't last long.

A gray sedan pulled into the lot and began to circle. At first Anett thought the driver might be a county employee who could let them inside, but then he rolled down his window to ask Anett if she had access. He parked, walked up to the permit department building, tested the doors, peered inside, and walked around its footprint. Anett asked the tall, curly-haired man if he worked there. He didn't, he said. The man then asked if she needed help or a ride, but something about him felt creepy to her. "I didn't feel comfortable putting residents in a stranger's car," she said. So she passed on his assistance, yet the stranger didn't leave, fostering more anxiety. "It didn't make sense," Anett said. "I didn't understand why he would come to a random location in the middle of the night and try to get in."

Anett patrolled in a wide circle around the residents, keeping a close eye on them until the headlights of her sister's Audi appeared across the parking lot. She was ecstatic, relieved to have her sister by her side, even though she knew the impossibility of fitting the residents into her small car. Their wait was not over. Her phone finally charging in her sister's car, Anett tried to call Cynthia and Marie but couldn't get through. Their phones were likely dead too. She tried Debie Smith and Jane Torres. No luck. *What am I supposed to do if Joey doesn't return?* she thought.

Fountaingrove Parkway, About 3:30 a.m.

Joey Horsman was convinced he would need a miracle to survive. When he crossed over the median in hopes of making it east to Stagecoach Road, he was trying to follow the path to safety his wife had taken an hour earlier. But he soon found that, too, was not an option. Stagecoach was swallowed by flames pouring from the small shopping center on the corner. Joey knew he had only one other way out—continuing east on Fountaingrove Parkway into the very teeth of the firestorm. It was a path that even firefighters had abandoned. He called Stacie again "and I just kept telling her, 'Sorry.'" Then he hit the gas and accelerated into the flames. "Not only was everything on fire, but the wind was gusting so hard. Literally, the flames...within a milli-second, would go from 40 to 50 yards and just explode in the air," he said.

Like a scuba diver descending into the depths, Joey felt a wide, external pressure compressing his body as the van propelled up the hill, crumbling sticks and other brush in its path. The sides of the vehicle seemed to squeeze inward as he gunned it. He passed through the shaft of smoke and flame, maneuvering around debris where he could, unsure of whether this was a path to his deliverance or certain destruction. Then, somehow, it was over.

"And all of a sudden, it just opened up," he said in a deposition, "and I wasn't surrounded by fire anymore." He found himself at the top of the hill where only the smoldering remains of houses and other evidence of the firestorm's ruinous handiwork was visible. He continued through the waste-land until he reached the intersection of Fountaingrove Parkway and Brush Creek Road, where he came upon a roadblock with multiple police cars present. "Everything's on fire," he told one of the officers, who was surprised to see anyone coming east down Fountaingrove Parkway. "Everything's gone up there," Joey said. "Everyone needs to get out."

Having reached the east side of town, he knew it would take a while for him to get back to Anett and the other residents. So he called Sonoma County dispatch where his call registered at 3:52 a.m. "Just dropped off eight elders at 2550 Ventura," he said. "They will need help. They are from Villa Capri."

Because of traffic, it took Joey another 30 minutes to traverse the few miles back to Ventura Avenue. On the way, he called Stacie to let her know he had survived, and they stayed connected as he worked his way back to the county complex. As he pulled into the parking lot, he found Anett and the residents still waiting for them. "Did you get to Villa Capri?" she asked him. He told her he hadn't. He couldn't even see the facility from the road because of the flames, he reported. Both feared for those who were left behind.

"[Joey] thought nobody had made it," Anett said, a sentiment that terrified her. "I thought maybe my coworkers didn't make it," coworkers who, unbeknownst to Anett, had planned to throw her a baby shower on Tuesday.

Villa Capri

As Melissa Langhals drove her Jeep from the visitor parking lot to the portico, flames devoured the downslope side of Villa Capri. The entire hillside vineyard adjacent to the complex was on fire, and there was no time to spare. Melissa hopped out to find Kathy banging on the front door's window with a flashlight. At some point in the shuffling, someone had moved the chair that had propped open the front door, and now it was closed and locked, leaving 24 Villa Capri residents alone inside.

The few elderly residents inside were of no help. Most, like Alice Eurotas, had been rushed out of their rooms without an opportunity to grab their hearing aids or glasses. Even if they could hear Kathy's pounding over the roaring winds or could see the women through the thickening smoke inside, most were incapable of lending a hand. At least nine were in wheelchairs. A number of others were from memory care.

It was around 3:45 a.m., and Kathy and Melissa were stuck outside, looking in at frightened, frail elderly residents counting on them for survival.

Neither woman had even a momentary urge to flee, although even if they had wanted to, their escape route was blocked.

Kathy had seen plenty of TV detectives use a Maglite to break glass, and she was certain hers would do the trick. She banged and banged on the window with the heel of the heavy flashlight, but the glass wouldn't crack. They looked around for something heavier. From her Jeep's cargo space, Melissa grabbed a tow hitch, the one she used to pull her 1975 Tahiti Tri Hull Runabout to Lake Sonoma. She and Roxanne had a favorite campsite there where they used to spend almost every summer weekend boating, fishing, and kayaking. Melissa had sold the boat six months earlier but, in a stroke of luck, she still had the hitch.

Positioning herself in front of the door, Melissa heaved the heavy metal device toward the window. It shattered the glass on the first try. She reached through the broken window and pushed open the door from the inside. Melissa then propped the door open with the hitch while Kathy ran to pull sheets and blankets off beds and lay them over the glass to protect several barefoot residents. Kathy worried she and Melissa might get in trouble for breaking the window.

Just past the entrance, on the concierge desk, Kathy caught sight of three sets of keys and walkie-talkies. She suddenly realized how valuable it would have been if at least one employee had stayed behind. Neither Kathy nor Melissa could communicate with some of the disabled residents, and they didn't know them by name. One lady moaned, and Kathy didn't know whether she was injured. And what about the woman with the catheter? Could Kathy pick her up? She had no idea. Plus, if Kathy knew their needs maybe she could alleviate their stress and dissipate some of the panic bubbling up.

Melissa repeatedly called for help over the radio, hoping someone might hear her. Kathy tried pulling the fire alarm. *Perhaps an emergency vehicle might respond*, she thought. But nothing happened. And where was her husband? *Mark should have returned by now. Maybe he got tangled up taking care of residents at Coddingtown.* She was losing hope that she would see her husband arrive. Yet he had promised to return for her, and Mark, "Straight Arrow," was a promise keeper.

Kathy grabbed a set of keys from the concierge desk and took them to the nurse's office. The former middle school teacher who always anticipated the next fiasco wanted to access the big binders containing residents' medical records. She thought staff would need those at an evacuation site. But none of the keys worked.

Before she and Mark retired, they had aced fire drills hundreds of times, and every K–12 emergency training session or drill always identified a method of communication and a leader. There was always a plan. Everyone had a job. But tonight, Kathy realized, no one was in charge, and there had been no method of communication. Kathy, Mark, and Melissa—and Elizabeth, Cynthia, Marie, Anett, Joey, Joel, and Pouya—each operated individually with minimal coordination. And now the task of saving the last two dozen residents rested solely on Kathy and Melissa. Working together to come up with a realistic plan would be the only way they and the residents were going to get out of this impossible situation. The women agreed to first load Melissa's Jeep with a few of the 18 residents in the lobby. Then they would bring down the final six residents who were still upstairs—all sitting in wheelchairs.

Kathy and Melissa shouted to the able-bodied seniors in the lobby to climb into Melissa's Jeep if they could, and two men and three women, including Henrietta Hillman, rose to do just that. But the Jeep only held four passengers, so one woman climbed on a man's lap in the front seat. Henrietta said that woman was "a nervous wreck," and the man's wife, who sat in the backseat with Henrietta, also seemed anxious. Once the Jeep was full, Kathy urged Melissa to leave. "I won't leave you here alone," Melissa repeated. Besides, they had only completed the first part of their plan. She left the residents in her Jeep, even though they were growing impatient. "They kept asking about a driver," Melissa said, "and I said, 'If any of you want to drive, please feel free to take it, because we have to get the rest of these people out of here.'"

Back inside, she and Kathy headed upstairs to the second-floor landing. When Kathy and Mark had conferred before he left, she offered to stay at Villa Capri so she wouldn't have to lift residents in and out of the Suburban. But now she faced the more-daunting task of carrying residents in wheelchairs down two flights of stairs. And she knew she and Melissa would have to do it alone; Mark was not coming back.

To this point, the two women had brought to the lobby only the residents who could walk. Carrying residents would require brute strength, but neither Kathy nor Melissa was in top form. Kathy's back surgery put constraints on what she could lift, and Melissa's recent hip replacement surgery limited her as well. The first resident underscored the difficulty of their situation. Melissa grabbed a sheet and wrapped it around the lady's waist to strap her to her chair. Then she and Kathy each took a side and rocked the chair's large rear wheels down one step at a time.

It worked for a few steps, but then they lost control. They were able to tip the chair sideways so both Kathy and Melissa fell but the woman just slid sideways in the seat. She wasn't hurt, but her prosthetic leg fell off. Kathy picked up the limb and, unsure of what else to do, tossed it down the stairs ahead of them. She and Melissa strained to tip the chair upright and wrangle her down step-by-step. When they reached the bottom, Kathy returned the woman's limb, with an apology.

Insatiably thirsty from exerting herself in the dry, smoky building, Kathy had often filled a coffee cup with water from a pitcher near the reception desk, right under a large, two-foot-wide battery-operated wall clock. Time seemed to be flying by too quickly for the tasks at hand.

It was after taking another gulp of water that Kathy looked outside and saw one of the Jeep's occupants wandering away. She called to Melissa, and they ran outside to corral the woman.

Varenna, 3:45 a.m.

R.J. Kisling hit speeds in excess of 80 miles per hour as he drove north on Highway 101 from Petaluma toward the menacing glow atop the hills of northeast Santa Rosa. Police cars, fire engines, and other emergency vehicles passed him with indifference. As he exited on Bicentennial Way, R.J. saw an ABC7 van parked on the overpass filming live with its camera lights beaming, creating a bright patch of illumination on an otherwise bleak scene of emergency lights and fire in the distance. At that moment, R.J. was on speakerphone with his sister, four years his junior, who happened to be watching that very Channel 7 broadcast from her San Rafael home. "I just saw your truck pass in the background," Steffany told him.

Her brother's brown GMC Sierra pickup was easy to identify, as most nonemergency vehicles were going the other direction. "Fire is *everywhere*," she said, her voice elevating as she emphasized the last word. R.J. didn't respond. He was concentrating on getting uphill. At the Bicentennial Way merge with Fountaingrove Parkway, a police officer stood with his flashlight beam sweeping the middle of the street. R.J. pulled over and hopped out.

Speaking loudly to be heard over the wind, he asked the officer whether Varenna had been evacuated.

"I think they have been," the officer shouted back. R.J. asked if he was certain.

"I'm pretty sure," he said. "But it's like a war zone up there."

R.J. jogged back to his truck, unappeased, the officer's "pretty sure" replaying itself in his mind. He made a U-turn. R.J. needed to see for himself. He buzzed past the officer who, with little more than a glance, made no attempt to stop him. As R.J. headed up the hill, the smoke grew thicker as ash rained down, making it difficult to navigate. He turned right onto Altruria Drive in hopes of finding a clearer path but found only a more circuitous route through a dark and desolate neighborhood on a roadway that was just as hazardous. A flickering crown of red and orange divided the dark hill from the blackness of billowing smoke above him.

Guided by two female voices, the placid instruction from his GPS and the serious tone from his sister, R.J. pushed ahead. "Literally, the road is covered in fire," he told Steffany. "The trees are down, burning in the street. I'm driving over this stuff, over burning trees, or going up on the sidewalks to get around them." For a moment, R.J. feared the Varenna complex was gone. It was hard to imagine any structure, let alone people, enduring in these conditions. He could barely see six feet beyond the hood of his truck. But then, suddenly, there it was. "I see the entrance," he reported. "It's dark. There's nobody there."

This initial report came as a relief to both of them, reviving their hopes that the retirement home and its 228 residents had been evacuated. With no vehicles and no lights or movement inside, R.J. contemplated how he could turn around and get out of there. Should he try going over Fountaingrove heading toward Stagecoach Road this time? As much as he was unhappy with his original path, the second route seemed like suicide. Either way, he was confident his visit to Varenna would be short-lived.

"Are you sure?" Steffany asked after he reported seeing no one. "Are you sure? Go check his apartment."

R.J. parked at the ornate circular fountain bordered by a flowering hedge. He grabbed his headlamp as he exited his truck, and, for the first time in his 35-minute journey, he lost cell service. He also lost his sense of relief. R.J. entered the darkened lobby to find a group of residents seated on chairs and couches. "What are you guys doing here?" R.J. asked them incredulously.

One gentleman stood up and approached. "Are you the firefighters?" he asked. "Are you here to rescue us?"

The situation was worse than R.J. feared. Not only had the building not been cleared, many residents, he quickly discovered, were still in their rooms. As he was peppered with questions, he reminded himself he had a specific task to execute: find his grandfather. R.J. turned his attention to room 101, the first apartment off the lobby, where Papa lived among his oil paintings. R.J. walked in to find an empty apartment and signs of a hurried exit, including a mix of clothes strewn on the bed and batteries spread on the kitchen counter. It appeared Papa had mustered a go-bag before heading out. Not knowing Papa's whereabouts left R.J. unsettled, but now he had the others to worry about.

He ran back to the lobby. "Where are the fire hoses? Where are the extinguishers?" he asked two young women wearing dark green polo shirts with an insignia on them. They appeared to be staff workers. One woman showed R.J. one extinguisher encased in a wall near the dining hall and another nearby. He brought them both to the entrance. *We may need these at some point*, he thought.

R.J. took a look outside. Through the smoke, he could barely make out the outline of his truck. Flashes of embers and ash surged through the courtyard like fireflies. He calculated he could fit maybe a dozen people in the bed of his truck and a couple in the cab if needed. But given what he drove through to get there, he knew that was only an option of last resort. The odds of residents surviving those conditions were slim.

12

Souls

The Firestorm, 4 a.m.

Tubbs Fire distance to Villa Capri and Varenna: Surrounding the property
Over the previous two hours, the fire had hopped Highway 101 and burned its
way west toward the Santa Rosa Plain, home to approximately half of the popu-
lation of Sonoma County as well as the Russian River Valley where chardonnay
and pinot noir grapes grow in abundance. Vineyards and their treeless expanses
make great firebreaks, but vineyards in this area are dotted with wild oak wood-
lands, perfect lily pads from which a spotting Tubbs Fire could leapfrog its way to
the dense redwood forest that starts a few miles west of Highway 101. If the fire
reached that thicket of second-growth forest, there wouldn't be much that could
stop it running clear to the Pacific Ocean 15 miles away.

Fire crews began arriving from all over the state to help in the region. In
all, more than 250 wildfires erupted throughout Northern California beginning
on October 8. Of those, 24 became major fires, including the Nuns Fire, which
swept through areas of Sonoma Valley up to a state park at Santa Rosa's south-
eastern limit. Simultaneously, the Atlas Fire scorched more than 51,000 acres in
Napa and Solano counties and claimed six lives, while the Redwood Valley Fire
in Mendocino County killed nine people and destroyed nearly 550 homes and
other structures. But none compared to the Tubbs Fire in terms of devastation
and loss of life.

As the fire ripped through a neighborhood called Coffey Park, residents
packed up and left quickly, if they could. Some did not make it out in time,
including 56-year-old Karen Sue Aycock, a retired roofer who perished after
seeking shelter in her bathroom. Tamara Latrice Thomas, who was paralyzed,

died around the same time after being trapped in her second-floor bedroom in a board and care home. She was 47.

Marin County, San Rafael, 40 Miles South of Varenna, 4:04 a.m.

It had been nearly 15 minutes since Steffany Kisling had heard from R.J. He had told her there were still people inside Varenna, but she had not heard much else before they lost their connection. She called R.J.'s wife, Betty. "I know his frickin' personality," Steffany said. "I know he's going to go down with the ship." She was angry—pissed at him and upset with herself—knowing she was the reason he was there in the first place. She had called to wake him, knowing full well he would get in his truck and head over to Varenna. Steffany had other reasons to be anxious as well. She and R.J. had lost their father just two months earlier, after he took a fall in his home in Escondido, California. It was a sudden and unfathomable death. The idea of losing more family members so soon was too hard to imagine.

Between periodic calls with Betty, Steffany dialed R.J. over and over without success. But then Steffany's phone rang. It was her brother. She quickly conferenced in Betty. "Take as many residents as you can and get out of there," Steffany pleaded. But R.J. told them that plan was not going to work. Residents were shaking, coughing, and sweating, and the smoke was far worse outdoors.

"Then start putting them all in the pool if you have to and get in with them," Steffany said. He said he had considered that, but he first needed to get them out of their rooms. This was discouraging news to Steffany as she had assumed the residents were, at the very least, already out and waiting to depart.

"I'm coming to help you," she said.

"No!" R.J. snapped. "That makes no sense. Besides, you're never going to make it."

"I'm coming anyway," she said.

Betty interjected to announce she was going to call 911. Certainly someone had called by this point, Betty reasoned, but she had to do something. Betty's landline call would prove pivotal. For reasons that remain unclear, when she dialed 911 at 4:04 a.m., it resulted in the first radio call, according to dispatch records, notifying emergency crews there were still people inside the retirement complex.

"How many people are still there at Varenna?" the dispatcher asked Betty. She relayed the question over her cell phone to R.J., who made a quick count.

"About 12 to 14," he told her. "But there could be still more in their rooms."

As Betty completed her call, Steffany headed for Varenna. After a quick stop in Petaluma to swap cars with Betty, whose Toyota 4Runner thankfully had a full tank of gas, Steffany found herself speeding 95 miles per hour on Highway 101.

"Nobody was going north except random civilian cars, people who are batshit crazy like my brother who are going into the flames," Steffany said as she, too, headed straight for the fire line.

Highway 101 and River Road

Capt. Mike Stornetta had managed to make it from Palo Alto to the Windsor Fire Protection District station, where he left Rocket and found an available vehicle, a Type 3 four-wheel-drive-class fire engine common in mountainous or rural districts that specialized in rapid deployment, pick up, and relocation during wildfires. It was just the engine he needed. He had also been able to assemble a small team of three crew members, including one volunteer and a veteran firefighter, Jason Jones, who had to be picked up at a utility substation on River Road just west of the highway because he was unable to make it up to the Windsor station. As Jason jumped on board, Mike noticed he had burn marks on his car. It seemed that all firefighters had their stories that night.

"REDCOM: Engine 7265 available for assignment par four," Mike radioed, referring to the number of crew on his team. Stornetta and his colleagues waited for their assignment. The dispatcher directed them to head immediately to the Varenna complex on Fountaingrove Parkway where possibly 50 or more elderly people needed help getting out. They were "surrounded by fire," the dispatcher said. "You are the only apparatus available to respond at the moment." Mike confirmed, "On the way," and turned to his companions. "Did I just hear that right? Did she say '15' or '50'?" he asked. They couldn't tell. Either way, it was dumbfounding.

Varenna

R.J. surveyed the lobby. The two uniformed women he had seen earlier were now nowhere to be found. Everyone else, it appeared, was a resident. One woman had a chocolate Labrador with her. Another resident wore a yellow reflective vest and looked as if he knew what was going on, so R.J. asked him for details of the emergency plan. The man explained residents were told to wait in their rooms, but some had come down when the alarms sounded.

R.J. spotted a guest registry on a credenza near the entrance. "Everybody!" he announced loudly. "We need to get a list of everyone who is here. Would you all please write down your names on this registry? And please include your room numbers." One man explained he had difficulty moving a pen, so R.J. wrote for him. After the registry circulated, R.J. counted 15 names. More people arrived by the minute.

R.J. decided to take it one step at a time. First, he needed to get everyone out of their rooms. He started running down the halls, pounding on doors and directing residents to the lobby. Each time he passed through the lobby, residents pressed him with questions, asking if he was going to take them to safety. He assured them he was there to help, but he said nothing about getting them out of the building.

One resident's personal caregiver tapped him on the shoulder. "Would you be so kind as to help me?" the young woman asked in a Jamaican accent. She needed help carrying down the woman in her care who lived on the second floor and used a wheelchair. R.J. strapped on his headlamp and followed her up the grand staircase. What he found startled him. Scattered about the landing were at least a half dozen residents, some in wheelchairs, others perched on their walkers. Almost everyone seemed anxious, and most were apprehensive about descending the stairs. R.J. sensed they were waiting for direction—and help.

He got to work bringing the residents downstairs however he could, including the woman whose caregiver brought him up to the landing. Some he picked up and cradled. Others he guided down holding their side as they took each step. One man was exceptionally large and needed assistance to walk. He told R.J. he was recovering from recent heart surgery. "You're going to have to be last," R.J. told him. "I can't carry you. But we'll get you down." The man nodded in gratitude for the encouragement, and a woman with short blonde hair, who R.J. assumed was his partner, thanked him as well.

When his turn came, the man stood with R.J., and they began their descent. R.J. could smell something burning, like rubber, plastic, or roof tar. He was certain the building had caught fire somewhere. Despite the adrenaline racing through his body, R.J. couldn't push the man faster. He and the resident took one step. They stopped for the man to take a deep breath. Another step. Stop. Breath. After the third step, R.J. had to take a break, and he leaned the older gentleman against the wall. *I don't know if I can make this*, R.J. thought before quickly adjusting his attitude. "You can do this," he encouraged the resident as they resumed their journey. It was only when they reached the lobby floor that R.J. noticed the heavyset man was barefoot. R.J. ran back upstairs and retrieved a pair of shoes and yellow socks for him. The man and woman thanked R.J. profusely.

R.J. checked on the other residents in the lobby, some of whom asked for water, in addition to items left behind in their rooms. R.J. reminded them he was only one person, and he was not on staff. Then he slipped away to evacuate more apartments. It was hard, disorienting work. Every hall was dark except for emergency lights and green exit signs. Every door was white. And each time R.J. returned from delivering a resident to the lobby, he had to remember where he left off. He often had to find a stairwell or return to the lobby to get his bearings. R.J. feared he was beating on some doors more than once while missing others entirely. He cursed himself for not bringing something to mark the cleared rooms.

After reaching the end of a first-floor hall on the northeast wing, R.J. realized he had been there before. Dismayed, he turned to leave. But after a look back, his eyes fell on one particular door. He couldn't remember if he had cleared that apartment, but he was overcome with the sense he should double-check. He tried the unlocked handle, swung the door open, and announced himself, but received no answer. As he walked into the bedroom, an open window acted like a portal to another dimension. The landscape was burning outside, and the wildfire cast a flickering, hazy glow onto the room's furnishings. The wind howled as it pushed smoke inside, and embers blew through the open window, landing on the curtains, carpet, and decor. It was then, through the dim, spectral light, R.J. saw a figure lying in bed. The woman's eyes were wide, glued to the man standing over her, his headlamp beaming down. She made no sound. R.J. closed the window and stamped out any embers he could find. He offered to help her up, but the woman shook her head. He insisted, but she refused. "You don't understand," she said, her voice almost a whisper, explaining that, in the stress of the night, she had soiled herself.

R.J. ran to the lobby for the caregiver with the Jamaican accent, who agreed to help. After some trouble finding fresh incontinence briefs, the caregiver cleaned and changed the resident and helped her to the hall. As the three of them walked downstairs together, R.J. offered quiet thanks for whatever instinct called him back to that room. The resident was paralyzed with fear and shame and, if he hadn't closed her window, the entire wing might have caught fire.

It had seemed longer, but R.J. had been working for roughly 30 minutes, and his plan to gather the residents and wait for the professionals to arrive was not looking promising. He needed a backup strategy. R.J. thought if he could figure out which side of the building would burn first, he could take the residents to the pool in the back or the fountain in the front. But that was a lousy idea, and R.J. knew it. The residents would never survive the conditions outside.

A few minutes later, R.J. was escorting a resident down a hall when he saw lights—the unmistakable flickering of red lights signifying an emergency vehicle outside Varenna's front entrance. He gave a sigh of relief just as a young firefighter in turnout gear walked into the lobby and looked around. "How many people?" he asked. A couple of residents looked toward R.J. "Thirty-four, so far," R.J. said. He had recently completed a count. The firefighter studied him, then turned and exited, saying he needed to talk to his captain.

Moments later, the front door swung open, and in burst Capt. Mike Stornetta. From his perspective, the scene was surreal, bordering on eerie. All Stornetta could see were the shadows of people sitting in wheelchairs and walkers or milling about in the dark. Here and there, flashlights and headlamps cut through the haze casting a blue-green backlight that only added to the haunting spectacle. Sometimes, worried faces turned to him, their eyes glinting with the reflection of the flashlight in his hand.

Stornetta approached a man wearing a headlamp, assuming he was in charge. "How many people do you have?" he asked, as if he didn't trust the answer his junior crew member had just given him.

"Last I counted, it was 34," R.J. said.

"Is this everybody?" he asked.

"No way," R.J. said, before explaining that each time he went down a hall he found more. "But I've never left the Main Building. I have no idea if all of the other buildings [are] clear." Stornetta asked for the master keys to the rooms. "I've already looked for them but haven't been able to find anything," R.J. said.

Up to this point, the captain had been under the impression that the man in the headlamp was a Varenna manager. R.J. noticed the captain's frustration with his answers. "I just came to get my grandfather," he said before lowering his voice. He told Stornetta he had no idea where anything was: vans, keys, flashlights. Nothing. He didn't even know where the staff had gone. He hadn't seen the two women with the polo shirts since he arrived. "These people were left here alone," R.J. told him quietly.

Stornetta was disgusted. He walked outside to brief the three-man crew he had cobbled together at the station. "We've got a bunch of elderly people in here," he told his team. "But first we need to do an assessment of this structure. Let me know if anything's on fire. I need you guys to go do a hot lap and tell me what you see." Then he radioed REDCOM. They were going to need assistance and buses—at least two—to get all these people off the ridge, he reported.

Meanwhile, R.J. tended to the residents in the lobby who continued to shower him with questions. "How come nobody came and got us earlier?" "How come nobody told us to evacuate?" "When are we going to be taken to safety?" He had no answers, and as grateful as he was to see these men in turnout gear, he was certain no one was going to make it out before the hilltop was overrun by the approaching inferno.

As Stornetta was making the call, a Santa Rosa ladder truck pulled up, followed soon after by an engine from the Mountain Volunteer Fire Department. The crew included firefighters Caroline Upton and Tony

Albright, who had seen the Tubbs Fire at its roots and had been working nonstop since 10 p.m. when they received that first call for a smoke check on Tubbs Lane. The married volunteers had left their utility truck behind and teamed up with Capt. Tony Riedell, a 12-year department veteran.

Relieved to see both teams, Stornetta immediately tasked the Mountain VFD crew with defending Varenna's structures. They headed toward the complex's western edge overlooking the lake where one casita was on fire, casting flames into the already ash-filled sky. As Capt. Riedell and his team approached the casita, they saw a couple firefighters fighting the blaze with only shovels, axes, and other hand gear. They quickly plugged into a hydrant and disposed of the flames eating away at the front porch, preventing any interior damage.

At that point, the Varenna complex was essentially surrounded, and the fire was closing in "in stages," Riedell said. One round of flames would come through "hot and fast, and then it seemed like the fire was gone . . .but then here comes another run of fire coming at you." Given what they were witnessing, the Mountain VFD team held out little hope of saving the structures. With any luck, they might be able to buy some time for the people inside to get out. "We needed to protect all those people who were just staged there in the lobby that couldn't get out," Riedell said. "That was the concerning part."

***

At 4:14 a.m., an unknown caller reached 911. "Several elderly people are still trapped," dispatch reported concerning Varenna. "Building is catching on fire. Four people still in building."

At 4:16 a.m. a Santa Rosa police officer—call sign OCEAN3—called dispatch with urgency in his voice.

> OCEAN3: We need to know as much as we can about 1401 Fountaingrove. Who's calling it in and where they're at, because this building is on fire.

Dispatch: We are advised that there were three elderly residents still inside the North Building and all employees had evacuated.

OCEAN3: The building is on fire. Who called this in?

Dispatch: Looks like we have had multiple employees call in. I don't have names on them. Just phone numbers…. It looks like one party is a Betty Kisling. We have multiple phone numbers in the call, but one person was an employee, but he didn't sound like he was on-site.

It was about this time that Santa Rosa Police Officer Dave Pedersen arrived at Varenna in his patrol car. Capt. Mike Stornetta approached and quickly briefed him about the senior residents who were still in the lobby and how a search was underway for more. Pedersen—call sign GEORGE5—called dispatch at 4:21 a.m.

Pedersen: I need a bus up here Code 3. We've got 25 elderlies up here…1401 Fountaingrove. If the bus will come up to the fireline, I will come down and drive it the rest of the way if I am able to.

Dispatch: Copy. GEORGE5 requesting ambulance Code 3 for elderlies.

Pedersen: Not an ambulance. Twenty-five souls need to be transported down from this hill. I need a bus.

Another officer who heard the request chimed in, describing his hazardous drive up Fountaingrove Parkway. "I had flames over the top of the patrol car to get here, so I don't think a bus driver is going to want to do that," he reported. At 4:22 a.m. a third officer's voice came over the radio. "We are coming up to the entrance. Do you want us to go right?" he asked, a turn which would have taken them to Villa Capri, where Kathy and Melissa, at that moment, were still working to extract two dozen frail residents. Instead, one officer told the new officers to drive straight up to Varenna. "I've got fire guys up here with me," he said. "We're not going to leave these people."

***

The beams from two flashlights panned across the lobby windows followed by a loud knock. Varenna's main doors had been propped open for a time, but because smoke was billowing inside, someone had closed them, and the doors locked shut.

Bob Mitton, who had been sitting in the Bistro café area with his wife, Mimi, and their dog, Cocoa, got up to answer. Standing before him were two police officers, Dave Pedersen and his partner, Eric St. Germain. An alarm was beeping on the control panel to the right of the front door, and Pedersen didn't see any staff. "Can anyone help give us some directions?" the officer asked. Bob spoke up, prompting the officers to train their flashlights on him. "Do you work here?" Pedersen asked. "No, but I live here," Bob said.

Pedersen asked if Bob knew the complex and where people lived. When Bob assured them he did, Pedersen summoned him to join them. Pedersen told Bob they had received a report of people trapped in one of Varenna's north buildings, and that the building was on fire. "The firefighters will have to deal with [evacuating] this [Main] Building," Officer St. Germain said as he motioned them outside to the north. As they walked, Bob gave the officers a brief overview of the grounds, noting the locations of the North and South buildings as well as the casitas.

Then, instinctively, Bob and Officers Pedersen and St. Germain started running toward the North Building. Flames licked the sides of the structure. Conditions had worsened in a hurry.

***

At 4:25 a.m. a Santa Rosa police officer called dispatch.

> I'm here at Varenna.... We've got about 30 people in wheelchairs, and we need a bus up here ASAP.

Officer Pedersen chimed in from the North Building.

> We're finding more people. The number is growing up here.

The dispatcher responded that buses would be on their way as soon as possible. The problem was, four CityBuses were already en route to Kaiser Medical Center to transport noncritically ill patients away from the fire at the hospital's doorstep. Ambulances took those requiring medical support, while the remainder of Kaiser's 130 patients, many still in hospital gowns, found rides with doctors, nurses, and other staff. As they left, trees and shrubs burned on the edge of the hospital parking lot. Two miles north, the fire would soon arrive at the doorstep of Sutter Hospital in Larkfield, resulting in the commandeering of more buses and ambulances to transport 77 patients there to safety. Buses and ambulances were in short supply across the county.

Villa Capri

As Kathy and Melissa tore out of the lobby to catch a tall, thin woman in a light-colored bathrobe wandering away from Melissa's Jeep, a ray of white light swept through the smoke near the turnoff to Villa Capri. It was a beam of police car headlights, and they had passed over the right turn toward Kathy and Melissa and pointed uphill toward Varenna. The women chased after the cruiser, screaming. Melissa wildly swung her arms as Kathy waved her flashlight. The police car paused, and, for the first time in hours, Kathy and Melissa felt a sliver of hope.

Sgt. Steven Pehlke and Officer Andrew Adams were responding to Betty Kisling's 4:04 a.m. 911 call and instructions to head straight up the shared driveway toward Varenna. Kathy and Melissa ran to the car and told the officers of their dire situation before racing back inside to check on the residents. Pehlke and Adams sped around to the back parking lot and saw the rear of the building blanketed in flames. They returned to the front, parked, and entered Villa Capri, where Pehlke saw the elderly residents gathered in the lobby. "The building was completely full of smoke," he reported later. Adams noted, "Most of the residents were confined to a wheelchair, barely dressed, some had catheter bags hooked to their wheelchair.... Not a whole lot of people could walk."

And there were still five people in wheelchairs on the second-floor landing. Pehlke and Adams carried one down, leaving four up top, including Melissa's mother, Virginia. The flames that earlier gnawed at the shrubbery outside her bedroom window were now devouring her apartment only 250 feet from where she sat.

***

Two minutes after Pedersen reported "25 souls" needed rescue from Varenna, Pehlke—call sign SAM22—radioed from Villa Capri's lobby.

> *SAM22 at Varenna. I'll give you the exact address. We have about 30 people in wheelchairs, and we need a bus up here ASAP.*

But Pehlke wasn't at Varenna; he was at Villa Capri, at 1397 Fountaingrove. Not 1401. The shared, split driveway with two separate addresses had created confusion in the response. The dispatcher asked Pehlke to advise on which part of the property they were located, and for the first time, Villa Capri was identified over the airwaves as a separate entity, albeit not by name.

> *I need a bus at 1397 Fountaingrove Parkway. Front building at Varenna in Fountaingrove.*

The dispatcher asked how many buses he would need, but Pehlke didn't answer directly. Instead, he conveyed there were at least 30 people inside, including some who couldn't walk. Seven officers heard Pehlke's plea for assistance and sped to Villa Capri. When they arrived, none of the officers saw a single Oakmont employee on the premises, but they likely all noticed the two women in charge.

Melissa asked the officers to carry the four remaining nonambulatory residents, her mom among them, down the stairs from the second-floor landing. One officer hesitated, she said, saying that type of work was reserved for firefighters. "These people are dying of smoke inhalation right now," Melissa pleaded. "They're too heavy. We can't do it." The officers agreed to help, but they ordered Melissa to leave with the five residents already loaded into her Jeep. She refused. "I'm not leaving without my mom," she told them.

One officer forced a flashlight into her hand and told her to shine it for them. She stood at the top of the stairs as the officers lifted each resident and wheelchair and carried them to the lobby. Officer Adams, already on duty for 16 hours, and another officer together carried the last residents, including Virginia, down the stairs. Then the officers checked every room in the burning building one last time to make sure all residents were out of their rooms and assembled in the lobby.

"There was broken glass everywhere," Adams said. "[Residents] were in their bare feet. So we'd run and literally go into somebody's room and take a pair of shoes or put slippers on them, so they could walk through glass." Kathy Allen performed a similar service gathering eyeglasses and dentures for those rushed out of their rooms without their essentials.

The buses were taking forever to arrive, and police worried the worsening fire and smoke might trap the remaining residents inside. So officers began to put residents into detectives' cars and patrol units to start bringing them down the hill. As the officers helped residents into their vehicles, Kathy approached one of them. "Where are you taking everybody?" she asked. He told her not to worry about it and said, "That's not your concern."

Kathy was absolutely concerned. "No, you don't realize. These people have dementia," she told him. She worried memory care residents would not be able to speak for themselves. They might not know where they came from or worse, who they were. She recalled the officer responding, "Our concern is their safety and getting them out of here. We're not worried about where they are going."

New Vintage Church, About Six Miles Southeast of Villa Capri and Varenna

Gena, Sheri, and Gena's parents had been among the first to arrive at New Vintage Church between 3:30 and 4 a.m. and found a hectic scene. It was not only a last-minute shelter for Villa Capri and Varenna residents, but those from the Fountaingrove Lodge and The Terraces as well. Gena watched as Joel Ruiz pulled up in the Villa Capri shuttle and several residents were carried out and reunited with a wheelchair or walker. The church was mostly quiet inside, although Gena said some residents from memory care shouted out in fear and confusion. One woman meowed like a cat. "Some were freaked out. Some were very verbal. Some were very scared," she said. It was difficult to witness.

While Gena took care of her parents inside, Sheri talked with church volunteers outside. The expanding red glow of fire cresting the ridgelines made them question whether the church was truly a safe place. "Since we just ran from that situation, we decided to move on to get ahead of any potential evacuations that might occur there," Gena said. Around 4:30 a.m., Gena called Tammy Moratto to tell her they were not staying.

Mark Allen had also arrived at the church with his seven residents. He was glad to be delivering his charges somewhere he thought was safe, and he was pleasantly surprised to see the church had so quickly mobilized parishioners, who helped him unload the seven seniors, including his mother.

At first glance, New Vintage Church resembled an elementary school campus, with several gray, white-trimmed outbuildings connected by a long concrete walkway. Inside the main building was a dome-shaped sanctuary lined with stained glass windows that bathed the room in hues of purple, blue, and green during daylight hours. It featured theater-style seating surrounding a broad, elevated stage, where, on Sundays, contemporary musicians played concert-style services under colored lights and in front of a movie-theater-size screen, a production aimed at attracting Millennial and Gen Z worshippers. This morning, though, the vibe was markedly different. The light was artificial, the stadium seating was filled with displaced elderly, and the large screen blared breaking fire news.

Having the TV on describing the widespread devastation upset Mark. "So now that the residents were just evacuated from a fire—to have to experience being ripped out of your bed at two o'clock in the morning—and they [had] to witness what it was doing to the rest of the county as they're sitting there," he said. All of that struck him as "fairly traumatic."

Grace Tract, About Three Miles South of Villa Capri

When Beth Eurotas-Steffy's husband woke her around 4 a.m., she looked outside and saw a "fireball in the sky." She immediately texted her sister Gloria to alert her to the fire. Beth's neighborhood was under an evacuation warning, and she and her husband were packing to leave. Gloria had silenced her text message alerts that night, but a neighbor called around 4:30 a.m. to warn her about the fire. That's when Gloria saw Beth's texts and responded with her first thought, "What about Mom?"

As Beth threw belongings into a car to meet her husband's goal to "leave in five minutes," Beth hurriedly texted Gloria back: "She's in assisted living. If the fires are anywhere near Fountaingrove, I'm sure they had her off the hill hours ago." Gloria tried to call Villa Capri, but the lines were dead. She texted Beth that she was going to go up there. "No," Beth countered. "Mom would want us to take care of ourselves." Beth's husband experienced a traumatic fire as a child and was urging her to leave. "We need to head south," Beth texted Gloria. "You can follow us."

Beth did persuade her sister, in part. Gloria didn't rush to Villa Capri, but neither did she follow Beth out of Santa Rosa. "I'm not leaving without knowing Mom is OK and where she is," Gloria said. Alice was most likely fine, Gloria assumed, even though no one at Villa Capri answered the phone. "It's a huge corporation. They've got to have a call-down list," she said. "We should be getting a call any time, even if they are in chaos or don't have power." Gloria stayed home to wait for news of Alice, while Beth and Don headed to a friend's house in nearby Rohnert Park, out of the path of the fire.

Beth would later reflect on that rushed text exchange with Gloria. "I assumed an assisted living facility such as Villa Capri would care for their residents 24/7/365, especially in a disaster. I was so certain they had Alice off the hill hours before," she said. "I made a huge assumption," one that would reverberate with her for years. "I thought my assumption was safe, but as it turns out, it was anything but safe."

Varenna

Steffany Kisling drove through the same apocalyptic scene R.J. had passed through an hour earlier. When she reached the intersection of Bicentennial Way and Mendocino Avenue, a police car blocked the intersection, but Steffany didn't stop. She just steered around the roadblock with a wave to the officer and kept going.

As she drove up Fountaingrove Parkway, Steffany could see the charred shells of 8,000- and 10,000-square-foot homes already gutted. Burning branches and debris filled the streets. The scene reminded her of World War II war zones she had seen in films she watched with her father and Papa. She felt she entered—borrowing a phrase from one of those films—"the gates of Hell." She thought of her mom. *There's a good chance she's losing two of her kids tonight,* she prayed. *Just be with her, Lord, and let her know that we're happy we did this. Give her the understanding that these are the children she raised and have her be proud instead of in mourning.* As Steffany headed up Varenna's driveway, it was all the more alarming to see Villa Capri, where her grandmother had lived, in flames. Her only comfort came when she saw fire engines and police cars in front of Varenna. *Thank you, Lord,* she thought.

Steffany walked inside the Main Building at about 4:45 a.m. and noted about 50 people in the lobby. She scanned the crowd and then, out of the darkness strode her brother. Having spent the past hour worried what, if anything, she'd find as she made her way into the fire zone, she was relieved to see him. The feeling was not mutual.

"What the fuck are you doing here?" R.J. asked his sister.

"I told you on the phone that I was coming to help," she said, standing there wearing black sweatpants and a gray sweatshirt embroidered with letters that said "Make it happen"—and sporting her usual defiance—it was clear Steffany was ready to work. She put it to him squarely. "If you're not leaving, I'm not either." It wasn't the first time they had come to loggerheads, but she had never seen R.J. so angry.

"He had already made his decision and was already resigned that he wasn't going to see his family again," she said. "I brought the real life back to him. That's what he was frustrated about, and he was also concerned for me. Now his sister is going to die too."

Steffany asked what she could do to help, and R.J. managed to put aside his frustration to fill her in on what was happening. Then, before he said anything else he knew he would regret, R.J. turned and walked away to join firefighters in clearing more apartments upstairs.

Soon after, a deputy Santa Rosa fire chief who had taken over from Capt. Stornetta as incident commander at the scene, gravitated toward Steffany. He told her two residents had yet to arrive in the lobby, and neighbors feared they were still in their apartment. The couple apparently lived in a unit near the indoor pool on the mezzanine level, the chief said. He asked her if she knew how to get there. Steffany did, but only by way of the elevator. They could walk around the outside, but she wasn't sure if they would be able to get back in from the terrace level one floor below. "Where's your key?" the deputy chief asked.

"I don't have one."

"Why not?" he responded with an edge to his voice.

"I'm not an employee," she explained, clarifying. "I'm just here to help my brother."

The chief was clearly frustrated, as they all were, at the lack of any staff members on-site. Steffany led him and another member of his crew outside and down the wide staircase overlooking the pool to try the doors on the mezzanine level. One opened. As a group, they walked past the gym and various offices until they reached the apartments.

The firefighters knocked and shouted outside the units but heard nothing and continued working their way down the hall. That's when Steffany heard a voice—an internal one. *They can't hear you.* The words came to her so clearly as to be almost audible. *They can't hear you.* She called to the deputy chief. "They can't hear us!" she said. "We need to go in and check the bedrooms."

The deputy chief conceded and turned back, starting with the room he had just shouted into before shutting the door. This time, both he and Steffany walked inside, announcing themselves. There they found an elderly couple, still in bed. As she had feared, the couple were both hard of hearing and weren't wearing their hearing aids. Steffany helped the woman into her motorized wheelchair, and as they were leaving, the woman politely asked if she could put on a coat. Steffany helped her into a red jacket from the front closet. Another firefighter aided the unsteady man out of bed. Steffany stepped outside as he dressed because—as the gentleman explained to the ladies present—he was not wearing pajama pants.

The crew escorted the couple back to the landing by the pool, taking a path around the rear of the complex to avoid the stairs. The view from the terrace was horrific. What looked like bonfires dotted the hills beyond the lake and the golf course, but they were the hollowed-out shells of stately homes burning in uniform devastation. As if to emphasize the point, a nearby explosion rocked them. Again, Steffany's thoughts returned to her mother. *Mom's going to be so mad if we both die tonight.*

***

Officers Pedersen and St. Germain ran with Bob Mitton through the North Building halls calling to anyone who might still be inside. "Some people you could throw a housecoat over them and tell them to run like hell to the main lodge," Bob said. But other residents were hesitant, reminding him that they had been told to stay in their rooms. "Sorry," Bob replied as diplomatically as possible, "that does not apply when your building is starting to burn. This building is on fire. This is a wildfire." If Bob's career-forged diplomacy didn't persuade them, Pedersen stepped in. Leaning through the door, he would say, "I think you'd better do what Mr. Mitton says or we'll have to carry you out." Usually, that was all that was needed to convince the holdouts.

Hoping for rescue were Richard Williams and his wife, Carole, who could not fall back to sleep after their earlier attempt at escape via the parking garage. She had hoped to get direction from Oakmont managers, but no message ever came. It made sense to Carole that you might shelter in place if there was a small fire in the building, say, if a candle caught a curtain. *But if the fire came from outside, that was a different story*, Carole thought to herself as she waited in the dark. *It could hit from anywhere and sweep over you in an instant. In that case, you would want to leave the area, right?*

Oakmont never made that distinction, Carole said, not in any of the trainings or discussions they held for residents. At one point she turned to Richard and said, "Maybe this is it." Richard said nothing. *I hope we die of the smoke before the fire gets us*, she thought. But that didn't mean Carole wanted to go quietly. She alerted neighbors, starting with the couple across the hall who were "dead asleep."

Then, before she knew it, Bob showed up. His arrival came as a tremendous comfort and a huge help, since he had Officer Pedersen with him. Pedersen got Richard out of bed and dressed for the second time that night, then tied his shoes and helped him down the stairs. Richard sat on his walker while Pedersen pushed him down the hill toward the Main Building. Carole prepared damp washcloths they held over their faces as they journeyed the

300 feet through the smoke. It was a perilous trip. At one point, Richard fell out of his walker and hit the pavement with a thud. "It was awful," Carole recalled. Fortunately, Richard was only bruised, and they were able to join Bob's wife, Mimi, and the others in the lobby.

Bob stayed in the North Building where Capt. Stornetta and his team joined him kicking in doors and shouting for residents. In one room, Stornetta looked out the window and over the tennis courts. Everything was red beyond that point. Seeing a huge, active fire in such a familiar place was a gut punch. Long before Oakmont built Varenna, Stornetta and his friends camped, explored, and shot BB guns in these hills and fished for bass in the lake. When he was first hired at the Windsor Fire Protection District, Mike rented an apartment for a year and a half in the Oakmont staff building across from Villa Capri. Now, all of it, including his childhood home where his parents still lived, was at risk of obliteration.

"When we force entry into these apartments, the first thing we need to do is go shut the blinds," he told his crew. It was bad enough that residents had to wake to strangers in their apartment. "They're already going to be panicked," he said. "I don't want them to look outside and see those conditions."

Stornetta and his team left the North Building for the north-side casitas, one of which was burning. It was the Lemmerdings' house, overlooking the golf course. Capt. Riedell, Caroline Upton, and Tony Albright were on the attack within minutes, keeping the exterior damage to a minimum. "Thank God that they did, because we would have been way bigger problems if we wouldn't have done that," Stornetta said later of putting out the casita fire.

At one point, two officers tried to encourage a pair of elderly residents to move a little faster toward the Main Building. Just as they were hurrying, a cloud of hot cinders swarmed the couple like hornets. Stornetta shouted at the group, but his voice was swallowed by the roar of the wind. He watched as the two police officers hugged the residents to shield them from the embers, a move that may have saved their lives.

Firefighters know how painful this type of ember contact can be. Hours earlier, Capt. Riedell sustained a significant injury when a similar wall of hot air, gas, and embers, known as an ember cast, had flashed over him while he rescued a man mesmerized by the firewall in an open field. The ember cast blew up from beneath Riedell's engine and hit him square in the face as he was climbing back into the cab. He protected his airways, but the cloud of ash and gas burned his eyebrows and eyelashes to painful extremes.

Stornetta watched a similar ember cast bounce off the police officers' uniforms. They then ran/walked the rest of the way, half-escorting and half-carrying the two elderly residents. The older gentleman had a hard time hurrying and, at one point, tripped and fell. The officer helped him up quickly but continued to encourage the man to move forward. "We've got to keep going!" he shouted in the wind.

Satisfied all the north-side units were vacant, Bob and the first responders ran toward the Main Building, coughing and teary-eyed. "When we got past the front door of the Main Building, we were faced with intense heat and smoke," Bob said. But he and Pedersen didn't duck inside for respite. They headed straight for the South Building to repeat the process. "My flashlight would only shine up to a few feet," Bob said. "I had a shirt over my mouth. When we got to the South Building, I couldn't find the front entrance." The smoke was blinding, so Bob put his hands on the building to feel his way to the front door. "We were under the impression this building was going to go at any time."

Bob made clear to the officers that he didn't know anybody personally in the building. Even so—after the professionals banged on a door and shouted, "Santa Rosa police! There's a fire emergency!"—Bob went in first to check on the residents. He preferred that. It was better than residents first seeing someone in a uniform, he believed.

Sometime around then, Carole and Richard Williams had joined Bob's wife, Mimi Vandermolen, in the lobby, doing what they could to support the growing number of residents still emerging from their rooms. "Everyone was sitting in the hall, living room, and coffee shop and most were paralyzed with fright," said Carole, who helped hand out surgical masks and water bottles. She accompanied three women on individual trips back to their units to retrieve medications, hearing aids, power cords, and other items. "They were all too afraid to go alone," she said.

Carole also helped R.J. as much as possible. "He realized no one was in charge. Literally there was no one who knew anything," she said. "[R.J.] clearly assessed that we were all just deer in the headlights. He was concerned some people would be left." All the while, she and Mimi were amazed at how many residents R.J., firefighters, and others were escorting—and in many cases carrying—to the lobby.

"Everybody was scrambling around. There wasn't much order to anything," confirmed Santa Rosa Police Officer Orlando Macias, one of the officers who responded to the Varenna call. "There was no order. There was no real communication," he said. "If you talk about a perfect storm, that was it." Since no one seemed to know where the master keys were, Macias radioed for a battering ram. When it arrived, he began bashing in apartment doors while others, mostly firefighters, rushed inside. They did this for more than a dozen apartments and found a few residents in the process before someone finally showed up with keys.

The forced entries were a painful process, one that ended up costing Macias his career. When he used the battering ram on one door, he blew out the tendons in his wrist. He didn't notice it at first, but the next day his wrist was swollen and miserable, resulting in a series of medical examinations and physical therapy sessions. Ultimately, the injury forced him into retirement.

"I would say it was a complete disaster on all ends," Macias said.

Villa Capri, Front Parking Lot

Kathy and Melissa had had enough of the officers who kept telling them to leave, that their services were no longer needed now that buses were en route. Melissa was indignant. Her car held five residents, none of whom was her mother. There was no way in hell she was leaving without Virginia. Only when her mother was loaded into a police car did Melissa comply, and she encouraged Kathy to leave as well. "I'm not leaving until everyone else is gone," Kathy said.

The five residents in Melissa's Jeep had been waiting there for quite some time. One officer told Melissa to follow his patrol car to the Veterans Memorial Building across from the Santa Rosa Fairgrounds, where other police vehicles were headed. Melissa tried to follow, but as soon as they pulled out of the parking lot, the firestorm surrounded them. High flames flanked both sides of the street. "When I say high, it was like building-high, not walls of flames," Henrietta Hillman said. Melissa lost track of the police car in the intense smoke and missed the soft-left turnoff for Bicentennial

Way, which would have taken her out of the blaze and to Highway 101. Instead, she found herself surrounded by more flames on the lower part of Fountaingrove Parkway. "Both sides of the road were on fire, including the center median," she said. There was no way she could continue down onto Mendocino Avenue. She had to turn around.

Melissa made a U-turn and inched along through the elements until she found Bicentennial Way. She made the right and saw an apartment complex burning on her left. A CityBus passed her traveling the opposite direction. She hoped it was heading to Villa Capri, both for the residents' sake and to mollify her anxiety at leaving Kathy. At the intersection with Mendocino, an officer manning a barricade directed her across the overpass to merge onto 101 South. "I'd have gone the other direction," a resident in the back seat said disapprovingly.

Melissa thought the barb came from Henrietta, but Henrietta claimed it came from the woman next to her. Henrietta had developed a newfound respect for Melissa and claimed she wouldn't have passed a comment like that. "I knew that Melissa knew what she was doing," Henrietta said. She had done a 180 from the beginning of the night, when Henrietta had sized up Melissa as bossy and wondered who gave her the authority to take over. "And now," Henrietta said in retrospect, "I must say I'm grateful she did."

***

After Melissa's departure, Kathy and Sgt. Pehlke raced to load some of the remaining residents into patrol cars while Pehlke listened intently to the police radio and kept dispatch updated whenever a patrol car left with residents. In one police SUV, resident Dorothea Collins held her large golden dog by a string Kathy had tied to its collar. The officers didn't want to take the dog without a leash.

Alice Eurotas recalled the moment she was waiting downstairs and Kathy told her she could go. Alice left eight others in the lobby and climbed into the front seat of a patrol car loaded with three others. Until that point, Alice had thought only Villa Capri was on fire, but as they headed down Fountaingrove Parkway, she saw otherwise. "I didn't know the whole fucking town was on fire," she said. "And then it dawned on me why we didn't have a fire engine come to us." Everyone rode in stunned silence until Alice asked the officer where he was taking them. "To the Vets Center," he told her.

Ruth Callen had been helped into the back seat of a detective's unmarked car with a few other residents, including one man known fondly as "Tall Bill." After hours of sitting in fear inside the building, she grew anxious waiting for her "getaway car" to leave. "I thought if the car didn't start, I was going to get out with my walker and take a left and take a right," she said. "You'd be surprised what people can do in an emergency."

When the patrol car finally headed down the driveway to make its escape, Ruth saw flames attacking the exterior of Villa Capri. "Oh God, there was a ring of fire," she said. She thought of her best friend, Joellen Mack, who had been seated beside her on the second-floor landing. In all the confusion, Ruth couldn't remember whether Joellen had made it down, and she felt very bad about not finding her before she left. Despite the night's heaviness, Ruth tried to lighten the mood. "Guess what, kids?" she quipped. "We are not barbecued chicken tonight. We got out."

Veterans Memorial Building, About Five Miles South of Villa Capri

When Melissa arrived at the shelter, volunteers scrambled to escort Henrietta and the others inside where, serendipitously, former Villa Capri Activities Director Elizabeth Bruno was passing out water bottles. Elizabeth had been watching patients arriving from Kaiser and Sutter hospitals when she heard someone call out above the din, "Villa Capri! Villa Capri!" She turned to see Tall Bill, wrapped in a blanket, walking through the entrance.

"Bill, what are you doing here?" she asked.

"They left us," he told her. "They left us."

Elizabeth was stunned. "Where's everyone else? Where's Henrietta?"

"Turn around," Bill said.

Elizabeth spun to see the queen of Villa Capri walking in, striped blazer pristine, pocketbook over her arm. The 91-year-old grabbed Elizabeth, and they hugged. "I'm so glad it's you," Henrietta said, clutching her handbag and her walker. Behind Henrietta came several more residents, including Ruth Callen and Alice Eurotas. Volunteers pushed two of the seniors in on rolling desk chairs.

"What's happening?" Elizabeth asked the woman.

"We went up and evacuated people. The staff just left them," Melissa said. "Do you work there?"

Elizabeth responded without thinking. "Yes," she said incorrectly, her muscle memory kicking in from 10 years of Oakmont employment. "Where are their meds? Where's their paperwork?" Elizabeth asked.

Melissa didn't answer. Instead, she turned and walked away. So Elizabeth began to do what she had done for a decade: take care of Villa Capri residents, this time without any staff to assist her. "I was it," she said. Elizabeth swaddled a nearly naked resident in a blanket to ease her embarrassment, and she found a volunteer doctor to evaluate one of the women from memory care who kept falling over. Elizabeth's phone was almost dead, but she knew she had to make one call. "Henrietta," she said, turning to her friend. "If there's anything you can remember, what's Margie's number?"

Though she had been up all night and among the last to escape, Henrietta, ever so calm, managed to remember her daughter's number. Elizabeth got Margie's blessing to take Henrietta when an Oakmont corporate marketing director walked over, phone to her ear. "Do you know these people?" she asked Elizabeth. Elizabeth confirmed she did—and far better than this staffer, Elizabeth soon realized. The woman clearly couldn't discern Villa Capri residents from those from Varenna.

Elizabeth was miffed. "Why did they send you? You don't even know these people," she said.

"I don't know," the manager replied. "I just need to be here."

Elizabeth suggested she take photos of the residents and send them to whomever she was speaking with, so they knew which residents arrived at the shelter. The woman heeded her advice, but it didn't make Elizabeth feel any better. A little while later, in walked the person who had been on the other end of the line. It was Tammy Moratto, Elizabeth's former colleague. "I'm so glad it's you who was taking care of them," Tammy said to Elizabeth, and the two women embraced.

Outside the building, exhaustion overcame Melissa. Her passengers were safe, but she didn't see her mother arrive at the shelter. Melissa had risked her life to ensure Virginia made it off the hill, even withstanding orders from the police to leave at the 11th hour, but now she couldn't find her mom. As maddening as it was that Virginia's whereabouts were unknown,

Melissa realized she needed to check on her own home and get some rest before resuming her search. At 4:50 a.m. Melissa called her partner with the news that Virginia made it out, but that Villa Capri had burned.

"I'm coming home," she told Roxanne. And with that, Melissa burst into tears.

Villa Capri, Parking Lot

Sgt. Pehlke radioed dispatch at 4:50 a.m. from Villa Capri.

> *I'm down to nine people that I need to evacuate.... Everyone seems to be in a wheelchair.*

A back-and-forth exchange ensued among dispatchers as to whether they should still send a bus or more patrol cars. A male dispatcher wondered aloud whether any buses were still headed up the hill. Besides hospital evacuations, rescues were needed seemingly everywhere, and police, fire, and EMTs were stretched thin.

> *I'm not sure how we're going to handle them,* one dispatcher said.

> *Are they able to get them into a bus or cars?* another asked.

> *We will get 'em in,* Pehlke said.

Moments later, an officer warned the channel that getting to Varenna and Villa Capri from the east was no longer an option. "Fountaingrove [Parkway] is completely engulfed," the officer announced. "Impassable. We have to go around the other way." A minute later, at 4:51 a.m., another officer checked on the status of transportation for those still at Varenna.

> *I'm looking for those buses up here,* the officer said.

> *We're working on getting more right now,* a dispatcher responded.

But the situation at Villa Capri was far more critical. There was no more time the residents and their rescuers could possibly wait. Finally, a little more than half an hour after Pehlke's initial call for buses, which, to his partner Andrew Adams, "felt like an eternity," the first bus arrived at 4:57 a.m.

The driver pulled the 40-foot blue and gray Santa Rosa CityBus into Villa Capri's parking lot, where officers lined seven residents, still in their wheelchairs, down the bus's wide center aisle. Kathy noticed one who couldn't speak was wearing only a sports bra and Depends briefs. She covered the woman and other elders with blankets from Villa Capri.

Though Kathy was too busy with the first bus to notice, a second bus arrived, driven by a man wearing a blue pajama top, black jeans, and a tan fishing hat. Two hours earlier, the peculiarly clothed CityBus driver, Gary Basile, had herded five cats into carriers and grabbed a hard drive, photos, and tax records before fleeing his Chanate neighborhood with his wife and daughter. He didn't have time to don his uniform before getting to work rescuing others around the county.

"I'm out of here," he had told his neighbor. "This fire is going to run."

Considered an emergency services worker, Basile knew he was supposed to get his family to safety then report as soon as possible to the transit center, where a dispatcher sent Basile and another driver to Villa Capri. But both were given the wrong address: 1600 Fountaingrove Parkway, a vacant lot nearly a half mile east of their intended destination.

As Basile navigated bus No. 001 toward Fountaingrove, he passed within a block of a burning gun shop where ammunition was exploding like fireworks. Across the freeway he saw Kaiser hospital employees loading patients into four or five CityBuses with his colleagues at the wheel. But when he reached the corner at Mendocino Avenue, orange-vested volunteers refused to let him cross into Fountaingrove.

"I'm dispatched to 1600," he told them.

"Well, you're not going this way," they said.

Basile tried to negotiate, but they refused. That's when two Santa Rosa Police officers pulled up next to him and overruled the volunteers. "Follow me," the officer driving said. The officers were returning to Villa Capri after dropping off a woman resident at Kaiser hospital. As Basile approached the senior living complex, he saw nothing but red sky over his neighborhood directly south. *My house is gone*, he thought. He would later discover the fire came within one-eighth of a mile but spared his home.

Basile followed the officer's car into the shared driveway that led to Varenna at 1401 Fountaingrove Parkway and Villa Capri at 1397. "All I remember is I'm glad the police officer pulled up next to me because I would have been looking for 1600," he said. "And if you go up any further, you end up at Stagecoach, which was in total flames."

As Basile approached Villa Capri, he noticed the first driver had pulled his bus all the way into the narrow, gooseneck-shaped entrance to the parking lot. Basile was adamant he would not do the same. "When you drive a tractor-trailer," he said, "you never go anywhere if you don't know you can get out," which is why Basile opted to park only his bus's nose in the entry before hopping out to survey the scene. Police officers scurried in and out with residents as flames topped the backside of the two-story building. Embers blanketed the driveway with a coat of neon red-orange. Basile worried one of his tires might blow.

When Basile boarded the other CityBus, he found several elderly residents screaming and crying. He asked the driver, a man named Ken, what was going on. "The workers left," Ken told him. "No workers." Basile got off Ken's bus, and a police officer raced toward him pushing a man wearing only underwear seated in an extra-large wheelchair. Basile lowered the wheelchair ramp on his bus and tied in the passenger. Once on board, Basile wheeled him to a space behind the driver's seat. The driver expected more seniors in wheelchairs, but the officer gestured to a collection of leftover walkers instead. As Basile loaded the devices onto his bus, another officer approached. "Did we get them all?" Basile asked, referring to the residents.

"Don't worry about it," the officer said. "We'll put the rest in squad cars. Get out of here now."

Basile did as he was instructed, putting the bus in reverse and backing down the driveway. With the officer directing him, Basile inched the bus toward Fountaingrove Parkway, narrowly missing a tree. He needed to correct his trajectory a few times but managed to reach the bottom of the hill thanks to the officer's hand signals. As soon as he did, the officer shouted, "Go down the hill! Get out of here! Now!"

Getting out was not so easy for the other driver, however. Ken had driven all the way into Villa Capri's parking lot, through and past the curved entrance, which meant he couldn't reverse straight down the driveway. He would need to somehow find a way to turn his bus around, the one loaded with the most fragile residents and Kathy Allen.

Kathy quickly realized it would be impossible for Ken to turn around. The parking lot simply wasn't big enough for the bus to maneuver. They were in a difficult situation, perhaps the most precarious of the night. Kathy clung to the swaying wheelchairs nearest her while the driver attempted what felt like an infinite-point turn, reversing and driving forward inch-by-inch. The bus hit the curb so hard at one point, it listed severely. For the second time that night, Kathy was afraid. *Oh my God, we're going to tip over*, she thought. She sensed Ken starting to panic. He was having such a difficult time backing up that she wanted to get out and direct him, but an officer had appeared through the smoke to do just that. Ultimately, Ken realized he would never be able to turn the bus around within the parking lot, so he executed a very large three-point turn, reversing out of the jam they were in, pulling the bus up the main driveway, then backing the bus's rear end into Villa Capri's parking lot.

As he did, the passengers were jolted and jostled. Louise Johnson clung to her wheelchair's armrests in the dark, seeing flames through the bus's back window. Bess Budow moaned and cried in her wheelchair in the front row. Ken reached back and placed one hand over hers to comfort her as he steered with the other. Another resident fell out of her wheelchair onto the floor, trapping her catheter underneath her body. Kathy tried to lift her as the bus lurched to and fro, but the resident was too heavy, so Kathy covered her with a blanket while she remained on the floor for the drive.

The bus was finally pointed downhill, but to complete their escape Ken still needed to make a left out of the parking lot, around the small gatehouse in the shared driveway's median. The bus was too big to make the tight turn so Ken had to scoot back and forward once again, chipping away at an angle. The heat of the fire pressed in from all sides, until it became clear they could never win this game of inches.

Deciding he no longer had time to finesse his way out, Ken hit the gas and plowed through the side of the gatehouse—destroying part of the structure and part of the bus in the process. The impact from the collision jarred the sensitive passengers. But then the turbulence was over. They cruised smoothly down the rest of the shared driveway, and Ken made a right onto

Fountaingrove Parkway, guiding the bus carrying Louise, Bess, Kathy and the rest to safety.

Within minutes of their departure, the entirety of Villa Capri was consumed by flames. As with most of the 5,600 homes, apartments, businesses, and other structures in the Tubbs Fire's path, Villa Capri continued to burn for hours until reduced to rubble and ash. Santa Rosa Police Detective James Vickers, who had assisted at Villa Capri, visited the remains of the facility over the next couple days. Beyond the field of destruction, he could see Villa Capri's 26-passenger bus still sitting in the parking lot, unscathed. "And I remember saying if they had just left the keys to the bus somewhere where we could see them," he recounted, "we could have used the bus."

13

Rescue

The Firestorm, 5 a.m.

Tubbs Fire distance to Villa Capri and Varenna: Villa Capri engulfed

Around 5 a.m., the crew of Engine No. 6 from the Berkeley Fire Department linked up with four other engines from the San Francisco Fire Department to form a strike team responding to Sonoma County's appeal for mutual aid. Although the firefighters were under the assumption they were headed to battle a large grass fire, as they drew closer to Santa Rosa, a red glow stretched across the hills to the east like a burgeoning sunrise. This was clearly more than a grass fire.

The convoy had been asked to rendezvous at a staging area set up in the Kmart parking lot on Cleveland Avenue, just off Highway 101, a mile and a quarter from Varenna and Villa Capri. But when they arrived, they discovered that would be impossible. Flames ascended from multiple corners of the 100,000-square-foot structure. In a YouTube video that went viral, one crew member recorded the moment they passed the big box store. They didn't stop, they would later explain, because the building was already lost. The team eased its way north, looking for a safer place to stage. But their options were limited. The Mountain Mike's pizza parlor next door was also on fire, as were other buildings nearby, including an Applebee's restaurant.

"Is that a gas station there?" one firefighter asked as the convoy slowed to a halt, leaving the Berkeley crew in front of a Chevron station with an adjoining McDonald's. Huge, undulating flames pulsated from the blown-out doors and windows. "I guess you just let some of this stuff just burn, huh?" he asked. The sound of glass breaking and other popping noises could be heard as the fire seemed to intensify. Gas stations, unlike how they are often depicted in movies, rarely explode, even in dire situations like this. But that conviction seemed to

wane as they watched. "I can actually feel the heat, pal," one firefighter said from where they idled. "Do you feel that?"

Unsure of where to go, the convoy continued up Hopper Avenue. But as they looked left and right, the crew couldn't orient themselves. All that was visible was a rolling landscape of blackness illuminated periodically by individual cauldrons of flames, like scattered bonfires on an endless beach of lava rock and black sand.

"At first I wasn't sure what I was looking at," the videographer later acknowledged in subtitles. "It looked like a large field." Then they realized what was before them. This was Coffey Park—an entire neighborhood burned to the ground. The firefighters were stunned. "This...this is over 100 homes," one said.

In fact, it was more than 10 times that number. Within just a few hours of jumping Highway 101, the Tubbs Fire had swept deep into the west side of Santa Rosa, destroying a square mile of mostly detached middle-class homes on the northern edge of the city. This was a part of town that was flat and densely populated. It was about as far from a wildfire-risk zone as you could find in Sonoma County. But fed by Diablo winds gusting in excess of 70 miles per hour, the Tubbs Fire had found Coffey Park anyway.

"This is like a frickin' bomb went off," one firefighter said as they continued past the darkened debris field where no structures—not even their framing—was visible. "Foundations, barbecues, and chimneys. That's all that's left."

The strike team eventually reached the front lines of the destruction and helped stop the fire near railroad tracks that cut through the heart of Coffey Park. But the damage had been done. In the final count, the Tubbs fire destroyed more than 1,400 homes in this one neighborhood—nearly 25 percent of the total number lost countywide. But the toll was even greater in Fountaingrove. When the smoke cleared enough to take inventory, emergency officials determined the Tubbs Fire consumed nearly 1,600 homes scattered among the hills surrounding the Varenna and Villa Capri complex. All told, the Wine Country Fires destroyed more than 5,334 homes throughout Sonoma County, including roughly 3,000 in Santa Rosa, representing nearly 5 percent of the city's total housing stock.

New Vintage Church, Around 5 a.m.

Caregiver Elizabeth Lopez found her way to New Vintage Church thanks to a text from med tech Marie So telling her of the new meeting spot. After pulling into the parking lot, Elizabeth helped Viola Sodini and Bill and Wanda Lee out of her minivan, sat them down inside the multipurpose room designated for memory care residents, and brought them water. The residents looked scared, so Elizabeth talked to them softly to try to calm them.

She was having a hard time staying calm herself. Elizabeth had promised to return to Villa Capri, so she headed out to do just that, telling an Oakmont employee her plan. No, he told her. It was of no use. Firefighters were there, and she should not go back. The presence of first responders assuaged Elizabeth's anxiety enough to stay put, but still she worried that without enough cars, they couldn't get everyone out.

Elizabeth searched the church, looking for answers from one particular person. On her rounds she spotted Marie and Health Services Director Jane Torres, but the one person Elizabeth sought was nowhere to be found. "Have you seen Debie Smith?" she asked her coworkers. They hadn't. "She didn't show up," they told her.

It upset Elizabeth that she didn't know Debie's status or that of Villa Capri, but she left between 5:30 and 6 a.m. to go home, where her parents were caring for her 9-year-old daughter. As soon as Elizabeth arrived, she went to check on her sleeping daughter and gave her a kiss. "I was in shock," she said. Though Elizabeth had less than two hours of sleep in the previous 24, she tossed and turned when she finally went to bed, unable to get the images of the previous 10 hours out of her head. "I was scared that they didn't get everyone out," she said. "If something happened to the residents who stayed behind, it would be my fault, because I said I was going to be back."

***

A little more than half of Villa Capri's residents had arrived at the church, but at least 24 were still out there, and no one had heard from Kathy. It had been about two hours since Mark had driven away from Villa Capri. Since arriving, he'd gotten his mother situated, moved arriving seniors into various rooms, and dashed to a nearby store to purchase incontinence briefs and wipes. He hadn't worried about his wife, nor had he tried to contact her.

He didn't think he needed to. "I didn't have time to think about Kathy as a school bus was supposed to pick her up," he said.

At 5:10 a.m., his phone buzzed. It was Kathy, texting that she was with seven residents. "I was surprised she was on a CityBus on the way to Elsie Allen High School," he said. At least she was alive. "I knew she was OK and out of harm's way."

So, too, was Joey Horsman, who had miraculously survived but was only now pulling the Sprinter van up to New Vintage Church with Anett and the eight residents, including his grandmother, Len Kulwiec, and Norma Porter. Despite being the first group to leave Villa Capri, at a little after 3 a.m., they were the last to arrive at the church, almost two hours later. In between, Joey had driven through the heart of the firestorm on his unsuccessful second rescue attempt, found his way back to the county building to pick up the group he had dropped off, and had driven them to the Veterans Memorial Building shelter, which he deemed too crowded for the residents. Anett found out about the church, so they headed there.

Joey and Anett had unloaded half the residents when Joel Ruiz, the corporate maintenance manager who had driven the Ford Econoline, raced over to Anett, concerned about one specific passenger.

"Where's Norma?" he asked.

Anett pointed toward the sanctuary.

"Are you sure?" Joel asked. "Are you sure you know which resident is Norma?"

Anett had done Norma's laundry once a week and memorized her face and short white hair from the daily resident roster. She knew what Norma was wearing that night. "She was one of the first people to get out, and she was in a purple robe," she told Joel.

Joel didn't seem to trust her response. He asked her again if she was sure before walking inside to find Norma himself. After all she had been through in the past few hours, Anett was taken aback not just by his questioning but by what Joel didn't inquire about. "Honestly, I was like, *Oh, OK, well here I am, pregnant. Fuck me, then*," she thought but didn't say aloud. "He was concerned about one resident when he should have been concerned about everybody."

Anett made sure the eight Sprinter-delivered residents were settled before taking care of herself. Her back and feet ached, and she worried about how the night's stress, not to mention the smoke she inhaled, might affect her pregnancy. She needed to rest, and she sought out Jane Torres to ask for permission to leave. Anett found Jane sorting seniors, trying to place each new arrival with assisted living friends in the sanctuary's stadium seating or with fellow memory care residents in the multipurpose room. Bedbound residents were placed in a different room off the sanctuary. Jane asked Anett to stay longer. They needed all the help they could get.

Joey also went looking for Jane because he still believed dozens had perished at Villa Capri. He was visibly shaken as he told Torres about his near-death experience. Much to his relief and disbelief, she informed him everyone made it out alive. Joey also had a second reason to connect with Jane. His grandmother needed round-the-clock care, and so he asked the nurse if she had a plan, a place they could take residents from the church. He recalled Jane replying, "Not at the moment."

Varenna

Inside the lobby, Mimi Vandmolen reassured fellow residents while at the same time worrying about how her husband, Bob, was faring. Without cell service, she had no way to reach him. Mimi noticed the menacing glow getting closer through the floor-to-ceiling windows that overlooked the terrace where she and Bob had enjoyed their Sunday brunch less than 24 hours earlier. They had taken in so many majestic sunsets from this vantage point, but now those same hues of yellow, orange, and deep red threatened their existence.

Large embers landed on bushes outside. *If this thing goes up, what am I going to do?* Mimi wondered. She studied her options and concluded the lake below offered her the best escape route. Although it was a long way down, there was a tram that ran down the hillside to the dock, a tram that reminded her and Bob of Europe's funiculars. With any luck, the rail system would still be operational. If not, Mimi would walk Cocoa down the winding path and either jump in the water or commandeer a boat. But as she studied the route, her view suddenly changed. "Within minutes those windows went orange because all the houses across the lake caught on fire," she said. *I don't know if I can go down there*, she thought. She looked around the lobby at the mass of residents, many with serious mobility issues. They certainly couldn't make that trip.

Moments later, at 5:35 a.m., a Santa Rosa police officer radioed about the situation at Varenna. "We have approximately 70 people up here that are going to need to be transported by bus," he said urgently.

> *"Can you confirm if the buses are going to be able to make it up there?"* the dispatcher replied. *"Or do we need more [police] units?"*

There was a pause before the officer made it clear they were going to start loading residents into patrol cars. They couldn't wait any longer.

***

Katheryn Mann, 86, was still waiting in the hall outside her Main Building apartment for help. Ever since her daughter had called and woken her hours earlier, she had done what she was told to do in case of fire. She sheltered in place, but no one had come for her. Her floor's fire captain hadn't checked on her, and no one else had knocked on her door. Katheryn yelled for help in the hallway, but no one answered. She grew more nervous by the minute. She had mobility issues and couldn't manage the stairs alone. "I was left to fall through the cracks," she said.

Suddenly, the third-floor fire door flung open, and in strode two men, one of whom her granddaughter had contacted on Katheryn's behalf. "I was never so glad to see two strapping police officers," she said. One officer put a mask on Katheryn. "They put [an] arm under each arm and carried me down three flights of stairs to this lobby," where the smoke was so thick, Katheryn couldn't see the end of her arm. Her eyes watered, heavily enough to drip down her face. Although the lobby was bustling with residents, Katheryn wasn't given the chance to interact with anyone. The officers continued to lead her straight outside and into a patrol car. "I wondered whether people thought I was being arrested or something," she said later with a coy smile.

***

Over in the North Building, Frank Perez, clad in his neon safety vest, running sweatshirt, and trusty Nikes was returning to his first-floor apartment, having just checked the smoke-filled garage. Smoke detectors were going off "like mad," he said, because the smoke had been building up since he had fought back the flames that had breached his patio door.

That's when he encountered a police officer doing a final sweep of rooms. "Come with me," the officer instructed him. "We have orders to take all of you to the Main Building that's further away from the fire."

But before they left the North Building, Frank rounded up three other residents from his floor, including his neighbor Ruth. The four of them locked arms at the elbows to support one another. "I was wearing my running cap, but, of course, the wind just blew that right off," he said. "So I had to cover my eyes to keep the embers out since we were leaning into the wind."

Frank said the lobby was packed with about 50 people, and while there was talk of buses coming for them, none had yet materialized. Frank checked in with friends for about 10 minutes until the officer who pulled him out returned. He had an SUV, he told Frank. "You get in it, and I'll get four or five other people." Frank resisted. He didn't feel right leaving while so many others were waiting. But the officer would have none of it. "That's an order," he said.

Outside, while waiting for buses, officers had begun filling available patrol cars, but there were far more residents than seats. A fire crew at the bottom of the hill attempted to ensure a safe route for the SUV as Frank and the others left the hill, but flames still raged on both sides of the road as they passed through.

***

Bob Mitton and Officer Pedersen continued going room to room in the South Building, having abandoned all niceties. "By the end, we just ran in and grabbed people, saying 'FIRE! FIRE! You have to get out,'" Bob said. The situation's intensity was magnified by what they heard through the screaming wind. "Every 20 or 30 seconds, another propane tank would explode [in the distance]," he recalled. "It sounded like someone was bombing us." And the air quality was terrible. "We had all been coughing." Bob tried wearing a surgical mask as they ran between apartments, but the mask made it hard to inhale enough air to catch his breath and hard to communicate. He used it sparingly. When the smoke grew unbearable, Bob lifted the bottom of his T-shirt to cover his nose and mouth. With the South Building cleared, Bob and Pedersen prepared to return to the Main Building, but before they could get outside, two paramedics rushed over and put oxygen masks on their faces. Bob's nose started gushing blood.

During this time, four or five different firefighting crews were still battling fires outside, trying to maintain a safe zone around Varenna. Although they were occasionally called in to support evacuations, "I wasn't really looking for people," Capt. Riedell said. "I was more looking out for whatever fires were sneaking up on us into those buildings."

According to Caroline Upton, the Mountain Volunteer Fire crew's main job "was to make sure the fire at Villa Capri didn't make a run and compromise where everyone was sheltered." It wasn't easy. The fire came in waves, meaning, at times, the flames were too intense, too close to the driveway to allow safe passage for the buses and emergency vehicles. It was arduous work made more complicated by the campus' design itself. Varenna's narrow driveways and hillside paths made maneuvering fire engines increasingly difficult. "We had trouble backing our Type 1 [traditional fire] engine out of there because of the tiny little road that runs up to those homes," Riedell said of the casitas.

What was clear to many of the first responders, Pedersen included, was that if firefighters had not arrived when they did, Varenna would have been lost as the fire at Villa Capri accelerated. Riedell reported the air shook as flames exploded the oxygen tanks within the smaller assisted living building only 100 yards downhill. "I guarantee you that the [Varenna] complex would have gone down," Riedell said. "The structure fire we put down on the edge of the complex would have just rolled through all of those structures leading right up to the Main Building. If one of them were to start and get going, it would have caught the next one and the next one, and it would have just moved its way up."

But their efforts were successful. At 5:35 a.m. firefighters reported they had contained the fires enough that a large-scale evacuation could take place. An officer radioed their progress to dispatch. "Buses should be able to make it up now," he said.

Two minutes later, dispatch confirmed buses were headed their way "Code 3," meaning with urgency and an escort. At 5:40 a.m. a Golden Gate Bridge district coach rolled up in front of the Main Building. A second bus followed minutes later. When they came into view, residents in the lobby cheered.

Bob and Officer Pedersen had just made it back. Bob was still coughing, and the front of his shirt was bloodstained, but Mimi was grateful to find him alive and in one piece. Bob, on the other hand, was simply grateful for the chance to sit down. "Man, you're hard to keep up with," Officer St. Germain, only two years out of the police academy, said to Bob when they had a chance to rest. "How old are you?"

Bob, 73, ignored the heart of the question. "When I have fire burning up my derrière," he said, "I can move pretty quickly."

After the buses parked, any firefighters not involved in defending the perimeter converged at the main entrance to load residents milling about in their nightgowns or pajamas, some with pets by their sides. R.J., Steffany, and firefighters Caroline Upton and Tony Albright joined in helping seniors climb the steps and get seated while Capt. Riedell loaded as many walkers and wheelchairs as possible in the undercarriage luggage compartment. At one point, Officer Macias calmly encouraged an elderly woman wearing a sky-blue bathrobe with pink embroidered flowers as he helped her onto one of the buses. "Grab onto my shoulders," he said. "Like we're dancing, OK?"

Without equipment to help lift the seniors, R.J., Steffany, and Tony and Caroline were left to improvise, and for Caroline, that meant using her petite stature to heave people up. After helping a resident up the first step, Caroline, shorter than 5 feet, 2 inches tall, would stay on the ground, properly positioned for a creative albeit awkward maneuver. "My head and shoulder were such that I was standing even [with] where their butt was," she said. "I was joking with them, 'OK, now put your butt on my shoulder'…and so when I'd stand, I could shove, sort of push them into the bus." One after another, Caroline boosted the elderly residents from behind to get them up the four steep stairs. Tony was not surprised by his wife's tenacity. "Caroline is the little engine that could," he said.

Riedell later acknowledged his frustration with the loading process. "When they prepare to evacuate these people, they need to have the equipment to help those who have a disability and have difficulty moving around," he said. The scene outside the bus was unforgettable for Caroline, with "a sea of walkers" lined up along the sidewalk. It was an image "permanently embedded in my head," she said. "I really should have taken a photo of all of those walkers," she said. "Never in my life have I seen so many."

What stood out to Capt. Stornetta was the poise the residents demonstrated throughout the ordeal. Although fire was visible all around, "There was no panicking," he said. "They all were calm and gracious." Maybe it shouldn't have been a surprise, he thought. The balance of these residents were of the generation that had survived the Great Depression, polio, World War II, and wars in Korea, Vietnam, and the Middle East, as well as the tumultuous 1960s and the 2008 financial crash. Still, their calm and patience left a mark on Stornetta. "I was just really impressed."

The last residents to board the buses needed no assistance. They were Bob, Mimi, and Cocoa the Labrador, who had alerted her owners to something amiss four hours earlier.

At that point, Riedell and his Mountain VFD crew had a bit of a problem; they were running out of fuel. They hadn't had time to gas up before coming up Fountaingrove, and if they ran out, everything on the engine would stop, including the pumps. To make matters worse, Capt. Riedell had left his wallet behind. The same was true of all his other crew members. No one had a credit card to allow them to fill up at a local gas station, as so many other engines were doing that night. Faced with this dilemma, Capt. Riedell, Tony and Caroline, and others on Engine No. 7680 packed up, rolled off the hill, and headed back to their station to gas up, some 14 miles away.

Meanwhile, Officer Pedersen said goodbye to his friend Bob and headed upstairs inside Varenna to ensure all the rooms were clear. At 5:42 a.m. body camera video showed him standing with another officer in a dark hallway with only the glow of a flashlight visible in the distance. The video was fuzzy, but the audio was clear. Pedersen approached his colleague and said he guessed they could rest the battering ram now that they had master keys.

"I love the employees of this place," Pedersen said sarcastically.

The other officer chuckled and issued a word of caution in response: "Don't send your loved ones here."

14

Exodus

- -

The Firestorm, 6 a.m.

Tubbs Fire distance to Villa Capri and Varenna: On and surrounding the property

Not all evacuations of senior living complexes that night were as chaotic and haphazard. As the clearing of Varenna continued, Monique Dixon stood in the darkened lobby of Brookdale Chanate, an independent and assisted living facility a mile south of Varenna and Villa Capri, her one hand holding a list, the other using a pen to point each of her 72 residents into small buses parked out front. Brunette and boisterous, the executive director was particularly commanding tonight, having just scaled a ladder to the roof to survey the blaze in the Fountaingrove hills. "We couldn't even talk over the roar of the fire," she said, getting goosebumps at the memory. "I took one look at [my maintenance guy] and said, 'We're out of here. Start loading them.'"

The regional maintenance employee joined two NOC caregivers and one med tech, as well as a receptionist, clinical specialist, registered nurse, physical therapist, activities director, and sous chef, many of whom had shown up without being summoned. They knew what to do if they encountered roadblocks. "Take the ticket. Let them chase you," Monique said she instructed her staff.

At first, Monique was anxious; the evacuation before them was strenuous enough. But she took solace in their unified presence. Before she issued her staff what she knew would be an hours-long series of orders, she offered this disclaimer: "I'm going to say 'please,' 'thank you,' and 'I'm sorry' up front. After that, you do what I want you to do."

In the four hours between when a manager woke Monique to report the smell of smoke in the building and when she stood in the lobby at 6 a.m. hollering for each resident by name, her team had mobilized.

After smelling smoke around midnight, the med tech and caregivers patrolled to pinpoint the source, checking every resident's room one by one. Their search included the room Monique lived in on the property. When the med tech realized the smoke was coming from outside, she alerted Monique, who jumped into jeans and boots and within minutes was wheeling locked medication cabinets, which secured prescription drugs linked to an electronic system for tracking dosage and stock, to the still-working elevators.

She staged the carts on the ground level, plugged them in so their laptops would be fully charged, and printed copies of each resident's records in case they needed to bug out without the meds. She unplugged the fax machine and inserted a landline cable into the jack. Unlike contemporary phone systems that use the internet, the fax ran on a copper line, which she knew could still receive calls without electricity.

Then Monique gave an order to the maintenance worker: Call the bus company with which Brookdale was contracted for emergencies and have them send the buses immediately. She had one important stipulation. "I want those little buses," she said, "because Chanate [Road] is tight. It's very difficult to get a big bus up [here] and into the parking lot."

At around 1 a.m., she tasked the receptionist with calling family members listed on a hard-copy roster. "Brookdale Chanate may have to evacuate," the receptionist told them. "If you want to come get your loved one, do it now." The med tech, caregivers, and other assorted staff spent time waking, dressing, and escorting to the elevators any resident with mobility issues. Monique wanted all nonambulatory residents in the lobby before the power went out, which it did, right in the middle of their operation. Not missing a beat, she distributed to staff baseball caps with built-in brim lights, which lighted their paths and freed their hands for guiding unsteady residents. Once each room was vacated, the physical therapist entered, confirmed no one was left behind, then affixed a strip of blue painter's tape to each apartment door to indicate it was empty.

The residents made themselves comfortable in the library and flipped on the news, but that did not pass muster with Monique because it was causing panic.

She instructed her sous chef to whip up coffee and breakfast as a 4 a.m. diversion and served it in the ballroom, which "got people away from the TV."

It was dark when they started loading the buses. Monique stood at the entry while the receptionist and maintenance worker stood outside. The executive director would shout a resident's name, call out a bus number, and send the resident in that direction. The staff member standing at that bus would echo the name and number back. Monique, the receptionist, and the maintenance staffer each recorded on independent lists the combination of who went on which bus. Staff loaded med carts into each bus's wheelchair bay, and Monique insisted each bus carry a default caregiver, which this morning included the sous chef, much to his surprise. Residents' wheelchairs and walkers were stacked into Brookdale Chanate's shuttle, which the clinical specialist drove to a prearranged destination, arriving prior to the residents so they would be reunited with their specific equipment as soon as they stepped off the bus.

As the darkness gave way to the shadowy gray of dawn, the executive director ordered the buses off the property. At around 6:15 a.m., she and the maintenance worker did one last pass of "every single door, bathroom, everything." They opened a window so a cat could escape, put out extra water for a bird, and noticed someone had moved a fish tank to the floor.

"Everyone was accounted for," she said, and at 6:45 a.m., "I put a big blue X on the exterior door and left."

Elsie Allen High School, About Eight Miles South of Villa Capri

Kathy Allen watched as student volunteers unloaded the residents from the CityBus and at least one police car. "It just scared the heck out of me," she said of the well-meaning but inexperienced high schoolers escorting some of Villa Capri's most fragile elderly. "They were kindly taking the residents into the gym, but I felt like I was losing track of where my people were, not knowing what they needed. One of the ladies felt like she had to throw up the whole time we were on the bus, so I wanted to make sure she was taken care of."

Residents, including dementia patient Louise Johnson, were scattered in different parts of the gymnasium-turned-shelter in southwest Santa Rosa. Three of the seven from the bus were sent to a nurse in a makeshift medical area. One of them, Bess Budow, vomited, and the nurse had her lie on a massage table. "It was hard to corral them," Kathy said, although she ran into a friend who helped her herd the residents and push them into one corner.

At 6 a.m. Kathy called Mark to report her whereabouts and ask for a ride. She didn't have a destination in mind—she had no idea about New Vintage Church—just that she needed to get the residents somewhere more appropriate. Mark was relieved she'd found somewhere safe, but he turned furious when he learned no one ever made it back uphill after their initial trip down.

Back at the church, Mark found Joel Ruiz out front, unloading a van full of Oakmont residents he had rounded up from the different shelters. Mark approached him, incensed. "You left my wife at Villa Capri," he said. "She could have died." Joel's face went ashen. "Do you think you can go pick them up now over at Elsie Allen High School, where they were evacuated to?" Mark asked. Joel said he would, then Mark told Kathy, "Someone is on his way to come get you."

New Vintage Church

Vivian Flowers was terrified her mother might have perished. It had been five hours with no return calls, no communication from anyone with Villa Capri or Oakmont. Then her nephew rang with news that he found Viola at New Vintage Church. Vivian fought crosstown traffic to get there. On the thinly carpeted gray floor in the multipurpose room, she found Viola sitting in her light-blue nightgown, her arms bruised. She was without her dentures, glasses, shoes, and robe. Viola was confused but not scared, most likely because she was unable to comprehend the situation.

For Vivian, it was a different story. "I was bawling," she recalled. She hugged her mother over and over again, beyond grateful she was alive, but realizing how vulnerable her mother still was. Viola could not eat without her dentures or see well without her glasses. She was also without two vital heart medications, and replacing them would prove a logistical nightmare in a city where most pharmacies, still lacking power, were closed.

By comparison, when Vivian had unloaded buses at the Finley Center, her first stop in her quest to find her mother, she watched employees from other assisted living homes disembark with carts full of their residents' medications. "They had a plan," she said.

Petaluma

Cynthia Arroyo did not make it to New Vintage Church like her coworkers. Instead, after a harrowing drive where she lost her bearings and did a U-turn on Highway 101, she had transferred her three residents to Jane Torres and raced back to her house in downtown Santa Rosa to find her boyfriend had slept through the entire disaster. She woke him and demanded he pack, even though they didn't have an evacuation order. "I was so scared after everything I had gone through," she said. "I got some stuff and my dogs and drove to Petaluma," where she sat trembling in her car in a health clinic parking lot.

There, the beleaguered 21-year-old met up with her mother and five other family members. Her mom, who had diabetes, had grown ill with worry after Cynthia's terrified call as she drove lost through the firestorm. Now, Cynthia's mother needed medical treatment. As she waited outside the clinic, Cynthia received a call from Anett with an update on Villa Capri's fate. "Everybody got out, and it burned down," Anett told her. The news crushed Cynthia. "I was so scared," she said. "I was crying from what had happened. I couldn't stop crying."

Cloverdale, About 30 Miles North of Villa Capri

"Ruthie, Fountaingrove burned down. Where's Mom?"

That was the call Ruthie Kurpinsky received at 6:30 a.m. from her brother Chris Callen, a retired firefighter vacationing in Arizona. Soon after, her brother Tim called from Disneyland.

"There's a fire in Santa Rosa," he said. "Where's Mom?"

Ruthie tried to call their mom's cell phone but without success. She then tried Villa Capri, followed by Villa Capri's Marketing Director Roberta Murray. No one answered. Ruthie checked her email, cell, and landline for messages. Nothing. In the past, staff called within minutes if her mom had slipped out of bed or took a misstep. Ruthie kept a landline explicitly for this purpose, to receive incoming calls of a serious nature. This time, however, no call had come.

Right away, Ruthie posted to Facebook in all caps:

> *IF ANYBODY KNOWS WHERE THE VILLA CAPRI SANTA ROSA, CALIFORNIA RESIDENTS WENT TO, PLEASE TEXT ME.*

Three hours later, also in a panic, Ruthie's younger sister, Liz Schopfer, took to Facebook as well:

> *Don't know where Mom is! They evacuated Villa Capri! Please text me if you know anything!*

Ruth Callen's family—her five children, 12 grandchildren, 16 great-grandchildren, and countless nieces and nephews—joined forces to find her. They were, as Ruthie put it, "on a manhunt."

Varenna, 6:55 a.m.

Two Golden Gate Bridge district buses rolled slowly downhill toward Fountaingrove Parkway, giving the Varenna residents on board their first look at what rescuers outside had been dealing with for hours. Villa Capri was a bonfire, with flames pouring out windows and door frames. On the last bus were Carole and Richard Williams, who said residents looked on in uniform silence as they passed by. "We were shocked by the raging fire at Villa Capri," she said. "There was also a lot of flame on the west side of the road, so I was sure the South Building would also be a total loss."

R.J. and Steffany Kisling followed in separate vehicles. They had rescued dozens of Varenna residents but still didn't know what had happened to their grandfather. His gray Lexus was still in the garage. Unsure whether the complex would endure, the siblings had grabbed some of his oil paintings and a few changes of clothes before queueing up behind the buses.

Steffany videotaped the scene as they passed Villa Capri and drove down Fountaingrove Parkway. "I'm following a bus right now with a bunch of elderly people who were abandoned, left with no staff or anything, 70 people, and nobody knew they were there," she narrated in one video. "And the only reason they're getting out right now is because R.J. went to search for our grandpa and make sure he got out all right."

She repeatedly remarked how "crazy" the landscape looked, and though they were off the hill, safety still wasn't a guarantee. "As far as we knew, the entire world was on fire. That's what it felt like. There was no light at the end of the tunnel." Until there was. They soon emerged from the black cloud of smoke to discover dawn was breaking. "Suddenly it was daylight, and life was still there," Steffany said.

Capt. Stornetta and his crew from Windsor followed the Kislings down. Within a couple of hours, they were dispatched again to the Flamingo Hotel, Santa Rosa's landmark lodge located in the center of town, where Stornetta's job was much simpler. To get the guests out of their rooms as quickly as possible, he simply pulled the fire alarm, and they walked out from every room under their own power. From there, he and his crew returned to Fountaingrove and executed structure protection measures, trying to save untouched houses next to those actively burning. Later, when he had a chance to go by his family's home, he found, as he feared, the entire neighborhood was gone. "I didn't know where the street was to turn because all those landmarks that I've known for my whole life were gone," he said, sighing. "So many emotions."

When he drove away, the ground and debris that once marked his home were still burning.

15

Exhausted

The Firestorm, Sunrise, 7:14 A.M., Monday, October 9

As the sun rose over Northern California, reports of the Tubbs, Nuns, Atlas, Pocket, and other Wine Country Fires went global, with images of the devastation featured in print, television, and social media coverage. But because of widespread power outages, downed cell towers, and smoky skies ruining sightlines, many Sonoma County residents had only the radio for information about the destruction.

San Francisco Bay Area residents mobilized. They opened their homes to displaced friends and relatives, volunteered in shelters, and donated food, money, and clothing. Bay Area firefighters drove north to fight the still burning blaze. Police departments from around California sent officers to help beleaguered Sonoma County departments providing security in evacuated neighborhoods until National Guard troops could arrive. More than 100,000 Sonoma County residents had fled their houses, apartments, and mobile homes. Officials began to report death counts, and lists of hundreds of missing people circulated online. By afternoon, reporters told of the demise of entire neighborhoods from Fountaingrove to Larkfield to Coffey Park and the destruction of Santa Rosa landmarks, including Paradise Ridge Winery, Fountaingrove's Round Barn, and the Fountaingrove Hilton, all within a mile of Villa Capri and Varenna. Closer in, the entire shopping center housing resident-favorite Sweet T's was gone, as were numerous Keysight Technologies buildings across Fountaingrove Parkway from Varenna.

Anne Reynolds, the Red Cross division disaster director for California, deployed 150 to 200 volunteers—all requiring immediate background checks and on-the-job training—and worked with officials to take over shelter operations. Doctors and nurses teamed with Red Cross health services staff to identify medically fragile evacuees who needed care across all county shelters, and the Red Cross helped seniors obtain refills for prescriptions they had left behind.

New Vintage Church

It was "mayhem" according to Melissa, who had driven over when her sister called to suggest their mother might have wound up at the church. "They just had a big room full of people sitting in their wheelchairs or sleeping in corners. It was not organized whatsoever," Melissa said. She found Virginia, typically bedridden, propped in a corner by herself in someone else's wheelchair.

"How are you doing?" Melissa asked, relieved to have found her at last.

"I'm tired," Virginia responded. "I want to go to sleep."

Melissa wrapped a blanket around her mom and went in search of information about placement plans. The first staff member Melissa ran into was Jane Torres, but Jane didn't know anything about next steps. Then Melissa came upon the woman whose name had been on many people's minds, Debie Smith, who said she arrived at the church sometime after 6 a.m. Melissa anticipated interrogating Smith, but Smith turned the tables. Before Melissa could utter a word, the executive director fired a question at her: "Where did you leave the master keys to Villa Capri?"

"I left them on the glass table at the reception area," Melissa replied.

"Good," Smith said succinctly.

It took a beat for their exchange to sink in, but when it did, Melissa was apoplectic. "What the hell happened?" she asked Smith. "Why did things go so wrong? Why did no one have keys to the bus?" She continued on in a rush of emotion. "You guys left 24 people up there, and you're asking me about keys? If it hadn't been for Kathy and me, none of these people would be here right now. They'd all be dead."

Melissa said Smith's face didn't change, nor did she respond. She just turned to talk to someone else. But another Villa Capri manager overheard what Melissa said and walked over.

"Was what you said really true?" the manager asked.

Melissa confirmed it was. The manager looked at her, Melissa remembered, "and she was just appalled."

Inside the sanctuary, Len Kulwiec and Susie Pritchett sat next to one another in front of a large screen airing the news. The space was full of residents from all four Oakmont Senior Living properties on the hill in Fountaingrove. Len and Susie didn't recognize many faces. Among those strangers, Susie spotted a man carrying a small cage, and inside, his parrot. It saddened her. *If I'd only had a small cage like that,* she thought, *I could have put Tiffany in and had her right with me.* Susie's son-in-law Kevin eventually found her between the pews, and Susie threw her arms around him when he approached.

Len was wearing pajama bottoms, a navy robe, and slippers when his son found him in the lobby. Forever the king of Villa Capri—the guy the ladies loved, and the men loved to hate—the handsome Len cracked wise about his circumstances. "Michael, look at all these ladies in their nightgowns. Too bad we're not 60 years younger," he joked. Len relayed the night's events to Michael and credited Joey Horsman with his escape. "He saved my life," Len said in all seriousness.

As the Kulwiec men prepared to leave, Len saw Debie Smith. According to Len, he told her, "We're here, we made it, and I love you," and she said "I love you" back.

***

R.J. and Steffany followed the two buses to a shelter, where they were rerouted to New Vintage Church. When they arrived, Steffany ran through the complex, searching the crowded sanctuary for her grandfather. Unable to find him, she met up with R.J. and their uncle who'd arrived to help. They decided to split up and search the other shelters. Steffany was about to pull her car out of her parking space just as an Oakmont Senior Living shuttle bus arrived. A voice inside her told her to wait. Having operated on instinct for most of the night, Steffany trusted the voice, so she turned off her car and approached a woman who was helping seniors step off the bus.

"Have you brought my Papa here? His name is John Hurford," Steffany asked.

The woman, it turned out, had been rounding up Oakmont residents from the emergency shelters. "He's already here," the woman said.

Steffany ran through the church again, eventually spotting Papa near the restrooms, chatting up the ladies waiting in a long line. "I found him eating his animal crackers and drinking juice, barefoot," she said. The typically well-groomed and finely attired John Hurford had a fleece vest on inside-out over his plaid button-down shirt and tan slacks. His disheveled comb-over made him look like a cockatiel, Steffany thought. "He was very discombobulated when we found him," she said. She hugged him. "Hey, you," Papa replied in a voice so casual it almost worried his granddaughter. She didn't want to upset him, so she tried to stay calm. "He had no idea where he was until that point," she said.

The Kislings learned that at 3:30 a.m., as Varenna Executive Director Nathan Condie prepared to leave, he instructed John and two women to climb into his Kia Forte. "I never felt like I was in an emergency," John said, yet for weeks to follow, he was under the impression that Varenna had burned to the ground and all his belongings were lost. He only relinquished that belief when residents returned home many weeks later.

Satisfied that Papa was OK, Steffany began helping other seniors who told her, "I'm hungry, I'm thirsty, I'm cold." She brought them water, escorted them to the restroom, and found blankets to wrap around them.

R.J. and his uncle arrived soon after, and once R.J. was assured his grandfather was in good hands, he set off for home in Petaluma, where he parked his ash-covered truck, pockmarked with ember burns, and jumped out. He was still running on a heavy dose of adrenaline when he walked inside. "Go rake the clothes in the front yard!" he barked at his eldest son.

Puzzled, the young man looked to his mom.

"He means leaves," Betty said. Their son should rake the leaves off the lawn. The wind had taken a toll on their yard, and R.J. was worried about the dead leaves as potential fire fuel.

Reeking of smoke and sleep-deprived—and rather than stopping to eat, shower, rest, or consider his herculean accomplishment—R.J. tossed belongings in boxes and shoved them into a trailer that held their camping gear. The Nuns Fire was only five miles away, and considering what far-flying embers had done to spread the Tubbs Fire, it was reasonable to think Petaluma could be next. As he packed, he agonized over the Varenna evacuation. "My biggest fear was 'Did we leave somebody behind?'" he said.

R.J. was right to worry.

Varenna

Sheila Van Pelt noticed one thing out of the ordinary as she woke up early on October 9 and took her dachshund Lulu for their usual walk down by the lake. She usually took the funicular on the return trip back up the hill but that wasn't an option this morning as the power seemed to be out. It took the 79-year-old a while to walk back up, and when she reached Varenna, she discovered a second unusual occurrence. "Everyone was gone," recounted her daughter-in-law, Terry Van Pelt. "There was not a soul anywhere. [Sheila] had no idea what was going on. No warning. She had no power. No water." Terry said. "She went back to the apartment and waited for someone to come and get her and no one ever did."

Over in the South Building, Sally Tilbury, neatly ensconced in her well-appointed bed, head resting on an ironed pillowcase, had "heard some commotion" and stirred overnight, according to her daughter Mary Tilbury. Sally disconnected from her CPAP machine and walked to the window, which she closed because of what she thought was swirling dust. Hours later, when Sally arose in the morning, the power was out, and it was deathly quiet. She smelled smoke, and when she looked outside, she saw the fire's devastation. The well-read, politically conservative woman's mind immediately leapt to what she had read in the *Wall Street Journal* about rising tensions between President Donald Trump and North Korea's Kim Jong Un. She thought the North Korean president "had dropped the big one on us."

But Sally was not going down unkempt. The meticulous woman balanced her bedside flashlight on her walker and dressed herself for what she thought was the end, tying one of her signature silk scarves around her neck. Then she made her way to her safe, from which she donned her most prized necklaces and all her rings. If Sally was going to perish in a nuclear holocaust, she was going to do it wearing her jewels and her lipstick. Then she sat in her living room and waited to die—for roughly four hours.

New Vintage Church

It was 8 a.m., and Kathy had reuniting to do, both for residents with their walkers and wheelchairs and for herself with her husband. But her mission was interrupted—twice. As Kathy entered the church, a familiar Villa Capri concierge named Sheryl Bishop gave Kathy a hug and asked if she was OK. "Oh my God," Sheryl said. "I don't believe what's happening."

"Sheryl, no evacuation plan," Kathy said bluntly.

"It was in a binder," Sheryl replied.

Kathy was not impressed. "Your workers didn't know it was there."

Sheryl apologized.

Former executive director Tammy Moratto also stopped Kathy, to ask if she'd seen Bess Budow. Kathy didn't know the residents' names or that Bess was the one whose wheelchair the bus driver steadied as he banged his way through the Villa Capri gatehouse. Kathy told Tammy she didn't know Bess. The brief interaction rankled Kathy. "[Tammy] didn't even ask me any questions, like, 'Is it OK up there? Did you get everyone down?'" Tammy didn't ask for any outcomes, not about the residents, the building, nothing, Kathy recalled. "I thought Tammy or someone would come up to me and say, 'Thanks for getting those people out of there,'" Kathy said. "No one wanted to talk to me."

Kathy walked into the sanctuary, where she found Mark with his mom. Kathy had remained calm and collected all night, but that changed when she saw her husband. Their reunion was not joyous. "What the hell happened?" Kathy demanded. "Why didn't you come back?"

"Tammy said they'd send school buses up to get everyone," Mark said in his defense.

Kathy made clear he was mistaken. "No school bus came to get us."

Mark went numb. "Oh my God," he said. "I got down [to Coddingtown]. Tammy said a school bus was coming to get you." The knowledge that he almost left his wife to die overwhelmed Mark. "It was hard to believe Tammy would have told me something that didn't happen," he would later reflect.

A drained Kathy walked outside to call her children, who both lived out of the area. She told them she, their dad, and their grandmother were safe. "They were like, 'OK from what?'" Kathy said. It was still just after 8 a.m. on a Monday morning, and they hadn't yet heard what was happening in Sonoma County.

***

Anyone who showed up at Dawn Ross's friends' house was quickly enlisted in the search for her parents, Bill and Wanda Lee. About 10 people, including a niece in Sacramento, formed a detective corps that sent emails, checked evacuation centers, called every Oakmont-related number they could find, and scoured all Oakmont websites. They thought surely the company would post something. By 9 a.m. Dawn's nerves were frayed. "It had been eight hours with no word if my parents were dead or alive," she said.

It was deeply troubling, given everything she had done over the past five years to keep her parents happy and safe. Not to mention the fact that she had forked over $22,000 a month for their round-the-clock care. She sent email after email to anyone who would listen about the unsatisfactory care she witnessed at Villa Capri.

On October 6, two days before the fire, Dawn had emailed the new memory care manager Janice Wilson and copied Debie Smith to relay an incident in which her parents' personal caregiver found Bill lying in bed with soiled briefs. Dawn's email had not garnered a reply from either Janice or Debie—until three days later, on October 9, at 9:06 a.m., when Dawn received the following message:

> *Hi dawn, your parents are at 3300 Sonoma ave. new vintage church. They are ok.*

Dawn responded immediately.

> *Thank you. We are on the way. Our house burned down.*

***

Like Vivian, Dawn, and Ruthie, Gloria Eurotas had been expecting a phone call from Villa Capri staff telling her where they had taken her mother, Alice. And like Vivian, Dawn, and Ruthie, no one called. Gloria waited and worried, growing increasingly upset. "There was a big chunk of time when we didn't know if she was alive or where she was," Gloria said. "There should have been a phone tree to contact everyone. [Oakmont staff] had our numbers."

Finally, at 10 a.m., Gloria's phone rang. It was an unfamiliar number, but she answered. "Guess where I am?" Alice chirped. "Guess what happened?" A shelter volunteer got on the line and confirmed that Alice was safe at the Veterans Memorial Building, but Villa Capri residents were being sent to New Vintage Church. Alice would be among them. As it happened, Alice actually remembered Gloria's number, a number she hadn't dialed in quite some time.

Gloria navigated through the morning's yellow-gray haze to arrive at the church around 10:30 a.m. She waded through a sea of seniors, Red Cross staff, and church volunteers until she came upon her mother wandering aimlessly in her hot-pink robe and Birkenstocks. She had her walker but not her glasses or hearing aids. "It was pitiful," Gloria said. They hugged.

Alice seemed confused yet pleased to see her oldest daughter, led her to a table where a volunteer was writing names on butcher paper. "I'm taking Alice," she told the man, before realizing her mother had never even been checked in. "They didn't know her name before that," Gloria said. According to Jane Torres, because the staff lacked a resident roster, she and Smith were trying to create one from memory, attempting to track who they'd seen at New Vintage Church, who might have left with family, and who was still missing.

Although Gloria was prepared to leave, Alice wasn't quite ready. A chef from one of the four Oakmont communities, aided by church and Red Cross volunteers, had prepared pancakes and eggs, and Alice was not going to leave without a plate. After breakfast, Gloria left her mom with a volunteer so she could retrieve her car. As she pulled around, she saw Debie Smith running through the parking lot with another Oakmont employee. "She looked pretty frantic," Gloria said. "She was flustered and running around trying to connect with residents." Gloria told her she was taking Alice.

***

After hours of searching shelters for her grandmother Sally Tilbury, Jessica Kilcullen found herself at Finley Community Center, where she and her son bobbed through rows of hunched-over elderly, crouching down at each person to see if they recognized faces from Varenna. They didn't. Jessica's mom sat in the car at each shelter, frozen in fear and shock.

At one point, Jessica saw a Facebook post about New Vintage Church, so they drove over. "Where is Sally Tilbury?" she asked the young woman who seemed to be overseeing the operation. She didn't know. "You don't even know who's here? You haven't taken roll?" Jessica asked, stunned. Having heard enough, Jessica climbed the stage and stood in front of the large screen featuring ABC News live coverage. Hundreds of pajama-clad seniors blinked back at her. She yelled at the top of her lungs, "Has anybody seen Sally Tilbury?"

An older gentleman told Jessica he hadn't, which heightened their panic. Then a young woman who Jessica remembered as "Nathan Condie's right hand," told Jessica "maintenance man Tony" was heading up the hill to Varenna for medication. Jessica asked for his cell phone number and called to ask him to check Sally's room.

It was around noon when Jessica, her mom, her son, and a cousin paced in the church parking lot waiting for Tony to return. When he pulled up, they could make out Sally's profile inside. They rushed the van and opened the door. Sure enough, Oakmont staff had found Sally in her apartment. The four generations crushed together in a tearful hug so strong that Jessica's son had to support Grandma Sally to keep her on her feet. "I'll never forget waiting for that guy to show up and the door to open, and we all just fell to our knees like 'Oh my gosh, she's alive,'" Jessica recalled. "She was in her unit, and nobody got her." Sally relayed she had sheltered in place as instructed. "I couldn't believe it," Sally told them. "I thought they dropped the big one."

Sally wasn't the only one found when staff returned to Varenna that morning. Sheila Van Pelt was discovered too, as were at least two other Varenna residents.

***

Dawn Ross arrived at New Vintage Church around 10 a.m. to find Bill and Wanda in their pajamas, her father sitting on a folding chair, and her mother lying across three chairs positioned in a row. Her mother had a "big lump" on her head; neither had their glasses. "They just started sobbing when they saw us. My dad kept saying, 'There was fire everywhere.'"

Dawn spent a few hours consoling them. Around 1 p.m. she spoke with Debie Smith, who said they were trying to figure out a plan and were considering bringing in cots for the residents overnight. Dawn called her brother in San Jose to have him pick up Bill and Wanda; Dawn couldn't host them because her home was leveled. In the meantime, Dawn would buy clothes, food, blankets, and pillows for her parents, her husband, their son, and herself. She told Smith she was running to Target and would return in two hours. When she arrived at the store, she was struck by what she saw. "Target looked like a world of zombies," Dawn said. "We all had the same look on our faces. 'What just happened?'"

***

It was only after a friend brought her a cup of coffee and they sat on a bench that the previous 10 hours caught up with Kathy. "It took that long to realize what happened," she said. "It took that long to finally break down and cry." No one would have blamed her if she had insisted on going home to rest and to process the night, but Kathy kept going. She helped Red Cross volunteers serve breakfast, and as she brought meals into the memory care room, she saw Jane Torres "frantically" trying to assess residents' dietary and medical needs without their charts. As Kathy delivered a plate, Jane had to figure out, off the top of her head, who could eat what.

Then Kathy went in search of the Ford Econoline shuttle to retrieve a stack of adult briefs she had stashed in the back, but in the morning's tumult, a thief had stolen the van from the church parking lot. Mark heard the commotion as the crime transpired. "All of a sudden we heard screeching and a crash. Someone had gotten in the bus and hit two cars" before driving off, he said. Witnesses described a man wearing a baseball cap and a bright blue shirt bumping cars on his way out of the church parking lot and heading south. Police found the banged-up shuttle abandoned a few hours later.

Although the front lines of the Tubbs Fire were still nearly four miles north of the church and the winds had died down significantly, fear was still spreading rapidly. Given the emerging evidence of the devastation in Coffey Park, concern grew that even the flat, residential area around New Vintage Church was now no longer safe. Kathy couldn't remember who yelled the order, but after serving breakfast and cleaning up, she heard someone suddenly shout, "You're going to have to evacuate the church!"

Nell Magnuson, still wearing her "shabby" maroon robe and tattered gold sandals, was mid-interview with a *Washington Post* reporter, discussing all they'd lost overnight. The October 10 article read:

> *"'Our whole lives have turned upside down. We don't have a clue what's going to happen. It's just losing everything. All the pictures, my whole life,' [Nell] told The Post. But before her concerns could be addressed, the fire began to threaten the church. 'You caught us just in time,' Magnuson said as she headed for the exit. 'We're being evacuated again.'"*

Kathy and Mark made for the exit as well, having decided they finally had enough for one night. They put Helen in the Suburban, and, a dozen hours after they left Sebastopol, the couple drove home exhausted and, as they recalled, reeking like a campfire. But there would be no rest for the weary. Mark and Kathy became round-the-clock caregivers for a distraught Helen, who, at 89 and with dementia, had just lost her home, her possessions, and access to her stable circle of friends.

***

At 2 p.m., a stranger from San Carlos, an hour and a half south of Santa Rosa, called Ruthie Kurpinsky with a clue about where her missing mother might be. He had seen Ruthie's plea for help on Facebook and told her to check New Vintage Church. Neither Ruthie nor her sister had heard anything from Villa Capri.

Ruthie lived 45 minutes away, so she enlisted a nephew who found her mother, Ruth Callen, wrapped in a sheet at the church. Underneath she was wearing her favorite floral and leopard-print designer nightdress. She had lost her robe somewhere along the way. Without her glasses, Ruth didn't recognize her grandson, and it took her a moment to realize he was family.

"[My mom] said that was her happiest moment," Ruthie said. "She knew she was going to get out of there." Ruth told her family she had sat among "a million people" at the Fairgrounds but knew no one until a bus brought her into the church. She had arrived "cold and hungry," she said. And it was clear the church was not an end point either. Ruth's grandson stepped outside to tell his aunt Ruthie that because of concern about the fires possibly spreading, "they want them out of here."

Though she had feared for her life all night, Ruth's sense of humor remained intact as she bantered with her progeny about her now unhoused status. "OK kids! Who wants me now? I'm up for grabs!"

Her youngest daughter, Liz, volunteered to house her, so Ruthie arranged a series of rides to get their mother from Santa Rosa to Marin County to Sacramento to Auburn, a journey of more than 150 miles. Ruth had a one-liner for that situation too: "Hell, I've been in five getaway cars today and I didn't even rob a bank!"

Although she seemed to take it all in stride, Ruth's signature humor dissipated when she arrived at Liz's home. Ruth continuously worried about the fate of her best friend, Joellen Mack, whom she'd last seen sitting in a wheelchair at the top of Villa Capri's stairs, and she struggled to remember who rode with her in the police car that took her to the first shelter. "My mother isn't a crier. She doesn't cry," Ruthie said. "And then she cried all night at my sister's. She cried for hours."

Santa Rosa Memorial Hospital, About Four Miles South of Villa Capri

Sherry Minson's phone had rung that morning with a call from Maritza, the caregiver whom Sherry paid to sit with her mother, Bess Budow, for 12 hours every day at Villa Capri. "Where's your mom?" Maritza asked.

Sherry was puzzled. "What do you mean?"

"You haven't heard?" Maritza asked. She proceeded to tell her about the fire.

Sherry was aghast. No one from Villa Capri had called to tell her what happened or relay her mother's whereabouts.

After hearing about the fire, Maritza tried to drive to Villa Capri but couldn't get there. She searched senior care facilities that might have taken in residents, and she called caregivers she had befriended during the year she worked for the Minsons. Eventually, Maritza found out about the church, and since Sherry lived an hour and a half away, Maritza raced right over.

But officials there turned Maritza away from New Vintage because they were moving residents again. The three women were left wondering, once again, what had happened to Bess. "Finally," Sarah said, "my mom gets a phone call from someone she doesn't know at the company. 'Everyone has been put on buses to one of our two other facilities, Concord and Albany. But we don't know yet who's been sent where,'" the caller told Sherry. Sherry and Sarah, who had started to drive north from the San Francisco Peninsula, began to reroute to the East Bay Area to check Oakmont facilities there. But then someone at the church told Maritza that Bess had been rushed to Memorial Hospital. She had taken a fall.

Memorial operated the city's only functioning emergency room after both Kaiser and Sutter were evacuated. And because so many injured residents had flooded Memorial's ER, the overwhelmed staff couldn't confirm to the Minsons whether Bess was there. "They said it was a madhouse," Sherry recalled. Unable to hear and thus communicate, Bess had been admitted as a "Jane Doe."

Maritza arrived first and eventually located Bess in an emergency room treatment bed. Bess, who usually recognized Maritza's voice, was unresponsive at first. "I told her I love her, and she'd be OK," Maritza said. "For me, it was very sad." Maritza was by Bess' side when Sherry and Sarah walked in. "[My mom] was having a tremendous amount of pain, and they suspected a broken hip," Sherry said. She also had a broken tooth, a wound on her heel, and bruises on her body.

Because of the fire, Memorial had paused nonemergency surgeries, so Bess was transported to Petaluma Valley Hospital for immediate care. Over the course of 12 hours, Bess had gone from her bed with rails at Villa Capri to a wheelchair, a bus, an emergency shelter, a chair at the church, an ambulance, a hospital bed, a second ambulance, and another new hospital bed. In all the shuffling and stress, Bess' blood pressure dropped, and her heart rate slowed. Doctors wouldn't be able to operate on her for four days.

"As a nurse, I knew it was extremely painful while the broken bone is flopping inside there. There's no way to stop that pain without stabilizing it," Sherry said. "She was crying and saying she wanted to die."

Kaiser Hospital, San Rafael

About the same time Bess was reunited with her family at Memorial Hospital, a Varenna resident lay in another hospital bed 30 miles south. Her face was scraped, swollen, and badly bruised, especially her forehead, and she needed a few stitches near her hairline. Her arms and knees also bore severe scrapes and bruises. Unlike Bess, Edel Burton was capable of telling medical staff her name, but she couldn't recall phone numbers for her relatives. She was also missing her beloved dog, Abigail. Minutes after Varenna maintenance employee Andre Blakely had dropped her at Kaiser in Santa Rosa, staff there helped Edel into a hospital gown and rushed her into a stranger's pick-up truck to transport her to Kaiser in San Rafael, an hour south.

Edel's relatives, meanwhile, had been searching for her since 4 a.m. One relative, B.M., who asked to use only her initials, had unsuccessfully called two Varenna numbers. She tried other numbers listed on Varenna's web-site, eventually reaching Tammy Moratto around 8:40 a.m., according to a detailed timeline B.M. recorded the following day. Moratto told her all Varenna residents were safe and enjoying a hot breakfast at New Vintage Church. She took Edel's name and B.M.'s phone number and promised to call back in an hour.

When Moratto didn't call back, B.M. and her husband headed to the church, arriving around noon. After B.M. and her husband had searched all the church's buildings, Oakmont staff told her Edel was likely on a bus to Concord. "We checked every bus manifest we could and physically got on two buses," B.M. said.

Desperate to find Edel, B.M. tried asking one last Oakmont employee, and the woman said she hadn't seen Edel or her dog all day. She led B.M. to Nathan Condie, who suggested Edel may have driven herself away from Varenna or left with another resident. "We explained she did not know anyone well enough to leave with them and that she would have needed assistance to get out of the building if there was no power," B.M. wrote. "Nathan said he knew [Edel] had been evacuated. When pressed, he admitted he did not have a master list of the evacuees and was just going by what he believed to be true."

Nathan's assurances that employees and fire officials had checked every apartment didn't sit well with B.M., who drove to the bottom of Bicentennial

Way and appealed to an officer to check Edel's unit at Varenna. Forty-five minutes later, the officer confirmed apartment 302 was empty. Thus began a search of emergency shelters and the one hospital still operating, and an attempt to file a missing person report with Santa Rosa Police.

Finally, close to 3:30 p.m., a creative Kaiser social worker used the networking site LinkedIn to find and contact B.M.'s son. Two hours later, B.M. arrived in San Rafael to find Edel in surprisingly good spirits. "She's a very strong Norwegian woman. She was shaken, but she had already started to block out some of the trauma," B.M. said.

The ordeal to locate Edel incenses B.M. to this day. "Oakmont flat out lied to me," she said. "They told me [Edel] was safe and sound at the church, and she was not. And they had no clue she was missing." But nothing makes her angrier than the call she received at 6:18 p.m., while she was in the process of getting Edel discharged from the hospital. Nathan called to say Oakmont staff located Edel at Kaiser in Santa Rosa. When B.M. informed him that Edel was in San Rafael not Santa Rosa—because Kaiser Santa Rosa evacuated—he acted surprised, B.M. said. She explained Edel's injuries to Nathan and was met with what she felt was a "throwaway attitude," as she recorded in her notes. "His response was, 'A few residents did sustain injuries. At least she's alive.'"

New Vintage Church

Having worked through the crowd at Target and purchased clothes for five people, Dawn Ross drove back to the church. Previously bustling with volunteers, employees, residents, and even a buffet line, New Vintage was vacant. "We get back, not a soul. Completely empty," Dawn said. She was at a loss.

"Are you sure this is the right church?" Dawn's friend asked.

For a second, Dawn wondered if they had gotten the address wrong, but they were in the right spot. They saw piles of food left inside, including juice boxes and granola bars. The only person they could find told them the staff, the volunteers, and the residents had all left. He mumbled something about Concord or Albany. "There was no note or other indication as to where everyone had been taken, and no note or call from Debie. Nothing," Dawn later said. "At this point, we were mentally and physically exhausted, and more upset than I can describe," she recalled. "We could not believe that my parents were lost to us again."

She sat in her car, and at 3:23 p.m., replied to Smith's email from 9:06 a.m.

"Came back for my parents. Where are they?"

Henrietta Hillman on her 90th birthday.
Photo courtesy of Corky Cramer.

Ruth Callen. *Photo courtesy of Ruthie Kurpinsky.*

Len Kulwiec. *Photo by Anne Belden.*

Louise Johnson and her three sons. L to R: Craig,
Clinton, and Eric. *Photo courtesy of Eric Johnson.*

Alice Eurotas in Villa Capri's courtyard October 7, 2017, in a photo
she asked her daughter Beth to send to her brother to show him
that "we are both old now." *Photo courtesy of Beth Eurotas-Steffy.*

Bob Mitton and Mimi Vandermolen and their
dog, Cocoa. *Photo courtesy of Bob Mitton.*

Steffany and R.J. Kisling. *Photo by Anne Belden.*

Gloria Eurotas and Beth Eurotas-Steffy with their
mother, Alice Eurotas. *Photo by Anne Belden.*

Kathy Allen. *Photo by Anne Belden.*

Villa Capri caregiver Anett Rivas. *Photo by Anne Belden.*

Villa Capri caregiver Cynthia Arroyo. *Photo by Anne Belden.*

Villa Capri caregiver Elizabeth Lopez with her
infant son. *Photo by Anne Belden.*

Varenna maintenance technician Michael Rodriguez. *Photo by Anne Belden.*

Varenna maintenance technician Andre Blakely. *Photo by Anne Belden.*

Bess Budow. *Photo courtesy of Sherry Minson.*

Virginia Gunn and Melissa Langhals. *Photo courtesy of Melissa Langhals.*

Dawn Ross with a photo of her parents, Bill and Wanda Lee. *Photo by Anne Belden.*

Attorney Kathryn Stebner. *Photo courtesy of Kathryn Stebner.*

Department of Social Services executives strategize before their November 16, 2018 mediation with Oakmont attorneys. From left to right: Attorneys Tara Rufo, Sean Abalos, and Kevin Mora; Community Care Licensing Deputy Director Pam Dickfoss, and Adult and Senior Care Program Administrator Ley Arquisola.

Attorney Michael Fiumara. *Photo by Anne Belden.*

District Attorney Jill Ravitch on election night,
September 14, 2021. *Photo by Paul Gullixson.*

District Attorney Jill Ravitch and her sister, Amy Friedricks, on election night, September 14, 2021. *Photo by Anne Belden.*

Kathy and Mark Allen and Melissa Langhals at the April 2019 reunion. *Photo by Anne Belden.*

Frank Perez on his back patio. *Photo by Paul Gullixson.*

Noella "Nell" Magnuson. *Photo by Anne Belden.*

PART III
FALLOUT

16

CHAPTER -

Outrage

The Firestorm, the First Three Days After

The Tubbs Fire would burn for 22 more days, becoming the most destructive wildfire in California history, at least for the time being. In all, Tubbs destroyed 5,600 homes, including nearly 5 percent of all the housing stock in Santa Rosa, while devouring a combined 382 square miles of land, an area equal in size to Dallas.

It proved to be the deadliest of dozens of fires that burned throughout Northern California that October. Initial reports indicated more than 10 people had died while hundreds more were injured and missing. Power was out for much of the region for days. The firefight required the service of 30 air tankers, 73 helicopters, 2,000 National Guard members, 500 law enforcement officers, and 11,000 firefighters, of which 177 were from out of state, including teams from Canada and Australia. Thousands of residents whose homes were destroyed or fled areas of mandatory evacuation sought refuge in emergency shelters, hotels, campers, campsites, or the homes of friends and family members. Many were holed up for days awaiting news about when they could return home, and whether their houses and apartments were still standing.

Journalists descended on the county to attend daily press briefings broadcast around the world from the Sonoma County Fairgrounds, featuring Cal Fire and local fire officials, law enforcement leaders, meteorologists, federal emergency management experts, and an array of federal state and local elected representatives. "This is truly one of the greatest, if not the greatest, tragedy that California has ever faced," Governor Jerry Brown said after touring the damage on Saturday, October 14, along with U.S. Senators Dianne Feinstein and Kamala Harris. "The devastation is just unbelievable."

But the fire was not done. Although Cal Fire crews felt they were getting the upper hand with the Tubbs 25 percent contained by October 13, a branch of another fire erupted southeast of Santa Rosa late that Friday, forcing the evacuation of hundreds more homes. Many of those who awoke to police sirens and bullhorn warnings to leave as soon as possible were residents who had just returned after being forced out for several days. "We're not out of the woods yet," Brown warned residents.

Oakmont Corporate Offices

Oakmont Senior Living sought to assure family members of Varenna, Villa Capri, and Fountaingrove Lodge residents that the evacuations had been orderly and all residents were safe and accounted for. The first email sent out to family members of Villa Capri residents at 10:05 a.m. on October 9 was short and straightforward:

> *Subject: Evacuation Location for Villa Capri*
>
> *Hello Friends and Families,*
>
> *We wanted to notify you that Villa Capri at Varenna evacuated early this morning due to the wildfires in Santa Rosa. We are currently located at the New Vintage Church at 3300 Sonoma Avenue. We will continue to update you as things develop.*
>
> *Oakmont of Villa Capri*

A second email arrived just before midnight and appeared in red-brown typeface, all caps.

> *CURRENTLY WE HAVE EVACUATED OUR COMMUNITY DUE TO THE FIRES IN THE CITY OF SANTA ROSA. OUR RESIDENTS FROM FOUNTAINGROVE LODGE, VARENNA, AND OAKMONT VILLA CAPRI (ASSISTED LIVING) HAVE ALL BEEN SAFELY TAKEN TO OR DIRECTED TO EVACUATE TO OAKMONT OF MONTECITO [at address, phone number].*

ALL MEMORY CARE RESIDENTS FROM OAKMONT OF THE TERRACES AND OAKMONT OF VILLA CAPRI HAVE BEEN SAFELY EVACUATED TO BELMONT VILLAGE SENIOR LIVING [at address, phone number].

WE HAVE BEEN INUNDATED WITH PHONE CALLS. HOWEVER, IF YOU NEED TO GET A HOLD OF US, PLEASE LEAVE A MESSAGE FOR OUR OAKMONT MANAGEMENT TEAM AT [phone number]. YOU MAY ALSO CALL BACK THIS NUMBER PERIODICALLY FOR UPDATES.

FOR URGENT MATTERS ONLY PLEASE CALL CRYSTAL ROBINSON AT [phone number].

OUR FOCUS CONTINUES TO BE ON THE WELFARE AND SAFETY OF OUR RESIDENTS AND STAFF.

On Tuesday, October 10, Oakmont posted the following on its website:

All Oakmont Senior Living residents and staff are accounted for, safe, and settling into new living arrangements after wildfires forced evacuation of our four Assisted Living and Memory Care communities in Santa Rosa. Our primary goal is to ensure the safety of our residents and to reassure their families. During this process we will continue to update our website and send out emails to our residents and families every 48 hours.

***

For Beth Eurotas-Steffy, the first indication that all had not gone as smoothly as Oakmont Senior Living was portraying began with a coat, or, more precisely, the lack of one.

Amid those frenetic first hours of Monday, October 9, Beth was relieved to find out where her mother, Alice, was and that she was safe. "Alice is at a church, and she only has her nightgown and Birkenstocks," Beth recalled her sister telling her by phone. That fact struck her as odd. *That's weird. If they are evacuating them, at least let them put on a jacket*, she thought.

Beth and Gloria considered themselves lucky to have snagged Alice before she was taken across San Francisco Bay to Oakmont of Montecito in Concord. The sisters had been taking care of their mother since they were teenagers, after Alice had divorced their father, whom Beth described as a "deadbeat dad." Alice had once doted on Beth and her older sister, Gloria, like a 1960s TV mom. "She used to sew our clothes, and she wanted us to be twins, so she'd sew us the same outfit," Beth said. But things changed with the divorce. The girls, ages 12 and 13 at the time of the split, lived with Alice and visited their dad every other weekend. He didn't pay child support, so they moved from one seedy apartment to another around San Mateo on the San Francisco Peninsula. That's when their mother went down a dark path, frequenting bars and throwing back margaritas with other legal secretaries while eschewing familial responsibilities. "There were nights she wouldn't come home," Beth said. "I remember twice I had to go clean vomit out of the car because she had gotten drunk. I feel like I took care of myself, and I took care of my mom." As a reflection of this sudden shift in dynamics, both daughters soon stopped calling her "Mom," referring to her by first name only thereafter.

Decades later, the sisters were still calling their mother Alice—and still taking care of her. On the evening of Monday, October 9, Beth called Gloria's house to do just that.

"How are you doing?" Beth asked her mother.

Alice kept a lighthearted front. "When you get to my age, you can handle anything," she said.

Beth asked her what had happened, and Alice's answers startled her. "Helen's son took care of me." Beth assumed her mother was confused. She knew Alice was referring to Helen Allen's son Mark. *But why would Mark have been up there? What about the staff?*

The next day, Beth followed through while Gloria was at work. She found Alice wearing an old sweatsuit of Gloria's. "I really need a bra," Alice stressed. Beth told her she was working on it and asked Alice again what had happened the night of the fire. "I was woken up by Helen's son," she said.

Beth again thought she was confused. "How did you know it was Helen's son?"

"Well, two things," Alice replied. "He looks just like Helen, and he used to come to lunch all the time, and I'd see him with Helen, so I knew it was Helen's son who woke me up."

"Well, where was the staff?"

"Oh, the *nocturnal* staff?" Alice said, always proud she knew the word. "They only have two or three on staff. You know, I bet they got scared and left. I don't blame them. I would have got scared and left too if I was in their shoes."

Beth dove deeper. "Are you sure Helen's son woke you up? You sure it wasn't a staff member?"

Alice was unwavering. "I never saw staff. I only saw Mark and this woman who helped me get down the stairs," she said. Alice described the assistance from Kathy Allen. "She took the walker in one hand, and she took my arm in the other hand, and then I held on to the railing with the other, and it was really dark and smoky, and somehow we got down the stairs together." Each time Alice repeated her story, she persuaded Beth that she wasn't confused.

"What struck me was how calm she was," Beth said. "The more she talked, the more calm she got. And the more she talked, the more upset I got."

Beth resolved to learn more about what happened that night. The initial emails Oakmont sent out said nothing about family members helping with the evacuations. "I needed to find someone who knew what happened," she said.

These were the first of many questions that would launch Beth Eurotas-Steffy on a dogged, multiyear mission for accountability—and to set the record straight.

*****

Beth was not the only family member asking questions.

Vivian Flowers, after hurriedly trying to replace her mother's teeth, glasses, and prescription drugs, had spent two nights comforting Viola as she cried about her lost belongings and worried about her Villa Capri friends. "It was such chaos that when she closed her eyes, her subconscious would bring it back," Vivian said.

Two days later, on October 11, an Oakmont corporate employee called Vivian to follow up. The employee told her everyone had evacuated Villa Capri safely, that they were in Pleasanton, and that her mother Viola was doing fine.

Vivian decided to play along. "Really?" she said.

"Yes," the Oakmont employee confirmed, "and everybody is doing fine."

"That's a surprise," Vivian responded, "because my mom is sitting right next to me."

There was a slight pause on the line. "Thank God she's safe," the woman said.

Vivian hung up on her. "I was pissed!" she said, still incredulous as she recalled that exchange years later. "They didn't know, two days later, where everyone was."

Ruth Callen's daughter had a similar experience. An Oakmont employee working from Escondido, California, phoned Ruthie Kurpinsky to find out how her mother was doing in Concord. "My mom is not in Concord," Ruthie told the man, who went silent, but sounded as if he was typing furiously.

"They didn't know where everyone was," Ruthie said. The person Ruthie really wanted to hear from was Villa Capri marketing director Roberta Murray, whom Ruthie had called several times on October 9. Roberta finally called back two days later.

"Why didn't somebody call me?" Ruthie asked her. "Why wasn't I called?"

Roberta answered vaguely, Ruthie said, saying something about Debie Smith trying to get to Villa Capri.

"Roberta, I used to run a supported living home for someone who was disabled," Ruthie told her. "Someone was always in charge. Who was in charge?"

Roberta replied that they had had a problem with staff leaving.

***

Dawn Ross also had plenty of questions on the afternoon of October 9, beginning with "Where have they taken my mother and father?" Dawn was distraught as she drove away from New Vintage Church the afternoon of October 9. Her house had been consumed in the fire, and she hadn't slept in hours. On top of that, she had no idea where Oakmont Senior Living had taken her parents, Bill and Wanda Lee.

Her family drove to their beach house where they could determine their next step. In the meantime, Dawn's sister-in-law began making calls to find a new assisted living home that could offer dementia care. When she called Belmont Village, a new facility about to open in the East Bay city of Albany, she asked whether a room was available and was shocked by the response she received after providing Bill and Wanda's names to the man on the phone.

"I'm looking at them," he told her. Bill and Wanda had been bused there by Oakmont staff.

When Dawn's brother and sister-in-law arrived in Albany soon after, they found Bill and Wanda in strangers' clothes lying on an air mattress. They also found that their health was rapidly deteriorating. Bill had been struggling with level-three kidney disease for three years. Immediately after the fire, he went to level four, according to Dawn. At the same time, Wanda, who had to have the mysterious bump on her head checked out at Kaiser, began to reject food. "I don't eat anymore," she told the family. "I don't need to."

Dawn said it seemed clear to her the sudden change in their health was due to the trauma of the botched evacuations as well as the stress of "being shuffled off to a brand-new place without family nearby." Dawn was most disturbed, however, by the lack of communication from Oakmont from the time of the fire to their relocation to Belmont Village, especially considering her parents didn't know Dawn's number and couldn't use a phone. "They are completely dependent on these people," Dawn said. "How do you not have an emergency contact list? I have a list of all of my employees' phone numbers. I would think you would have a list of all your residents' emergency contacts. Why is that not in 10 places? To me, it's so inexplicable."

She sought an explanation when she ran into Villa Capri Executive Director Debie Smith while visiting her parents. Dawn asked Debie point-blank, "Why didn't you call me to let me know where my parents were?"

Dawn recalled Smith telling her the fire had destroyed all their files. "I can't believe the company wouldn't have a backup list on the server, at the main office, at your house. That's crazy," Dawn replied. According to Dawn, Smith did not respond.

Belmont Village

During and immediately after the evacuation, Villa Capri staff didn't have a printed or digital roster of all the residents. As eyewitness testimony and depositions would show, they instead relied on their own mental assessments of who they had seen and who was missing.

"When they evacuated everybody to Concord and Albany, I don't think they knew where all the people were at the time," said Kimberly Lange, Oakmont's regional health services manager at the time. "They were trying to find them. They were telling everyone that everyone was accounted for, but it took one or two days to figure out where everybody was."

Lange wasn't making calls to family members herself, but she heard that regional operations people were. She was too busy trying to figure out how to get residents their vital medications. "They had no medical charts. They had no medications. They literally came with the clothes off their backs," she said. The problem was rooted in the fact that Northern California Oakmont facilities were still using paper charts. This meant Villa Capri residents needed all new medical records, which required new physician reports. In the meantime, managers had to rely on the knowledge of family members and staff, along with what pharmacy records they could locate, to get emergency refills.

Belmont Village, a complex owned by a senior living chain affili-ated with the University of California, Berkeley, but not associated with Oakmont Senior Living, had room for all the memory care residents from Villa Capri and The Terraces because it hadn't officially opened. But the complex lacked furniture, as well as a full slate of employees. So some Villa Capri and Terraces employees came along to care for the residents. Local nonprofit organizations, East Bay Area neighbors, and fellow Oakmont residents themselves donated clothes, air mattresses, and other supplies to help.

But some residents did not adjust well to the new accommodations. Lange, whose job had involved overseeing health services at 13 Bay Area Oakmont facilities, said seniors with dementia don't do well when transferred abruptly. "We don't typically take our memory care people out of memory care that often because it's too hard on them," she said. Many with dementia took medication such as Seroquel to keep them calm and reduce anxiety, but they missed out on their regular doses the first night or two after the fire, Lange said. "I think the ones that were really distraught and traumatized couldn't vocalize what they'd been through."

Caregiver Elizabeth Lopez witnessed many residents stressed or not eating when she reported for duty at Belmont Village. "They were saying 'I want to go home,'" she said. "They missed their home. They missed their family."

Concord

Frank Perez was among the many who experienced severe health problems immediately following the fire. After a traumatic night in which he stomped out flames inside his Varenna apartment and assisted neighbors before racing to safety through the thick smoke, Frank was first taken to Oakmont of Montecito in Concord, where his brother from Santa Cruz located him. He brought Frank home with him to get out of the thick smoke that had blanketed the Bay Area. On his third day in Santa Cruz, Frank collapsed. The family rushed him to a hospital where doctors discovered he had signs of smoke damage to his lungs. As a former long-distance runner, breathing had never been an issue for him. "It's a good thing you were in great physical shape," the doctor told Frank. "Maybe you wouldn't have survived." Nonetheless, his breathing issues persisted. Frank would have a long wait to get back to his second-floor apartment at Varenna. Hours after he fled, the fire crawled back up the hill and again attacked the North Building. Frank's apartment was a total loss.

The fire also damaged the apartment below his—the one belonging to Bob Mitton and Mimi Vandermolen. Firefighters were able to stop the flames and limit the damage to a small area of their unit, but Bob and Mimi would be unable to move back for seven months, and their return would be short-lived. Bob and Mimi had also first landed in Concord, where he said staff "fed us and tried to be good to us," though they were surprised when staff passed around glasses of wine. "I thought that's the craziest thing. They should be getting water. They're dehydrated," Bob said.

Bob and Mimi were most focused on Cocoa, who was trembling and hyperventilating. They wanted to find a quiet hotel room, but Bob's phone was dead. He asked a volunteer for help. They started chatting, and, while charging Bob's phone, the woman called area hotels. Nothing was available. "She looked at the dog and us and said, 'I'm taking you home,'" Bob said. He and Mimi lived with the woman and her husband for nine days. Their new friend fed them, took them shopping, made their medical appointments, and, a week later, helped Bob get past the National Guard so he could sneak his car out of a Varenna parking garage. "We had nothing to pack," Bob said, so with just a few new outfits and plastic bags of medicines, the couple drove north to a second home they owned in Vancouver, Canada.

Besides the couple who had adopted them, Bob Mitton had made another fire-related friend, Officer Dave Pedersen. On October 11, Bob emailed him to reconnect after their wild night rescuing residents.

> *Subject: Hang in there*
>
> *Constable David,*
>
> *From the safety of a shelter in Concord I wanted to make contact with you and offer encouragement for the challenges you and your colleagues have been confronting for the past three days. I was with you at Varenna in the early morning hours as we swept the North and South buildings during the firestorm. As we pulled away in the safety of the bus I must say that I suffered a strong sense of guilt that I was an able person who should have stayed on to help you. You and your partner have been in my thoughts ever since, and I do hope that you are safe and well. I will be back in touch when all of this is over and we will have that beer together. I'm buying!*
>
> *[Bob Mitton]*

Pedersen responded less than 12 hours later, despite having worked around the clock for days.

I am so glad you and your wife are in a safe spot. I cannot express what a great help you were to us. We would have been flying blind without you.

Varenna survived too. I'm thinking in part, because it took us so long to evacuate everybody and the fire department just kept watering down that hill, buying us time. Of course, the view sucks right now, but what are you going to do?

That was the most intense night of my 28-year career and I don't ever hope to have another like it. We are all very tired, but we press on knowing we have lost many and many have lost much.

I look forward to that beer and take care.

Dave

***

After staying up all night and sitting at the church most of the day, Nell and John Magnuson hoped to get some much-needed sleep at Oakmont of Montecito in Concord. "Of course they were completely overwhelmed, but they did their best," Nell said of the staff. "When we got there, they had nice food for us, but there was no place to sleep."

The couple spent the night on an air mattress in a room with three other couples. "That was the most hellish night I've ever had in my life," said Nell. "My husband is 6-foot-2, and he can't get up from the floor." When he tried, he slid under his walker. Eight times during the night, Nell, still wearing the burgundy robe in which she had fled, had to walk down the hall to ask two employees to help lift John to his feet. The next night, a permanent resident volunteered their one-bedroom apartment so the couple could have a bed. "I was in Concord for two or three days in a bathrobe," said Nell, who lamented leaving her iPhone next to her purse at Villa Capri. "I thought, 'I'll come back.' So dumb."

Santa Rosa

Norma Porter, mother of Oakmont Senior Living cofounder Cindy Gallaher, was not among those transported to Concord. With Cindy and Bill Gallaher dealing with the loss of their own home, one of Norma's sons drove two hours from Folsom, California, to pick her up at New Vintage Church and take her to stay with family friends in Santa Rosa. However, those friends soon had to evacuate their home as well, so Norma and the family spent the night on cots in an emergency shelter. It didn't faze the ever-positive 92-year-old.

"I slept six hours straight," she said. "It always surprises me how well I slept." The next day, her son brought her to Folsom, where she lived until a spot opened up at the Fountaingrove Lodge.

Day Four: Word Leaks Out

Within hours of the evacuation, R.J. and Steffany Kisling searched for news reports and social media posts to see what was said about Villa Capri and Varenna, but details were scarce. The first mention of the Tubbs Fire's impact on the Oakmont Senior Living communities was in a *Press Democrat* article on Monday afternoon. "Residents of two large senior living complexes, Oakmont of Villa Capri and Oakmont of Varenna, both on Fountaingrove Parkway, were evacuated," the story read. "Oakmont of Villa Capri was destroyed; details about damage to other buildings in the complex were not available Monday night."

Early Tuesday, Betty Kisling, R.J.'s wife, took to Facebook, offering an account of her husband and sister-in-law's rescue of more than 70 Varenna residents. Her intent was not to brag or shame anyone, she said, but to warn others. "Please don't assume the home where your elderly family lives has a plan.... Don't assume that someone else has called 911," she wrote near the end of the thousand-word post.

She ended with a message of gratitude: "I'm so thankful that everyone made it out from this situation okay. Steff has told me not to think of the 'what ifs' because it's too upsetting to even contemplate. I thank God that

R.J. went and that Steff insisted on busting down doors to check rooms, and that the residents, firefighters, Steff, and R.J. all made it out safe. Prayers for all of those affected by fires all over our state."

Later that afternoon, *Press Democrat* reporter Martin Espinoza shot two Facebook Live videos from the grounds of the retirement complex. In the first 36-second video posted at 1:55 p.m., Espinoza stands in the Villa Capri back parking lot as his camera scans the building's ruins, and the 26-seat Villa Capri bus still parked nearby, against the hillside. In the second live-streamed recording, this one nearly nine minutes long, Espinoza heads up the hill toward Varenna, where he encounters two employees outside a garage near the Main Building. One, Chris DeMott, describes helping to get residents out of the building around 3 a.m. "All of them were evacuated," he says. "All of them are accounted for except for one resident," adds Mika Alcasabas, standing alongside him. "And we're here to check her house," DeMott says.

The workers said they were also there to retrieve medical records for the evacuated residents, Espinoza reported. He then toured the west side of the Main Building overlooking the lake. "This is the Varenna retirement facility, which still, well, a lot of it looks pretty good," Espinoza narrated, unaware of the great lengths that firefighters had gone to earlier to save the complex. "It all looks pretty good, doesn't it?" he asked Mika as she walked ahead of him around the back deck.

"Yes, but we don't know about the casitas yet," she responded. "And the North Building looks like it did catch on fire."

They then moved to the front of the complex, where Martin directed the camera down the hill, past blackened trees and brush, toward the ruins of the buildings below. "That is Villa Capri and the memory care center, and that is completely gone," he says. "It's so… It's so amazing how the rest of it survived."

Among those watching were R.J. and Steffany Kisling, who knew all too well the story of how Varenna survived. What they didn't understand was why these two workers were the ones who had been sent back to the site. "There's no way Oakmont would send up entry-level [employees] to make sure the building is empty," R.J. said.

R.J. was right to be suspicious. As it turned out, DeMott, a maintenance worker, and Alcasabas, who worked in the Varenna dining room, had gone to the complex along with one other coworker of their own volition. They had walked a mile up the hill from a checkpoint. No Oakmont managers had approved their adventure. They later said Varenna residents in Concord had asked them to retrieve cell phones and feed pets, including cats and at least one bird, left behind during hasty exits. DeMott said he was scolded via a voicemail message left by operations vice president Ken Garnett who was "less than enthused about us going up there and being interviewed by the *Press Democrat*."

Mika remembered Garnett calling her into an office in Concord when they returned. "You shouldn't have done that," he told her. He wasn't cross, she said. He was primarily concerned for their safety, but she believed the reprimand was likely a result of the media coverage. "I just burst into tears. What the fuck were we supposed to do? Nobody felt like anything was happening fast enough," she said. "I felt compelled to go."

Among the 182 comments left beneath Martin Espinoza's Facebook videos were urgent pleas, such as "Can you get my parents [sic] bird out of M109B?...My dad needs his meds too but no answer on the verenna [sic] hotline." One woman hit on a key point she felt other commenters were missing: "They lost a resident!?!?"

Frustrated that the full story wasn't being told, Steffany couldn't hold back. "Over 70 residents were left behind at Varenna/Fountaingrove, Santa Rosa. No staff were on the premises," she posted under the video, encouraging the *Press Democrat* to do more investigating. "Ask them the tough questions and see if they have logical answers with no holes in their story/claim about how they evacuated everyone, what time they evacuated everyone off the property and the names of the employees that evacuated everyone," she wrote. "Then ask the residents the same questions. Then ask the firemen and the police and the bus drivers that came to help with the evacuation after my brother found the residents abandoned, and we called 911, who was there helping them load the residents on the buses? #varenna #fountaingrove #coverup."

Steffany posted three more times among the comments, but there was no mention of evacuations gone awry in an October 10 article in which Espinoza reported tales of survival in Fountaingrove and mentioned Villa Capri and Varenna. "On Tuesday evening, parent company Oakmont Senior

Living released a statement that said all residents had been accounted for and are receiving care and services at another Oakmont Senior Living community and a partner facility in the East Bay," the story noted. It ended with a quote by Chris Kasulka, president and CEO of Oakmont Management Group. "Our focus continues to be on the care, welfare, and safety of our residents and staff. We want to thank our staff, residents, and Oakmont families for all of their support during this difficult time."

But it didn't take long for the real story to surface. Betty's post received some 90 comments and 53 shares. In one comment, Steffany Kisling added photos and videos, including a photo of Villa Capri when she arrived around 4:45 a.m. showing flames rising from the building's Fountaingrove Parkway side, and a video of flames devouring Villa Capri's skeleton as she followed the buses out at 7 a.m.

One of Steffany's students at her flight attendant training school saw the post and contacted San Francisco ABC7 News reporter Melanie Woodrow, who was in the field covering the Wine Country Fires. Soon after, Woodrow interviewed R.J. and Steffany about what happened and sought comment from Oakmont Senior Living. Not satisfied with the answers she was getting from Oakmont, Woodrow tweeted October 12, looking for more sources.

> *#Oakmont followers—looking to speak w/anyone re: Oakmont of Varrena [sic] & associated facilities if you are still looking for loved one.*

Woodrow broke the story on the evening news October 12, broadcasting live in front of Golden Gate Transit buses, the type used to ferry the last 70-plus seniors from Varenna. She started off saying all 400 residents of Varenna and Villa Capri were safe, according to an Oakmont Senior Living representative. But then the story switched to R.J. Kisling, who described how he arrived to find residents had been left behind, many of them still in their apartments, sleeping. He told of how he had insisted that firefighters, once they arrived, break down doors to make sure everyone was out. "The repeated question was, 'How come nobody came and got us?' 'How come nobody told us we were evacuating?' And from the fire department, 'Where is the staff? Where is the master key?'" R.J. explained in Woodrow's report.

He ended the interview with a question: "Why did nobody stay behind to ensure that everybody was evacuated?"

Oakmont defended the company's actions after Woodrow requested a response. "While we were in the process of shuttling residents to a designated location, authorities refused to allow staff to reenter the area because of the existing danger, and indicated they would take responsibility for evacuating remaining residents.... Our staff remained in communication with authorities to ensure that all of our residents were safe."

Woodrow followed Oakmont's statement with an interview of Santa Rosa Police Capt. Rainer Navarro, who disputed the company's claims that employees were barred from getting through checkpoints. "We were not stopping anybody from helping save lives that night," he said. "We had not set up any roadblocks at the time. We weren't preventing anyone from getting in at the time."

The following day, on October 13, shortly before 5 p.m., Woodrow broke additional news in a tweet.

> JUST IN: Dept of Social Services investigating evacuation at Varenna Oakmont Sr. Living to determine if staff followed evac plan #ABC7NOW.

Three days earlier, on October 10, a concerned county resident had reported to the California State Department of Social Services' (DSS') Community Care Licensing Division that Varenna's staff had mismanaged the evacuation and that residents had been left behind. Licensing Evaluator Dina Alviso logged the complaint and recorded a formal allegation against Varenna that "facility staff failed to evacuate residents during a fire." Over the next 11 months, Alviso and her colleagues would interview 10 Varenna staff and Oakmont employees, 10 residents, and other witnesses, including first responders and city officials. They would also collect police reports, body camera footage, resident and personnel records, Varenna's operations plan, and its disaster and emergency manual in an attempt to suss out what happened.

The DSS team's job broadened on October 16 when another resident called DSS to complain, but this time about Villa Capri. The DSS regional office recorded three allegations in this case: "Facility staff failed to evacuate residents during a fire," "staff failed to inform family of evacuation," and "staff neglect resulted in resident sustaining serious injury." The Villa Capri investigation would overlap and ultimately eclipse the Varenna investigation for multiple reasons. But in the beginning, Alviso, her boss Carla Nuti-Martinez, and other licensing evaluators got to work tracking down residents and relatives of both communities.

The timing of the DSS investigation and Woodrow's reporting soon became intertwined. In some instances, the spotlight she shined illuminated the botched evacuations to family members, who, up to then, had been in the dark. Dawn Ross, for one, was outraged by what she saw on the news and called DSS to offer her perspective on the evacuation and the mismanaged reunification. Her complaint contributed to the first and second allegations against Villa Capri. Sherry Minson's engagement with DSS underpinned the third allegation, that staff neglect caused Bess Budow to break her hip.

That same day, October 16, Kathy and Mark Allen gave their first public account of what happened at Villa Capri in a TV interview with Woodrow. Kathy repeated her refrain, "We asked [the staff] specifically 'Do you have an evacuation plan?' because we wanted to help out, and they said no. They were waiting for their director." The story also included Andre Blakely, the Varenna maintenance employee whom Woodrow questioned about whether Varenna had an emergency plan. "I wasn't taught if they do," he said.

As part of her reporting, Woodrow called out on social media a contradiction between two Oakmont statements issued one week apart. On October 12 Oakmont claimed, "When the order came simultaneously to evacuate all four communities in the early morning hours of October 9th, staff, nearby residents, and residents' family members began evacuations immediately." But Oakmont's October 17 statement to the *Press Democrat* said, "We voluntarily evacuated as it became clear the fire was getting close and we had been unable to reach authorities because 911 and non-emergency lines were clogged. We hadn't received an evacuation order from emergency authorities." Woodrow posted screenshots of both statements and tweeted the following:

> *Which is it? Varenna Oakmont Sr. Living told @abc7newsbayarea October 12 it received evac orders, now tonight says it didn't. Side by side.*

Woodrow's reporting also noted that in September, one month before the fire, San Francisco elder care attorney Kathryn Stebner had filed a lawsuit against Oakmont Senior Living accusing the company of fraudulent practices that allegedly deprived residents of needed care and exposed them to risk of injury. The suit, filed on behalf of four senior citizens, including an 88-year-old Santa Rosa man, claimed that Oakmont fees were based on "budgets driven primarily by desired profit margins." As a result, the lawsuit alleged, Oakmont Senior Living facilities were understaffed and residents "run the continuing risk of not having their care needs met and of suffering frustration, pain, discomfort, humiliation, and/or injury from inadequate care and supervision."

Stebner told Woodrow understaffing likely played a role in the messy evacuation as well. "I saw your report," the attorney bluntly told Woodrow, "and I wasn't super surprised."

Oakmont Senior Living co-owner Cindy Gallaher refuted Woodrow's reporting directly to residents and families by sharing, via email, the experience of her mom, Norma Porter. "My own mother was living at Villa Capri. She told me a few days afterwards that she was comforted and impressed by how calmly and smoothly the evacuation was there," she wrote.

Crystal Robinson, vice president of sales and marketing for Oakmont Management Group, told the *Press Democrat* "an Oakmont Senior Living executive staff member who was on location evacuated the final residents," although she did not indicate at which facility that occurred. This was the company's first assertion that an executive team member had been on-site until the end. Oakmont had "been extremely busy attending to the welfare and safety of our residents." The story indicated that all 430 of the residents were "accounted for, safe, and settling into new living arrangements.... Their safety always has been—and always will be—our first priority," Robinson said.

To those residents and family members who knew what happened, however, Oakmont's statements only raised more questions about what happened—and fed a growing outrage.

One Week Later

Although Oakmont Senior Living claimed the evacuations were orderly and all residents were doing well, the physical and psychological toll on residents, staff, family members, and first responders was beginning to come into full view, and it was extensive. Several residents, including Bess Budow and Louise Johnson, would not recover from the injuries and trauma they experienced.

The post-fire decline for Bess, who had broken her hip during the evacuation, was rapid. Given her mother's slow heart rate and low blood pressure, Sherry Minson knew hip surgery was risky, but she felt there was no choice given Bess' pain level. Sherry released physicians from liability and pushed them to operate. Even then, they had to wait. Although doctors had diagnosed Bess' broken hip on Monday, October 9, they couldn't operate until Friday, October 13. "She was in pain the whole time," Sherry said.

Bess survived the surgery, but the hospitalist said she was so weak she likely wouldn't make it through the night. Sherry and her daughter Sarah rushed to her bedside. Though she wasn't consistently lucid, Bess worked one hand out from under the blanket and pulled out her nasal cannula prongs so she could speak. "I'm in a lot of pain," she told them.

The Minsons faced a heart-wrenching decision. Giving Bess pain medication would lower her blood pressure and interfere with her heart medication; it also could kill her. But withholding medication, Sherry felt, would dishonor her mother, who had made clear in her end-of-life wishes that she didn't want to be in pain. So, bundled in winter coats because the ICU was so chilly, Sherry and Sarah sat beside Bess as the ICU nurse administered whatever pain medications she needed, each resting a hand on her to make sure she stayed swaddled up to her chin in blankets. They expected her to stop breathing at any moment.

Much to their surprise, Bess' condition improved, and she was soon moved out of ICU. A few days later, Bess was alert and talking, her cheeks rosy. Sarah shot a video of her grandmother lying in her green hospital gown. "How are you feeling, Mama?" asked Sherry, whose long hair was as white as her mother's.

"I'm feeling awful," Bess answered.

"You're still such a feisty lady," Sherry said.

Bess rallied her strength. "I love you so much also," she said. "That's all we have is each other." Bess squeezed her eyelids closed, as if holding back tears. The Minsons shared the video with Melanie Woodrow, who aired it in one of her newscasts.

About two weeks after Bess' fall, an Oakmont representative in Southern California called Sherry. "He was calling to sell a new spot" in an Oakmont facility, she said. "He didn't know she was in the hospital." A week after that, Sherry saw another incoming call from Oakmont Senior Living, this time from regional marketing director Tammy Moratto. "I was so disgusted at that point I didn't even pick up," Sherry said. These were the first calls they had received from Oakmont following the fire.

Then Bess steadily deteriorated. The hospitalist said her body had stopped processing protein and her skin was starting to break down, signaling the beginning of organ failure.

***

Louise Johnson was also on a downward spiral. Despite her dementia, Louise, who had only lived in Villa Capri's memory care for three weeks, had been lucid, healthy, and happy in her new accommodations, according to her children. She liked her room, decorated with her own oil paintings, and enjoyed pointing out the courtyard flowers in the garden to her family members. "She didn't have a care in the world," her son Eric said. He had even joked with his siblings that their mother was so healthy, her care costs would likely consume their entire inheritance. But things changed quickly after the fire.

"I saw flames coming from the back of the bus," Louise told her daughter, Jonell Jel'enedra, who was hiking on Spain's Camino de Santiago when she got word of the natural disaster back home. "I looked back, and I saw flames," her mother told her via cell phone.

Though Anett Rivas had placed a medical mask over Louise's nose and mouth during the evacuation, the life-long asthmatic had sat for roughly three hours in the smoky lobby before she was loaded onto a CityBus with Kathy Allen. She was among the last seven residents to leave the building before the Tubbs Fire consumed it. She spent the next couple of nights on an air mattress on the floor of Belmont Village.

Wanting to get her out of that situation, Louise's two oldest sons quickly wrote a check for $6,000 to secure permanent accommodations there, ensuring she didn't need to move again. Located on an urban city block, Belmont Village wasn't as fancy as Villa Capri, but, according to Eric, the staff was friendly and overly accommodating if not a bit helter-skelter, having to merge employees from Santa Rosa with those from Belmont.

From the first time Eric visited with Louise after the fire, he was concerned about her health. Despite her Lewy body dementia, which left Louise hallucinating that she had 15 children under her care, she previously had no problem recognizing him. This time was different. When Eric first arrived, he told her he was moving a bed and other supplies into her new room, at which point Louise went off to an art class. Thirty minutes later, Eric spotted her painting a daisy in a recreation room with 10 other residents. "She stared at me for 10 seconds before she realized who I was," he said.

"Oh, Eric, what are you doing here?" she asked in surprise.

His mother did not look well. "She had this pallor to her that she didn't have at Villa Capri," he said. "Her skin was gray. Her whole complexion had turned ashen." The quality of her artwork also had fallen precipitously. "She's an accomplished artist. The art project she was doing looked like something a 4-year-old would do." His mother's worsening condition frightened him. "She was 90 percent there two weeks earlier. At Belmont, she was like 20 percent," he said.

He called his brother Craig. "Mom has regressed tremendously," he told him.

Two days later, Craig called Eric with news. Louise had developed a bad case of the flu and was dehydrated. Belmont Village was sending her to the hospital. From there, Louise's condition rapidly deteriorated. Within a day she was on a ventilator. Eric and Craig had a long conversation and made the painful decision to remove life support. Louise died at 6:37 p.m. October 23, exactly two weeks after the fire. She was 87.

"We were very surprised actually," Craig said. "It was sudden. She was healthy, and then she was not. She was fine. Then the fire. She was transferred here, there, and everywhere. And then she died."

October 17: Excavation

For reasons that defy explanation, some houses were spared the wrath of Tubbs, but these were few and scattered far between. Although the loss for most was absolute, the urge among victims to sift through the remains to find anything that may have survived the intense heat was strong and immediate. Local Boy Scout troops built and donated hundreds of sifter boxes for residents to use to comb through the debris. In the days and weeks to follow, newspapers, TV, and radio stations captured emotion-packed stories of treasured keepsakes—wedding rings, coins, Christmas ornaments, jewelry, and sundry other items—pulled from the ruins. But before they could begin their searches, they had to wait many days and, in some cases, several weeks before authorities allowed them to access their properties.

Several Villa Capri residents and family members say they received promises from Oakmont staff that they, too, would have a chance to search through the remains of their apartments. Beth was eager to look for her mother's heirloom jewels. Nell Magnuson was hoping to find pieces of her international jewelry collection. Henrietta Hillman's son Corky planned to sift for pieces of his mom's $100,000 pewter collection. Ruthie Kurpinsky and her brothers hoped to find what remained of Ruth Callen's beloved lamp, Lydia. "I doubt it would have burned," Ruth's daughter Ruthie said. "We made a joke, 'We'll go get Lydia.'" But none of them got the chance.

As the Tubbs Fire continued to burn and vast stretches of Santa Rosa, including Fountaingrove, remained under mandatory evacuation orders, Oakmont Senior Living and a local contractor made daily site visits and, within a week, were able to get excavators and dump trucks past the barricades to begin clearing the Villa Capri site. How they did so remains something of a mystery, given that only police, firefighters, utility crews, and members of the media were allowed past the checkpoints at the time.

"This is still a very dangerous event," Sonoma County Sheriff Rob Giordano pleaded at a press briefing at the Santa Rosa Fairgrounds on Friday, October 13. Some 28,000 customers in Sonoma County were still without gas and power service, and earlier that day, fire crews had evacuated the Alexander Valley due to new fire threats. "I'm hearing a lot of people asking why they can't go back into their homes," Giordano said. He explained that utilities and other crews were working to restore utility services and making sure the areas were safe. "I really want to impress upon people, please stay out of the evacuation zones," he said. "Stay out of the burned areas. It's still extremely dangerous there."

Search and rescue teams and firefighters continued to comb through the ruins of Fountaingrove searching for fire victims as well as hot spots that could reignite the blaze.

Law enforcement officials were strict about the rules concerning access. As evidence, on October 17, two Santa Rosa brothers were arrested, and later charged, for bypassing the barricades in an attempt to walk to their mother's burned Fountaingrove home just a mile from Villa Capri. The men, who had hoped to begin searching for treasured items from their late father who lived in Germany and Poland through World War II, later pleaded no contest to illegally entering a disaster zone and were forced to serve two to three years probation and complete up to 180 hours of community service.

But the situation was different at the Villa Capri site. The same day police arrested the brothers, crews operating three large excavators, which had somehow arrived the day before, began demolition and excavation work. It was an unusual sight, so odd that word soon spread. At 3 p.m. on Wednesday, October 18, Santa Rosa Police Officer Michael Heiser received a call from a police sergeant assigned to the Sonoma County Emergency Operations Center asking about the construction activity occurring at the Varenna site. "There should be no construction activity occurring in the burn zone, as it was still restricted access," the sergeant emphasized.

Heiser, accompanied by other officers, went to check it out and found "several pieces of heavy equipment actively clearing the burned building site," he wrote in his investigation report. Officer Hector De Leon said he could see "at least one large cement slab was almost completely cleared off," and that "numerous pieces of heavy equipment and several equipment operators" were present.

Soon after, Santa Rosa Police Department's Lt. Michael Lazzarini and Sgt. Josh Ludtke arrived to halt the excavation work, saying Oakmont Senior Living and its contractor lacked the proper permits. They also said Oakmont was having the work done before the ruins had been searched for bodies and toxic materials. After learning that Oakmont's contractors had already removed most of the debris, Sgt. Ludtke directed Officer De Leon to drive to the dump site in Petaluma to determine what happened "and to make sure [the debris] was not processed or removed from there," according to De Leon.

Lazzarini noted in his report news stories alleging the facility had abandoned residents during the Tubbs Fire. "However, it was unclear from a law enforcement perspective [whether] people were in the building at the time fire destroyed it," he wrote. "The area had not been cleared by search and rescue teams sweeping the disaster zone."

Lazzarini questioned David Hunter, the director of construction for Oakmont Senior Living Construction, "regarding his awareness and certainty that no one was deceased in the building before his crews began" demolition and debris removal. "Hunter told me that it didn't matter if a corpse was in the building or in a dumpster at the dump site off Shiloh Road, because a corpse was a corpse," Lazzarini wrote. Ludtke provided precisely the same quote by Hunter in his own written account of what happened.

According to Lazzarini, Hunter "was adamant" that he had obtained permits for the removal, transportation, and storage of the debris, "which he admitted was likely hazardous waste. However [he] did not have proof of such permits in his possession, nor did he say he could furnish that proof," Lazzarini wrote. "I warned Hunter that he would be subject to arrest if he entered the property before it was cleared by officials with the City of Santa Rosa and County of Sonoma," Lazzarini wrote. "Fire Marshal [Scott] Moon and I told Hunter to cease and desist all clean up and construction [including demolition] activity on the site."

Santa Rosa police then posted National Guard troops at the entrance to the Fountaingrove property. Before leaving, Ludtke requested a list of all Villa Capri occupants "including staff and residents as well as any information as to where they were relocated and contacts to check the status of the occupants." Later that afternoon, Crystal Robinson, vice president of sales and marketing for Oakmont Management Group, sent Hunter a roster of residents in an email saying, "We have spoken to each one of these families multiple times throughout the week." Hunter forwarded the list to Ludtke that day.

However, city investigators soon discovered there wasn't much that could be done. Oakmont's contractor had already carted most of the debris away. Rather than search through what had been dumped at the disposal site, the police instead worked off the roster of residents and employees to ensure that everyone had been accounted for. Once assured, the National Guard troops were reassigned, and Oakmont was allowed to resume with "processing the debris." But the city made it clear that no further demolition work would be allowed without proper permits.

Hunter would later testify that, although they tried, neither he nor their contractor, M&M Services, ever found a single item or remnant of personal property during their sorting process. Residents and their family members, as well as community members, were outraged.

"It was also quite upsetting for us to learn, through the newspaper, that within days of the fire, Villa Capri unlawfully crossed the security barriers, began clearing their lot, and that the [police were] being sent to the disposal site to make sure they were not hiding bodies or any other evidence," Dawn Ross said. When Dawn and her family were finally allowed back into their own neighborhood, they didn't want to sift through all the ash on their property. Instead, each family member chose one thing they hoped to retrieve. For Dawn's partner, Jim, it was a box with his great grandparents' rings. For their son Joshua, it was a heart-shaped box with silver dollars he had collected after losing teeth as a child. Dawn hoped to find a lockbox containing cash and her mother's watch and wedding ring.

"We were each able to go right back to where we thought it would be, and we each found it," Ross said. Dawn found her box inside the carcass of a file cabinet where her office had once stood. The cash had burned and the jewelry melted, but her mother's diamond was intact. "I had it made into a necklace," she said.

When residents received clearance to return to Fountaingrove, they drove by Villa Capri, but Oakmont's private security guards blocked their entrance and refused to allow them access—even after they explained that their parents were residents. Other family members, including Mark Allen and Jessica Kilcullen, had similar experiences, noting that guards were abrasive. Among those who tried to see the site was the family of Ruth Callen, who didn't have insurance for her lost possessions. Unlike most of her friends at Villa Capri, Ruth wasn't wealthy. So once it had burned, she needed help replacing everything. But to process her claim, FEMA told her someone from the agency would need to see the fire-damaged site for themselves. A FEMA representative agreed to meet her daughter, Ruthie, outside the front gate of Villa Capri, but a security guard prevented them from entering. "I was in shock," Ruthie said. "It was all clear and covered with tarps." According to Ruthie, the FEMA representative was also surprised that the site had been cleared considering that, at the time, nearly 90 Sonoma County residents were still on a missing persons list.

Few family members of Villa Capri residents were more angered than Joey Horsman. His home on Crown Hill Drive, just a mile from Villa Capri, had also burned. But he had hired a local gun company to help him recover a gun safe he kept at the residence. They were able to open it there, and he salvaged some guns inside, Horsman said. In his duties, he also accompanied National Guard troops to other sites where they had found safes. "I would go out with a platoon of anywhere from 20 to 100 National Guardsmen, and I would coordinate the search effort.... And if they located anything such as a safe, a pet, a gun, anything of value, they were to notify me."

His grandmother, Inez Glynn, had a safe in her Villa Capri apartment, and Horsman told Villa Capri Marketing Director Roberta Murray and Executive Director Debie Smith that he wanted to search for that as well. Inez had grown up in Germany and immigrated to the United States after World War II. Among her life's tragedies, she lost a 3-year-old daughter. In her safe was her deceased daughter's stuffed animal, along with a jewelry collection that included a diamond necklace. In hopes of locating the safe, Joey took pictures of the rubble during one of four visits he made to Villa Capri—the day of and after the fires. He and his wife had even poked around in the debris and found the charred remains of one resident's cat. It didn't feel right to him to dig through other people's stuff, he said in his deposition. So he waited for permission to search for Inez's belongings. A few days later, he was visiting his grandmother, who was temporarily housed in Albany, when he received a call from a fellow officer who told him he was watching excavators clear the rubble of Villa Capri. Joey raced back and tried to stop the debris removal, but he was too late. He said he spoke with a few Villa Capri managers to express "just how kind of ridiculous it had been" regarding his grandmother's safe and about them "taking everything away and not letting myself and the other residents have a chance to retrieve any salvageable things that could have been there." But Oakmont officials continued to claim that nothing from the ruins was salvageable. Joey protested to the point that company officials told him to contact Oakmont's attorney. So he contacted Christian Holland, general counsel for Oakmont Management Group, who, according to Joey, told him that the company would "sift through the debris" that had been taken off the site and videotape the process.

"I expressed to him, you know, that that wasn't the ideal situation, but I appreciated that effort," he said. Joey told Holland he was worried someone would find and keep his grandmother's diamond necklace. That was when the conversation went sideways. Holland responded that finding the necklace was unlikely because everything was in ashes. "I explained to him that, no, that's not true," Joey said. "I'd been up there. It wasn't all ashes. And that above all else, the safe—I can't even count the amount of safes that I've recovered during this fire. And I said, 'That safe is still there. It's steel. It's not going, it's not going to melt.'"

Their argument "got pretty heated" at that point. Holland later testified that Joey was "quite upset" and was "insistent and focused on those possessions. He wanted those. That was for his inheritance." Holland acknowledged he told Joey the debris removed from the site would be "sifted" and that the process would be videotaped. But instead of being "sifted" through the kind of wire mesh–lined boxes that local Boy Scouts had built, the debris was, according to Hunter, "sorted," meaning someone observed as the large sections of demolition material were removed and recyclable items were separated while the rest of the debris was shifted from one container to the next or from one truck to another. It was this process that failed to produce a single personal item or fragment.

The Santa Rosa Fire Department vowed to look into what happened, but, given the demands in the aftermath of the fire, the investigation would take seven months to complete.

One Month Later: In Pursuit of Justice

When it came to speaking out, and speaking up for others, Beth Eurotas-Steffy was a late bloomer. Very late. Admittedly timid as a child, Beth was more likely to stay indoors while her sister Gloria, born a mere 10 months before her, was out in the neighborhood. "Beth was afraid to ride a bike," Gloria said. Beth stayed much the same through her teens, preferring to play classical guitar alone in her room while her outgoing sister led a robust social life. "I didn't have any friends. I was the one no one really wanted to pick for the volleyball team," Beth said. She wasn't bullied, just ignored. "I was invisible."

While Gloria left home for college, Beth did not. She wanted to major in music, but her parents refused to pay for such a degree, so at 18, Beth moved out, living in various apartments on the San Francisco Peninsula and supporting herself with a job at the Belmont Police Department, where she worked her way up to dispatcher. She thought she might want to be an officer, but after spending six years there, she realized she wasn't cut out for it.

She followed her mother and sister to Santa Rosa, and, after working as a temporary secretary at Hewlett Packard, she discovered what she wanted—to work full-time for a stable, thriving company like HP. Beth had taken night classes at community colleges, first on the Peninsula and then at Santa Rosa Junior College, before transferring to Sonoma State University. Four nights a week, Beth worked all day at HP and then was in class until 10:45 p.m.

One day in 1990, Beth was wrapping up a long workday and preparing to transition to her student role when an HP engineer leaned over her 4-foot-high cubicle in the company's open-floor-plan office. "I hear you're going to school at night," he said, in all seriousness. "Why are you doing that? You'll only ever be a secretary."

To this day, Beth remembers it clearly. "His arms were dangling into my work area, and he said that with a smirk on his face." Inside, Beth was seething, "but being very shy and lacking self-confidence, I just kept working and did not respond. I even felt apologetic." But the moment had left its mark. "From that day forward, if I ever questioned why I was going to classes four nights a week and studying all weekend while working full-time, I only had to picture his face and hear his words, and I got back to focusing on my goal," she said.

The first order of business was to finish college. "Once I set my mind to something, I do it, but I don't always do it the easy way," she said. "I just can't quit." Seventeen years after she started college, at age 35, Beth earned a bachelor's degree in business management. And something changed in her. She felt accomplished. She went on to earn a marketing communications certificate and then completed a yearlong leadership training program in Santa Rosa. With newfound confidence, Beth's career took off at HP and its spinoff Agilent Technologies, where she worked her way from administrative positions into managerial ones. Ultimately, she became a marketing manager who created and implemented global communications programs. But her dedication had its downside. "I was a little too into my job," she admitted, but "it was important that I was well respected."

It was also important to her to give back. She wanted to let young women know they had the ability and confidence to go to college right after high school instead of following her lengthy trudge. She mentored teenage girls at two Santa Rosa high schools and counseled at-risk teenage girls through a local nonprofit before joining its board. That early work would be the start of 25 years of community service.

Beth, in her thirties and forties, had finally bloomed. Although slight of build at five feet, three inches, Beth, with her shoulder-length brown hair and disarming smile, had become a force in the community. "She is strong, tenacious now; bull-by-the-horns when she wants to fight for justice," Gloria said.

That bullfighter emerged the moment Beth watched Melanie Woodrow's October 16 news report in which Kathy and Mark Allen told how they had helped save Villa Capri residents. Their story matched Alice's unbelievable tale of Helen Allen's son waking her and his wife helping her descend the stairs. The pieces were there. She just needed to start bringing them together.

"I wanted to find the people who risked their lives to save the last 24 people," Beth said. As she scoured Facebook and Google, more news unfolded. Beth followed reports of the state DSS investigations into three of Oakmont Senior Living's Santa Rosa facilities. She was horrified by the video of a hospitalized Bess Budow in agony. The more she learned, the more concerned she grew. But it was the *Press Democrat*'s article about the investigation into Oakmont Senior Living's clearing of Villa Capri's debris without a permit that spurred her into action. "That was when I just lost it," she said.

Near the end of each of the three conversations Beth had with Marketing Director Roberta Murray and Regional Marketing Director Tammy Moratto, she had asked about the Villa Capri site and insisted she wanted to comb through the ashes to see what she could find of her mother's heirlooms. "Each time they said that they will have someone on their team carefully go through all of the ashes/remains and collect all that they find and then contact all residents, including me, to have us come to a certain location to identify what is ours," Beth said. "When I pressed them and said I really want to do it myself, they said it was too dangerous for me to do it, that it is toxic." They would even go into detail about the process that would be used to go through the ashes, Beth said. "They said it will be very organized and to please trust that they will do a very careful job and find all that they could find, as if it was their own family heirlooms they were looking for."

Thus she was crushed and angered when she learned that didn't happen, and that nothing, not a single item, was found. The bullfighter was enraged. Beth sprang into action, and having retired two years earlier, she could devote as much time as necessary to the cause. She started by posting a message October 27 in a newly formed Santa Rosa firestorm group on Facebook.

> *Looking for Mark and Kathy Allen, the couple who helped evacuate Villa Capri residents. Sure seems they saved many lives, including my Mom. Want to thank them.*

A friend of the Allens saw the post and put them in contact. Beth first connected with Mark by phone and then met Kathy in person at a coffee shop where, at first sight, they hugged for an extended period. Beth thanked Kathy profusely, to the point of embarrassment.

"Please don't thank me so much," Kathy pleaded. "I just did what you would have done."

But Beth had not rushed to Villa Capri, and as she listened to Kathy's story, learning for the first time about Melissa Langhals' heroics, she realized that by the time she and Gloria were awake and texting, Kathy and Melissa had already broken through the glass front door and were ushering residents out of a burning building.

It had been Beth's idea for Alice to move into assisted living. Beth had chosen Villa Capri because it was closer to her home, and she had coaxed and prodded Alice into going. "I should have asked 'What's your plan for emergencies?' I should have done more due diligence up front." Now her mother was getting shuffled from one temporary home to another. Although Alice maintained a tough "shit happens" outer shell, Beth knew she was hurting on the inside.

Beth took notes of the Allens' accounts, recorded Alice retelling her experience, and wrote a numbered list.

1. *There was not an evacuation plan for Villa Capri.*
2. *The Allens were told the executive director (Debie) was on her way, and she never showed up.*
3. *The employees did not know where the keys to the buses were.*
4. *At least two of the three employees left. Details are sketchy.*

Armed with those four facts, Beth charged in two directions at once. First, she contacted the Community Care Licensing Division, the local office of the state DSS that oversaw complaints about senior living residences. She connected with Carla Nuti-Martinez, the licensing program manager, whom she would continue to press for information, refer sources to, and pressure for action.

The same day she also sent an email to Kathryn Stebner, the elder law attorney she'd seen in one of Woodrow's broadcasts and offered to help connect Stebner with more victims. Stebner returned her call, and around the one-month anniversary of the fire, Beth traveled to a Windsor coffee shop to meet her.

As she walked up, Beth recognized Stebner's spiky salt-and-pepper hair from TV. At that moment, Stebner was talking with Melissa Langhals, whose natural blonde hair had begun turning gray immediately after the fire.

Beth hugged Melissa. "I think you may have saved my mom's life," she told her.

Over the course of the hour get-together, Beth was impressed by Stebner; she had been fighting for seniors' rights since 1987, and Stebner was outraged by what she'd heard about how the senior residents and their families had been treated during and after the Tubbs Fire. *We have a savior*, Beth thought. *Someone who's going to help us get justice and accountability for the victims.* To

Beth, justice and accountability meant three things. "I wanted [Oakmont] to admit fault, and I wanted them to be forced to tell the truth and be forced to make changes so it wouldn't happen again," she said.

Beginning in early November, as state social services investigators dug into the case and began interviewing witnesses, and as Stebner began collecting plaintiffs, Beth was in full fighting mode. And like the self-supporting 17-year night school student, she would not back down.

Meanwhile, Kathy and Melissa were wrestling with themselves, questioning their own actions during the night of the fire, and struggling with images they could not forget. "[Melissa] cried a lot. A lot. And just seemed to lose faith and motivation. It was really hard on her," her partner, Roxanne Campbell, said. Suffering from depression, Melissa could not talk about that night without tearing up. "I'm pretty sure I should have been going to therapy," she said. "But I figured everyday life would just help me get through it. I never want to go through anything like that again. That was horrible, horrendous, and if it hadn't been for my mother and me, leaving her there last, I would have just grabbed her and left probably like everybody else."

Kathy, exhausted from the round-the-clock care of her mother-in-law, could not stop reliving October 9. "I play it over and over in my head, usually at night, and I'd wake up thinking about it," she said. "It took a long time to stop doing that. I kept thinking what I should have done." She questioned why she, the daughter of a San Francisco fire battalion chief, didn't know more. Why, for example, did they load the short bus and van with residents who could walk instead of those in wheelchairs? "We left the difficult people for last. That was not smart," she said. Her postmortem spanned from larger issues to the petty. For example, one man had asked her to retrieve his glasses, but she wasn't able to. "Why didn't I go back?" she asked herself. "I know, I didn't have time. But I still beat myself up."

She also worried about her demeanor during the rescue. "I felt like I was being mean all night, pushing people around," she said. "The lady with the amputated leg—her [prosthetic] leg came off. I just threw it down the stairs because I knew I'd get it. I hope those people weren't traumatized because I was mean to them."

The Allens' son Michael said his parents didn't want to talk about what happened on October 9. "It's not like they're out there promoting what they did," he said. "I think it was a genuinely traumatic experience. They were doing what they felt were the best options at the time."

The what-ifs were not reserved for the family members who risked their lives ferrying residents off the hill. Vivian Flowers said she spent a good amount of time crying and feeling guilty that she didn't go rescue her mother, Viola Sodini. In hindsight, she wished she had just driven around the barricades.

And Gena Jacob, who alerted Villa Capri employees that the fire was headed their way around 1:45 a.m. when she picked up her father, had since learned that she was wrong to assume higher-ups were orchestrating an orderly evacuation.

"I was disgusted that families couldn't be there to get their own mothers or fathers, and they had to go through what they went through," Gena said. "Why are we paying the big dollars to have our parents in these places if they are not going to be protected?"

Her wife, Sheri, tried to relieve Gena's guilt that she left Villa Capri taking only her father. "I know you," she told Gina. "If you would have known people weren't going to be there, you would have stayed and risked your life."

***

The three Villa Capri caregivers who helped with the evacuations also struggled in the months that followed. All three had trouble sleeping; nightmares and tears filled Elizabeth Lopez's attempts to get much-needed rest between her multiple jobs and single parenting.

Elizabeth called Anett Rivas after the November 22 birth of her daughter, Maya, and the pair processed what they'd been through. "It was a crazy night. It was bad," Anett said. But that didn't stop the former coworkers from doing their own second-guessing. "Maybe if we would've known exactly where the bus keys were, we could've moved the residents ourselves," Elizabeth said. "If we started evacuating sooner, maybe it would be a lot better. Maybe if we had a supervisor/manager on board, it would have been a lot better."

All three Villa Capri caregivers felt especially angry toward Debie Smith. "I honestly think once Marie made the first phone call, [Debie] should have been there, no matter what," Elizabeth said.

Cynthia Arroyo read news reports that police said they didn't stop anyone from going and helping. "Why didn't Debie end up showing up? If Joel made it up the hill, and all these family members made it up the hill, why didn't she make it?... It would have been nice to have her as our backbone," she said. "Or at least the Gallahers, the ones who actually own the damn place."

***

Former Varenna maintenance worker Michael Rodriguez often dreamt he was back inside Varenna, sometimes looking for his friend Andre Blakely. In other dreams, he was just looking for a way out of the complex. "I'd wake up in hysteria, freaked out, heart beating," he said. Michael visited a therapist and "bawled out" during a few of the sessions. "I got it out for a couple of weeks, and then the nightmares reoccurred," he said. "Sometimes I get antsy before bed because I'm worried that I will relive that nightmare." He was also tormented by the memory of leaving Andre behind and then hearing him on the errant cell phone call pleading with Edel Burton to help him "or we are both going to die here."

"I apologized to Andre for months," said Michael. "He told me I did all I could."

Finding peace would be a slow process, for both of them. For a long time, Andre would wake at 2:30 a.m. "And if I smelled smoke, I would get panicky," he said. He also worried about Edel. Her relatives had picked up her dog, Abigail, from his house on October 10 and "forced Andre to take $100 as a small token of our deep appreciation," Edel's relative B.M. said. About three weeks later, Andre's wife told him he had received mail from Utah. Inside was a check for $1,500 and a card that read: "We'd like to thank you for your heroic act of saving our sister the night of the fire." Edel lived with her relative B.M. as her bruises healed. She and her family agreed that she could not return to Varenna. However, when B.M. called to arrange a time to pack Edel's possessions, Varenna staff told her Edel would have to wait until residents could move back into their still-evacuated apartments.

"We said, 'Fine, and we will tell every resident we see what happened,'" B.M. recalled. "They said, 'How about next week?'"

November 20, 2017: Allegations of Abandonment, Elder Abuse

Though Beth was the one who first met with Kathryn Stebner and began actively recruiting families to participate in a class action lawsuit, it was Kathy Allen who ultimately convinced the elder law attorney to take the case. "I just heard her story," Stebner said. "The fact that she was so brave in what she did. And then when I met Melissa, I'm like, 'I'm doing this.' No one's ever done a case like this."

Stebner was already familiar with the company, having just filed a civil action against Oakmont Management Group in September regarding billing and staffing policies. Six weeks after the fire, Stebner and Associates filed the first claim regarding the botched fire evacuations in Sonoma County Superior Court on behalf of four residents—Bess Budow, Helen Allen, Virginia Gunn, and Alice Eurotas—and two family members, Beth Eurotas-Steffy and Mark Allen. The lawsuit accused the owners and operators of Villa Capri of elder abuse, negligence, false imprisonment, and emotional distress, claiming they subjected residents "to a foreseeable risk of harm, and did in fact cause them to be seriously injured, by its policy and practice of failing to adequately staff its facilities and develop and implement an adequate emergency evacuation plan before and during the Tubbs Fire on October 9, 2017."

The crux of the case, and the point that drew widespread media attention, was the allegation that Villa Capri staff had abandoned residents. The lawsuit claimed that as the fire approached, staff members did not evacuate any of the residents and waited for an executive director who never arrived. Two hours later, as the building filled with smoke, employees, with the help of family members, ferried some residents to safety. "But Defendants abandoned at least a third of the residents, including Alice Eurotas, Virginia Gunn, Helen Allen, and Elizabeth Budow, other residents in wheelchairs, and other residents with dementia who were physically and cognitively incapable of escaping a burning building without assistance." The residents survived, the lawsuit stated, only because of the "herculean efforts" of family members. The suit also accused the Villa Capri owners of "false promise," negligence, and emotional distress related to the removal of the fire debris, which gave Beth standing to join the lawsuit. It claimed the company razed Villa Capri without the proper permits and without warning residents or family members or giving them an opportunity to see if their belongings had survived. "Instead, Defendants carelessly dumped Plaintiffs' and other Villa Capri residents' personal property, including irreplaceable heirlooms, photographs and jewelry, in the landfill," it stated.

The civil suit also delved into the nuts and bolts of California's health and safety codes for licensed residential care facilities for the elderly and claimed Villa Capri had violated codes regarding emergency plans, fire drills, staffing, and training.

For example, California Health and Safety Code requires residential care facilities to have a written disaster and mass casualty plan that must include a fire safety plan, transportation plan, relocation sites that can provide temporary accommodations, supervision of residents during an evacuation or relocation, and a way to contact emergency responders. One clause of the code specifically states that "persons providing night supervision from 10 p.m. to 6 a.m. shall be familiar with the facility's planned emergency procedures."

The lawsuit claimed Oakmont management didn't properly hire or train enough staff or develop and implement evacuation procedures. It also alleged that because Bess Budow and Virginia Gunn were bedbound and dependent on others to perform all daily living activities, they shouldn't have even been allowed to reside at Villa Capri without the required waivers from the state. Bess Budow was the only plaintiff to also sue for the care she received prior to the fire. "Defendants were responsible for meeting the basic needs of Elizabeth Budow, but Defendants knowingly did not have enough staff at Villa Capri to ensure that she was monitored and provided with the treatment she needed," the lawsuit stated. Once Bess became nonambulatory, Villa Capri managers knew or should have known they couldn't provide her with the required care, "yet they recklessly continued to retain her as a resident to continue collecting payment."

For Stebner, everything came down to staffing. "When you've been doing this for a really long time," Stebner said, referencing her 30-year career in elder rights law, "It's the staffing, stupid. Because if you don't have enough people, I mean, bad things happen."

ABC7 News reporter Melanie Woodrow and *Press Democrat* reporter Bill Swindell both filed reports about the lawsuit on November 20, the day Stebner filed the suit, with headlines that included the words "elder abuse," "negligence," and "abandoned." The *Los Angeles Times* quickly followed with "Lawsuit accuses Santa Rosa senior home of abandoning residents as wildfire approached."

December 2017: Three Deaths

Three weeks after the trauma of the fire, Bess Budow's organs were failing, and she was no longer a candidate for assisted living or a nursing home. On November 1, the Minsons moved her into a small board and care home with a hospice connection on the San Francisco Peninsula. Bess' skin, an organ itself, was opening into painful sores. Sherry told the hospice nurse to give her mother as much pain medication as she could withstand.

With her personal caregiver, Sherry, or Sarah by her side around the clock, Bess continued to decline. When Sherry visited on December 11, Bess' lips moved but no words came out. "I kissed her goodbye and said I'd be back tomorrow." Two hours later, Bess died.

The Minsons had Bess cremated and her remains tucked into the grave of her husband, Norman Budow, a World War II veteran buried in a national cemetery in Santa Fe, New Mexico.

***

Four days later, the residents of Villa Capri lost a third housemate and friend. Virginia Gunn's health declined quickly after October 9, according to her daughter and rescuer Melissa. Virginia couldn't get out of bed or even be turned at the board and care home in Rohnert Park where she had been moved, so she spent her days and nights lying on her back. "She pretty much went into herself. I couldn't hold a conversation with her," Melissa said.

While they knew Virginia was sliding, her passing was sudden. Melissa and her sister had decorated her new room for the holidays. They were on their way to visit on December 15 when the care workers called to say that their mother was gone. Her death came just two months and six days after the fire. Melissa was convinced the events of that night hastened Virginia's death. "I know that 100 percent," she said. "She was doing great. She went downhill so fast after the fire."

Virginia was cremated and the family celebrated her life with balloons, flowers, and stories at Melissa's brother Carl's home in Santa Rosa. "We all knew that's how Mom wanted it to be."

***

One week later, another Villa Capri family was in mourning. Bill and Wanda Lee, who were used to having family nearby in Santa Rosa, continued to be unhappy in Albany, and it was taking its toll. Wanda maintained her hunger strike, and the family had little choice but to bring in hospice care. On December 22, Wanda took her last breaths. "She ended up dying of starvation," Dawn said. "I truly think the fire, that whole experience, was kind of the last blow."

It was also the last blow for Dawn's trust in high-end assisted living facilities. "Maybe that's how those big, beautiful places are. A lot of show. They put all their money in the facility and not in the staff or the training or the care," she said. Wanda Lee was the fourth Villa Capri resident to die within 10 weeks of the Tubbs Fire. All the families attributed the deaths to the trauma their loved ones experienced during the hasty and mismanaged evacuations.

17

Dichotomy

Art of Seduction author Robert Greene suggests a person with "an elusive, enigmatic aura" will draw people into one's inner circle and make them want to know you more. But by the same token, "The moment people feel they know what to expect from you, your spell on them is broken." California developer William "Bill" Gallaher had maintained such an aura within the community that has known him best, the Wine Country region encompassing Sonoma County. But to call Gallaher merely enigmatic and elusive would be an understatement and something of a disservice.

As a developer of dozens of retirement communities throughout the West over more than four decades, builder of shopping complexes, founder and director of banks, and controlling partner and/or investor of an assortment of businesses from bars to country clubs to nonprofits to green energy companies to race cars and golf courses, Bill Gallaher has dedicated significant amounts of time and wealth toward his native county. If nothing else, he is a man committed to making an impact, at least on his terms. He also has seldom been shy about showing it and defending it, sometimes in unquestionably conspicuous ways. As those who know him well will attest, Gallaher is at times irascible; other times, gracious, and engaging. But he is above all else loyal—and dedicated to his work and family. But to the community at large, his aura has been that of a complex and unpredictable public figure, a native son who has shown his hometown abiding devotion and gratitude while, as a business leader, demonstrating to that same community, at times, an unyielding wrath.

Perhaps, the best example of Gallaher's dichotomous public persona was on display in 2009. That spring, budget cuts had placed the Santa Rosa High School woodshop program on the verge of elimination. One April day, as 70 students protested the cuts to passersby on the front lawn of the city's iconic high school, the set for several Hollywood movies, including *Peggy Sue Got Married*, the principal received a call on behalf of the Gallahers, offering to donate $85,000 to keep the program alive.

"I'm floating," said Santa Rosa School Board president Donna Jeye in a newspaper story the following day. She described it as "a community member stepping forward in a time of need. It's wonderful."

"I went to Santa Rosa High, and I took woodshop," Bill Gallaher told the *Press Democrat* at the time. "It was the class that saved me. I was a terrible student. I don't know how many classes that I missed in my senior year... but I made wood shop every day, and I loved it."

His benevolence was not a surprise to those who knew him well. As one former business associate noted, Bill Gallaher "grew up with a hammer in his hand." Contracting was a natural fit for Gallaher, whose career took off in 1986, when the man who started the eastern Santa Rosa retirement community known as Oakmont, due to failing health, sold the Gallahers the remaining 480 undeveloped lots to finish. Donating funds to save such programs was a familiar means of philanthropy for Gallaher, who said at the time of founding a community bank that he drew his inspiration from another well-known local business leader and benefactor, Henry Trione. The impacts of Trione's benevolence were ubiquitous in Sonoma County, none greater than the 5,000-acre Trione-Annadel State Park, on the northern edge of Sonoma Valley adjacent to Santa Rosa. Trione had spent more than $1 million to save the oak-studded mountains from becoming a housing development in the 1970s. Shortly after stepping down as a director of Sonoma National Bank to start his own banking venture in 2004, Gallaher said in an interview that he had been inspired over the years by the Trione family's success. But he didn't like talking about his own plans or ambitions, certainly not ahead of time. "It's kind of like bragging about what you're going to do," he said. "I don't like doing that at all. I'd rather do the thing and let it speak for itself."

For Gallaher, those declarations came in many forms. In 1990, Bill and Cindy founded North Bay Adoptions, a nonprofit international adoption agency based in Santa Rosa that within five years had helped place more than 300 children in Sonoma County homes. In 1996, they supported

Santa Rosa's Sister City program by joining Mayor Sharon Wright and a delegation of other community residents in making a trip to the city's newest "sister city" in Pak Cheju, an island community 100 miles off the southern tip of South Korea. With both causes, there was a personal connection. Bill and Cindy adopted three of their five children from foreign countries: Korea, Peru, and Vietnam.

"There's a very endearing side to him," said Doug Bosco, a lawyer and businessman who represented Sonoma County in the state Assembly and, later, Congress from 1978 to 1991. He had come to know Bill Gallaher when Boscoe sought $10 million in start-up financing from Community National Bank, later renamed Poppy Bank, for Sonoma Clean Power, a government agency that allows county residents and businesses more say in the sources of their electricity. According to Bosco, Gallaher didn't hesitate in supporting the venture and, as a result, received a Leadership Sustainability Award from the Santa Rosa-based Leadership Institute for Ecology and the Economy in 2013. "He's a rogue," said Bosco. "He likes being a rogue in some ways. But he's done some amazing things for the community." Bosco was later invited to join the Community Bank board where he developed deep respect for Gallaher's business acumen, especially with financial matters. "I think he could run any corporation," Bosco said. But he acknowledged that Gallaher has another side, one that would go to great lengths to correct perceived injustices or what he sees as a misuse of taxpayer funds. "It's a take-no-prisoners approach," Bosco said candidly. "You wouldn't want to be on his bad side."

Even as their network of business holdings grew, the Gallahers maintained family connections in just about all their pursuits. All five of the Gallaher children had ownership and/or management positions in many of Gallaher's 57 active businesses, but no one has been as closely tied to the family businesses as their eldest, Molly Gallaher Flater. With financial support from her father, Molly, at age 22, partnered in 2006 with her boyfriend to open a bar known as Upper Fourth. Equipped with posh interior trappings and an onyx bar, the tavern, commanding a prime location in downtown Santa Rosa, proved to be a popular gathering spot for the 20- to 30-something crowd in Sonoma County. But with little notice, the bar suddenly closed in September 2009, and all employees were let go. At the time, Molly Gallaher Flater told the *Press Democrat* that the closure was not based on economics but because of "new opportunities." Namely, she had secured a job through her parents at an Oakmont retirement community in Palm Desert.

In early 2017, Molly, again with support from her family, started another venture, Blue Gate Bank. As with First Community Bank, Blue Gate had quick initial success, reporting $145 million in assets within 12 months. Nonetheless, the enterprise was short-lived. In 2018, Poppy Bank's holding company acquired Blue Gate for an undisclosed price. At that point, Molly took a seat on the Poppy Bank board with her father, the chairman who held controlling interest, and his brother Patrick Gallaher, who owned stock in Poppy along with his wife, Joan. Molly also took on new roles and responsibilities within Gallaher's other holdings. By 2021, she was serving as the CEO of Gallaher Homes Management Group and COO of Gallaher Companies, where she oversaw the companies' senior living, multifamily, and commercial portfolios. In addition, she also was a part owner of Gallaher continuing care communities in Redding, Fair Oaks, and Orange.

Close family friends and employees also assumed ownership positions. Among them was Komron Shahhosseini, who, according to Bill Gallaher, came to know the family through a personal relationship with one of Gallaher's daughters and became a trusted member of the family business soon after. In April 2019, Shahhosseini, promoted to regional director of site acquisitions and development at Oakmont Senior Living and Gallaher Companies and was a founder and board member of Blue Gate Bank, joined the board of Poppy Bank. Shahhosseini also was a part owner of the Gallaher continuing care communities in Redding, Fair Oaks, and Santa Clarita, as well as the Canyon Oaks Apartments. In 2009, Supervisor Shirlee Zane appointed Shahhosseini to the Sonoma County Planning Commission, where he served for more than 12 years and became a lightning rod for controversy surrounding Gallaher's and Oakmont Senior Living's broad political influence surrounding local development decisions.

Bill Gallaher led an assortment of other deeply rooted family businesses as well. By the age of 18, Gallaher's son Will began racing in F1600 Formula cars, competing at tracks along the West Coast. He then moved into the United Auto Racing Association. Around that same time, Gallaher's other son, Marco, also began racing, but with the Sports Car Club of America. During this time, the family founded Gallaher Brothers Motor Sports LLC, designating each member of the family, including the five children, as part owners.

However, within a few months of the Gallahers saving the woodshop program at Santa Rosa High School in 2009, the community would see another side to the family man and community benefactor. Locals bore witness to the resentment and provocation of a developer whose views on housing development were clashing with a region that had taken an abrupt shift at the end of the 20th century away from the sprawl-inducing land-use practices that had dominated much of California for generations. In short, Gallaher's hometown was changing, and it was no longer as welcoming to his projects as it once was. Sonoma County voters demanded policies that protected open space areas, provided green "buffers" between developed communities, and prevented developments on ridgelines and watersheds in favor of city-centered, transit-oriented development. And they were electing public officials who would pledge to defend these policies. On top of that, the Great Recession had taken its toll on the North Bay as it had on the rest of the nation, with its deepest impacts felt in the housing and development sectors. However, in July 2009, when Gallaher laid off seven of 18 employees at Oakmont Senior Living, he didn't blame the economy. He blamed the city.

"I held off laying people off as long as I could," Gallaher told the *Press Democrat*. "It's directly related to the projects in Santa Rosa." In particular, he criticized city planners who were holding up approval of two of his planned housing developments. One was the 142-unit Fountaingrove Lodge project he had first proposed five years earlier for a site just down the hill from the recently opened Varenna campus. The other was a larger 200-unit Elnoka Village condominium complex near the retirement community of Oakmont, a project that had been in planning for more than four years. "We're tired of it," Gallaher said. "We're tired of being kicked in the teeth."

By then, Gallaher had built nearly 1,000 homes in Sonoma County, including 650 houses for senior citizens in eastern Santa Rosa's Oakmont neighborhood and in Windsor. In addition, Aegis Assisted Living was operating nearly three dozen senior care facilities in California, Washington, and Nevada. But Gallaher was having misgivings about Sonoma County. "I really made a tactical business error when I bought so much property around here," Gallaher told the *Press Democrat* in that same 2009 interview. Despite the setbacks, he made clear that he was committed to finishing what he had set out to do. "I'm too ornery to give up," he said. "They've met their match with me."

In an interview with *North Bay Biz* magazine in November 2009, Gallaher complained again about the difficulties of getting his 63-acre Elnoka Village project approved in Santa Rosa. "I could do three projects in Palm Desert in the same amount of time it takes to do one in Santa Rosa—and accomplish much more without the hassle," Gallaher said. In the story, Gallaher, a third-generation Santa Rosa resident, once again threatened to sever ties with his hometown. "We're done sugar-coating it," he said. "We've worked and worked and tried to do it, but it's an endless, endless road. There's always a new study that needs to be conducted or an application that has to be resubmitted." He made clear that Cindy Gallaher shared his growing antipathy with local planners. "My wife says I'm out of my mind," he continued. "But we won't buy more property here. I don't want any part of that. If anyone asks me, I warn them not to come here. I hate to say that, because it's my hometown."

City officials offered a different perspective. According to Chuck Regalia, director of community development for Santa Rosa, Oakmont Senior Living had twice withdrawn its development permit applications for Elnoka Village, which brought a halt to all city work on reviewing the project, only to have the process started again later when the plans were resubmitted. "They must be willing to meet us at least halfway," Regalia said. "Successful projects have a good idea, combined with a good staff that stays engaged in the process and is able to be there when decisions must be made."

So far, he said, he had not seen that from Oakmont Senior Living.

***

Whether it was in response to his growing frustration with evolving land-use regulation or not, records show Gallaher and his family began to take a more active role in local political campaigns. When former Santa Rosa

Mayor Sharon Wright, a one-time employee of Oakmont Senior Living and an ally of pro-development interests, ran for the Sonoma County Board of Supervisors in 2008, Bill Gallaher gave her $1,000, the spending limit at the time. So did Cindy Gallaher. So did Steven Gallaher, Bill's brother, a builder with OSL Construction. So did Bill's other brother, Patrick, and Patrick's wife, Joan Anne Gallaher. Keith Fitzsimons, OSL vice president, also gave $1,000, as did Joseph Lin, CFO of OSL; Stephen McCullagh, project manager at OSL, and Komron Shahhosseini.

When Wright made it to a runoff for the November general election, where individual spending limits increased to $2,500, Bill and Cindy Gallaher gave another $5,000. In the end, however, Wright, who was heavily supported by the construction industry, lost to Shirlee Zane, who received the bulk of her financial support from labor unions. Although the clash between business and labor sentiments was not new, it had become amplified with the election of slow-growth majorities on city councils in cities such as Santa Rosa and Petaluma that year. Going forward, the involvement of Gallaher, his family, and his business associates in political campaigns seemed to only accelerate.

In August 2014, Windsor Town Councilwoman Deb Fudge came under fire for voting to approve Gallaher's requested changes to his Bell Village development, one of the largest mixed-use projects ever proposed in her town just north of Santa Rosa. While running for a county Board of Supervisors seat, Fudge had received an $11,000 donation from Bill and Cindy Gallaher. That year, Gallaher's political activity spread to ballot measures as well. In October, Gallaher and his family members contributed $35,000 to defeat a Santa Rosa measure to raise city revenue by extending a utility tax to include cell phones. The donation was made under the name of Young Hoon Kim LLC, the birth name of Gallaher's adopted son, Will "Billy" Gallaher. Measure N, opposed by a number of conservative business leaders, ultimately went down in defeat. But those donations paled in comparison to what was coming in 2016 and years to follow. By 2015, Gallaher's appeal to have his Elnoka property exempted from the city's new ridgeline restrictions—rules that had been put in place, in part, due to criticism that the development of Varenna and homes in Fountaingrove had marred views from below—had run into stiff opposition from neighbors, residents of the original Oakmont neighborhood where Gallaher got his start building homes. In a letter to the city, one area resident urged Santa Rosa to block the project and avoid "another Fountaingrove fiasco."

By then, Gallaher had expanded his plans for Elnoka Village to include 475 houses and apartments inside a gated community that would include assisted-living and memory-care residents. But the city's Planning Commission vetoed his proposal. And, when he appealed, the City Council also rejected his plans.

The situation was further complicated by the fact that in early 2017, Gallaher had come in as the top bidder on a massive piece of county-owned land in Santa Rosa that once was home to the Sonoma County Hospital. He proposed building up to 800 homes on the vacated property off Chanate Road for up to $11.5 million. Gallaher, who said he and his wife once roamed the open space area as children, called the site "a rare opportunity for any developer, but particularly rare for a native of the county." Although the county owned the property, the new Santa Rosa City Council would have final say on the development because of the site's location within city limits.

This set the stage for the 2016 City Council election, which would prove to be the costliest in city history. Although Santa Rosa had a $500 cap on individual campaign donations, due to the U.S Supreme Court's 2010 *Citizens United* decision, there was no limit to the funds independent expenditure committees could spend on behalf of candidates so long as the committees reported the spending. When all was said and done, independent expenditure committees, as well as candidates, raised and spent more than $525,000 in the City Council race, all for a job that paid only $9,600 per year. What was notable was that nearly $200,000 of those funds came from a single source—a member of the Gallaher family. But even the reporting on that fact became the center of a prolonged legal battle.

With a week to go before the election, the *Press Democrat* reported on October 28, 2016, that Scott Flater, Molly Gallaher Flater's husband, had donated $130,375—the final tally would be $195,000—supporting three of the six candidates in the race. "We've talked for years about the effect of Citizens United on money in politics, and I think this is really Santa Rosa's first taste of it at the local level," said candidate Chris Rogers, who had not received Flater's support. Sonoma State University political science professor

David McCuan, an oft-quoted observer of local political campaigns, noted in one story that Gallaher had a history of "sprinkling money around" to family members "to maximize payments to—and potentially influence with—council candidates." McCuan added, "Bill Gallaher uses his family as a shell game, and has for a long time, in order to channel support to candidates of his liking."

In the end, voters elected two of the three candidates supported by Flater and the Gallaher family. But the outcome would not be the last word on the campaign. A month after the election, Bill Gallaher and Scott Flater, a 40-year-old father of four who listed himself as "homemaker" in campaign filings, sued the *Press Democrat* and McCuan for defamation. The lawsuit claimed the articles about Flater's spending and McCuan's "shell game" comments had damaged their reputations by falsely suggesting the money had come from Flater's father-in-law. Bill Gallaher flatly denied it. "Plaintiff William Gallaher has never used anyone, including family members, to make political contributions on his behalf," the suit claimed. The suggestions that funding from Gallaher's family, and specifically Flater, were actually from Gallaher himself caused "upset, embarrassment, humiliation, and anguish," the suit alleged.

An attorney for the *Press Democrat*, however, countered, arguing the paper had "fairly and accurately" reported on the source of the political contributions and had made multiple efforts to interview Flater and Gallaher, but they repeatedly refused to comment. "The *Press Democrat* will vigorously defend its reporting on this matter of significant public interest," the attorney said.

Nevertheless, the *Press Democrat* lost in its initial attempt to have the lawsuit tossed out on First Amendment grounds. The paper claimed both Bill Gallaher and Scott Flater were public figures and, thus, under established libel law, needed to prove the writer or publisher acted with "actual malice" by demonstrating a "reckless disregard for the truth." But in an unexpected turn, a superior court judge found that, indeed, Flater was a public figure, but Gallaher was not—because Flater's name and telephone number had been printed on campaign mailers purchased with the donated funds. Gallaher, despite his high profile as a developer, the chairman of First Community Bank, and operator of 25 senior living facilities in California, including four in Sonoma County, was still a private figure, the judge found. In his case, Gallaher would need to prove only that the allegedly false statements in the stories were made with ordinary negligence.

The suit accused the newspaper of acting with malice anyway, creating a showdown in the court system between the Santa Rosa builder and his hometown newspaper. Meanwhile, the lawsuit had a chilling effect inside the newsroom concerning coverage of Gallaher and his properties. In the weeks and months to come, attorneys and newsroom editors closely vetted stories, editorials, and columns concerning Gallaher, his projects, and the lawsuit itself out of concern for further litigation. The newspaper, in the end, became cautious on how it reported on Gallaher and Oakmont Senior Living and their influence in the community, a situation that grew ever more tense internally in the days to come surrounding coverage of what happened at Villa Capri and Varenna on October 9 and the controversies that followed.

This was not the first time that Gallaher had pursued legal action against critics. In 1998, two retired homeowners of the 200-unit Brooks Creek retirement community in Windsor submitted a complaint to the Sonoma County Grand Jury claiming their homes, built by Gallaher's company, had code violations and that the city had failed to ensure they were properly inspected. One owner claimed his fireplace had been installed improperly, while another, a former building official, said the incorrect installation of clothes dryer vents posed a fire hazard. The Sonoma County Grand Jury investigated and concluded that the Windsor building department needed to look into the allegations, toughen its inspections program, and improve how it responded to citizen complaints. The town soon hired an outside expert to inspect the homes. Gallaher Construction, however, responded by filing a $4 million libel suit against the two retirees, claiming they had defamed the company by suggesting it had built unsafe houses. The company also accused the two men of trespassing and secured a restraining order preventing them from visiting their construction sites.

"We're a couple of guys living basically on Social Security," one of the homeowners, Ed Corley, told reporters at the time.

"People may sue me for $4 million, but it isn't going to scare me one damn bit," said Ed Ellwanger, the other homeowner and former Sonoma County building inspector.

Ultimately, the company and the retirees reached an out-of-court settlement in which both sides agreed not to discuss the terms. Nonetheless, Gallaher Construction conceded to fix the problems in 52 Brooks Creek houses.

Thus, by the time the fires hit in October 2017, Gallaher was already embroiled in public controversy on several fronts, in addition to his battle over his proposed Elnoka project, his bid to develop the massive Chanate property in the heart of Santa Rosa, and his deepening involvement in local political campaigns.

Gallaher and Oakmont's track record of litigation and political activity also had become a deterrent in the willingness of many within the community to engage in public debate about Gallaher, his company, or their projects. "You have to be careful about what you say," noted one elected official who declined to speak on the record. "Gallaher has shown he has money to burn, and he's not afraid to use it."

***

Just five weeks after the fire, Gallaher and Flater faced a setback in their defamation suit against the local newspaper. In an extraordinary twist, a former general counsel for Oakmont Senior Living declared that Gallaher had indeed approached key company employees offering to reimburse them for any political contributions they made "at his direction," thus contradicting the very basis of the lawsuit. Jeffrey Breithaupt, OSL's general counsel for 18 years until 2015, said in a sworn statement that it was "common" for Gallaher to make such offers for contributions to City Council and Board of Supervisors candidates. Gallaher had directed Breithaupt himself to collect the checks and deliver them to the campaigns, the attorney said.

Breithaupt acknowledged that he personally had made contributions at Gallaher's request on several occasions and that, each time, Gallaher had reimbursed him with a check from his personal account.

Given that Gallaher and Flater had claimed their reputations had been damaged by the suggestion that Flater's political donations may have come from Gallaher himself, the attorney for David McCuan called on them to dismiss the matter. "There are too many far more important things going on in Sonoma County for Mr. Gallaher to continue this lawsuit," the attorney, Karl Olson, said.

But Gallaher and Flater didn't back down. They pressed ahead with the case, which by then had been elevated to the state appellate court in San Francisco.

18

Investigation

Early 2018, Lawsuit Adds Plaintiffs

The complexity and trajectory of the lawsuit by Villa Capri residents and family members changed significantly in the early months of 2018. After Virginia Gunn and Bess Budow died, attorney Kathryn Stebner added wrongful death allegations to the civil claim and expanded the plaintiff list to include both women's heirs: Melissa Langhals and her three siblings; and Bess' daughter Sherry Minson. Sherry and her daughter Sarah had heard of Stebner's pre-fire September class action lawsuit but were initially worried Bess would lose her apartment at Villa Capri if she signed on, so they opted out. After Bess died, Sherry wanted to see Oakmont brought to justice.

These were not the only additions. Four other residents signed on as well. Ruth Callen's firefighter sons felt it was the only way to force change. For her daughter Ruthie Kurpinsky, encouraging Ruth to join the lawsuit boiled down to two things. "I asked my mom if there was ever a fire drill, an actual fire drill. She said, 'We never had a fire drill.'" The second issue was the lack of generators. "I understand it's not even a state law to this day. That's a huge problem," Ruthie said.

Len Kulwiec also joined. "With the generator, we could have had the elevator working. They didn't have an evacuation plan. They never did a fire drill with the [residents]," the WWII vet said in early 2018. "I thought there was negligence." Nell and John Magnuson joined for the same reason. "They were at fault. That was gross negligence," she said. "The whole thing was a mess. They are so lucky.... If those volunteers hadn't come, I think we all would have died."

These nine new additions and the wrongful death claim were not the only notable changes. Within the amended lawsuit, Stebner called attention to a letter Oakmont Management Group officials sent on December 8 to departing Villa Capri employees, those who could not find work at another Oakmont property while they waited for Villa Capri to be rebuilt. The letter appeared to offer money for silence. Oakmont said it would give those employees one payment between $700 and $1,500 "to assist you in transitioning to new employment following the wildfire that destroyed Villa Capri." But the money came with strings attached. To get the payment, employees had to state they had no knowledge of Oakmont Management Group (OMG) breaking any local, state, or federal laws or regulations, and that if they learned of such practices, they would tell management—and no one else. Oakmont also required these employees to waive any rights to sue the company for employment rights violations. Vice President of Human Resources Karen Ellis signed the letter, and below her signature was a place for the employee to countersign, accepting the offer—and the terms.

Two employees leaked the unusual letter to Stebner. "I've never seen that before," the attorney said, asserting that some employees without job prospects might have ignored the fine print because they needed the cash. One of those employees who later said she didn't understand the letter's nuance was Elizabeth Lopez, for whom a new job at Varenna didn't pan out because of the modified night shift hours she required. Elizabeth had questions but didn't raise them. She couldn't afford to. As a single mother, she needed the money. She signed the letter and received $750 in return, the equivalent of about a week's pay.

Elizabeth was one of 20 Villa Capri employees who signed, according to Ellis in her deposition. She said amounts varied based on whether the staff was full-time, part-time, or on call. She later testified Oakmont's legal counsel wrote the letter, which she understood to be a standard severance letter, that is, until it reached the press. "I saw an ABC news story, local news, which…alleged that I had participated in some sort of hush money scheme, which was not true," Ellis said.

The news segment caused a new round of negative attention for Oakmont, and this time the company went directly to residents with a letter rebutting the "hush money" claims, instead calling their offer a "good faith gesture." It said the corporation paid all Santa Rosa Oakmont employees two weeks' salary and a bonus to those who came in to work in the two weeks after the fire. Management also distributed money to those employees who lost their homes, including $42,000 from Oakmont Senior Living ownership. Managers also claimed they tried to find jobs for displaced employees at other Oakmont facilities or with other local assisted living companies. "Employees were not required to accept the payment, and by accepting the payment, they were not being 'silenced,'" the letter stated. "To the contrary, we specifically asked departing employees to advise us of any unlawful practices or potential problems so we could address them and ensure the needs of departing employees and residents who needed alternative living arrangements were met."

The letter called the lawsuit a "set of misrepresentations" and slammed Stebner's reputation, calling her law firm "unscrupulous." It stated, "Once we have the opportunity to review the allegations, we will mount a vigorous defense against these unfounded claims." Also signed by OMG president and CEO Chris Kasulka and Varenna Executive Director Nathan Condie, the letter closed by touting the company's "extraordinary efforts to assist our employees, who we view as our most valuable asset.... Our response to the North Bay fires was driven by our genuine care and compassion for all of our employees and residents."

***

Two days after Oakmont defended itself to its customers, its attorneys filed their response to Stebner's lawsuit. In nine pages, Giovanniello Law Group attorneys Alexander Giovanniello and Paul H. Kang denied each allegation and refuted the notion that residents had been damaged "at all." These denials were not a surprise to Stebner, but their defense strategy was.

When a lawsuit is filed, the plaintiffs' attorney lays out the allegations, after which defense attorneys present their own evidence to exonerate their client or mitigate the legal consequences if their actions are proven unlawful. These sets of evidence are called "affirmative defenses," and of the 34 that Oakmont's attorneys presented to counter Stebner's allegations, eight appeared to blame the residents for not being better prepared to save themselves. They also blamed the rescuers for the injuries or damages the residents suffered. One of their affirmative defenses said the plaintiffs—residents Bess, Helen, Ruth, Len, Nell, John, and Virginia, and rescuers Melissa, Kathy, and Mark—did not conduct themselves "in a reasonable manner or as a responsible person would have" in similar circumstances. Oakmont was saying the residents and rescuers caused or contributed to their own losses, which was why nothing was Oakmont's fault.

Stebner called it victim blaming. Typically, she said, defense attorneys delete from their list of affirmative defenses any common legal arguments that don't apply to the situation at hand. She assumed the Giovanniello Law Group would decline to use the standard "it's their fault" finger-pointing because of the circumstances, "But they didn't. I never normally look at those, and then it just struck me that they are blaming the residents themselves," she said.

Oakmont's attorneys also argued that if the company was found at fault, then the court should determine the degree of responsibility of everyone involved and prorate damages accordingly. In other words, Melissa, Kathy, Mark, and even the police and firefighters should also be held liable, and they should pay too.

Those nine pages infuriated the families and rescuers alike and spurred many into action. Joey Horsman and his grandmother Inez Glynn responded by joining the suit. Dawn Ross initially declined her parents' involvement, saying she would give people the benefit of the doubt because it was a crazy night. When she read Oakmont's legal response, "then I was pissed," she said. "They need to be punished, and they should not be operating old folks' homes." She called Stebner to try to add her parents' names to the suit.

Vivian Flowers was already angered over the excavation debacle and the fact no one ever called to check on her mother, but the suggestion that the victims and the rescuers owned some of the blame put her over the edge. "I was absolutely livid," she said. "I was up there quite often, and my mom was one of the better ones. There were a lot of bedbound and wheelchair-bound who didn't talk. What do you mean help themselves? What were they supposed to do in a locked facility?"

Community members shared similar sentiments in *Press Democrat* letters to the editor. "I would really like to know why these nonambulatory, frail elderly people were on upper floors with no generators for the elevators and lights in case of fire, earthquake, or other emergency," wrote Dori Coleman of Windsor. "And to blame the residents, shame, shame. I pray that I will be called for jury duty."

Other Oakmont residents were unmoved. Henrietta Hillman, who lost nearly $1 million in possessions and exhibited both physical decline and depression afterward, could not be convinced to join the lawsuit. Mary Lou Delaney's family also declined. "The Tubbs Fire caught everyone by surprise. If you said 5,000 homes are going to burn, I'd say you're crazy. That thing roared through," said her son, Tim Delaney, who was grateful for those who risked their lives to save residents. "Moving 80 slow-moving residents down the stairs, power's out. I am utterly amazed everyone made it off of that hill." But as the DSS investigation showed, everyone did not make it off the hill at Varenna. Yet none of those left behind opted to sue either. According to Sally Tilbury's granddaughter, Sally perceived litigiousness as unbecoming and refused to sue despite her family's urging.

Since the balance of Stebner's plaintiffs were elderly, and some increasingly frail, the judge bumped up the trial date to August 3. This was good news for Ruth, Alice, Len, and the other surviving residents who might have to testify, but it worried Stebner and her team. Her plaintiff count was now at 17 up from the initial six, and she would have to review thousands of pages of documents and identify and depose a longer witness list—all within the next five months.

***

Stebner knew she was up against a formidable opponent. Since its founding, Giovanniello Law Group had handled thousands of cases "representing health care providers, corporations, professionals, private businesses, and insurance companies" in California, Arizona, Nevada, Washington, and New York. Its founder, Alexander Giovanniello, lectured nationally to skilled nursing and health care facilities on elder abuse, malpractice, and other liability issues, and conducted training seminars on how to defend skilled nursing facilities. His company's website boasts of stopping plaintiffs' efforts to punish his clients, while forcing plaintiffs "to capitulate." The firm claimed it obtains "reasonable settlements in cases that otherwise would have resulted in large verdicts" favoring those who sued.

These attorneys knew all the moves, Stebner said. One was to turn the tables and blame the residents and rescuers. Another was to stall at every possible opportunity in the discovery process, the phase when the two sides exchange information about witnesses and evidence they will present at trial.

As standard procedure, Stebner created a list of the information she would need from opposing counsel, information including budgets, emergency plans, employee shift assignment sheets, and training records. Oakmont's attorneys objected to these requests, even claiming some bordered on harassment. They balked at producing Villa Capri's emergency response plan because they said it was "confidential proprietary information protected by trade secret protection." At the same time, they also suggested the fire may have destroyed the emergency plan, and therefore it no longer existed. "Defendants are only required to produce records within its possession, custody, or control," the response stated. Stebner was floored. "They wouldn't give us anything," she said.

That "anything" included access to staff members for sworn testimony. Stebner wanted specific employees to give depositions on areas where their knowledge intersected with the allegations in question, namely staffing, budgeting, and construction debris removal. She also wanted a list of employees who were present at New Vintage Church when Bess Budow broke her hip.

First, the opposing firm refused to schedule depositions because it said the whole matter should go to arbitration, rendering testimony under oath pointless. But then Giovanniello Law Group refused to hand over Villa Capri's maintenance director and other employees for interviews "on the grounds that [the request] is overbroad, vague, and ambiguous." Attorneys there also rejected access to three key witnesses: Oakmont attorney Christian Holland; Oakmont Management Group's cofounder, president, and CEO, Chris Kasulka; and Oakmont Senior Living owner Bill Gallaher.

After being stymied for months, Stebner started filing formal court motions to compel Oakmont's participation and fine her opponent for wasting her time. "I had to fight for every little thing, every little scrap, in the shortest period of time known to humankind," she said of the process. While the lack of documentation hindered her preparation, Stebner was particularly focused on deposing Holland, Kasulka, and Gallaher, the three people who had intimate knowledge of the company's decision-making, budgeting philosophy, and corporate ethos, all of which she believed sealed her clients' fate between October 8 and 9.

Oakmont Management Group's in-house counsel Christian Holland cited attorney-client privilege as the reason he could not testify, but Stebner produced his Oakmont website profile that said he served as not just legal counsel but as "risk manager," someone who "provides oversight for resident safety, employee safety, and compliance initiatives." When it came to Gallaher and Kasulka, Stebner highlighted that Gallaher owned one-fifth of Oakmont Management Group and 70 percent of Varenna at Fountaingrove, LLC, a trade name linked via permitting paperwork to both Oakmont Management Group and Oakmont Senior Living. Stebner also submitted to the judge copies of OSL's website with profiles of Kasulka and Gallaher and commentary about the two companies' ties to one another. She argued that both Kasulka and Gallaher were "closely involved in making decisions regarding Oakmont's properties, including Villa Capri," and that "Mr. Gallaher clearly has information and decision-making regarding the lack of care, neglect, and reckless conduct that created the basis for Plaintiffs' claims." Plus, Stebner said, Gallaher's mother-in-law, Norma Porter, lived at Villa Capri. "As a family member of a resident, Mr. Gallaher clearly has direct information regarding what information, assurances, and actions took place to provide for residents' safety," she wrote.

The Giovanniello Law Group objected, claiming Holland, Kasulka, and Gallaher were protected by the "apex doctrine," a legal principle shielding from depositions those at the top of a corporate organizational chart. Giovanniello's attorneys argued Holland, Kasulka, and Gallaher had nothing to do with day-to-day operations, and deposing them would be a waste of time. However, Stebner was sure all three knew more than any manager or executive director beneath them in the reporting structure, and regardless of what they claimed, Stebner believed "all roads lead to Gallaher."

Judge Patrick Broderick of the Sonoma County Superior Court heard the arguments at a June 8 hearing and was clearly not impressed by the defense counsel's arguments. In fact, he leveled $8,750 in sanctions against Oakmont and the Giovanniello Law Group for stalling the discovery process for 75 days. He agreed their "delaying tactics constitute bad faith actions." After that, every motion Stebner put before him, she won. "Judge Broderick is part of the community," she said. "My sense was that he wanted this all to come out for the community. I think he really cared."

The judge also required Oakmont to provide Stebner access for deposition to every Villa Capri memory care director since 2016, several Oakmont Management Group executives, employees most knowledgeable about the demolition, and all employees present at Villa Capri from midnight to 6 a.m. on October 9, as well as those present at New Vintage Church. And Broderick replied to their apex doctrine defense with a note of frustration. "I will say the defendants' argument is not well taken that these are busy people," Broderick said. "I don't accept that argument. In fact, I'm concerned about that argument." Broderick ruled in Stebner's favor on all three apex witnesses in question.

"You get to [depose] Gallaher," he told her.

March 2018: Oakmont Pushes Ahead

Despite the extent of the firestorm devastation and array of investigations, lawsuits, and public debates, Oakmont Senior Living showed no signs of slowing in its development plans, specifically in the scarred Fountaingrove area. Not only had work begun on rebuilding Villa Capri and repairing Varenna in early 2018, the company continued with plans for a fifth senior housing complex, Emerald Isle, to be located half a mile from Villa Capri's ruins in Fountaingrove. Targeted for a 12.5-acre hilltop site surrounded on three sides by fairways from the Fountaingrove Country Club golf course, the project was within chipping range of homes destroyed by the Tubbs Fire. This rubbed many residents the wrong way, none more so than Beth Eurotas-Steffy.

Beth learned about the proposal while reading a March 17, 2018, column in the *Press Democrat* that emphasized that the city's design review board had already given final approval to OSL's plans to build Emerald Isle. "The Emerald Isle project, which would offer a mix of assisted living and memory care, will house roughly 70 people. If no appeal is made to the City Council, the project will now be built," the column read.

"That was when I took my marching orders," Beth said. She began by emailing each City Council member as well as planning officials, conveying her disbelief that city officials would approve a new senior care facility when Oakmont Senior Living was still under state investigation for mishandling evacuations at another site less than 2,000 feet away.

One City Council member got back to her and walked her through the steps for filing an appeal. She had only two days before the deadline. She also needed to come up with $493 to cover the filing fee. Beth turned to social media, posting how she would be willing to accept any support to file the appeal. Several readers responded. One community activist who was already battling Gallaher and Oakmont Senior Living on other fronts met Beth at a coffee shop and slapped her hand on the table. Underneath was a $100 bill. "If anyone asks, I didn't do this," the woman told Beth.

Beth received seven other donations, all from strangers who read her social media post. One $25 gift came from a woman who included a note: "This is from my personal account, because my husband would be angry if he knew I was doing this," she said. "But you go, girl!" In all, Beth received $401 in donations. She made up the difference out of her own pocket and, with help from her newfound activist friend, filed the appeal within hours of the deadline.

"The Design Review Board completely ignored the ongoing investigations into and litigation about the inadequate evacuation during the recent Tubbs Fire of other assisted living properties owned by [Oakmont Senior Living]," Beth wrote in her appeal, concluding the city's reasoning in support of the project was "fatally flawed." Emerald Isle, which the planning commission had already approved, was set to be reviewed before the Santa Rosa City Council, where the public would have a chance to debate the project's merits in the aftermath of the fire. But each time the project was listed on the council's agenda, Oakmont asked for a postponement. "They were using delay tactics," Beth claimed. "The hearing date was changed two times because they kept saying it didn't work for them."

Beth took the opportunity to do more homework, meet with more city officials, and strengthen her arguments and presentation for the City Council hearing. After multiple delays, the hearing was reset for September in 2018. But just a few days before, Oakmont suddenly announced it was dropping the Emerald Isle project as proposed. Beth was left with mixed emotions. She wanted a chance to make her arguments publicly, but given all the losses she had endured over the past year, "I considered it a win," she said. It wasn't Gallaher's only development setback that summer. Two months earlier, more than 300 residents packed a July public meeting to address his plans to build up to 867 rental homes, a grocery store, amphi-theater, and dog park on the Chanate Road site of the old Sonoma County Hospital. The town hall meeting, a requirement of the city, was the public's first opportunity to weigh in on what Gallaher had in mind for the 82-acre parcel. It did not go well.

A few spoke in support of the plans, noting how studies showed the region needed more housing. Gallaher's project manager, Komron Shahhosseini, still a member of the Sonoma County Planning Commission, told the crowd that 20 percent of the housing units would be reserved for very low–income residents, meaning two-bedroom apartments would be available for about $950 a month, well below the then market rate of roughly $2,700 a month. That would benefit working-class residents who have "really been truly priced out of the community," Shahhosseini told the crowd. But most attendees spoke against the project. Some objected to its size and density, others to traffic concerns. Still others noted how the property was less than a half mile from the southern edge of both the Hanly Fire of 1964 and the Tubbs Fire. On the night of the 2017 fires, most roads in and around the area had been cut off, one resident testified. "The only way to get the hell out of the way of this fire was to come out on Chanate Road and go down onto [Mendocino Avenue]," the neighbor said. "That was it." Building this many housing units would make that route even more unusable the next time around, he said.

What wasn't up for debate that day, but was on the minds of many, was a lawsuit filed by Friends of Chanate, a neighborhood opposition group that claimed the county had failed to adequately study the project's envi-ronmental impacts before voting to sell the massive site to Gallaher. On July 26, Gallaher's bid to purchase the Chanate Road property and convert it into one of the city's largest housing projects in memory was torpedoed by a superior court judge, who ruled in favor of Friends of Chanate that the county had rushed the sale. The county ultimately decided not to appeal, and by October, the Board of Supervisors voted to scrap the project and start over. Gallaher would again make an offer to develop the site when the county put the 72-acre property out for bid a second time. But this time his offer, for just $9 million, was rejected.

Summer 2018: Residents and Family Testify about Their Suffering

Beginning on June 5, attorneys for both sides began questioning more than 40 witnesses, from residents and family members to police, doctors, experts, and Oakmont employees. First to be deposed under oath were the plaintiffs. For Stebner to prove allegations such as elder abuse, negligence, and the infliction of emotional distress, she needed to first show that residents and rescuers had suffered and continued to suffer from the chaotic evacuation.

In sworn testimony, residents Len, Ruth, Alice, and Nell each recounted the night's events. John Magnuson, Viola Sodini, and Inez Glynn were deemed incapable of testifying because of their dementia or health limitations, and three of the lawsuit's residents had died by June. In those cases, as well as for Alice and Ruth, family members testified how their parents' mental or physical health worsened after October 9, 2017.

During his deposition, Len Kulwiec told attorneys how he saw a red horizon through the window blinds that night. "I'll tell you—it was a moment of terror because it reminded me of World War II," he said. He recalled rolling down the stairs and how his injured knee stayed swollen for a week. He asked his doctor if he could fix it and was told, "No, I can't because you are too old. I wouldn't dare operate on you." The knee now required a brace and still caused him pain. He also had trouble falling asleep following the fire and was taking sleeping pills, he testified. However, he wasn't asked about his emotional pain. "My dad still has PTSD," said Len's son Michael, who was not deposed in the case. "I had to get him blackout curtains because anytime he sees red out of the window, it causes him distress."

Ruth Callen brought her trademark humor to her deposition. When Giovanniello Law Group attorney Paul H. Kang asked Ruth if she'd ever been convicted of a felony, she quipped "Not yet." Early on, Kang asked Ruth if she kept a diary or journal.

"No. I just keep a grocery list."

Despite these periodic infusions of humor, Ruth was no longer the same social animal. She had moved into Brookdale Windsor, and although she knew some former Villa Capri residents there, she didn't partake in crafts or watch movies as she had before the fire. "I just don't feel like it," she said in an email to an attorney at Stebner's firm. She was also distressed about her uninsured belongings that had burned. "I miss my antique lamp ['Lydia'] and pictures and my peach painting," she said.

Ruthie Kurpinsky, deposed immediately after Ruth, said her mother had steadily declined since the fire, becoming forgetful, especially in her word choices, requiring stronger antidepressants and help with dressing and showering, and needing a wheelchair instead of her walker. "We talk about my mom before-fire and after," she said of conversations with her siblings. "Mom didn't have so much confusion as she does now."

Sonoma County Sheriff's Deputy Joey Horsman testified both on his own behalf and that of his grandmother, who he said would seem to understand one moment but forget the next that her home had burned in a fire. A week after moving to Belmont Village, Inez Glynn was hospitalized for a month with myriad health issues, including norovirus and pneumonia. Joey believed his grandmother's lung issues were associated with the time she spent in the smoke during the evacuation. Joey also recounted his near-death drive through the fire tunnel on Fountaingrove Parkway, as well as his own vivid flashbacks and other post-traumatic stress disorder issues. Before the fires, he was diagnosed with severe sleep apnea, a condition that required him to wear a CPAP mask at night. After the fires, he couldn't bring himself to wear the mask. "I'm not sleeping much," he said. "My body feels like it rejects it. It takes me back to that feeling of everything closing in on me." He testified it was difficult to talk about the night without crying. "I'm experiencing anxiety and claustrophobia, which was never something that I experienced before."

Several family members went further than associating the fire trauma with their relatives' decline; some claimed the fire had hastened or outright caused their parent or parents' death.

"My mother died on December 22, 2017," Dawn Ross wrote in a sworn declaration. "I strongly believe her life was cut short because of the terrifying events on the night of the fire. My father died June 13, 2018. I believe his life was cut short by the loss of my mother and the events on the night of the fire." His was not the only spring 2018 death. For six weeks after the fire, Helen Allen had slept on a blow-up double bed in Mark and Kathy's family room. The couple took care of her around the clock, helping her to the toilet in the middle of the night, changing incontinence briefs, and trying to find easy-to-feed foods she could maneuver into her mouth. After the fire, she could no longer stand on her own. "It was raising a 130-pound baby," Mark said.

His mother was also continually upset. "She tossed and turned and moaned and cried at night," Kathy said. "We'd have to sit with her and rub her back and tell her it was okay." Helen would cry out the same questions: "Why am I here? When am I going home?"

"There was a fire," Kathy would remind her.

"Oh, yes," Helen would say. "Kathy, I don't know how long I can do this. I don't want to do this anymore."

Exhausted from the 24/7 care and unable to console Helen, the Allens found her a spot at The Vineyard at Fountaingrove, a memory care community. They hoped she would improve surrounded by potential new friends, but her sadness continued. "She was done," Kathy said. "She kind of gave up."

In March 2018, Mark took his mother to the doctor, and when loading her into his car, he smacked his head on the door. "Mark, are you okay?" Helen asked. Her sudden engagement surprised him. For the next two days, she perked up. She ate well, talked with other residents, and even played balloon volleyball. On the second night, Helen wanted to stay up late and watch television. A caregiver came in to say goodnight. She leaned over, kissed Helen's forehead, and said she'd see Helen tomorrow.

"Maybe," the 89-year-old responded.

Helen didn't wake up. "Maybe subconsciously, she decided to enjoy the last two days on this earth," Mark said. "But those two good days came after five months of emotional pain. I count her as one of the fire victims."

***

To back up her clients' claims of trauma, physical injuries, and wrongful death, Stebner deposed medical experts, including geriatric psychiatrist Dr. Mary De May from the University of California, San Francisco. She had interviewed several plaintiffs and testified they suffered from trauma, anxiety, depression, fear, and agitation as a result of the chaotic evacuation, and the trauma was exacerbated by how the evacuation occurred. According to Stebner's summary, the doctor said the "residents went through added stress, prolonged smoke inhalation, a haphazard transfer from upstairs to down by people unfamiliar with their needs or not trained to perform such a transfer, and a sense of terror as they watched a wall of fire encroaching them as they sat trapped inside the facility…. Several people appropriately thought they were going to die at Villa Capri." The evacuation's stress and trauma also hurt residents with dementia—even if they couldn't recall the night—as evidenced by family members' reports of weight loss and a decline in their conditions.

De May talked with Kathy, Mark, Melissa, and Joey and testified they, too, experienced psychological trauma and continued to carry it with them. Stebner planned to apply the rescue doctrine to argue that Oakmont created a situation of peril that caused the need for rescue, therefore the company was responsible for any injury those four suffered.

An internal medicine expert, Dr. Steven Fugaro, testified Len's knee injury was a result of the evacuation and Inez Glynn's month-long hospital stay for chronic obstructive pulmonary disease was probably caused by smoke. Fugaro told attorneys that Oakmont's "wrongful conduct" was a substantial factor in causing the deaths of plaintiffs Bess Budow, Virginia Gunn, and Helen Allen. Virginia's doctor, Andrew Wagner, said he had documented her "PTSD nightmares from experiences of evacuation during fire and feeling helpless waiting for her daughter to rescue her from Villa Capri."

Oakmont's attorneys, however, brought in their own psychiatrist who acknowledged the residents suffered emotional stress but testified that he didn't believe the stress would impact their long-term health. And Oakmont's medical expert, internist, and pulmonologist, Dr. William Kline, said he believed the three deceased women's medical trajectory would have been the same had there been no fire that night. He did not believe the evacuation or Bess' hip fracture affected either her life expectancy or hastened her death. He said he didn't think Virginia Gunn's PTSD affected her life expectancy, nor did he think Helen Allen's death was hastened by the events, according to Stebner's trial brief. The Oakmont attorneys' trial brief noted that Virginia's death certificate identified colon cancer as her cause of death, Helen's listed heart attack and dementia, and Bess' listed complications from vascular dementia as her primary cause, plus a left hip fracture as a significant contributing factor. "The medical records show how it was the pre-existing comorbidities of Ms. Gunn, Ms. Budow, and Ms. Allen that caused their respective demise," defense attorneys wrote. "Accordingly, Plaintiffs' Wrongful Death Cause of Action is without merit."

***

With six weeks to go before trial, Stebner found herself in a fight that could derail her entire case. Oakmont Senior Living was blaming PG&E, the power company whose power lines were suspected of starting many if not all of the Wine Country Fires.

"They wanted to argue all this wouldn't have happened if PG&E hadn't messed up," Stebner said. She worried Oakmont would attempt to "try a case within a case" and "muddy the issues and confuse the jury" with massive amounts of irrelevant information.

"Simply put," she wrote in her response to the judge, "after all the depositions [in the fire investigation-related case] have been taken, there has been no admissible evidence…that PG&E was the cause of the Tubbs Fire, nor has there been any admissible evidence that the city, county, local law enforcement, and/or any other individual entity was a substantial factor in causing plaintiffs' injuries during (the) fire."

The whole matter came down to a five-minute hearing on June 15, where Stebner, exhausted from the rapid pace of the case and back-to-back depositions, was dismayed to find Judge Elliot Daum substituting for Judge Broderick, who knew the case and had already ruled in her favor. Stebner felt she was carrying the weight of the residents' stories and that everything they'd endured before, during, and after the fire would be for naught if this "random guy who didn't know the case" ruled for Oakmont, she said.

But Judge Daum denied Oakmont's motion to file a cross complaint that would include PG&E. "And I started bawling in the courtroom, in front of the defense attorney," Stebner said. "I told the judge, 'I was so scared you were going to do it because all of these people are depending on me.' I was like, 'Thank you, thank you, thank you.' It would have derailed everything."

Each motion Stebner won represented a battle victory, but she felt she was losing the war. "The case was moving as quickly as the fire," she said. "They knew."

What the Giovanniello Law Group knew was how to run out the clock during the discovery process, how to press their opponent under their thumb, preventing Stebner from collecting the information she needed to thread a cohesive and damning story she could tell the jury in August. Whatever work Stebner and her team could complete by August 3 would be the only work she could use at trial. If her opponent's initial strategy was to stymie Stebner with a trickle of evidence, their 11th-hour approach was the opposite. Documents flooded Stebner's office in late July as if bursting from a fire hydrant.

"Everything was being dumped on us in the very end," she said, noting it's a common defense tactic. "Defendants don't want to give you something unless you make them, and [then] they want to give it to you late because they don't want to give you time to look at them." The documents amounted to 50 to 100 boxes, Stebner said. Adding to the overload, a week before trial, Stebner and Associates received all 911 records from the night of the fire, totaling 5,000 calls in all. She enlisted every member of her 10-person firm to help with the analysis. "My entire law firm came to a stop on this case."

***

It was one thing to see the physical and mental toll the October 9 fire had taken on her clients and others at Villa Capri and Varenna and to understand the mounting evidence of operational failures, lack of emergency planning, and negligence on the part of Oakmont Senior Living. It was another thing to prove it all to a jury. Now that she had been granted access to the top echelon of OSL executives, including Gallaher himself, Stebner had the opportunity to put them all on the record under oath. This was her chance to make her case.

Evacuating a senior care home in the middle of the night would likely be hard on most elderly residents under the best of circumstances, but Stebner sought to show how Oakmont's "redundancy of errors" before, during, and after the fire at Villa Capri turned an already stressful situation into a perilous one that traumatized, injured, and even led to deaths among her plaintiffs. To that end, Stebner and Associates began deposing employees, starting with those who were at Villa Capri the night of the fire, before moving on to managers and corporate executives. The answers they provided—and what they didn't say—addressed outstanding questions regarding Villa Capri and Oakmont.

A few days before her deposition, caregiver Cynthia Arroyo was on the job at Varenna when a Giovanniello Law Group attorney showed up. Debie Smith, who had also taken a management job at Varenna, found a room where they could talk. According to Cynthia, the attorney went over questions Stebner might ask during her deposition. Cynthia shared her fire story and how she transferred the three residents to nurse Jane Torres' car at Coddingtown Center, in part because she was shaking and traumatized from driving through the firestorm. He instructed her not to panic if she couldn't remember certain things. "He said to use the words 'I'm not sure' or 'I don't recall,'" she said. A nervous Cynthia heeded his advice under oath and said "I don't recall" 72 times, "I don't remember" 75 times, and "I don't know" 51 times during her four-hour deposition.

Anett Rivas said she received similar advice. "I do remember them saying if you don't recall or aren't certain about questions, don't answer if you're not sure," she said. During Anett's deposition, Kathryn Stebner repeatedly accused Giovanniello Law Group attorney Paul H. Kang of coaching the witness in one of dozens of contentious exchanges between Stebner and Oakmont's attorneys. At one point, Stebner said to Anett, "So instead of being coached by your lawyer, like, every other question, I just want you to know—if you don't know something, you can say you don't know." Anett repeated that refrain 70 times throughout her deposition. Seconds later,

Kang responded to the charge. "First of all, I'm not coaching the witness," he said. Neither caregiver provided much help to Stebner's case. Nor did Marie So, who said "I don't know," "I don't remember," or "I don't recall" a total of 103 times over four hours.

But the fourth employee on duty on October 8 wouldn't return attorney phone calls and refused to appear for a deposition until she received a subpoena. "I didn't want nothing to do with it," Elizabeth Lopez said. "I'm done. I put my life in danger and for whatever you just gave me, it's not worth it. What about *my* family?" Attorneys "stalked" her, she said. They tried to serve legal papers several times, and her parents told them Elizabeth wasn't home. "One time they said, 'We've been sitting in front of your home watching you,'" she said. Finally, a process server handed her papers. "What happens if I don't show up?" Elizabeth asked. "They will put out a warrant for your arrest," she was told. Elizabeth complied. But when the single mom showed up on July 26 at the tail end of the deposition process, she wasn't about to be coached by attorneys for either side. And she had no problem recalling everything.

***

The depositions in the Stebner case addressed the sequence of events on October 8 and October 9, 2017, as well as issues of emergency preparations, training, and management practices at Varenna, Villa Capri, and Oakmont Senior Living in general. At the heart of the sworn testimony were eight central questions, which Stebner posed to the "employees most knowledgeable," those whom she had won the right to depose:

Was the building adequately equipped for an emergency?
Villa Capri was among the highest-end assisted living facilities in the county. It had a movie theater, fine artwork, and chandeliers, but was it equipped with flashlights, batteries, portable generators, and other basic emergency supplies? During the final power outage at 1:53 a.m., battery-powered emergency lights barely cut through the smoky hallways. Half of the flashlights the caregivers found in the laundry room didn't work or lacked batteries, so they borrowed some from residents' rooms to light pathways and

rooms for fall-risk residents. Since flashlights were a scarce commodity, they used their own cell phones for lights, a move that would cause phones to die when most needed..

Villa Capri Executive Director Debie Smith testified she thought the staff knew where to find flashlights because they talked about them in monthly meetings. Stebner asked, "Did [Marie] ever tell you that the flashlights—the batteries weren't working, some of them?" Smith answered, "Not that I recall."

When Stebner asked how many flashlights were available, Smith said, "We had flashlights in each fire extinguisher case. We had flashlights in, I think, every department head's office, at the front desk, in the kitchen. I don't know—I don't know how many per se, but they were in the maintenance director's office."

But in her conversations with Marie, Debie did not mention that more than 100 flashlights with fresh batteries were inside an emergency supply box in the locked office of Maintenance Director Tony Moreno. Moreno testified that, once a month, he tested the flashlights and changed batteries as needed. Also in the box were rolls of blue tape for marking doors, masks, bottled water, and an unknown number of glow sticks; he testified he routinely checked their expiration dates and hadn't needed to replace any in the two months he'd been on the job. He reported all his activities and routine inspections to Smith. The keys to Moreno's office were in a locked drawer behind the front desk. Moreno said Debie called him the night of the fire, forgetting that he was out of state on vacation and unable to help.

Moreno also shed light on whether Villa Capri had portable generators. The short answer was no, but they were supposed to.

Regional Operations Vice President Ken Garnett had selected models that could charge communication devices and run oxygen concentrators and sent ordering instructions beginning in January 2017 to each community's maintenance director. Villa Capri had seen turnover in that position, and no one had followed up. Moreno, only on the job since August, testified he "was in process to order one generator" for Villa Capri, but had not yet done so.

Yet in an October 16, 2017, report on ABC7 News, Oakmont representatives told Melanie Woodrow "…we have three backup generators on-site" but they did not specify at which community or how large the generators were. Executive Director Nathan Condie testified that Varenna did have two portable generators located in the golf cart storage area of the basement, but nobody was directed to look there. Even if they existed, two portable generators at Varenna would not have helped beleaguered employees at Villa Capri, and they certainly wouldn't have been enough to power elevators in either facility.

Where were the bus keys?

The depositions provided answers but also more questions. Debie Smith testified that a lockbox inside the activity director's office at Villa Capri held the keys to both shuttle buses parked out back, along with keys to a large Lincoln Town Car. The lockbox required a combination but was usually left unlocked. However, the activity director's office, located just a few steps off the lobby, was locked, and the key into that office was stashed behind the front desk.

The concierge who spent 10 minutes at Villa Capri during the fire did know where the keys were, according to testimony, but she wasn't aware of her fellow employees' desperate search for them. The executive director knew their location too, but she didn't tell Marie during their conversations. "It was my expectation that the med tech would know where the keys are," Smith testified. Marie testified she did know where to find both the bus and office keys, but she said she was too busy getting residents to the lobby to even try to get to them.

But Elizabeth Lopez's testimony contradicted this. Stebner and Associates attorney Karman Guadagni asked her whether Marie knew the bus keys' location, and Elizabeth asserted all three caregivers had asked Marie about the keys.

> Guadagni: Do you remember Marie's exact words in response to your question?
>
> Elizabeth: She said, I don't know where the bus keys at, I don't know where's the vans keys, I don't know where they're at.

It's unclear whether Marie knew on the night of the fire the keys' location or forgot in the stress and chaos. But even if she had produced keys to the 26-seater shuttle, it's unclear who would have driven the vehicle. No one on duty that night had been trained to do so.

Why could family members but not Oakmont employees get to Villa Capri the night of the fire??

Aside from Joel and Pouya, who worked for corporate, no Villa Capri managers familiar with the residents showed up to help. "We were just sitting ducks out there," Cynthia said.

Gena Jacob, Mark and Kathy, Melissa, Joey, and even Elizabeth Lopez's boyfriend all made it through or around checkpoints between 1:40 a.m. and 2:45 a.m. Varenna employees Chris DeMott and Mika Alcasabas said they drove around an unmanned barricade around 2:35 a.m. to help at Varenna. But no one else made it to Villa Capri during that critical evacuation window. Several Oakmont employees, however, said they tried.

Tammy Moratto, a corporate marketing employee who was Villa Capri's executive director for three years, testified that she attempted to get into Fountaingrove at two locations. At Bicentennial and Mendocino avenues, a man in a black outfit told her the roads were closed. "I said that we had a building up at the top that I needed to get to. And he said, 'I'm sorry, ma'am, we will take care of it. We're not allowing any people up.'" Stebner pressed her on whether the man said he would take care of it, and Tammy couldn't recall if those were his exact words. "I can't say that for sure. I felt that they would. So what words he used, I don't recall."

Stebner then asked if Tammy told the officer that "the building" was an assisted living facility filled with elderly residents in desperate need of rescue. "I didn't say at that point," Tammy testified. Instead, Tammy called Ken Garnett, regional vice president of operations, who said he had also failed to get through checkpoints. So both headed to Coddingtown to set up a communication center. When Nathan Condie arrived, he and Garnett testified they tried to get into Fountaingrove but were prevented by a "volunteer" at one barricade and by fire crossing the road on another route. However, 15 minutes earlier, R.J. Kisling had managed to get through, and

Steffany Kisling didn't bother to converse with anyone. She breezed through the checkpoint and sped up the hill.

Debie Smith, notified by staff of a power outage at 11:30 p.m., never showed up. VP Kevin Garnett offered a possible excuse in his deposition. "You know, we didn't have a policy per se that said you had to go there if the power was out," he said.

Why did the executive director never show up at Villa Capri?

Debie Smith testified that when she was notified about the power outage at 11:30 p.m., she considered driving to Villa Capri but felt from her conversations with Marie that "everything was taken care of." She said she thought the med tech would know what to do, but a moment later, Smith admitted she didn't know if the caregivers had been trained for a power outage.

> Stebner: So when you were sitting there contemplating whether you should go up there during the time that the power was off, were you thinking about the fact that you had three really new women up there and actually one was pregnant? Was that sort of running through your mind at all?
>
> Smith: No. What was running through my mind was, are the residents okay? Do they need me to be there…?
>
> Stebner: Okay. So did you take that into account, the fact that there was no elevator and you had people in wheelchairs and you had people with walkers upstairs? Did you take that into account when you made the decision not to go up there?
>
> Smith: I knew PG&E were on their way, and I knew the residents were sleeping and in bed from my conversations with Marie. So that's what I was thinking about.

Smith said she didn't know about the fire until Marie called her, which most likely occurred between 1:45 and 2 a.m. According to Marie, Debie said she was on her way there. Smith testified she left immediately and tried to drive to Villa Capri from her home in Windsor, roughly 15 minutes away. As she headed south on Highway 101, she saw a couple cars speeding north on the wrong side of the highway. The direct route from Windsor to Villa Capri would be to drive south on Highway 101 to Santa Rosa Exit 492 at Cleveland Avenue and from there take the Mendocino Avenue highway overpass east to Fountaingrove Parkway. But on October 9, Smith exited at River Road, a mile and a half before Cleveland Avenue and four miles north of Villa Capri, where she encountered roadblocks at the intersection of Mark West Springs and Old Redwood Highway, a back way to the complex. "There were police cars barricading it and police officers redirecting traffic," she said. "It was very smoky, very loud, very—ashes and fire right there. They had their masks on. It was hectic. And they were directing traffic so you couldn't go right on Old Redwood Highway, and you couldn't go up further on Mark West Springs Road."

Stebner asked what she did next. "So then I drove home," Smith said, acknowledging she did not try another route. On her way back to Windsor, she said she called Ken Garnett and Joel Ruiz, "maybe" tried Jane Torres, and "may have" called Memory Care Director Janice Wilson and Maintenance Director Tony Moreno as well. Smith told Joel to rush to Villa Capri, while she sent Torres and Wilson to Coddingtown. Back at home, Smith said she woke her husband and called 911. When she got through, "I was told that there were 25 fires burning in the area, and there were no resources," she said. She said she jumped back in her car and headed for Coddingtown, where Garnett had told her to meet. That's when, she testified, she got stuck in gridlocked traffic. Records show Smith made the 911 call at 2:24 a.m. and arrived at New Vintage church at 6 a.m. It's still not clear what happened in the interim.

Elizabeth Lopez, for one, was not buying Smith's story and was forthright about it under oath. "Let's say that she wanted to come to Villa Capri but couldn't because of roadblocks, what would be your thought?" Stebner asked.

"I would say it's a bunch of BS, honestly," Elizabeth replied.

Stebner asked why she'd say that. Elizabeth said she had already confronted Smith over this very issue a month or so after the fire, after an interaction on a different topic caused Elizabeth's bottled-up frustration to explode. Elizabeth explained to Stebner that, after the fire, Smith promised Elizabeth a job at Varenna, but it didn't work out because managers there couldn't accommodate Elizabeth's modified night-shift hours. Elizabeth filed for unemployment but was rejected.

She called Smith, who told her, "Elizabeth, right now we don't have the time to pick and choose." This angered Elizabeth, who felt Smith had broken her word.

"She promised me a job, same pay, same hours, same days," Elizabeth told the attorney. So Elizabeth hurled at Smith the question she and her coworkers had wondered: "Where were you at that time [of the fire]?"

According to Elizabeth, Smith said, "I have family too."

"I'm like, 'Guess what? I have a daughter too,'" Elizabeth responded. "And I decided to stay and help the residents instead of me running to my daughter."

Was there an emergency plan?

If one did exist, no one from Oakmont was ever able to produce it—or provide any detail about its contents. Smith's absence stalled the evacuation, Cynthia Arroyo said in her interview, "because...we had no evacuation plan other than [to] get the residents out to the lobby." So even if Smith or managers had made it to Villa Capri, did an emergency plan exist for them to execute? "I know that we had an emergency disaster plan, but I wasn't really involved in the creation or the oversight of it," Chris Kasulka, then-president and CEO of Oakmont Management Group, testified under Stebner's questioning. Nor had she ever seen an emergency plan for any of the Oakmont communities she oversaw and had not asked to see them even after the fire, she said. But Kasulka said she expected Debie Smith and the Villa Capri staff would know the evacuation plan in case of a wildfire. And she expected Smith to make sure staff understood the plan.

Christian Holland had similar expectations. The OMG attorney who oversaw risk management for the corporation, also taught risk management classes at two colleges. Holland testified he studied state regulations and wrote and delivered a webinar to OMG executives in February 2017 titled "Disaster Planning Tools and Best Practices, Bi-Monthly Risk Management and Safety" with a goal "to create education and training for the executive directors." It included slides on disaster planning tools and best practices for all types of disasters, including earthquakes and wildfires, as well as guidance on making advance arrangements with local transportation companies and planning relocation sites.

The webinar was intended to supplement the company's disaster and emergency manual, which provided a template for executive directors to use to design a community-specific plan. Debie Smith, like other executive directors, was supposed to use Holland's manual to create a specific disaster plan for Villa Capri. Among the tasks, she was supposed to form a monthly disaster planning task force with the maintenance, business, and culinary managers.

"He's interesting because he gave a whole talk about 'This is what you need to do,'" Stebner said of Holland. "Actually, if they had done all that, none of these people would have been left." She tried to get Holland to agree, but when she pushed him on whether Smith and Villa Capri staff had followed the manual for the creation of a resident roster identifying those with special needs, for example, or developing evacuation procedures with alternate routes to and from Villa Capri, Holland deferred, saying, "This is just best practice." Like Kasulka, Holland expected the staff to know evacuation procedures, but he felt it wasn't his responsibility to follow up with each community to make sure his suggestions were implemented. That responsibility fell to VP of Operations Ken Garnett, whose job included making sure executive directors at 12 Oakmont properties were in compliance with their emergency planning. However, neither Holland nor Garnett could say whether Villa Capri actually possessed a site-specific emergency plan. Oakmont's attorneys would argue that not only did Villa Capri have a comprehensive emergency plan as the state required, but that it contained evacuation procedures for major disasters, including wildfires. But Oakmont could not produce it.

Sue McPherson, vice president of regulatory affairs and quality assurance for Oakmont Management Group, testified she told DSS investigators there were no digital copies of the plan. Instead, she gave them general Oakmont disaster manual sections on wildfires. "I explained this to them in the phone conversations that we could not find the Villa [Capri] document. It appeared to have burnt up. I could give them some of the basic things that were common for wildfire instructions, but that the details of that community's plan would have been—lived in the building, and it burnt up with the building."

The only person with intimate knowledge of the plan's contents was Smith, who told attorneys that the emergency disaster plan was kept at the front desk and in her office. "It was [in] a big red binder, and it was my expectation that, in an emergency, yes, that's where you go first." Smith said it was tailored to Villa Capri with maps, locations of shut-off valves, and evacuation sites. But when Stebner questioned her, Smith had trouble remembering the plan's specifics.

> *Stebner: So in terms of available vehicles, was there something in this plan, in the binder, that talked about what to do if you've got 70 people, but you've got a Lincoln and a van that holds 12 people?*
>
> *Smith: Not that I recall specifically.*
>
> *Stebner: At the time of the fire, was there a fire and disaster plan for the community which addressed the safety of the residents with dementia?*
>
> *Smith: I don't recall.*
>
> *Stebner: In the emergency disaster plan, were all nonambulatory residents identified?*
>
> *Smith: No.*
>
> *Stebner: Did the fire and evacuation plans include drills to assist non-ambulatory residents to a safe place?*
>
> *Smith: Not that I recall.*

From the staff meetings and online computer training sessions they had completed, Smith said she expected the caregivers to know there was an evacuation procedure or plan in case of wildfires. She recalled seeing Marie, Cynthia, and Anett at monthly trainings. But the training wasn't hands-on, the employees said. For example, Marie, Cynthia, Anett, and Elizabeth learned about the two-person carry in online training but had never actually practiced transporting nonambulatory people downstairs. Smith admitted they hadn't done hands-on training in the maneuver, nor had her staff participated in a simulated fire drill, one that sounded the fire alarm and escorted residents out of the building. Both Marie and Cynthia said they would have liked to have been better trained for the night of the fire. Even corporate maintenance specialist Joel Ruiz admitted he wasn't prepared. "Nobody trained me on what to do in a wildfire," he said. "We're not firemen."

> *Stebner: So my question is, you would have expected, based on all these trainings you did, that the staff that were there that night would know that there was some procedure or policy or evacuation plan on what to do with a wildfire? You would expect it because you talked about it all the time, right?*
>
> *Smith: More in the case of a fire. We didn't talk about wildfires as much as fires, internal fires, things like that.*
>
> *Stebner: What was your understanding as to what the disaster plan said in terms of what to do during a wildfire?*
>
> *Smith: I don't recall specifically. Of course, in any emergency, you would call 911.*
>
> *Stebner: Anything else?*
>
> *Smith: Fire department, emergency personnel.*
>
> *Stebner: Anything else?*
>
> *Smith: No.*

When Stebner asked Anett Rivas where the evacuation plan was kept, she said, "Evacuation plan?… Well, I didn't know there was a paper that had an evacuation plan for wildfire." And Elizabeth Lopez testified that she didn't know of the red emergency binder's existence at Villa Capri. Marie So said she knew there was a copy of the disaster and emergency manual kept at the front desk that night, but she didn't look at it or grab it.

Stebner: Is it fair to say that before this fire happened, you didn't know what to do if there was a fire off the building outside and how you were going to get all these people somewhere else? You didn't know what that plan was when you were supposed to evacuate, right?

Marie: Yeah. I didn't know, but I was waiting for further instruction from the management.

Cynthia, who had attended three of five monthly training sessions since she was hired, shed the most light on the evacuation plan's status when she testified, "They were teaching us how to use a fire extinguisher, and they were coming up with an evacuation plan, like where to evacuate."

Stebner: And what was your understanding based on those meetings in terms of where you were supposed to go to evacuate?

Cynthia: They were barely working on it, from what I know.

Presented with evidence that others heard an evacuation plan was in development and the fact that her maintenance manager had never heard of the safety committee he was supposed to be part of, Smith admitted she was "working on" an evacuation response. She had started it several months prior to the fire but had not completed it. Stebner summarized her take on these responses in a blunt one-sentence statement in her pretrial brief: "Executive Director Deborah Smith testified that the management knew of the need for a plan, but they were too busy to get around to it."

How was Oakmont able to excavate the Villa Capri site so quickly?

This was central to the questioning of David Hunter, director of construction for Oakmont Senior Living Construction. He testified he first visited the Villa Capri site one day after Villa Capri burned and began making plans to clear the site almost immediately. "We knew the debris had to be removed before we [could] go to the demo stage," he said. "It could not be left the way it was."

At that point, however, the fires were still burning out of control, cloaking the region in the dirtiest air ever recorded in Sonoma County history.

Throughout Sonoma County, barricades, many of them newly staffed by National Guard as well as Bay Area police officers, prevented entry into devastated areas.

Hunter said he was stopped at five such barricades as he tried to reach the complex on October 10, and each time, he sought a new way around. Finally, when he reached a roadblock off Chanate Road, he asked a uniformed fire official there for permission to pass. "I just told him I was trying to get to the properties at Fountaingrove, and we had a building burn down," he testified. Hunter asked, "If there's a way, I can get up there and check and assess the damage." Hunter showed his business card, and the fire official told him to follow him up.

When they arrived, the uniformed official left, and Hunter spent the next three hours walking the property as well as driving around Fountaingrove "looking at the whole devastation going on there." Of Villa Capri, there was little left, he said. The courtyard arbor remained standing "slightly burnt, and there was probably a few steel beams mangled," he said. He started making plans for what to do next.

Hunter returned to the property on Wednesday, October 11. At that time, authorities were repeatedly telling residents of fire-damaged properties to stay away. How Hunter got back up to the property, he couldn't recall under questioning. But he said he was not escorted by anyone after that initial encounter; he just showed his business card to those working the barricades. "They knew me," he said. "I don't know if the National Guard was on, but I went through the roadblock."

"People know you? Are you like a local celebrity?" a Stebner and Associates attorney asked.

"I've been around for 30 years in this area," Hunter said. "Yeah."

Hunter said he reached out to Northwest General Engineering on either October 11 or 12 to discuss the process for removing the debris. He was soon in contact with M&M Services, which operated Windsor Material Recovery Facility and specialized in sorting, recycling, and diverting from landfills as much material as possible. By the time Hunter connected with M&M, the company had already asked county authorities for a waiver from regulations related to the transportation and recycling of fire-related debris. Because the governor and the county Board of Supervisors had declared a state of emergency, the county agreed to suspend normal regulations for three specific areas: M&M's hours of operation, daily tonnage limits, and the location of two temporary transfer and processing sites in Windsor. But the county took no action authorizing the clearing of specific sites, particularly those within the jurisdiction of the City of Santa Rosa. Nonetheless, Hunter continued his trips to the Fountaingrove campus, visiting the property every day, and on Monday, October 16, excavation equipment arrived. Debris removal began the following day. By the time police halted it on October 18, the site was almost cleared.

The following day, Hunter emailed Fire Marshal Scott Moon a copy of the emergency waiver letter M&M Services had received from Sonoma County Department of Health Services eight days earlier. But the waiver said nothing about access to the site on Fountaingrove and nothing about Oakmont Senior Living or its contractor having authority to do work inside the city limits.

"David, other than the attached letter you provided, was there any other permit or approval documentation issued to Oakmont Senior Living or your contractor for the demo/debris removal?" Moon asked in his email response. Hunter replied, "At this time, no. We are being told that the City of Santa Rosa will give me a permit tomorrow over the counter when I produce the test results."

But when Moon reached out to city officials that day about the demolition permit, he was told otherwise. "Absolutely no permits are—or will be—issued in the burn areas until we ensure we have a cogent plan to do so," Jesse Oswald, acting chief building official, responded.

It wasn't until mid-May that Santa Rosa completed its investigation into Villa Capri's excavation. The city concluded that Oakmont Senior Living had no permit to do the work, but city officials would not issue a fine or citation because they had no authority to issue penalties other than to tack on fees for future permits. And in the interest of accelerating citywide cleanup and rebuilding from the Tubbs Fire, the city had since waived all such fees. So Santa Rosa officials said they lacked the means to issue a financial penalty to Oakmont Senior Living or any other entity involved. Furthermore, the site clearing occurred six days before the Sonoma County health officer issued an emergency order regulating debris clearance permits, debris handling, and property access in fire zones. In essence, the company swooped in and cleared the site before the rules for such work were established.

"They should not have done any of the removal until they had an actual fire debris permit issued to them by the city," Assistant Fire Marshal Paul Lowenthal said at the completion of the investigation. "They gained access to the site and initiated a process they shouldn't have." Fire officials said it was the only documented case of a fire-damaged building in Santa Rosa being demolished without proper authorization.

Meanwhile, Oakmont Senior Living, which continued to claim it possessed all the proper emergency waivers and permits it needed to clear the Villa Capri site and never admitted wrongdoing, was already rebuilding. By mid-August, the first-floor framing was up, making Villa Capri the only business of the 40 destroyed in the Tubbs Fire to have started reconstruction.

One former county Department of Health Services official, who was closely involved in the controversy surrounding the unauthorized excavation, said he was "astonished" at the lack of interest by the City of Santa Rosa in doing a more thorough investigation into how Oakmont got the excavation equipment up to the site. "The city of Santa Rosa has never explained their end of the bargain here and what really happened," said the official, who requested anonymity. "The city never thought this was a big deal in my analysis of it. The proof is in the pudding…. It's surprising to me there wasn't a larger outcry from the city government."

Who was ultimately responsible for what happened at Villa Capri?
In her quest to establish culpability, Stebner felt she needed to show that leadership failures at the top contributed to errors at the bottom. Although she grilled Marie, Anett, Cynthia, and Elizabeth about their actions during the night of the fire, she didn't plan to blame them. They were frontline workers who, for the most part, were just doing their best with the training and resources they had. In cases like this, "the people who work there are just as big a victim as the people who live there," she said. "I never point the finger at the caregivers; I always point the finger at the corporation."

That's because while it's easy to blame one person—the med tech in charge, the corporate maintenance guy who issues a few orders, or even the executive director—for poor planning or training, corporate executives establish the culture, according to emergency planning consultant Bo Mitchell, who was deposed as a witness for the plaintiffs. "[Change] has to come from the top," he said in an interview. "Change in an organization's emergency plan comes about from blunt force trauma from the outside, never by inspired leadership from the inside."

Under federal law, when something goes wrong, the CEO is actually the responsible party, Mitchell said. The safety of employees, visitors, or residents in assisted living was not the ultimate responsibility of Marie, Cynthia, Anett, Elizabeth, Joel, Pouya, or the rescuers who gave some orders to employees, or even the executive director. By federal law, Mitchell said, anyone who comes onto a workplace's premises, from employee to patient to family member, must be kept safe. "That's the employer's duty of care. No *employee* has a duty of care anywhere in the United States of America to keep somebody safe, including themselves at a place of employment," he said.

Safety ultimately comes down to the CEO, which begs the question: Which CEO? Would that be Chris Kasulka, then Oakmont Management Group (OMG) president and CEO, or Bill Gallaher, founder and owner of parent company Oakmont Senior Living (OSL) and partial owner of OMG?

The labyrinth of Oakmont's limited liability corporations could easily confuse the best of attorneys. The California secretary of state lists six limited liability corporations involving Varenna alone, including Varenna of Fountaingrove, OSL Varenna Employees, Varenna Care Center, Varenna Investors Group, and just plain Varenna, LLC. Most were registered by either Bill Gallaher or his daughter, Molly Gallaher Flater. Villa Capri is a subset of some but not all of these. Additionally, many companies use initials, such as OSL Santa Rosa Fountaingrove, OSL Construction, OSL Properties, and OSL Santa Rosa Projects, all with the same Windsor, California, address. And this structure was not specific to the Santa Rosa properties. Nearly every Oakmont property from Sacramento to Escondido initially had its own separate California corporation, registered by Bill Gallaher or Molly Gallaher Flater and using similar naming functions. In 2021, 18 properties were reregistered as Delaware corporations by a nondescript entity referred to as C. T. Corporation based in New York. Gallaher's name remains on the parent company, Oakmont Senior Living, still a California corporation.

"It's common in long-term care for facilities to be owned and operated by a relatively complex link of various entities," said Eric Carlson, director of long-term care services and support advocacy attorney for the nonprofit Justice in Aging. One entity might own the property, another one manages it, another is an investment trust, and among the entities a hierarchy may exist. "It's generally set up to isolate certain entities, so they are not held liable or responsible in the instance of debts or bad care or litigation." When corporations are sued, Carlson said, they use the complex ownership structure to separate out the liability and deny accountability. "They make various defenses saying 'We're just passive investors. We're not involved in these management decisions. What do we know? We shouldn't be held responsible for this.' Or 'We're out of state; you don't have jurisdiction.'"

Stebner was used to the game. As much as attorneys wanted to say OMG and OSL were independent operations, Stebner sought to prove both maintained a financial and managerial codependency. She tried to do so by asking top executives to read aloud parts of the contract pertaining to OMG's management of the communities that OSL built. OSL owned the land and buildings while OMG handled the budgets, staffing, and daily operations. She was able to get on the record that the parent company, OSL, retained final say over budgets, employee salaries, marketing plans, and capital improvements. Chris Kasulka explained under oath that expenditures of more than $1,500 required OSL approval and this meant getting approval from the OSL owners.

Ownership of OMG was commingled. CEO Kasulka owned 33 percent of OMG while Bill Gallaher owned 19 percent, and his daughters Molly and Nickie each owned 17 percent. Keith Fitzsimmons and Joe Lin, the CFOs of OMG and OSL, respectively, are also listed as part owners, as is Courtney Siegel, the president and CEO of OMG who took over from Kasulka during summer 2018. Besides financial connections, the heads of both corporations were interlocked from the start. Bill Gallaher registered the corporation in 2012. Kasulka said she worked with Molly daily and Bill "a lot more often" at the start. Once the management team was established, Kasulka conversed with both Bill and Molly weekly or as needed in 2017, and all worked out of the same office, she testified. But on paper, OMG was in charge of operations at Villa Capri, so Stebner pressed Kasulka on who should take responsibility for what happened during the fire. Kasulka refused, saying she merely created the team and was only "responsible for the overall vision and direction and strategic planning for the company."

> *Stebner: But in terms of the buck stops with you, you're the president and the CEO of a company who has a management agreement [that] says that…you're going to hire and fire staff; you're going to prepare the budgets. And so my question is: In terms of, like, ultimate responsibility, would you agree that as the president and CEO, that you had the ultimate responsibility to assure that the staff at the communities were sufficient in number and trained, ultimately?*

> *Kasulka: Yeah, I don't feel that—you know, I was—it was based on the needs of the residents, and I wouldn't be the person that would know that on a day-to-day basis. So I—you know, that would really be the team at the community; and if they needed help, they would be probably talking to the regional nurse or the regional operations person.*

> *Stebner: So the answer is "no" to my question? You would not have ultimate responsibility, correct?*

> *Kasulka: I wouldn't have direct responsibility.*

When pressed on her exact role within the company, Kasulka said her job was to create "the best-in-class" management company and operations team in the business. Although she sat in on the interview for hiring Smith, Kasulka said she didn't personally deal with budgets, staffing, or daily operations at Villa Capri. "I would still say that Debie Smith, as the licensed administrator, that is part of her responsibility, to ensure that she has adequate staffing at all times, including the night of the fire."

Why weren't more staff on duty that night?
Unlike federal staff-to-resident ratios for nursing homes, assisted living facilities operate under state law and, in California, simply need to "ensure that there's an adequate number of staff to support each resident's physical, social, emotional safety, and health care needs as identified in his or her current

appraisal." For assisted living, the staffing ratio is subjective. For example, at Brookdale Chanate, Monique Dixon said she once had 11 memory care residents who all slept through the night, and none of them were wanderers. That scenario called for fewer night shift employees than when she had 14 memory residents with three on hospice and two who wandered. According to Monique, these subjective ratios depend on "acuity," or the amount of attention the residents require. Twice-annual appraisals of residents dictated how much staffing Villa Capri would provide, Debie Smith testified. Bedridden residents such as Bess Budow would have more needs, thus higher points and greater costs for their care. "The more points means the higher the acuity," Smith said.

> *Stebner: One way for you to figure out your staffing levels is to, like, add up—you take all of the points of, like, everybody in the building and say, "I have, like, 2,000 points, but now I've got, like, 3,000 points, so I need to add more staff" or something like that?*
>
> *Smith: No.*
>
> *Stebner: Okay. Do you know what those points are even used for in terms of setting staffing? Do you even know?*
>
> *Smith: I do not know.*

Yet Smith said she and the health services director set staffing levels. Smith put four people on duty most, but not all, nights that Anett was scheduled to work once her pregnancy moved her to light duty. However, staffing schedules showed some nights when Anett worked with only two others. How such staffing decisions were made was also the foundation of Stebner's September 2017 class action lawsuit against Oakmont regarding the billing system at its California properties. She said the point system as advertised gave residents the reasonable expectation that if their points go up and they have to pay more, they will get more care. "That's not true. It's a static staffing model," Stebner said.

Had Smith added more staff, she might have run over budget, which, according to VP of Operations Ken Garnett's testimony, was developed by himself and Smith, and approved by CFO Keith Fitzsimmons "and the owners." Fitzsimmons had worked with Bill Gallaher for 15 years on the construction side before joining Oakmont Management Group and was also a part owner of OMG.

Staying within budget was also incentivized as part of Smith's compensation plan. "I was eligible, as executive director, for a quarterly bonus... if I met certain—if I met my budget," Smith testified. Financial incentives existed as well for the executives who were also OMG owners. If a community increased its profit year-over-year, then its corporate parent earned 10 percent of the difference, and from that 10 percent, owners took their share of the profit. For each $100,000 year-over-year increase in profit, for example, OMG would earn $10,000, and a part-owner like Chris Kasulka would take a share from that pool, in this case 33 percent or $3,300. This earnings structure exists for each of the more than 50 communities under the Oakmont Management Group portfolio, meaning owners could take home significant sums each year—sums based solely on a community's ability to keep costs low and revenue high.

Stebner questioned Kasulka about the virtue of this arrangement.

> Stebner: As someone owning 33 percent of a company, did you ever feel any conflict that when you were making decisions as to the safety of the residents, what you'll have to spend on them, that it would directly influence your pocketbook?
>
> Kasulka: Never, ever.

Budgetary decisions on staffing may have affected Kasulka and Smith's pocketbooks, but others controlled the purse strings.

> Stebner: And did you understand that ultimately OSL had to approve the budget?
>
> Kasulka: Yes.
>
> Stebner: And the people who were approving the budget at OSL, do you know if any of them had any background whatsoever in running a [Residential Care home For the Elderly]?

Kasulka: I don't know.

Stebner: Did you ever ask?

Kasulka: No, I never asked.

Stebner: Did you have a concern that the people who were making decisions about budgets for Residential Care homes For the Elderly, whether they had any experience in an RCFE or not?

Kasulka: No. That didn't—that didn't—that thought process didn't occur to me.

What Stebner was trying to show was Oakmont Senior Living was "basically a construction company. The people they hire are not well versed in caring for elders. These guys are 'build baby, build,'" she said. She homed in on this in her questioning of VP of Operations Ken Garnett, who Kasulka said had more direct oversight over Villa Capri's budget and staffing needs than she did.

Stebner: So who would decide, like, how many people would be on the NOC shift, for example, at Villa Capri, in October of 2017?

Garnett: The executive director.

Stebner: Okay. Well, doesn't she have a budget she works with?

Garnett: Yeah. Yes.

Stebner: But the number of caregivers on staff on the NOC shift in October of 2017 is essentially—that's decided by Molly [Gallaher Flater] and Bill [Gallaher], correct, in the end?

Garnett: They would have final approval.

Gallaher Deposed

Thursday, July 12, 2018—9:06 a.m.: Offices of Redwood Litigation Services, Santa Rosa, California.
Deposition taken in the matter of Sherry Minson versus Oakmont Senior Living:

> *Question [Kathryn Stebner]: Please state your name for the record.*
>
> *Answer: William Perry Gallaher.*
>
> *Stebner: And what is your date of birth?*
>
> *Gallaher: January 30, 1951…*
>
> *Stebner: Can you tell me about your educational background, please?*
>
> *Gallaher: I went to Proctor Terrace Elementary School, Santa Rosa Junior High, Santa Rosa High School, Santa Rosa JC, and Sonoma State.*

Despite drawn-out resistance from opposing counsel, Stebner finally got what she wanted, an opportunity to get the sworn testimony of Bill Gallaher. But it came late in the process, more than a month after a superior court judge had ordered Oakmont attorneys to make Gallaher available. At that point, Stebner had already interviewed all but a couple key witnesses, and the trial was just three weeks from starting.

The deposition took place over two sessions, the second occurring on July 20, at a litigation services office a mile down the hill from Villa Capri. Stebner's goal was to clarify who was ultimately responsible in terms of operations and budgeting at Villa Capri, who owned and was responsible for which companies, and what changes had been made at Villa Capri since the fire occurred.

> *Stebner: Have you brought any documents with you today [in response to Stebner's request to produce documents pertaining to ownership and operation questions]?*

Gallaher: No.

Stebner: Okay. Did you review any documents to prepare for today's deposition?

Gallaher: No.

Stebner: At the time of the fire, who owned the Villa Capri building?

Gallaher: It was in an LLC partnership.

Stebner: Okay. And who were the owners of that partnership at that time?

Gallaher: I don't know.

Stebner: To your knowledge, was there a lease between the owner of the property and the tenant?

Gallaher: I don't know....

According to the transcript, Stebner then produced a document showing Varenna Assisted Living, LLC, owned 100 percent of Villa Capri and that Gallaher himself owned 70 percent of Varenna at Fountaingrove with no other individuals owning more than 10 percent.

Stebner: Does this refresh your recollection as to the owners of Varenna Assisted Living, LLC or Varenna at Fountaingrove, LLC?

Gallaher: No.

Stebner: Okay. Do you think this is incorrect as well?

Gallaher: I don't know if it's correct or not.

Stebner: It also says that you're the only manager. Do you think that's true?

Gallaher: I don't know.

Early on the first day, Stebner established, with Gallaher's concurrence, that Oakmont, up to that point, had designed and built more than 50 senior communities throughout the West Coast comprising nearly 3,250 living units with a total market value of roughly $2 billion. Another 1,058 units were under construction or in the planning process, which would bring the company's total net worth to more than $3 billion.

Gallaher explained how each of his five children had ownership and/ or management positions with his companies and limited partnerships. He built his first state-licensed long-term care facility in Windsor in 1995, he said, and started Poppy Bank in 2005.

> *Stebner: And what was your purpose for starting that bank, if any?*
>
> *Gallaher: What was the purpose?*
>
> *Stebner: Uh-huh.*
>
> *Gallaher: I like banking.*
>
> *Stebner: Okay. Anything else?*
>
> *Gallaher: Provide services to the community, lending community....*
>
> *Stebner: And in October 2017, approximately how many branches of Poppy Bank were there?*
>
> *Gallaher: Nine or ten.*
>
> *Stebner: Okay. How many, if any, of those branches were inside of your buildings?*
>
> *Gallaher: There was one in Varenna, and there was—or is one in Varenna, and there's one in the [Fountaingrove] Lodge....*

From there Gallaher walked through the history of his construction career—from partnering with Dwayne Clark to found Aegis in 1997 to eventually forming Oakmont Senior Living and Oakmont Management Group. Stebner then asked about the night of the fire, and Gallaher relayed his family's harrowing experience in fleeing their mountaintop homes on Blue Gate Road before it, too, was swept over by the flames. Through it all, Stebner was taken by how calm Gallaher remained during questioning, his voice barely above a whisper at times. Nothing seemed to animate him, she said. By the same token, she said he also seemed to show a certain detachment not only to the events that occurred at Villa Capri and Varenna but to the operational details of his companies as well.

Stebner: How many Oakmont LLCs are there?

Gallaher: I don't know....

Stebner: Do you have any estimate at all as to how many Oakmont LLCs there are, even an estimate?

Gallaher: Twenty or thirty. Forty.

Gallaher testified he owned 80 percent of OSL, but he didn't have a role in managing operational budgets. "It's not my position to review these budgets and to make that decision," he emphasized. "If there's a capital improvement that's substantial, a remodel, a change, major change to the building, that's something that I would have a decision whether to do or not."

From there, Stebner pressed him on the specific experience his OSL managers had in overseeing the safety and the well-being of senior citizens.

Stebner: Are there people who are managers at OSL who have a specialty in assisted living?

Gallaher: Yes, there are.

Stebner: And who's that?

Gallaher: Joe Lin.

Stebner: And what's his background in assisted living?

Gallaher: He's finance.

Stebner: Okay. Anyone else, other than Joe?

> Gallaher: Keith Fitzsimons.
>
> Stebner: Okay. And what's his background?
>
> Gallaher: Finance....
>
> Stebner: What about your daughter, Molly? What is her experience, if any, in terms of her knowledge of assisted living facilities that you knew of prior to October 2017?
>
> Gallaher: She was involved in marketing.
>
> Stebner: Okay. Anything else?
>
> Gallaher: She never worked in an assisted living building, but she was involved in the marketing and still is involved in marketing.

Stebner would later share that, once again, her objective in this questioning was to underscore how the people making the financial decisions at OSL were primarily builders, designers, and finance people, individuals without clinical experience in caring for seniors. She felt she had already established from prior depositions that OMG executives didn't have final say over spending decisions. Rather, those responsibilities belonged to Oakmont Senior Living, and, for anything over $1,500, Bill Gallaher himself.

***

On the second and final day of Gallaher's deposition, Stebner focused her questions on the fire and its aftermath.

> Stebner: Did you have any understanding, one way or another, prior to the night of the fire whether there was an evacuation plan for wildfires at Villa Capri?
>
> Gallaher: No, I didn't know.
>
> Stebner: Prior to the night of the fire, did you understand that there was a risk of wildfires in the area by Villa Capri?

Gallaher: No.

Stebner: Did you know there was a previous fire in the exact place in 1964?

Gallaher: No.

Stebner: Where were you in 1964?

Gallaher: In Santa Rosa.

Stebner: How old were you?

Gallaher: Thirteen.

Stebner: Prior to the night of the fire, what was your understanding, if any, as to whether or not there was a risk of wildfires in the area of Villa Capri prior to the night of the fire?

Gallaher: I didn't think about any wildfires prior to that.

When asked whether he believed residents of Villa Capri should have had an opportunity to search through the ashes for their belongings, Gallaher said no. "We did look for personal property," Gallaher testified. "We had the company that removed the debris look for personal property," although nothing was found.

When asked if he had ever reached out to personally thank the family members who assisted with the evacuations, he said he hadn't. "I can't now because they are suing us," he told Stebner. Gallaher said he asked OMG's Courtney Siegel to thank the family members, but he never followed up to see whether it had been done.

Stebner: Do you know who saved your mother-in-law's life?

Gallaher: No.

Stebner: Do you know if it was a family member?

Gallaher: No. I don't know.

Stebner: Did you ever ask?

Gallaher: No.

Perhaps the most significant interaction during that final round of questioning occurred when Stebner asked Gallaher directly about his views of what happened at Villa Capri and what Oakmont Senior Living could have done differently. His response was unequivocal.

> *Stebner: Based on everything that you know now regarding the evacuation at Villa Capri, at any time in your own mind were you proud of the way that Oakmont Senior Living or Oakmont Management Group handled the evacuation at Villa Capri?*
>
> *Gallaher: Yes.*
>
> *Stebner: …Based on everything that you know now, in your own mind, did you also feel that Oakmont Senior Living and Oakmont Management Group was prepared for evacuation the night of the fire?*
>
> *Gallaher: Yes.*
>
> *Stebner: In your own mind, did you ever think about whether or not anyone at Oakmont Senior Living or Oakmont Management Group did anything wrong the night of the evacuation? In your own mind, did you ever think that?*
>
> *Gallaher: No.*
>
> *Stebner: In your own mind, did you ever think about anything that anyone could have done differently that night…? Did you ever sit down and think, "Okay, well, now, I have all this information. I know what happened. Let me sit down and think about, gee, is there anything at all we could have done differently?" Did you ever go through that thought process at all?*
>
> *Gallaher: No. No.*

Gallaher also made clear he saw no need for making any changes to the new assisted living facilities he was building.

> *Stebner: In terms of the assisted living facilities that you're building after the fire, have you made any changes in design or otherwise, as a result of what happened at Villa Capri in terms of changes about backup power, generators, number of vehicles, alarms, delayed egress, any changes whatsoever?*
>
> *Defendant's attorney, Alexander Giovanniello: I'm going to object....*
>
> *Gallaher: Not that I know of.*

To Stebner, the most awkward moment of Gallaher's deposition came nearly three hours into the first day of questioning when she asked him about his mother-in-law and how and when he learned about the events that transpired at Villa Capri. The exchange was picked up on the raw transcript of the interview.

> *Stebner: So you had a conversation with Chris Kasulka. She said, "Everybody's out. It was difficult." Who else did you talk to regarding what happened up there that night?*
>
> *Gallaher: I talked to Joel [Ruiz].*
>
> *Stebner: And would that be within a month or weeks or...?*
>
> *Gallaher. Yeah. Probably a month.*
>
> *Stebner: Okay. And what did Joel tell you?*
>
> *Gallaher: He told me that—geez...*

According to Stebner, the deposition was interrupted by something in the parking lot that was visible to Gallaher and others through the large conference room window behind her.

She turned to see what Gallaher was observing and turned back in disbelief. "There's a woman in a short white dress with large breasts" walking by, she said in a later interview. "I look at him. I was the only woman in the room. Even the guys were cringing."

> *Gallaher: Just distracting, for a minute. I'm sorry.*
>
> *Giovanniello: People walking by.*
>
> *Stebner: Um-hum.*
>
> *Gallaher: Where were we?*

Oakmont Denies Abandonment

The evidence that Oakmont managers and staff had left residents behind was overwhelming. Kathy and Melissa both testified they were the only ones who stayed with the final 24 residents from approximately 3:30 a.m. on. Two of the last residents to leave, Alice Eurotas and Ruth Callen, testified it wasn't employees who helped them down the stairs or into police cars. Two police sergeants and one officer also made clear they did not see any employees at Villa Capri when they arrived sometime after 4:15 a.m.

When Stebner questioned Oakmont executives, however, she said she was shocked by their denials and lack of attrition. "They never admitted in any deposition that the residents were alone without staff," she said. Stebner pressed one executive after another to own up. When asked who got the last residents out of Villa Capri, VP of Operations Ken Garnett said, "I do not know."

> *Stebner: Did you ever ask?*
>
> *Garnett: No, I did not.*
>
> *Stebner: Did you wonder?*
>
> *Garnett: Probably. I'm sure it crossed my mind sometime. I can't recall a specific time where I sat down and thought about it. We were pretty busy after the fact taking care of the residents.*

Under oath, Tammy Moratto said her standard response to people who asked her if residents were left at Villa Capri was, "Everybody got out alive and we did a great job." Debie Smith answered, "I don't know," when Stebner asked if anyone who worked for Villa Capri was there between 3:30 a.m. and 6 a.m.

> *Stebner: So is it your testimony that you've never heard from any source that, in the end, the only people up there with the elders were family members? No one has ever told you that, ever?*
>
> *Smith: I was not there. I don't know. I've heard different stories.*
>
> *Stebner: So I know you weren't there. I'm just asking you what you've been told.... So has anyone ever told you that, in the end, there were over 20 of your residents up there, but none of your care staff?*
>
> *Smith: No.*

Smith said her focus was on whether everybody was out and safe, not whether employees left while residents remained in the building. On Stebner's pressing, Smith said she had wondered and had talked to the employees after the fact.

> *Stebner: Did they tell you, "When we left, there were still residents there"?*
>
> *Smith: Yes.*

Smith testified she had never told the caregivers they needed to stay with the residents, but that she expected them to. "Just morally it's the right thing to do," she said. "We're responsible for these people, and as care providers and people that are in this industry, it's understood."

CEO Kasulka proved evasive when Stebner confronted her with similar questions about abandonment. "I think I came to understand that they were transporting residents down and weren't able to get back up and that may have been the case," Kasulka said.

> *Stebner: Other than your lawyers, did anyone ever tell you that there was a time when there were some residents up at Villa Capri that morning, but no staff? Yes or no?*
>
> *Kasulka: I'm not sure.*

With Stebner's help, Kasulka did remember she had been aware residents were left behind, but she couldn't recall who told her.

> *Stebner: When you found out that there was a time when it was the residents and no staff up there for a period of time, did you ever talk to anyone, any of your staff, and say, you know, "That shouldn't have happened"?*
>
> *Kasulka: I didn't have that conversation, no.*

One Oakmont employee, however, surprised attorneys on both sides with her forthrightness about whether employees left the last 24 residents. Caregiver Elizabeth Lopez described how she noticed Kathy and Melissa were locked out and offered to stay to help them, but Kathy told her to leave because Elizabeth had three residents in her car.

> *Elizabeth: After I leave, there [were] no staff members that I know of.*
>
> *Stebner: You were the last staff member to leave?*
>
> *Elizabeth: From the caregivers that were working that night, yes, I was the last one.*

Oakmont's "Real Story" Claims Enrage Families

On July 26, 2018, the same day Elizabeth Lopez stunned attorneys by laying bare her first-person account of what happened that night, Oakmont Senior Living published a new, multiple-page website that purported to do the same. The unsigned Oakmont Senior Living Story site claimed its purpose was to "provide an honest account of the actions we took to proactively evacuate our residents and provide ongoing support to them in the aftermath of this deadly natural disaster." Titled, "The Real Story Regarding Oakmont Senior Living & The Tubbs Fire," the new website included a retelling of the evacuations at Varenna, Villa Capri, the Fountaingrove Lodge, and The Terraces, a Q&A section, and a series of testimonials from residents and family members.

"Staff members, along with family members, evacuated the last residents," the online statement from Oakmont read, adding that "a total of seven employees successfully evacuated all residents at Villa Capri." The response by its staff was "heroic," Oakmont claimed, and told a tale that while occasionally accurate, more often did a delicate dance with the truth, leveraged convenient omission of fact, or avoided addressing critical questions altogether.

For example, OSL posed the question, "Did staff members provide information to the residents concerning the imminent danger?" The company's answer was misleading. "Yes, as soon as it was determined staff members needed to evacuate all residents, without the help of the Fire Department, residents were immediately notified, and the evacuation process began."

To the question, "Were there backup generators on hand that would allow elevators to operate?" the company was equally vague. "It would be extremely dangerous and contrary to all safety precautions to take the elevator during an active fire," it said.

And to the question, "Did Oakmont staff turn off fire alarms?" the company responded, "The fire alarms at Villa Capri were never turned off or silenced...." But no mention was made of employees turning off alarms at Varenna.

The most notable aspects of Oakmont's account concerned what details were left out. The retelling of events at Varenna, for example, made no reference to residents being told to go back to their rooms, or of Executive Director Nathan Condie and all other staff leaving and not returning. Furthermore, there was no discussion of family members, specifically the Kislings, finding residents left behind and helping with evacuations until firefighters and police officers arrived.

OSL's online recounting of events at Villa Capri had even more gaps. It included vague references to family members assisting but didn't mention the difficulty of getting second-floor residents in wheelchairs down to the lobby, of not having an evacuation plan, and of the missing shuttle keys. It also made no reference to residents who were dependent on staff to evacuate being left in the hands of family members, or of Kathy and Melissa's harrowing efforts to regain access to the building by breaking the front door glass. In fact, the statement made no mention of Kathy, Mark, Melissa, or Joey at all. "Police cars and a city bus loaded up the remaining residents and delivered them to Elsie Allen High School," the site noted instead.

Oakmont's Q&A section also addressed a number of issues that journalists had repeatedly raised in press coverage over the previous nine months. Although Oakmont representatives initially responded to media inquiries immediately after the fire, the company had declined to answer questions from reporters in the weeks that followed. The new website was the company's most detailed response to media inquiries in months.

One of the most pivotal questions was, "Did family members evacuate all residents from Villa Capri?"

The answer, again, was full of half-truths. "This was a team effort led by staff, with help from family members, which we greatly appreciated," the website read. "Staff members used their personal vehicles to transport residents to safety. Staff also used two buses to safely shuttle everyone off-site. Staff members, along with family members, evacuated the last residents."

Another question was, "Did family members who assisted in the evacuation at Villa Capri suffer from any emotional distress?" Oakmont skirted this one too. "We appreciate the efforts of family members who assisted in the evacuation," the site stated. "This was a catastrophic disaster for residents across Sonoma County."

One portion, titled "Thank You To Our Selfless Employees," read: "As the entire nation watched our beloved community bracing for one of the worst fire-related disasters in modern memory, we saw truly selfless acts from our staff, first responders, and residents that filled our hearts with hope."

The website also offered 25 testimonials, of which only four were signed with any identifying information. The rest were attributed to a series of initials or "family member of resident." One note, attributed to "LG and PLD, family member of Villa Capri resident," said, "My sister and I would like to commend the administration and staff of Villa Capri for the outstanding evacuation that happened early Monday morning." Another, from an unnamed Varenna resident's family, said, "We are grateful to the outstanding owners, management, and staff who were able to safely evacuate hundreds of residents the night of the firestorm." One unidentified Villa Capri resident's relative said, "Please send me info on where I can send a donation. Debbie [sic] (Villa Capri) and the entire staff need much recognition. They saved my Mom's life."

The testimonials were anchored by a lengthy statement from local attorney and Gallaher business associate Doug Bosco. Bosco's mother had lived at Villa Capri during the last three years of her life. Although she died there in April 2017, six months before the fire, he offered a full-throated defense of the company, noting that "without help from first responders," all residents "were rescued and brought to safety." As with the rest of the website, Bosco's 800-word testimonial, which he later said was based on information he gained from talking to OSL representatives, didn't once mention Kathy and Mark Allen, Melissa Langhals, or Joey Horsman.

During his mother's care at Villa Capri, "I got to know many of the staff and the management, and it really disturbed me that I see them sort of being blamed for everything. And I asked myself, 'Why is anybody being blamed?'" Bosco said during an interview six weeks later with local KSRO radio personality Pat Kerrigan. "Every single one of those people was rescued, every single one without getting harmed at all was brought to safety."

Yet residents, staff, and family members were not left unharmed. Four residents died within 10 weeks of the fires, and many residents and family members were left with lasting physical injuries, including lung damage and post-traumatic stress challenges.

The new website concluded with a letter from Cindy Gallaher addressed to "community members." "As a lifelong resident of Sonoma County, we share in the sense of profound loss left by the devastating fires that swept our area the week of October 9th," she wrote. She noted how she and her husband have a "deep and abiding connection with this land and community" and how their grandchildren are fifth generation Sonoma County residents. "Our local senior communities, the Fountaingrove Lodge and Terraces, Varenna, and Villa Capri, we consider our flagship properties," she said. "All were evacuated safely in the early morning of October 9th, and Villa Capri shortly thereafter was destroyed by fire." She said, "in an effort to soften the terrible sadness and loss we are all experiencing," she and her husband, along with business partners, were going to join the community fundraising effort by pledging to give $2 million directly to local nonprofit groups assisting with emergency housing, food distribution, and elder care.

Nevertheless, those who had firsthand knowledge of what actually did occur at Villa Capri and Varenna were aghast at Oakmont's claims. Mark Allen was particularly taken aback at Oakmont's response to: "Were there human remains in the rubble cleared at Villa Capri?" "No," the post read, "All residents and staff were accounted for." Oakmont could not have known this for certain, Mark argued, because it took them a while to account for everyone, and they had not spoken to him. "Nobody died because *I* went through the rooms and left each door open," he said. "And Kathy and a police officer went through before they left, and *they* closed the doors." What Oakmont Senior Living posted "made me physically sick," said Dawn Ross, so sick she couldn't finish reading because "it was too painful." She remembered thinking, "This is just lies."

Jessica Kilcullen, granddaughter of Sally Tilbury, one of the women left overnight at Varenna, called the new website "categorically wrong," and said it "kind of mitigated everybody's feelings."

It made Kathy Allen cry. "I started to read it and then I couldn't do it," she said. "They were basically calling us liars."

The accusations weighed on Beth as well. "When I read it, I openly sobbed," she said. "I couldn't believe they had the audacity to say what they were saying, that they were good guys. Some of the statements in there are such blatant lies. Whoever wrote that website should be ashamed."

Melissa Langhals was also upset but offered a different perspective. "It was totally a shitshow. Of course they're going to say crap like this because they're trying to save their own butts," she said.

There were other eyes on the Oakmont Senior Living Story site, including those from California Advocates for Nursing Home Reform. "They put on their website how brave the staff members were," said Executive Director Pat McGinnis. "It was disgusting."

Her colleague, advocate Mike Connors, assessed Oakmont's approach from a different perspective but was also concerned. "They're engaged in a campaign of influence. They were obviously trying to exert any pressure they could," he said, knowing that the case would eventually come to a very public trial. "Their website was to give the impression that they and staff performed heroically, and the residents of their community were enormously grateful for how wonderful they were."

What also stood out to Kathy, Mark, Melissa, and others was Oakmont's unwillingness to get the full story of what happened before presenting its tribute to its "heroic" staff members. No one from any Oakmont company ever reached out to any of them to interview them concerning what happened that night or to offer support. Nor did the website include any testimonials from employees involved in the evacuations. The only employee testimony came from a corporate employee who lost her home in the fire. She spoke of how gracious Oakmont had been in "offering a generous financial package" to help recoup her losses, find housing, and set up "counseling services at my office so that I could meet with someone to talk about everything for free." She did not reference the evacuation or the residents. And she was not present at either Villa Capri or Varenna that night.

August 16, 2018: Settlement or Trial

Mark and Kathy Allen picked up Beth Eurotas-Steffy at a park and ride off Highway 101, and the three drove to a mediator's office in downtown San Francisco for what was billed as a settlement conference, a last-ditch effort to see if the parties involved could avoid trial. *Why would we want to avoid a trial?* Beth thought. It was August 16, 2018, the day before jury selection was slated to begin. Attorneys for both sides had compiled a witness list of 154 people for a trial that was expected to last six to eight weeks.

Inside a long, narrow conference room with a wall of windows overlooking the financial district, Beth sat in a comfortable dark leather chair around a rectangular table. Nearby were Mark and Kathy, Deputy Joey Horsman, and Sherry and Sarah Minson. Kathryn Stebner told the group that the Giovanniello Law Group, on behalf of Oakmont Senior Living, had made a settlement offer. She presented the plaintiffs their options: settle or go to trial.

Stebner herself was torn. From the start, her intention was to air the events of October 8 and 9 before a jury. She wanted to try the case. It felt personal. But as a trial lawyer, she had to see past her own goals and weigh the risks to her clients; two-thirds of the elderly plaintiffs had already died or couldn't testify because of dementia or declining health. "I had to look at what it would be like for them to go through this and the potentialities of loss." And the potential to lose was palpable.

The Giovanniello Law Group's trial brief challenged that the plaintiffs couldn't prove with "clear and convincing evidence" their allegations of elder abuse, negligence, false imprisonment, intentional infliction of emotional distress, or the other claims. Abandonment was the basis for the elder abuse charge, and Giovanniello argued that Oakmont employees didn't intend to abandon anyone. "Indeed, Villa Capri never deserted its residents, that is, the staff never left the residents without the intent to return to Villa Capri," Giovanniello's trial brief stated. Caregivers Cynthia and Elizabeth planned to return to Villa Capri for more residents, and Marie So left her purse there, expecting to return on the bus with Joel. Nathan Condie, Tammy Moratto, Ken Garnett, and other employees said authorities prevented them from getting to the complex. Could Stebner prove intentional abandonment against this argument?

Similarly, considering any emergency plan had burned with Villa Capri, could Stebner meet the "clear and convincing" threshold that no plan existed or that Oakmont hadn't properly trained staff, since the employees on duty had completed mandatory computer trainings, and other training records had burned? If Oakmont managers were abiding by state regulations for staffing numbers and training, how would Stebner prove they weren't sufficiently staffed?

Stebner knew her clients were not suing for the money, which if they won, would be the only restitution the verdict would bring. But a settlement could force change. A loss would bring neither. "There's a lot of things you can't do with a verdict that you can do with a settlement," she said. "I had to tell [my clients] the risks and the benefits in a very objective way, which is challenging when you want to go get [Oakmont], especially when you are all ready to go." Beth recalled Stebner cautioning the group that going to trial was not a guaranteed victory. "She hammered that home a lot, that everyone could end up with nothing. Seemed so clear she did not want to go to trial."

Over the course of 10 hours, Stebner hopped among her clients in one conference room and Oakmont representatives and their attorneys in another, trying to forge an agreement. In between, she pulled each plaintiff individually aside for private discussions. Beth likened it to a used car dealership sale, when the salesperson has to take a number to the "manager" in the back.

Beth, however, was not shy about expressing to the group what she wanted; she fought "tooth and nail" to go to trial, she said. "I felt it was imperative that the details from Villa Capri that night be exposed in a court of law. That, at least to me, was so much more important than any amount of money. But she had trouble convincing the others. As they sat together all day, Beth said, "Details, fears, emotions shared began to make us all sad, stressed, and weary, especially the ones who were actually there that night. The more time that went by, some of them just wanted to end it now and move forward. Put that horrible night behind us. And others of us felt justice was more important."

One by one, the plaintiffs left the conference room to speak individually with Stebner and another attorney in a separate room. When they returned, each remained close-lipped. Beth was the last to be called. She sat across a narrow table from Stebner and her associate Karman Guadagni, who told her it looked like a settlement was underway, but they all had to agree. "And I was the only holdout," Beth said. "I felt such pressure. It was horrible." Beth reiterated her goals of holding Oakmont accountable, getting justice for the victims, seeking appreciation for the heroes, and enacting new legislation to prevent a repeat of the bungled evacuation. "Without the trial and the publicity that goes with it, all of these goals will be much harder to achieve," she said.

Stebner told Beth she could have all of the law firm's trial material that was already loaded in a car, ready to go to the Santa Rosa courthouse if no settlement was reached. She promised to help Beth get the story told. Exhausted, emotional, confused, hungry, and disappointed, Beth felt she had no choice but to relent.

All of the plaintiffs and their families had agreed they were going to accept the settlement offer, which, according to more than one source, stood at $3.75 million. After attorneys took their share, the money would be divided in varying amounts among the 17 plaintiffs, depending on the extent of individual injuries, trauma, or death. In the end, the individual amounts received "were hardly worth it all," noted one recipient.

Beth regretted the decision immediately, especially when she learned Oakmont's insurance would likely cover the full settlement amount. She felt betrayed. In an email she wrote to one of Stebner's associates, Beth said she had felt alone and pressured to go along. "I had no one on my side. Ironic. That is how the victims likely felt at Villa Capri that night," she said.

Beth was not the only one with regrets. In hindsight, Stebner regretted not taking the case to trial. "It's very difficult to settle something on the footsteps of the courthouse," she said years later. "It's a big letdown to do it, on a personal level."

In the movie that often plays in her mind, Stebner pictures two specific scenes from October 9, 2017, that she believes happened in tandem: Nathan Condie driving away from Varenna with residents loaded in his car, while Kathy and Melissa toss a tow hitch through Villa Capri's front door to get back inside. "It's [at] the exact time," Stebner said. "Just the juxtaposition of him driving away in his Kia. If I tried the case, I was going to have a visual of that, because that visual is the whole case. Those two scenes next to each other is basically everything you need to know."

But it would not be a picture painted for a jury to visualize.

State Investigators Issue Their Findings

While Kathryn Stebner fought Oakmont in court, the state DSS, which is charged with overseeing health and safety codes and regulations that dictate how California's residential care homes for the elderly operate, continued its investigation in parallel. For 11 months, regional DSS staff worked through a long list of interviewees, with each of their narratives recorded in writing and attached to either the Villa Capri or Varenna complaint. The goal was to determine whether the staff abandoned residents and failed to notify family members of the evacuations, and whether negligence resulted in Bess Budow's broken hip.

If during the course of these investigations DSS found code violations, then the department could propose a variety of penalties ranging from fines to license suspension. Typically, a DSS regional office handled investigations into residential care homes, but because the scope of these allegations was "egregious," according to an executive-level DSS employee, state-level administrators and attorneys got involved, and on September 4, 2018, Pamela Dickfoss, DSS deputy director for the Community Care Licensing division, signed the formal complaint, or "accusation," against Oakmont Senior Living, Oakmont Management Group, Debie Smith, and Nathan Condie.

Dickfoss and her team sought to revoke Oakmont's license to operate Villa Capri and Varenna and prohibit Debie Smith and Nathan Condie from working in the industry—for life. The proposed punishments were severe. In Oakmont's case it meant the company would need to relinquish both operations. For Smith and Condie, the terms specified they could never again hold a license in the field, own more than a 10 percent stake in a licensed facility, nor be a staff member with management responsibility in a care home. It also prohibited even their "presence in and contact with any clients of any facility licensed by the department."

The accusations and proposed penalties were based on 11 months of investigations that validated all but one of the allegations against Villa Capri and Varenna. After logging more than 30 interviews with staff, residents, and family members, and after watching police body camera footage and reading police reports, DSS attorneys determined both Villa Capri and Varenna's staff "failed to evacuate residents during a fire" and "failed [to] inform family of evacuation." When it came to the matter of neglect regarding Bess Budow, the state ruled the allegation "unsubstantiated." Essentially, even though Bess did break her hip, the state concluded something other than neglect could have theoretically caused her fall.

From the state's report, Sherry and Sarah Minson finally learned what had happened to Bess at New Vintage Church. Someone had set Bess in an armless chair in the designated memory care room, wrapped a blanket around her, and left her unattended. The Minsons were furious. "She was not capable of sitting up in a chair," Sherry said. "Nobody was watching her, and she simply fell over and hit the ground."

At the time, Jane Torres was sorting and escorting seniors into either the memory care room or the sanctuary and hadn't noticed Bess until the 92-year-old woman tumbled out of her chair and hit the floor. "What I remember is that I heard a noise, and I heard Bess moan. And I was across the room, but I recognized her voice," Torres said in her deposition. "So I rushed over to her, and I assessed her quickly, tried to make her comfortable."

The failures that DSS ruled were "substantiated" in its investigation—the failure to evacuate, and failure to notify family—were based partly on a sworn statement Dawn Ross gave in August 2018. "To me, it is criminal that Villa Capri had no emergency contact plan. When I asked why they had not called me, I was told they did not have electronic copies of resident files," Ross told DSS. "How is it possible that an assisted living facility caring for patients with dementia who are mentally unable to contact their family has no communication plan, no call tree, nothing on the cloud, not even a photocopy of emergency contacts? It is beyond belief and simply inexcusable."

The 18-page accusation found Oakmont, Debie Smith, and Nathan Condie violated regulations around personnel requirements, emergency procedures, emergency disaster plans, accountability, and residents' rights and safeguarding their personal property. In total, DSS enumerated more than 34 violations across 23 categories between the two properties.

The first factual allegation against Villa Capri found Oakmont and Debie Smith failed to ensure overnight staff were familiar with planned emergency procedures or had participated in emergency training, and that Smith's substitute was unprepared to lead in her absence. DSS confirmed none of the overnight staff knew where Smith stored keys to the buses. Marie and Elizabeth "had never participated in a fire drill involving evacuating all residents"; Anett "never participated in a fire drill involving evacuating all residents in response to an outside fire"; and Cynthia had never participated in any Villa Capri fire drill at all. And when Anett, Marie, Cynthia, and Elizabeth left, regardless of their plans to return, DSS said there were "20 elderly and infirm residents remaining at Villa Capri with no staff supervision."

According to this DSS accusation, if family members of Villa Capri residents had not remained to help, "more than 20 residents would have perished when Villa Capri burned to the ground after all staff left the facility." The situation stuck with an executive-level DSS employee who asked to be unnamed. "If it wasn't for the family members and the grace of God—you know, people got out of there because of them."

The bulk of the first factual allegation against Varenna was similar, that Oakmont "failed to ensure that facility staff members were able to provide adequate care and supervision to elderly clients at the facility on October 8–9, 2017." The accusation also said Nathan Condie directed residents back to their rooms "instead of continuing with the evacuation" because "he did not want to cause issues or make trouble for [Oakmont]." Condie left "without notifying staff that he was leaving permanently or directing them how to proceed," and he "left behind more than 70 residents with three on-duty staff members who were not trained in evacuation procedures."

The second set of accusations focused on the conduct of the executive directors. In Smith's case, rather than going to Villa Capri to help, DSS said she "returned to her home for an unknown amount of time before heading to an evacuation center" where she "eventually arrived…at approximately 6 a.m." The investigation found Condie knew when he left Varenna that the large bus was in the parking lot and its keys were in a desk drawer inside the building, but "[he] did not ensure that staff on-site, under his supervision, were aware of the location of those keys or tell them to use the bus to evacuate residents." Instead, Condie drove his personal car down the hill with four residents, despite knowing the bus could hold 26 people. He "did not ensure all residents at Varenna were awake or alerted to the situation when he left."

By virtue of these failings, DSS said neither executive director could do their job. Neither knew the requirements for providing appropriate care and supervision to their residents; neither knew the laws, rules, and regulations for their industry; and neither was capable of giving direction to others. Most damning, however, was that DSS accused both Smith and Condie of failing to possess "good character and a continuing reputation of personal integrity."

The third charge against Villa Capri involved the excavation and how Oakmont "decided to clear the Villa Capri site…using large equipment, without allowing residents or their families access to the site to search for personal belongings that may have survived the fire"—despite Oakmont promising at least two residents' family members otherwise. Dawn Ross's declaration factored in again here. "At this point, it was common knowledge no one was allowed in the burn zone, and that clean up would not be allowed until cleared by federal, state, and local authorities. It was beyond belief to think they had violated all these rules that the rest of us were abiding by," she said.

The last accusation pertained to how Oakmont corporate staff publicly portrayed the evacuation in the weeks and months that followed. DSS investigators said they lied. The state said Oakmont published to its new Oakmont Senior Living Story website "false and misleading statements" including that "a total of seven employees successfully evacuated all residents at Villa Capri," and that "the [evacuation at Villa Capri] was a team effort led by staff, with help from family members, which we [Oakmont] greatly appreciated. Staff members, along with family members evacuated the last residents." None of this was true, state officials concluded.

In addition, DSS regulators found that three maintenance staff members lied to DSS, although one walked back his initial statement. In an October 26, 2017, interview, Joel Ruiz recalled returning to Varenna at about 9 a.m. on October 9; he told DSS he "went to every room of the facility, including the casitas outside and found no residents—all residents had been evacuated." On November 2, Pouya Ansari told DSS he, Joel, and Tony Ruiz "checked all facility grounds to make sure everyone was out—all casitas, all rooms in the Main Building, and the garages on the property. Per [Pouya], all areas of Varenna had been evacuated." Tony claimed the same, at least at first. But after the DSS interviewer reviewed his statement, Tony changed it to say "that there were residents found during the return to the facility after the fires....one male and two female residents." It was Tony's revised statement that gave the DSS attorneys grounds for false claims accusations against his brother Joel and colleague Pouya.

Seven months after their October 2017 interviews with DSS, the three maintenance employees were deposed under oath as part of Stebner's lawsuit, and this time they all admitted to finding marooned residents. According to his deposition, Tony volunteered to drive back to Varenna on October 9 after he heard Nathan Condie say they needed emergency binders with residents' contact information. Under oath, Tony said he extinguished one small fire in front of the Main Building and another inside the North Building, then ran "door to door, room to room to make sure nobody was there." Tony told attorneys he ultimately drove four residents off the hill, including a man who had driven himself back to Varenna, plus another three residents he and Pouya Ansari found "as we were going into the building—into the area" on a trip to retrieve medications.

Pouya also recalled retrieving three residents from Varenna but under different circumstances. He said he made the trip for medications not only with Tony but with Joel, and that one gentleman was still in his room, awake. Pouya said they found the other two residents in the lobby, one of whom was a man in a wheelchair.

Joel's retelling put him and Tony together, but never mentioned Pouya by name. Joel told attorneys that as they approached Varenna, a woman walked outside with a little dog. The brothers helped the woman into the van, then planned to check "every single room at Varenna," but before they could begin, they heard "another resident...just yelling out, because he heard us drive up," Joel said. Joel and Tony found his room, and the man asked, perplexed, where everybody was. "And basically," Joel told attorneys, "he slept through the whole thing."

There are multiple areas where the three accounts conflict, but because Stebner's lawsuit pertained only to Villa Capri, Oakmont employees were never subject under oath to questions designed to pinpoint who was left behind overnight at Varenna. What is certain is that two women arose at Varenna October 9 to a shocking scene. Sheila Van Pelt, 79, had woken up in the Main Building and, according to her daughter-in-law Terry Van Pelt, "had no idea what was going on," and was ultimately discovered only when, per Joel's deposition, the three maintenance staffers saw her leave the building with her dog Lulu. They put the pair in the van for over an hour while the staff looked for other residents inside. "And they wouldn't let [Sheila] go back in to get her cell phone. An hour and a half, no water, no food. It was terrible," Terry said. "That poor woman was scared to death. It was disgusting how they treated her. It was like she had no rights." Sally Tilbury awoke in the South Building and thought she'd survived a nuclear holocaust. She was discovered in her room only after her granddaughter Jessica called Tony Ruiz and instructed him to check on her during one of his trips up the hill.

According to the DSS accusation, at least three residents "learned the following morning that an evacuation had taken place while they were asleep." At 8 a.m., these three "were confused and questioning everyone's whereabouts." DSS documents included a roster that said Varenna staff left behind Sheila Van Pelt, Sally Tilbury, and Royal Wald.

There were multiple contradictions in the testimony of Joel, Tony, and Pouya concerning when, where, and who among these residents were found, contradictions that weren't made clear until DSS subpoenaed Stebner's detailed and under-oath questioning. These depositions revealed more disparities and showed that ultimately no one knew exactly how many residents were left behind overnight.

DSS also may have been unaware that when Oakmont's VP of regulatory affairs and quality assurance, Sue McPherson, submitted a mandatory narrative of what happened during the fire, as required by the DSS, she never interviewed any of the caregivers. In her deposition for the Stebner lawsuit, McPherson said she interviewed eight Oakmont employees, but only three—Pouya Ansari, Tony Ruiz, and Joel Ruiz—were present at Villa Capri or Varenna the night of the fire. Another three, Debie Smith, Tammy Moratto, and Ken Garnett, were in Santa Rosa that night but not on-site. The seventh and eighth, Christian Holland and Courtney Siegel, lived in Southern California.

Stebner pressed McPherson under oath about why she did not interview Elizabeth, Marie, Anett, and Cynthia. "I obtained my information from the executive director," McPherson said. But Debie Smith also never formally interviewed the four caregivers about their experiences. "If there had been time to obtain every little detail, it would have been helpful. There was not time to do that," McPherson testified. In her rush to meet the DSS deadline, McPherson admitted to attorneys that she took some of her information from an Oakmont Senior Living press release that said "the final residents were evacuated by Oakmont personnel."

"So it is your opinion that the details you put into that narrative [were] more important than finding out whether the people that were there that night even knew what to do? Is that your testimony?" Stebner asked during the deposition. "Yes," McPherson replied. She then testified that she destroyed all notes she took during the interviews she did conduct.

On September 6, DSS served Oakmont Senior Living, Oakmont Management Group, Debie Smith, and Nathan Condie with the conclusions of its investigation. DSS also sent copies to the California Department of Justice and the Sonoma County District Attorney's Office, both of which could choose to investigate separately. At that point, Oakmont Senior Living, which claimed in an unsigned statement that the state's findings were "unsubstantiated and unfounded," had 15 days to appeal before an administrative law judge. The state set a series of hearings to begin in December, with a prehearing conference on November 9 at DSS offices in Sacramento, during which both sides would present the basis for their arguments. For DSS, Dawn Ross's sworn testimony would prove pivotal.

"In my opinion, Oakmont Senior Living is a bad actor," the practicing attorney wrote. "They provided substandard care, failed to protect their vulnerable residents during the fire, failed to timely notify family members during and after the fire, transported residents out of the county without family consent, and illegally crossed the fire line. I firmly believe they should lose their license to care for seniors, especially those with dementia."

Beth Eurotas-Steffy agreed. She wanted Oakmont's failings laid bare in public hearings. "They should not be allowed to build or manage another facility. What happened is wrong, and someone needs to be accountable," Beth said. "No one is above the law."

***

On September 12, Nathan Condie notified residents and their family members that Varenna "is the subject of a license revocation and administrator decertification action initiated by DSS" in hopes of drumming up support. In his letter, he gave contact information for Pamela Dickfoss and the "local long-term care ombudsman." "Write your state representative to share any firsthand experiences in support of Varenna's efforts during the evacuations and thereafter," he wrote. "Our hope is that [by] hearing resident stories directly, DSS and the greater community will have a clear picture of what occurred the night of the Tubbs Fire." Multiple residents did.

Some took an understanding tone, stating the Oakmont staff "did the best they could under incredible circumstances," or that "considering the general state of confusion…I think our evacuation was immensely success-ful." Another resident said, "I could tell you a million things in hindsight that should have been done differently, but given the reality of the situation, I think that they did the best they could under the incredible circumstances."

One letter was scathing. "Nathan did not know what he was doing when he was hired, obviously not during the Tubbs Fire evacuation, and still doesn't. Why is he still here? [Oakmont] should be fined and made to bring Varenna up to standards," the South Building resident said.

But multiple letters took a more analytical angle, offering DSS a bit of perceptive insight. "We feel that the Oakmont Management team has, in many ways, tied Nathan's hands," one resident said. "I believe that at times it can be difficult for him to take the lead, as it appears OMG has given him few guidelines, and he has to go to them for almost any resident request, let alone the lack of information during the fire. There was NOTHING in place for Nathan to fall back upon. We feel that he is being used as the scapegoat for the owners. This is grossly unfair." Another wrote, "We find your decision to remove [Nathan Condie and Deborah Smith] who we see as being scapegoated…being tantamount to economic crucifixion of these two basically good people. Clearly mistakes were made, but we think the major portion of responsibility for this less than perfect evacuation lies with the corporate management entity of Oakmont Senior Living."

***

The large, wooden conference table was packed with attendees inside a sec-ond-floor conference room at DSS headquarters in Oakland. It was late September 2018, and department staff were set for their first face-to-face with Oakmont representatives at an information-gathering session before the pre-conference hearing in mid-November. Around the table sat the expected parties from DSS legal and leadership departments and those from Oakmont management. There was one surprise attendee: Willie Brown, for-mer San Francisco mayor and longtime Speaker of the California Assembly. Bill Lockyer, former California attorney general and past president pro tem-pore of the California State Senate, had also been invited to attend but did not. Neither man had a personal connection to the case, but both were prominent figures in California politics with a combined 89 years in public office. But their involvement was not by request of the state—it was Oakmont that had arranged for them to attend.

According to one executive-level DSS employee who requested anonymity, an Oakmont representative told the state that Lockyer was now "part of their legal team" and that Brown was considering joining as counsel. "I think [Oakmont] was trying to...bring in all the big guns, and I don't know if I could say scare us, but intimidate us," a DSS employee said. Brown listened intently throughout the meeting but, in the end, made no significant contributions to the discussion. Also in attendance was DSS Director Will Lightbourne, Deputy Director Pamela Dickfoss, Program Administrator Ley Arquisola, and multiple DSS attorneys. It had been a long year, and the DSS team was feeling pressure from multiple directions. In addition to Oakmont and its pressure campaign, lobbyists from the California Assisted Living Association (CALA) were worried how the investigation of Villa Capri and Varenna might mar the industry. The association "was trying to diminish it down a little bit," the DSS executive said. Varenna represented one of the largest residential care homes for the elderly in the state, and CALA "was trying to get us to understand this was something nobody could control."

On the other side of the argument was Pat McGinnis, executive director for California Advocates for Nursing Home Reform (CANHR), who was horrified at Oakmont's performance and wanted its licenses revoked. "The place was on fire for God's sake. These people would have burned to death if their relatives hadn't come," said McGinnis, whose nonprofit fights for the rights of long-term care residents and elderly Californians. "I'd never seen anything like this, and I've been in this stuff for many, many years. [It was] a complete lack of responsibility, shirking your responsibility, and leaving these people to fend for themselves."

Neither CALA nor CANHR representatives attended the meeting, but their positions influenced the dialogue. While Brown looked on, DSS staff shared the findings of their investigation. Oakmont representatives used CALA's arguments in rebuttal. They continued to repeat the refrain that the Tubbs Fire was "unprecedented, and no one died."

"They were trying to get out of it," a DSS executive said, "and, you know, we just held our ground."

The state-level team at DSS was unmoved even though there were members of leadership who "were concerned that the case would be dismissed" if it went before an administrative law judge, as acting assistant program administrator Stacy Barlow told Beth in a later call. "They were concerned that the judge would throw the case out and then [DSS] would not have been able to put [strict compliance] terms on the facility." They also worried the case might not be winnable against Oakmont's high-powered attorneys and public relations campaign.

This is why some in DSS leadership wanted Dickfoss and her team to "have something else besides [license] revocation in your back pocket, not saying you have to use it, you just have to have it," a DSS executive said. But the team was unwilling to put anything else on the table. "We were getting pushed from all different angles that we had to have another option when we negotiate, other than revocation," the executive said. "I said I would quit over this because there are people who have done less than them, and we revoked their license. I want to go all the way to court. I don't want to mediate something lesser than what is due. I don't want to lessen it just because he [Gallaher] doesn't want this on his record."

The DSS employee's persuasion worked; Director Lightbourne agreed the circumstances were egregious enough to warrant license revocation. "Go for it," Lightbourne told his staffers.

***

On November 16, 2018, DSS staff and Oakmont representatives met one last time before the case went before an administrative law judge for a final ruling. This time, the group sat around a conference table on the seventh floor, and unlike their original meeting room that featured two walls of windows with views over a grassy quad or into the hallway, this conference room was windowless and deep within the DSS legal department. The state's staff and attorneys didn't want any distractions.

The DSS team had something else planned to help focus the discussion. Unbeknownst to Oakmont, two days prior to the meeting, DSS attorney

Tara Rufo did a little research and uncovered a surprising tidbit of information that Sonoma County residents knew all along. Rufo printed out a document illustrating this newly discovered rebuttal argument and brought it to the meeting.

According to a DSS executive who was present at the meeting that day, there were 14 to 16 participants in all. Among the DSS attendees were Pamela Dickfoss and Ley Arquisola, Senior Assistant Chief Counsel Sean Abalos, Assistant Chief Legal Counsel Kevin Mora, and Senior Staff Counsel Tara Rufo. Oakmont Management Group sent President and CEO Courtney Siegel, while Oakmont Senior Living sent CFO Joe Lin, as well as both companies' attorneys. Bill Lockyer, the political powerhouse rumored to have been part of Oakmont's legal team, didn't attend. Ultimately, he had opted not to join Oakmont's legal team.

As expected, an Oakmont representative commenced the meeting by reiterating the position they thought exonerated the company and the two executive directors—that the Tubbs Fire was "unprecedented" and that nobody could have prepared for such an event. Pamela Dickfoss interrupted. "Let's take 'unprecedented' out of your argument," she said. "There was a fire in that location in 1964 that Oakmont knew about." With that, Tara Rufo produced the document she had printed out—a map—and slid it across the table. The graphic showed clearly the Tubbs Fire wasn't unprecedented; the Hanly Fire had burned an eerily similar footprint 53 years earlier, a footprint that included the Fountaingrove hillside where Bill Gallaher pushed to erect Villa Capri and Varenna.

Dickfoss looked across the table and reminded Oakmont attorneys that the fire risk "was common knowledge when they were building up there, that it was part of the local discussion in the planning stages for Varenna" according to the DSS executive who asked for anonymity to discuss the private meeting. The pronouncement disarmed Oakmont's argument. It "blew the wind out of them in the very beginning," the executive said. "It really took the air out of the room."

Sensing that it had now earned the upper hand, DSS pushed Oakmont to agree to the license revocations for Villa Capri, Varenna, Debie Smith, and Nathan Condie. Most of all, DSS wanted Oakmont to admit, for the first time, that its managers and staff had abandoned the elderly and infirm residents of Villa Capri and Varenna that night and that family members and first responders rescued those remaining residents.

At first, Oakmont officials balked. "They had an excuse for almost everything," a DSS executive said. Oakmont blamed firefighters for absenteeism, but DSS countered, "You can't rely on first responders in something like this." Oakmont defended Nathan Condie, saying he was worried about his own home, to which DSS replied, "It's not what's going on in your personal life; you're personally responsible for these residents." Oakmont said "everyone got out safely," which made the DSS executive chortle in hindsight. "Yeah, but it was not, like, due to their responsibility."

It was still a "tough negotiation" despite the DSS staff pointing out weaknesses in each of Oakmont's arguments. "I don't think [Oakmont] thought we were going to have that strong of a case. I think they thought since it was 'unprecedented' that everybody would align with them," the DSS employee recalled. Oakmont wanted to settle for lesser penalties, but DSS staff refused. On six or seven occasions during the long meeting, Oakmont representatives asked for privacy to "caucus" among themselves. Through the door, the DSS team could see the Oakmont team making phone calls to someone they assumed was higher up, perhaps Bill Gallaher himself.

"At the very end, they knew we weren't going to budge, and it was going to court," a DSS employee said. "And I think they were afraid for it to go to court because they had all these lawsuits going on at the same time, and so if we revoked their license then it would have been even worse for their lawsuits, giving [the plaintiffs] more strength. And so whomever they kept calling, in the end, finally just said, 'Let's just go for [the settlement],' because they didn't want to go to court [where] they would have to do all the interviews and all that stuff will be public."

The state's case was so strong, particularly after learning the details of the Hanly Fire, that Oakmont settled without much change to the department's initial terms. The DSS director and staff were surprised the settlement took only one day of meetings. "In our eyes we won. We got them to admit [fault]. We got them to agree to our parameters," the employee said.

In the end, DSS got Oakmont to acknowledge publicly that residents had been abandoned. Soon after, OSL removed its Oakmont Senior Living Story website, which had said otherwise. The state also revoked Oakmont's licenses to operate Villa Capri and Varenna for two years, albeit with a caveat. DSS agreed to make the licenses probationary, meaning Oakmont would continue operating the two sites but under uncompromising supervision. The two-year probation began for Varenna when it welcomed back residents after cleanup and would begin for Villa Capri when it was rebuilt.

The settlement agreement also required Oakmont to improve in three areas—information management, notifications, and staffing—most of which fell under the umbrella of updated, site-specific emergency disaster plans that Oakmont was to develop for Villa Capri and Varenna. The settlement details read as a laundry list of requirements that one might expect to be standard practice, not appeasements made to avoid court. CANHR advocate Mike Connors said as much. "These are not mom-and-pop care facilities. These are advertised as luxurious assisted living communities you think would have all the resources in the world, all the plans made," he said. "And the exact opposite was the case."

Within 60 days, Oakmont also needed to create a system to manage a resident roster in the event of a future evacuation. The database needed to include whether the resident could walk unassisted, wore hearing aids or glasses, or needed oxygen or a wheelchair. This roster was to be available both remotely and on hard copy—filling a void Dawn Ross and others highlighted in their complaints.

As for notifications, the department required Oakmont to ensure Villa Capri and Varenna administrators and their substitutes, like med tech Marie So, "receive real-time emergency notifications from public safety agencies." Oakmont was also expected to come up with a procedure for "periodically confirming the location and status of each resident after an event," followed by a protocol to notify family immediately or as soon as possible after a resident was moved.

From a staffing perspective, the department required Oakmont to submit the job description and disaster-related responsibilities for administrators like Debie Smith and Nathan Condie or any substitute. The company needed to put an employee in charge of safety and security at each facility, and to update its staffing plans to ensure sufficient staff at all times, "particularly…between 10 p.m. and 6 a.m." DSS made clear it expected Oakmont to conduct emergency and disaster plan training with all new hires, and

Oakmont needed to prove all current staff, "including night staff," received new training.

DSS also required all staff to participate in quarterly drills according to health and safety code, but also added at least one annual evacuation drill to provide an experience "as realistic as possible" for staff who would need to escort elderly and nonambulatory residents off the property. "Live substitutes shall be utilized to stand in for residents who are unable or unwilling to participate in the annual drill." If Oakmont did not meet all these requirements, DSS could revoke Oakmont's licenses for good.

The same approach applied to Debie Smith and Nathan Condie. They were no longer going to be banned for life, but the executive directors were put on probation for two years with the opportunity to petition for full reinstatement after 12 months. As part of their probation, Debie and Nathan needed to receive a minimum of 40 hours of training on emergency disaster planning, facility staffing levels and resource allocation, preparing staff for an emergency, and communication with emergency services, residents, and their family members. Both were required to provide prospective employers with a copy of the settlement and notify DSS if either accepted a new job. And Oakmont could not hide the outcome either; DSS mandated the company post the full settlement on its website.

After 10 hours of negotiation, during which DSS attorneys drew up the settlement right there on the seventh-floor conference table, Oakmont representatives wanted to take the document home for review. State staff wouldn't have it; either Oakmont signed immediately or they were going to trial before an administrative law judge. At around 6 p.m., Oakmont Management Group President and CEO Courtney Siegel signed the settlement, and then she and the rest of the Oakmont team, along with their two attorneys walked out of the room. "I'll never forget, we walked out of the building…and we were just so elated," and everyone was hugging, the DSS employee said. "It's such a good memory because it was just in support of the residents. It wasn't like we wanted [Oakmont] so bad. It was like we wanted to set the tone for any other facility as well."

But the outcome received a mixed reaction from the community. Allowing Oakmont, Smith, and Condie to continue in their roles was anathema to some residents, their families, and community members. CANHR's

McGinnis also was disturbed. "Their actions were so blatantly irresponsible in endangering the residents of that facility," McGinnis said of the executive directors. "Why they got their license back, I have no idea." She said it was "ludicrous" that the three parties went back practically to business as usual. "That's one of the problems. You need to· set an example: 'When you do this, you can't ever have a license again.'"

DSS leadership didn't see permanent revocation of Oakmont's license as a suitable solution because of the additional hardship it would force upon Villa Capri and Varenna residents. "[I know] the residents' families would not think that, but there's also other things you take into consideration, and that's the community. Where would all these people go?" if Villa Capri and Varenna ceased operations, the DSS employee posed. "If you could turn things around and stay on top of [Oakmont, Smith, and Condie] to make sure that [residents] are safe, then these people could stay in the community where their families were. It's a lot of people to relocate out of the area, and it's not easy to have somebody just come in and rebuild." The DSS employee also said they considered the economic impact on job losses in an expensive county. "And so we had to take all that into consideration."

Beth Eurotas-Steffy heard this explanation firsthand when Stacy Barlow from DSS called with the news of the settlement. Beth had tracked the investigation for over a year, from when she first called to complain, until now, 13 months later. Barlow assured her that the victims' voices were heard during the process, but that a full revocation wasn't warranted because Oakmont Senior Living's compliance history as a whole had been very good. Beth was devastated. She had already been disappointed once, when Stebner's lawsuit settled rather than going to court. This second settlement was another blow. "When I pressed them on just what would warrant a license revocation, she said, 'Where there is intentional physical or sexual abuse. Premeditated crimes.' They said [Oakmont] did not have a history of non-compliance, and there was not anything intentional done," Beth recalled. Barlow's advice to Beth was simple. "The only suggestion they had for me was to be an advocate to fight for more legislation governing facilities." Beth had already planned to do exactly that.

19

Unsettled

Spring 2019: Employees Feel Shamed, Blamed

Former maintenance employee Michael Rodriguez was standing in line outside a Social Security office in downtown Santa Rosa waiting for it to open. It was late November 2018, and news had broken that week that Oakmont management, for the first time, had admitted to state regulators that the company left behind residents as the firestorm approached. People ahead of Michael were talking about the case.

"They abandoned those elderly people," an older man said.

A woman chimed in, "Those caregivers—they should be put in jail."

"Jail's not good enough. They need to go to prison," another man said.

Michael felt antsy, his anxiety kicking in. He took a big breath, thought twice, maybe three times, and then did something he didn't usually do. He spoke up.

"Hey, that didn't happen," he told them. "In fact, it was the opposite. I was there. I was rescuing those people. We were never trained. We were trying to get people out of rooms, and our manager was sending people back to their rooms." He explained how his best friend, Andre, had taken charge and started evacuating the building, how Andre had carried a woman, her wheelchair, and her dog down a long flight of stairs, how they had asked their boss for a plan, and he didn't give them one. The strangers' demeanor softened, but the incident scarred Michael and left him feeling like his good name was tainted.

He was not the only one. Cynthia Arroyo and Anett Rivas also felt blamed once Oakmont settled with DSS and admitted staff left before all the residents were out of the buildings. What appeared to be a win for the DSS turned into a loss for the caregivers on duty that night.

Anett read a *Press Democrat* article about the DSS settlement and came to one conclusion: "[Oakmont] defamed me and made me seem like I didn't do anything, that I left the residents," she said. "The supervisors from the facility signed [a document] that their employees had made a mistake and left. And they are making false accusations about me and ruining my career."

Cynthia felt defamed from the beginning, first by the residents' family members. "That night they were frustrated with Debie because she wasn't there, but when they came out in the press, it seemed their anger was toward us," she said. Then she heard Debie had signed a settlement saying it was the caregivers' fault. "That's when I was like, 'Screw them. I'll join the lawsuit and fight with the families....' We put our own lives at risk, and we're nothing to [Oakmont] other than staff."

Enter Michael Fiumara, a personal injury attorney for 30 years, who thought the employees were getting blamed for management's failures, and Oakmont had essentially abandoned them before, during, and after the fire. "Every time these people went out into public, they were shunned," he said.

Fiumara had always identified with the underdog. As a child, he grew up as one of 11 siblings in a "tenement slum house" in Brooklyn. Race riots burned his neighborhood, part of his house, and the front of his father's bicycle shop, so his family moved to a bungalow-style shack in a town without a post office in New Jersey's Appalachian foothills. Fiumara worked hard in school and earned scholarships to a top college and graduate school. In his own law practice, Fiumara represented Latino students who were disproportionately suspended or expelled from "zero tolerance" schools in administrative and juvenile court hearings, and he specialized in childhood sexual abuse cases. For example, he successfully sued the Roman Catholic Diocese of Santa Rosa in 2007 over the abuse of nine Latino children and young adults, winning a $5 million judgment.

Fiumara knew Andre from the gym where Andre trained Latino boys in both boxing and life skills. When Fiumara's husband, Gordon, was diagnosed with Alzheimer's, he hired Andre as a caregiver in 2015 until his spouse's death in 2018. "Andre was so kind, generous, and thoughtful, always taking Gordon to his favorite place on the Sonoma County coast," said Fiumara, who considered Andre family. After the Tubbs Fire, Andre told Fiumara what happened at Oakmont and introduced him to former Varenna and Villa Capri employees.

The attorney teamed up with former state senator and Santa Rosa City Council member Noreen Evans to file a lawsuit in April 2019 on behalf of the three former Villa Capri caregivers, Elizabeth, Cynthia, and Anett, and Varenna employees Michael Rodriguez, Andre Blakely, Maria Joffely Cervantes, Ma Teresa Martinez, and her husband Sigmund Martinez. "Noreen and I were the only two attorneys that cared enough to pursue this case, which turned out to be an economic loss for us, but we did what needed to be done, and we did what other attorneys failed to even consider doing," Fiumara said.

The lawsuit cast wide-ranging allegations, from fraud and defamation to workplace discrimination and failure to protect residents' belongings after the fire. It also alleged that rather than Oakmont taking responsibility, the corporation blamed its employees for leaving, then later tried to bribe and intimidate them from talking to DSS and the press. The core of the suit, however, was that staff were not trained or given tools to evacuate the buildings, and they risked their own lives to save elderly residents, something that was not part of their employment contract. The suit also repeated allegations that Oakmont had violated the law by failing to maintain an emergency evacuation plan and provide adequate staffing, including administrators and night supervisors who were familiar with planned emergency procedures. "It's reckless management, gross mismanagement," Fiumara said.

The lawsuit claimed each employee suffered from "severe emotional harm, including post-traumatic stress disorder." Michael's postfire anxiety and panic attacks also continued, and he experienced facial pain for the first three months after the fires. It eased with therapy but returned periodically over the next four years. Cynthia, who went to work at Varenna until she gave birth to twins in September 2018, found herself triggered every fire season, or whenever the weather was hot and windy. She and her partner often bickered during those times. "I get so stressed I can't get off my sofa to physically do anything," she said, tearing up. "I've stayed scared and traumatized." Anett battled insomnia during similar weather. "I don't even like to drive near Fountaingrove," she said. "I look up there and can't believe I overcame and went through that. I don't like to think about it."

The suit also included one Varenna resident, a move aimed at bringing the same level of scrutiny to Varenna's evacuation as Stebner's suit had done for Villa Capri. Joan Gilberry Coke, who had fled World War II London during the Blitz, was asleep in her North Building apartment on the night of the fire when caregiver Maria Joffely Cervantes woke her and helped her downstairs. The pair fled in Coke's car. "She had to go through a wall of fire, and she really had the flashback of being in war-torn Great Britain in the 1940s," Fiumara said. The lawsuit stated after the fire, someone stole items from Coke's apartment, including a yellow sapphire engagement ring her late husband had given her. "She said, 'I don't need the money, but someone came in and stole these items. I remember taking them off and putting them here [beside my bed] before I was woken up,'" Fiumara said.

Fiumara and Evans found themselves up against the same attorneys Stebner had fought for documents and depositions. Fiumara didn't think it proper for the Giovanniello Law Group to take the case against Cynthia and Anett, considering it had represented them in deposition hearings for Stebner's case. "They learned information from our clients, their vulnerabilities, their lack of sophistication," Fiumara said.

Like Stebner, Fiumara and Evans wanted the case to go to a jury trial. But Oakmont's attorneys forced the case into arbitration, claiming the Villa Capri employees had a built-in arbitration agreement, though they couldn't produce it because they claimed it had burned in the fire. "The judge believed them," Fiumara said.

Oakmont's first settlement offer was $3,000 for each caregiver, what Fiumara considered a "low-ball offer." It took two years to negotiate a settlement, during which time Joan Gilberry Coke died. The employees received their checks in April 2022. In the settlement, Oakmont did not admit fault. All parties were prevented from disclosing the amounts the plaintiffs received from Oakmont.

Fiumara felt the fact it went to arbitration kept the final settlement low for the caregivers. "It shows how the legal system can be used by the rich and powerful to minimize the overall compensation and true suffering of the minority class," he said. "These were low-paid, mostly female staff members who worked at this ritzy residential care facility, and they were paid very little. They were further marginalized when we sought damages for them."

Louise Johnson's Family Seeks Justice

Louise Johnson's family did not sue immediately. She could not tell her children much about the night of the fire before she died two weeks later. Once the DSS investigation revealed more about what their mother endured, the family met with attorneys Fiumara and Evans and filed a lawsuit on October 7, 2019, against Oakmont Senior Living, Oakmont Management Group, and its various connected limited liability companies. The suit alleged elder abuse, negligence, false imprisonment, breach of contract, and both negligent and intentional infliction of emotional distress for failing to comply with California law and thus failing to properly remove residents from Villa Capri.

Louise Johnson, as asthmatic, "was subjected to breathing toxic smoke and fumes for many hours, which worsened her respiratory condition, and was one of the last seniors evacuated from the Villa Capri facility," the lawsuit stated. "Following the fire, Decedent Johnson's physical, medical, and mental needs were not provided for by Defendants, and she became dehydrated and hallucinatory and passed away mere days after the fire."

Fiumara and Evans, who had a medical expert lined up to testify to wrongful death, pushed for a public trial. But the Giovanniello Law Group successfully argued this case into arbitration as well. Although all of Villa Capri's resident agreements had burned, the judge ruled it was reasonable to assume the Johnsons signed one that required arbitration and were thus ineligible to sue in court. After more than a year and a half of negotiations, the case settled in December 2021 for an undisclosed sum. "Because they settled, Oakmont obviously felt there was some merit to [our] argument," Fiumara said. The Johnson family, however, was disappointed. "The settlement was paltry," Eric Johnson said. "Craig and I spent hours and days collecting things for the attorneys. The settlement amount kept shrinking. We are done with it. Big Corp wins again."

Oakmont's Battles Continue

Meanwhile, Oakmont Senior Living continued to grow. In January 2019, Oakmont proposed building an 82-unit apartment complex for tenants 55 and older on the Fountaingrove site where Gallaher had earlier planned to build the Emerald Isle project, before Beth's appeal triggered its unraveling. This time, the proposal included no residential care component, which meant no state oversight, a proposition that received a frosty reception from Santa Rosa residents, who cited concerns about traffic and evacuation points. Ultimately, the proposal was spiked, and Oakmont sold the land on the open market.

Finally, during Oakmont's planning battles came another defeat—this one in court. In a unanimous decision on March 15, 2019, a state appellate court dismissed the defamation lawsuit Gallaher and his son-in-law had filed against the *Press Democrat*. The justices rejected their claims that the newspaper libeled them by implying the funds Scott Flater donated came from Gallaher and that campaign expenditures were a private matter between donors and politicians. Elections and campaign spending are of significant public interest, and any attempt to argue otherwise was "frivolous," the court ruled.

"The *Press Democrat* article reporting on Flater's enormous independent expenditures, explaining Flater's connection to Gallaher, and raising questions about the source of the funds spent by Flater were clearly in connection with an issue of public interest," the justices wrote. The *Press Democrat*, which had battled the lawsuit for more than two years, celebrated. "For a newspaper our size, this costly legal fight was a risky undertaking," then executive editor Catherine Barnett said. "So it is especially heartening that the court's decision vindicates both our reporting and our watchdog role."

The Gallaher family, however, did not back off on its political activity. Within the year, Molly Gallaher Flater, the 35-year-old chief operating officer of Gallaher Homes, embarked on her own crusade, this time to stop the renewal of a sales tax supporting Sonoma-Marin Area Rail Transit, a local rail transit line connecting Marin and Sonoma counties. "If I end up spending $1 million to save our community taxpayers from a $2.4 billion mistake then I feel it is worth every penny," Gallaher Flater said in a written statement at the start of the campaign. She said the train system had not lived up to promises made when residents first approved the tax, and she was opposed to the idea of renewing the tax for another 30 years. By the time the issue went before voters in March 2020, Gallaher Flater had donated $1.8 million. It ended up being the most expensive single contest in Sonoma County political history. As a result, Gallaher Flater got what she wanted, and the sales tax measure lost.

Their political spending was not reserved for Sonoma County. State and local spending records show that between 2003 and 2022, members of the Gallaher family and Oakmont Senior Living and Oakmont Management Group employees donated more than $350,000 to candidates, ballot measures, and political action committees in California. Of that, $250,000 came after the Tubbs Fire.

Beth Turns to State Leaders

To Beth Eurotas-Steffy, if the 17-page DSS settlement released on November 19, 2018, had a silver lining, it was this: Oakmont Senior Living had to acknowledge for the first time Villa Capri and Varenna residents had been abandoned, a stark contrast from their earlier contentions that Oakmont employees had evacuated the last residents. But it also meant, once again, that there would be no public airing of the details.

So, Beth opened another front in her campaign for accountability: the state Legislature. The first to agree to meet with her was Assemblymember Jim Wood, a Santa Rosa Democrat who also happened to be a forensic odontologist, a dentist with special training to identify dead bodies by examining teeth. He had helped to identify Tubbs Fire victims and was aware of what happened at Villa Capri and Varenna. "I wanted to get new legislation enacted so something like this can never happen again," Beth said. But after sitting with Beth for nearly an hour that April, Wood was frank that he did not see an opportunity for legislation, at least not at that point.

Wood had already voted that year to support A.B. 3098, which strengthened regulations for emergency plans at retirement care facilities. Authored by Assemblymember Laura Friedman, a Democrat representing Burbank, the bill required retirement facilities to develop more detailed emergency plans, install stair chairs on stairwells, make keys available to staff, and hold drills on a quarterly basis. Retirement facilities would have to designate nearby and out-of-area evacuation locations and make their emergency and disaster plans available to residents and family members upon request.

"California's residential care facilities for the elderly serve tens of thousands of older adults and adults with disabilities in communities across the state," Friedman noted at the time. "While every facility is required to have a general disaster plan whether they serve six or 60 residents, that plan is only effective if staff and residents know what to do during an emergency."

But to Beth and those guiding her from California Advocates for Nursing Home Reform, the bill was smoke and mirrors. Following a high-profile natural disaster like the Wine Country Fires, it was a time-honored practice among assisted living industry lobbying groups to draft and push for their own legislation before something more substantive, and possibly intrusive, came down the pike. This was the case with A.B. 3098. While the bill mentioned backup emergency generators, it did not require them. It mentioned the need for advance transportation planning but did not require facilities to have a standing contract with bus companies. And while it referred to having emergency plans on hand, it didn't require they address the specific needs of residents or spell out clear roles and training needed for each staff member in case of emergency. In short, the legislation did not ensure the kind of specificity that was needed to prevent a repeat of the Villa Capri debacle. "It just gave lip service," said Beth. "It didn't do anything substantive."

Because it was largely written by interests supportive of retirement community owners, the bill sailed through the Assembly and the Senate without a single vote of opposition, and the governor signed it into law on September 11, 2018. CANHR did not oppose it, but it did not support it either, saying instead that the organization was "recommending stronger protections." Executive Director Pat McGinnis said the law was too vague. "They have to make arrangements for transportation. What does that mean? You're going to call Uber?"

Beth wanted stronger protections too. In early 2019, with the help of CANHR advocate Michael Connors, Beth drew up draft legislation titled "Ensuring the safety of residents of Senior Residential Care Facilities during an emergency." The bill called for amending the California Health and Safety Code to include mandates for permanent on-site emergency generators, comprehensive, documented emergency/disaster plans, and a process to ensure all staff members are well trained, prepared, "and clearly understand their specific duties" during an emergency. But CANHR officials warned her that pushing for such significant and potentially costly reforms would not be easy. The senior living industry is hardwired to resist attempts at stronger regulation.

Still Beth pressed ahead. It was clear that if she wanted stronger legislation passed, she would have to work through the offices of North Bay state Senators Mike McGuire and Bill Dodd. McGuire, who represented Santa Rosa and northern parts of the county, was particularly aggressive in advocating for relief for fire victims, including partnering with a local credit union and the *Press Democrat* to activate a relief fund that guaranteed 100 percent of donations would go to fire victims. Within three months, the fund had raised more than $30 million, nearly two-thirds from donors outside the North Bay. But getting them to take a position on what happened at Varenna and Villa Capri was more of a challenge, Beth found.

After much pestering, Beth secured a 30-minute meeting with McGuire in July. To make the most of her time, she brought two subject matter experts, Kathy and Mark Allen. As soon as the Allens walked in the door, McGuire recognized Mark as one of his teachers from Healdsburg High School. Mark and Kathy relayed what happened on October 9, and Beth spent the last five minutes explaining her proposed legislation. She urged him to read it and carry it. "He seemed very interested and moved by the detailed account of what happened," she said. She left encouraged. But after several follow-up calls, "I was finally told he would not be carrying this legislation or even a portion of it," as he already had a number of bills in the pipeline.

Her last hope was Dodd, but he represented only a small part of Sonoma County, and it did not include Santa Rosa. However, Dodd had a particular interest in protecting senior citizens, and although he didn't offer to carry her legislation, he surprised her nonetheless. He submitted a bill in February 2019 that added "abandonment" to the list of offenses eligible for enhanced civil remedies for elder abuse under state law. Under the legislation, violators could be forced to pay up to $250,000 in civil damages, plus legal fees. He included a quote from Beth in a press release when the bill passed on the Assembly floor on a unanimous vote. "As a family member of someone who was left behind during the Tubbs Fire, I believe we can't adopt this protection soon enough," Beth said. "I appreciate so much what Senator Dodd has done, as well as other lawmakers concerned about the safety of seniors."

Although someone found guilty of criminal abandonment of the elderly could already be sentenced to up to seven years in prison under California law, Dodd was motivated to expand the definitions for enhanced civil penalties directly because of the events at the two Oakmont Senior Living facilities. "Deserting the frail and elderly when disaster strikes is not acceptable and can't be allowed to happen again," Dodd said. "These vulnerable people must be protected, especially with the growing wildfire threat. My bill penalizes caretakers who shirk their responsibilities and encourages more people to do the right thing."

The bill encountered no opposition, and Governor Gavin Newsom signed it into law on June 26, 2019.

20
CHAPTER

Revenge

A Criminal Investigation Begins

Among those horrified by the Tubbs Fire devastation and riled by reports of what occurred at Varenna and Villa Capri was Sonoma County's district attorney, Jill Ravitch. A no-nonsense career prosecutor who in 2011 became Sonoma County's first female district attorney, Ravitch had taken in fire refugees at her home near Sebastopol in the early hours of October 9, 2017, as had many west Sonoma County residents. "I must have had over a dozen people here," she said. Among them were two families who had lost homes in the blaze. Afterward, she focused on protecting wildfire victims from price gouging. One family who lost their home northeast of Santa Rosa soon found a listing for a home in Healdsburg at $3,700 a month. But by the time they scheduled a visit, the asking price had gone up to $4,700. Around that same time, another homeless family found a rental for $5,000 a month, but by the following morning, the price had gone up to $9,000 a month. Through the media, Ravitch reminded the community that such actions were illegal. State law prohibited the raising of prices by more than 10 percent after an emergency declaration. Within 60 days of the fires, her office had filed charges against six landlords for price gouging and had another 40 cases under investigation.

Ravitch also paid close attention to the investigations concerning Villa Capri and Varenna. "I was very angry that they went in and cleaned it up when everybody else was made to wait," she said. "This company just decided they were going to go in and do whatever they wanted to do." After DSS announced its November 2018 settlement, Ravitch questioned why state regulators had "backed away" from the stronger sanctions first proposed.

She asked her investigators to get the state's reports "so we could see whether a thorough investigation was done," she said. "Once we digested what we had, we just decided that we needed to look further." She assigned the task to her consumer fraud division and an investigation team headed by deputy district attorneys Matt Cheever and David Kim. The team, including the office's elder abuse prosecutor, "looked long and hard" at what happened, Ravitch said.

Initially, their work was hamstrung by the fact that the Villa Capri residents' civil settlement had come with a nondisclosure agreement, "so we couldn't access a lot of the information that was the basis of the civil suits," Ravitch said.

They caught a break, however, in early 2019 when, because of the widespread media attention, the office of state Attorney General Xavier Becerra joined the effort, offering additional resources, expertise, and heft to the investigation. According to Kim, they worked six months around the clock in partnership with two attorneys from the attorney general's office. The team interviewed more than 40 witnesses, including residents and former Oakmont employees. They weighed filing both civil and criminal charges. "Everything was on the table," Kim said. "The investigation was very open," Ravitch confirmed. "We didn't know what we were going to find."

Finally, on September 3, 2020, Ravitch and the state attorney general's office announced the outcome of their investigation—an unlawful business practices civil action against the owners of Varenna and Villa Capri resulting in a $500,000 settlement. The civil action targeted the three main Oakmont entities: Oakmont Senior Living, Oakmont Management Group, and Varenna, LLC, the official owner of Varenna and Villa Capri. The complaint included three claims: that the Oakmont entities "failed to adequately plan for and train staff" to prepare for an emergency, "failed to timely and adequately notify residents of the need for an emergency evacuation," and that "many residents were left without care or support from defendants and with no means to evacuate themselves. These residents had to be evacuated by family members or first responders."

The complaint found the three Oakmont entities guilty of not having adequate emergency and disaster response plans in place and for "failing to provide care, supervision, and services" for residents. The complaint also accused the Oakmont entities of other deficiencies, including a lack of proper training, a lack of qualified staff on night shift, and failing to maintain facilities "in conformity with the regulations adopted by the State Fire Marshal."

"This judgment will help ensure the safety of seniors and send a message to all facilities that undertake the care of vulnerable members of our community that they must be prepared to protect their residents during a disaster," Ravitch said at the time the settlement was announced.

Bill Gallaher signed the settlement twice, once on behalf of Oakmont Senior Living and once for Varenna, LLC. President and CEO Courtney Siegel signed for Oakmont Management Group, and the Oakmont entities agreed to pay $205,000 in penalties each to Sonoma County and to the state, and $45,000 to the district attorney's office as well as to the state attorney general's office to cover investigation costs. In addition, for five years, each facility was required to have on-site generators, a contract with a local bus company that could transport residents and staff in an emergency, and a designated and trained employee on every shift who would be responsible for resident and employee safety and overseeing potential evacuations.

Each OSL facility was also required to have the following: a plan for maintaining residents' health information, including medications; a plan for ensuring that managers and staff subscribe to emergency notifications; a plan to ensure adequate notification to residents in the event of an emergency, whether or not alarms are functioning; and a plan for tracking residents' whereabouts and notifying their families in the event of an evacuation. In addition, the three Oakmont companies agreed to retain a qualified "independent monitor" who would ensure the facilities complied with the mandates.

During the investigation, the district attorney's office and the state attorney general's office considered criminal charges, Ravitch said. "But causation is very difficult in a criminal case," she said. "You have to prove it beyond a reasonable doubt, and unfortunately, by the time we were able to really dig in and investigate it, much of the evidence was gone." And several witnesses had already died.

County attorneys instead focused on holding the organization accountable for its business practices and assuring their failures wouldn't be repeated. "I felt very strongly that I wanted to give [the residents] some sense of safety in the future," Ravitch said. Because they were never certain if it was going to be a criminal investigation or civil action, nothing was filed until the case was settled, Ravitch said. At that point, they announced both the lawsuit and the settlement agreement at the same time.

Oakmont spokesman Nathan Ballard said in a statement that the companies settled the case to avoid "years of litigation over this long-past dispute…. This settlement will also protect our team members from the threat of unwarranted criminal prosecution arising from any conduct occurring before or during the fire," he wrote. "We are confident that we would have prevailed should this matter have proceeded further, but for the sake of our team members, residents, and stakeholders in the midst of the current COVID-19 pandemic, we are pleased to lay this matter to rest."

Not all were happy with the outcome. Once again, Beth Eurotas-Steffy was angry and disappointed. Before the settlement ink was dry in the residents' lawsuit, Beth had encouraged the Sonoma District Attorney's Office to pursue criminal charges. Much like her mother's lawsuit and the DSS case, the DA and AG's investigation was ending in a settlement rather than a public reckoning. Once again, she feared, "there wasn't going to be any accountability." Yes, Oakmont would be required to hire an independent monitor to oversee the mandates of the injunction. But the independent monitor would be paid by Oakmont Senior Living, Beth pointed out, and the monitor's reports would not be public documents. Plus, none of the settlement money went to the victims themselves, she noted. "I was disappointed not for me but for the victims there that night who were left to die."

To Oakmont, a $500,000 fine was "pocket change," Beth added. She then turned her full attention to her ongoing search for remedies through the state Legislature.

***

Fifty days later, on Friday, October 23, Ravitch was sitting in her car outside her home talking on her cell phone to a police reporter when a figure approached from across the street. "I've got to get off because there's some guy coming up my driveway who I don't recognize," she said.

Having someone enter her private space at home was not something she took lightly.

"Excuse me," she said upon exiting her car. But the man continued toward her front door. "Excuse me," she shouted again, this time louder. "Can I help you?"

The man turned. "Are you Jill Ravitch?" he asked.

"Well, yes, I am," she said.

With that he promptly walked over and placed some folded paperwork in her hand.

"You've been served," he said.

Ravitch opened the paperwork and was stunned by what she read.

"Are you kidding me?" she exclaimed in the direction of the departing figure, who did not turn around.

With that, Ravitch discovered she was now the target of a recall campaign.

At first, she thought it was a joke. Just a week earlier she had announced publicly that she would not seek a fourth term in office in 2022. But when she looked at the signatures on the official "Notice of Intention to Circulate a Recall Petition" in her hands, she realized it was authentic. The notice required at least 20 signatures to start the process of gathering petition signatures. This one had 27. The first signature was William Gallaher's. The second was Molly Gallaher Flater's, and the last was that of Cynthia Gallaher. In between were the names of many current and former business associates and employees of Oakmont Senior Living.

It was then she recognized what it was all about: retaliation. "When I realized that [Gallaher] was behind it, honestly, I wasn't surprised because I had been told that he was very upset at us," Ravitch said.

Gallaher declined interviews about the recall. But at the outset, he noted in a statement the recall effort was to assure "steady, competent public safety in our county." The paperwork served to Ravitch defined the reasons for the recall as "issues of inequality, injustice, and fire safety failure that have been ignored or inflamed by Ravitch," as well as failure "to pursue charges against large corporations that harm and pollute our community." It also claimed Ravitch had failed to publicize conviction-rate data, "prevented the disclosure of police body camera recordings," and used her official powers to pursue personal vendettas. But it cited no specifics. What was conspicuously absent was any reference to the investigation into what happened at Villa Capri and Varenna. "We think District Attorney Ravitch has been horrible, and we feel the voters deserve a chance to decide whether she should complete her term," Gallaher Flater said in an email statement to the *Press Democrat*.

Among those who joined the "Recall Ravitch" campaign, also among the 27 original signers of the notification to circulate a recall petition, was Orlando Macias, one of the Santa Rosa police officers on scene during Varenna's evacuation. Macias had blown out the tendons in his arm using a battering ram to knock down doors, forcing him to take early retirement. He said he signed the petition because he didn't agree with the district attorney's handling of the case involving Andy Lopez, a 13-year-old boy who was shot and killed by Sonoma County Sheriff's Deputy Erick Gelhaus in 2013 while carrying an airsoft gun resembling an AK-47. The death triggered protests, lawsuits, and debate that divided the region for months. Ultimately, Ravitch's office had concluded that there wasn't enough evidence to pursue charges against the deputy. Macias disagreed with that decision.

During an interview, Macias also acknowledged he had become friends with Molly Gallaher Flater, as their children attended school together. Macias said he didn't blame Oakmont Senior Living for what happened. "Everybody was abandoned that night," he said. "That was the reality. Everybody abandoned their post." Some police officers didn't show up for duty that night, as they were taking care of their families, he said. At Varenna, it was no different. "Everybody was scrambling around. There wasn't much order to anything…. There was no communication. If you talk about a perfect storm, that was it," Macias said.

Ravitch prepared herself for the battle ahead. Just a few days after being served, she was meeting friends for lunch at Monti's, a popular restaurant in the heart of Santa Rosa, when she was seated near none other than Bill Gallaher dining at a table with former Congressman Doug Bosco.

Never shy about such things, Ravitch got up to engage with the men. "Oh my gosh. What an amazing coincidence. Here we are in the same place," she said with a smile. She thought Gallaher would laugh or make some witty response. But he didn't. "He wouldn't even look up. He wouldn't acknowledge me," Ravitch said. "So I just sat down with my back to him and enjoyed my lunch." Their public showdown had begun.

***

Ravitch soon found she was not alone in battling this campaign. Friends, fellow legal acquaintances, and past election supporters quickly came together to form a committee to support her fight. "We need to stand together, resolute in combating this political bullying, because that's what it is," Rohnert Park Mayor Gerard Giudice told a crowd of people gathered at his restaurant, Sally Tomatoes, on July 25, 2021. The crowd applauded. The mayor then introduced Ravitch, who stepped to the stage. Behind her was a faux red-brick backdrop. In front of the podium was one of the signs organizers hoped attendees would take home and plant on their front lawns. "Stop the revenge," it read in red letters on a white background. "No D.A. Recall."

The mayor's introduction had captured the reaction of many in the community since the county Registrar of Voters Office had confirmed in early May that the recall campaign had qualified for the ballot. The election would be September 14, the same day that voters across the state would be deciding on another recall attempt, that of California Gov. Gavin Newsom. His recall was driven largely by Republicans upset with the first-term Democrat's liberal policies and aggressive COVID-response measures.

Some of Ravitch's supporters had held out hope that the attempt to unseat Ravitch might not qualify for the ballot. But when Ravitch learned those gathering petition signatures were being paid $10 for every valid signature they collected, she knew it was a false hope. Such paid signature campaigns were rarely unsuccessful. As they camped outside big box stores, signature gatherers raised dubious allegations, including that Ravitch would increase taxes, although her office had no taxing authority; that she was homophobic, despite being gay; and that she prevented the release of body camera footage as part of the Andy Lopez investigation, although no body camera video existed. Body cameras weren't issued to sheriff's deputies until two years after the shooting. Nonetheless, the Recall Ravitch petition received the 32,000 signatures needed to qualify for the ballot.

"Here's the deal. This is not about me.... I'm leaving," she told the audience from the lectern. "It's been great. I've enjoyed it. I've done my best. I think I've done some good work." She reminded the crowd she had already announced she would not run for re-election. "In 50 days, you are going to the polls because one guy is pissed off, and he's pissed off because I did the job that you elected me to do. Let's be really clear about that." The room broke out in applause. "What you need to understand is, this was an agreed-upon disposition," she said, reminding the audience of the general details of the settlement with Oakmont Senior Living. Oakmont's representatives "agreed that they could do better," she said. "And they agreed to the disposition that includes five years of oversight to make sure that those people are not put in harm's way the way they were that night." Apparently, the agreement was not satisfactory to Gallaher, she suggested, despite the fact that he signed it—twice. "I guess he had a tantrum," she said. "Because, what does he do? He comes after me. This is all about taking me out. And I'll tell you what. If he succeeds, then anybody who seeks elected office should be worried."

Furthermore, the recall effort alone could have a chilling effect on the willingness of policy makers to investigate and hold powerful and wealthy companies and individuals like Gallaher accountable. "You all can really send a great message by leaving here today and telling everybody you know," Ravitch concluded. "They need to vote 'no' on the recall. Because it's not just about Jill Ravitch. It's not just about the district attorney's office. It's about one man's vengeance. And it has to stop."

After the applause died down, she welcomed Mark Allen to the stage. It was the first time he had spoken in a public forum about the night of the fire. He had been hesitant to participate but encouraged to do so by Beth Eurotas-Steffy, who had offered to help Ravitch fight the recall. Before long, Beth was a member of the Stop the Recall Executive Committee, working mostly behind the scenes. As the lead organizer of the fundraising event that day, she felt the need for the audience to hear from one of the rescuers. Despite the post-traumatic stress that he and Kathy experienced and his reluctance to relive the night's details, Mark agreed to show up. But he was nervous.

"I taught high school for 34 years," he said after introducing himself. "I was a shop teacher." Think back on the fire drills you had in school, he told the audience. "You would all file out of your classroom single file and line up very neatly up against the wall.... We have been trained from our very earliest days to follow the rules," he said. "To get up, to follow your teacher, to go out the door and go to where you belong so we could take a headcount and know everybody's out of the building.... Unfortunately, this is my story—where none of that existed."

He then retold the events of October 9, from the Nixle alert going off on Kathy's phone and their calling Villa Capri, to his putting on his work boots, managing the harrowing rescue, and coping with the all-consuming self-doubt that followed. He highlighted how the staff's only evacuation plan was to get everybody downstairs and then "wait for Deborah to come and help us," he said. He told of the heartbreak he felt helping residents out of their rooms, and how he wheeled his mother down the back stairwell because he was too embarrassed to take her past the residents in wheelchairs who remained on the second-floor landing. "I'm getting chills right now just thinking about it," he said. He described how the grapevines lining the slope behind Villa Capri erupted in a rush of flames moments later as he pushed his mother through the parking lot. He compared it to the kind of eruption one might experience after accidentally leaving the gas on in a barbecue before lighting it. "Now multiply it by a hundred," he said. He also told of the moment he said goodbye to his wife, promising to return for another carload of residents, only to be told by Oakmont managers that school buses were en route when they weren't. "The gravity of it hits me now more than it did then," he said, "because the shop teacher doesn't internalize when things are going wrong in the shop. I've had accidents in the shop. And you have to act now to safely [fix] it. So you don't think about it. You just take care of it, take care of business. And that's kind of what it was [at Villa Capri]." From there, he shared the details of Kathy and Melissa's heroics. "The only reason nobody perished in that fire is because my wife and Melissa were there," Mark told the audience.

He concluded by sharing his frustrations at what came later, after Oakmont Senior Living "started letting everybody know that everybody was safe" and that Oakmont staff "did a great job." He also shared his angst when attorneys for the company said any injuries that occurred were "because of the volunteers that showed up." Oakmont attorneys noted how one of the residents suffered a broken hip during the rescue operations, and they appeared to blame Mark for her injury, he said. "They thought it was me because they thought it was that lady I helped out last. It turns out she fell off the chair while she was at the church under their care." Several in the audience groaned. He sighed deeply. "We had a settlement," he continued, looking down at his notes. "I can't tell you what it is, otherwise, I could get sued for letting you know.... We didn't get our day in court. This is part of our day in court."

The audience erupted in applause. For most, this was the first time they had heard the details of the rescue. And as the applause grew, Mark received a standing ovation. "Mr. Allen, I want to say thank you," said state Senator Mike McGuire, who followed him onstage. "Thank you for standing strong for not just your parents, but for tens of thousands of residents who are living in these communities across California." McGuire then encouraged the 150 or so people gathered to contribute to the campaign supporting Ravitch. During the auction-style appeal, the donations came in waves, starting at $1,000 or more, dropping to $500, and then $100. As they gave, some took a handheld microphone McGuire circulated to encourage others to do the same. "I am furious about this attempt at a recall, and I think we have to just tell Bill Gallaher 'No way,'" said a woman from Cotati who gave $250. The room again broke out in applause.

By the end of the night, the event had raised nearly $40,000. It was a significant sum for Sonoma County, but it was negligible compared to what they were up against. Gallaher had already donated $1 million, and within the next 50 days, he would contribute another $700,000.

A "Revenge Recall" Comes to a Vote

If the campaign to recall Ravitch wasn't already personal, it became substantially more so in the final weeks before the election. Fueled by Gallaher's $1.7 million, the Recall Ravitch campaign flooded the local market with radio and digital ads attacking the 63-year-old district attorney with a litany of unspecified allegations, including corrupt hiring practices, failing to disclose conviction rates, and trying to keep officer body cam recordings confidential. In addition, the more than 300,000 registered voters in Sonoma County received half a dozen direct mailers. One glossy, four-page mailer featured a dour-looking Ravitch next to a figure in a business suit smoking a cigar. The front read "Jill Ravitch—Good for Political Cronies…BAD for Sonoma County families." Inside featured another cutout of the DA with the headline "Sonoma County deserves better than corrupt hypocrite Jill Ravitch!" On the back was an image of a stack of $100 bills being handed over in a handshake. "Jill Ravitch's 10 years of Corruption, Hypocrisy & Failed Leadership Ends in 2021," the mailer read, just above a disclosure that the ad was paid for through "major funding from William Gallaher."

The smear campaign took a toll on Ravitch, who was not optimistic about the outcome. "I went to law school to be a prosecutor," she said in an interview a few weeks before the election. "To think my career will end by being called hypocritical, unethical. It's amazing to me that that will be the end of my career. I don't care if I get voted out. It's more that my reputation is gone."

The campaign saved the most personal mailer for the end. In the final days leading up to the September 14 election, voters received an 8.5 by 11 card with a grainy black-and-white image of Ravitch next to the bold-face words: "Killed Someone." The mailer was referring to the conviction of Ravitch's brother for vehicular manslaughter following a fatal accident in 2015. The accident, which occurred during a vintage car rally in Napa County, claimed the life of one of her brother's friends. According to the California Highway Patrol, John Ravitch was speeding in a Porsche during the rally and crossed a double-yellow line before colliding with a car driven by Jordan Hilsenbeck, who died at the scene. As a result, a Napa County judge sentenced John Ravitch to two years of probation, 15 days in jail, and 120 hours in a work program. Both Ravitch and the Napa County District Attorney's Office had made clear Ravitch played no role in the case. But the mailer implied something else. It pointed out that Ravitch's brother was given only 15 days in jail while she had prosecuted a man who was sentenced to a year in jail for illegally dumping sewage. "How do you think you would be treated by Jill Ravitch?" it asked.

Ravitch wasn't alone in being targeted. On the back of the flier, the campaign took a swipe at local elected officials as well. In east Santa Rosa, voters received a version that read: "Despite injustices like this, [Sonoma

County] Supervisor Susan Gorin and State Senator Mike McGuire still blindly follow and support Jill Ravitch," it read. Beside the text were grainy black-and-white photos of each official. Voters elsewhere received similar pieces calling out supervisors, council members, and mayors in the recipient's specific voting districts. All featured the same message, that these officials "blindly" followed the district attorney.

Some saw it as a "shot across the bow," a warning to elected officials of more recalls to come. "This is a scorched earth sort of thing," said Maddy Hirschfield, a local Democratic party leader and leader of the anti-recall campaign. "Now it's really evident that he has said to every other elected official out there, 'Don't cross me, or this is what happens to you.'" But some local elected officials were unafraid and continued to oppose the recall. "I understand the chilling effect that [the mailer] could have," Sonoma County Supervisor Chris Coursey told reporters. "I dress warmly."

Ravitch said she didn't mind the reference to the illegal sewage dumping conviction. That case involved the owner of a North Bay septic system cleaning business who was repeatedly dumping untreated human waste into a sewer network near his home, causing significant backups to the city's system. The individual involved had a history of similar conduct and prior convictions dating back more than 30 years. A harsh sentence was warranted, she said. But what galled her was the recall campaign's willingness to go after her brother. "This has been a year from hell because of this guy," Ravitch said of Gallaher as she sat with Hirschfield, reviewing the mailers two days before the election. "My brother doesn't deserve to get dragged through the mud by this guy in his effort to unseat me," she said. "I didn't think he would stoop this low." Her brother was paying a price "that he will be paying for the rest of his life," she said. "He lost his best friend. He made a mistake. And no matter what anybody says or does, he can never erase that in his soul." Using him in the attack ads against her was "just evil," Ravitch said.

Nonetheless, with 48 hours to go before the election, she tried to be hopeful, despite her campaign being outspent by a 12-to-1 margin. Unlike the opposition, which received the entirety of its funds from one individual, the "Reject Revenge" campaign was supported by more than 600 donors, the vast majority of whom gave less than $100. They had raised $142,000, enough to send out one single-sided "Reject Revenge—Reject the Recall" mailer to voters. The card listed the elected officials, including the county's two congressional representatives and members of the state Legislature who supported Ravitch. Rarely if ever had locals seen such unanimity among elected officials in a single cause. "I just want to send him a message that we will not tolerate this in Sonoma County," Ravitch said. "And I hope that that message will be loud and clear."

***

It wasn't until 7 p.m. on September 14 that the ranks of those at the "Reject Revenge" campaign watch party began to swell. COVID-19 vaccination cards were checked at the entrance to the Teamsters union hall in Santa Rosa while the presence of a taco truck encouraged the dozens of Ravitch supporters, some in masks, to socialize outside in the parking lot. As they did, Ravitch, looking relaxed in a floral blouse, circulated through the crowd, thanking everyone for attending. She was trying to be optimistic, she said. But as always with elections, everything would hinge on turnout, and it was anybody's guess how many voters ultimately would participate in a special election in the middle of a pandemic. Plus, observers shared their concerns about voters casting votes only in the gubernatorial recall campaign, not realizing that they needed to flip over the ballot to vote on the attempt to unseat the local district attorney.

Those gathered included a cross-section of campaign workers, labor leaders, retirees, District Attorney's Office employees, and others who had played a role in the David-and-Goliath effort to thwart the pro-recall forces. They also included a cross section of people who held various perspectives about Ravitch.

Among them was defense attorney Amanda Roze, who was disappointed when the district attorney didn't pursue charges against the sheriff's deputy in the Andy Lopez case, so angry in fact that she joined protesters beating drums outside a fundraiser for Ravitch's first reelection campaign in 2014. Yet Roze vehemently opposed the recall. "It's important to me that we don't let millionaires buy our election," she said. "We should not allow revenge to dictate who's our DA." Noticeably absent was Beth Eurotas-Steffy, who had worked tirelessly behind the scenes, galvanizing opposition, helping organize events, and, most of all, supporting residents in writing letters to the editor for local newspapers. She had helped place 23 published letters in all. But because of growing concerns about a COVID surge, Beth chose to watch the returns from home.

As the clock moved closer to 8 p.m., the hour when polls officially closed, guests filed inside, filling the rows of metal folding chairs lined beneath the wall-mounted big screen TV showing the county Registrar of Voters election web page. When the clock struck eight, cell phones chimed with text alerts from networks projecting that Gov. Newsom had survived the recall. Local results, however, were taking longer. But given that 52 percent of Sonoma County ballots had already been mailed or dropped off in advance of Election Day and counted, the attendees knew the results that were about to be posted would be decisive, with percentages unlikely to change much in the hours and days to come. At about 10 minutes past the hour, Ravitch was talking and had her back to the screen as the results appeared. The room exploded in cheers. A campaign worker prompted her to turn and look up. "Yes!" Ravitch exclaimed, pumping her fist in the air. She then grabbed her cell phone and called her brother.

Gallaher had lost. And it wasn't close. Of the first 125,000 votes counted, 100,646 were against the recall. Roughly 80 percent of voters stood by the district attorney and rejected Gallaher's attempt at retaliation. The attendees pushed away folding chairs as they pressed together, embracing, toasting, and exchanging high fives, COVID be damned. After her call, Ravitch looked up at the screen again with her arm around her sister, Amy Friedricks, who had driven up from Marin County.

"This," the normally guarded Ravitch said motioning toward the monitor, "This is vindication for my family." With that she put her head on her sister's shoulder and teared up. Friedricks was equally emotional. "I spent many months waiting for this night," she said. "The fact that it's such a strong statement...." She shook her head. "The truth prevails; that's the most important thing."

Internal polls showed they had reason to be optimistic going into that night, said Leo Buc, a political consultant and member of the Reject Revenge Executive Committee. But they didn't expect this landslide win.

"You don't see 80-to-20 wins in politics. Full stop," he observed. "This is a pretty clear rebuke of a pretty clear abuse of the recall system."

Gallaher and those behind the recall campaign, composed mostly of Oakmont employees, declined to speak on the record. But the campaign released a statement: "Over the past year, the goal of our campaign has always been to send a clear signal that self-serving politicians who put their own interests above those of the people they represent will no longer be tolerated in Sonoma County," it read. "We are proud to have helped give a voice to the more than 43,000 residents who put their name on the original petition to Recall Ravitch as well as the countless individuals who bravely stood up to speak truth to power and share their stories of Ravitch's misdeeds..." The unsigned statement concluded: "Every so often, it is critical to our democracy that elected officials are reminded of who exactly they serve. We are proud of the campaign we have run and the long-term impacts that this movement will have on ensuring accountably [sic] and transparency in Sonoma County politics, regardless of the recall's outcome."

For Beth, her celebration at home was subdued but no less joyful. "I felt a little bit of redemption," she said. Although it turned out to be a waste of money, the recall election, in some ways, had been positive, she reflected. It had allowed more people to hear about what happened at Villa Capri, to see the extent to which Oakmont Senior Living was willing to go to suppress the truth and retaliate against those who sought to hold them accountable, and it brought the community together with a unified verdict. It wasn't the public trial that she had hoped for all along. "But it was close," she said. "It was a start."

After the initial rush of excitement inside the union hall, Ravitch stood at the front of the room to address the crowd. She praised her consultants, the committee's executive team, and her brother and sister, who had told her, "You don't walk away from 30 years of service and let this guy win." She then raised her hand as if to toast. "Ding-dong, the bastard's gone!" she declared to a mix of laughter and applause. With that a voice called out from the back of the room: "Hopefully."

21

CHAPTER

A Warning

In the years since the abandonment and rescue of more than 100 residents of Villa Capri and Varenna, major weather events that put society's most vulnerable residents at risk have only accelerated in number. Of the 10 largest wildfires in California history, eight have occurred since 2017, including Butte County's devastating Camp Fire in 2018, which claimed 85 lives, becoming the deadliest and costliest on record. According to EM-DAT: The Emergency Events Database, the number of reported natural disasters—floods, storms, drought, earthquakes, volcanos, and extreme temperatures—has risen from fewer than 50 globally in the 1960s to as many as 350 to 550 per year in the 2000s. The United States used to see fewer than 10 natural disasters a year, until the 1970s when the number rose into the teens. In 2017 alone, the U.S. was impacted by 16 separate catastrophic events that each caused more than a billion dollars in damage, including three tropical cyclones, Harvey in Texas, Irma in Florida, and Maria in Puerto Rico; eight severe storms across the Midwest; two inland floods, one in California and another in Missouri and Arkansas; a crop freeze; drought in the Dakotas and Montana; and wildfires in the West, including the Tubbs Fire.

It's not just the sheer numbers that climate scientists worry about but also the increasing intensity of conditions that feed natural events like these. The U.S. Geological Survey has recorded longer, more extreme droughts, higher wind speeds, more intense and longer heat waves, and a decrease in snowpack, all of which provide conditions for "perfect storms." "This is true for fires, hurricanes, and floods," said Daniel Swain, a climate scientist with UCLA's Institute of the Environment and Sustainability. "[Climate change] is not making minor flooding worse or minor fires worse. It's making the biggest and baddest ones bigger and badder."

377

It's also introducing other regions' disaster types into new geography, with 2021 proving to be the nation's bellwether with myriad climate disasters happening in unexpected places during unexpected times of year. In February, a winter freeze in Texas became the state's costliest weather event ever when a polar vortex delivered snow, sleet, and freezing temperatures that killed 246 people, shut down roads for lack of plows, burst water pipes not buried deep enough to withstand cold temperatures, and triggered a massive energy infrastructure failure that led to heat, water, and food shortages.

As atypical as a freeze was for the South, so, too, was an extreme heat wave in the Pacific Northwest a few months later. The late June "heat dome" trapped hot air in a region where air conditioning is scarce. Seattle temperatures, for example, hit 100 degrees only three times in the last century, but the heat dome sent temperatures soaring past 100 degrees for three days in a row. The high in Portland, Oregon, hit 116 degrees. The two states recorded an official death toll at nearly 200, but a *New York Times* analysis of mortality data showed 600 deaths. Thousands of people crowded hospitals with heat-related illnesses.

And then in December 2021, a twister cut a 165-mile scar across Arkansas, Missouri, Tennessee, and Kentucky, none of which are part of Tornado Alley, where U.S. tornado touchdowns peak in May and June. According to John Allen, a meteorologist and climate scientist at Central Michigan University, most tornadoes survive for no more than 10 to 20 minutes, but the Quad-State Tornado spun for four hours as a result of atypical weather conditions. In the same *Scientific American* article, atmospheric scientist Victor Gensini said temperatures there were more characteristic of April than December, with highs around 80 degrees Fahrenheit, and they combined with "extreme amounts of vertical wind shear" to provide perfect conditions for a massive twister to flourish and kill 89 people in its path.

Two days before the end of the year, an unprecedented winter wildfire tore through Boulder County, Colorado, consuming more than 1,000 structures and killing two people. According to the Western Regional Climate Center, Boulder typically sees about 30 inches of snowfall between September and December, but during that four-month period in 2021, the city received only one inch.

And as is common with all climate disasters, those most affected are typically poor or elderly. People over age 60 accounted for 60 percent of deaths in Texas' deep freeze and 74 percent of Oregon's deaths in the heat dome in 2021. People over the age of 65 represented 75 percent of the Camp Fire deaths. The majority had mobility issues and died inside their homes or within steps of their front doors. Multiple senior victims perished as they huddled with their partners, including two couples who were found in recliners next to each other.

It's becoming an all-too-familiar pattern. During Hurricane Katrina in 2005, half the deaths were among people 65 or older. "The majority of those who died were trapped in their homes. They either drowned or had heart attacks, or things related to their health conditions caused them to die during the hurricane," said Cornell University's Elaine Wethington, a human development professor who was part of the Cornell Aging and the Environment Initiative. "Older people and younger [children] are more likely to die during disasters."

These two trends portend an inescapable reality: as weather events become more vicious, more senior citizens will be put at risk. And never before has the U.S. had so many seniors. According to the U.S. Census Bureau, about 10,000 Baby Boomers turn 65 every day, and by 2030, all 73 million Boomers will be at least 65.

By their sheer numbers, their desire for active lifestyles in retirement, and their pent-up wealth—much of it tied to the equity in their homes—Boomers are revolutionizing senior living. Their plans to remain social and active, and to stay out of what used to be called "old folks' homes," have given rise to the senior living industry. The over-65 set now has the option of moving to stately independent living establishments in which they can reside among their peers and where a continuum of care is available should they need it. But the companies that run "residential care homes for the elderly"—the industry term for assisted living facilities—are not always designed to provide health care, even though some marketing brochures suggest they provide health-related services and support.

"Senior living came about because as a society we said, 'These folks don't need nursing homes. I'm not putting my mom in a nursing home,'" said Monique Dixon, a senior living industry expert who was a former executive director and operations specialist at Brookdale Senior Living and former director of senior living at Avalon Senior Living. Instead, seniors are moving into senior living communities where they can live independently with the opportunity to add more support and oversight as needed.

Problems arise, though, when these same seniors need more intensive care. Many assisted living communities have adapted their licenses to accept more frail and vulnerable people with difficult health conditions. "Assisted living is darned-near skilled [nursing because of] the type of residents we are getting now and the age of residents we are getting," Dixon said. Yet assisted living facilities don't necessarily employ skilled medical staff to meet more complex geriatric health care demands.

The burden falls on residents and their families to be thorough in determining the precise level of care they or their loved ones will receive—and the true cost—if and when their mobility or health declines. Eric Carlson, director of long-term care services and support advocacy for Justice in Aging, a nonprofit that fights senior poverty via the law, said assisted living facility owners, investors, and operators typically come not from health care or medical backgrounds, but hospitality and real estate. "Oftentimes at high-end facilities, you don't get that much [health care]. You'd think if you were paying that much money, you'd get fabulous quality of care. That's not true," he said. Prospective residents and their families tend to get focused on superficial things. "The campus is gorgeous; the buildings are beautiful. It's set up as a luxury residence. But that doesn't necessarily mean the quality of care is that much better."

That's not to say all senior living organizations are weak when it comes to care. Charlene Harrington, a professor emeritus at University of California San Francisco's School of Nursing, has studied nursing home ownership, finances, staffing, and policy since 1980. Her research shows that nonprofit and government-run senior care facilities tend to have higher staffing ratios and fewer violations than larger, for-profit chains. While her study focused on nursing homes, she said these same for-profit chains tend to own facilities across the senior living spectrum and that "larger facilities and chain facilities are more likely to have lower direct care staffing ratios than smaller facilities."

Pat McGinnis spent years working in for-profit residential care facilities where she witnessed "horrible conditions" before founding CANHR in 1983. She says many for-profit assisted living facilities are "all about money. It's not about caring for the residents.... We need to strengthen laws about who can own these residential care homes for the elderly." McGinnis pointed out a key element in the industry is the way ownership is established. "More and more [RCFEs] are incorporated as limited liability corporations, so it's hard to know who owns it. So if someone has a bad track record, they can hide it under an LLC," McGinnis said.

Brian Lee, executive director of the nonprofit advocacy group, Families for Better Care, has also researched profitability and corporate structures of some large commercial nursing home and assisted living chains. "It's a total shell game to protect their profits," he said. His organization provides state-by-state report cards of nursing home care, educates residents and their families about their rights, and advocates for changes to laws and regulations that strengthen care and quality of life for residents. "Really, at the end of the day, these are just profit machines, profit factories for [the owners]," said Lee. "There's a lot of upfront investment to make the places look good, to make them marketable, to get families in there. Once they get you in, they know they have you. They charge you these outrageous monthly rates or upfront deposits. And they continue to thrive on their profits."

Profit margins are high because while owners continue to raise rates year-over-year, they strive to keep expenses low, particularly when it comes to staffing. "Labor costs are expensive," Lee said. "If they can shortchange the residents when it comes to staffing, they are going to do it. They cut corners all over the place to keep their profits high."

Other advocates back up Lee's claim. Cristina Flores, founder of a Bay Area–based eldercare advocacy organization, said staffing competes with the mortgage for the most expensive thing in the building. "It's a high-ticket item," Flores said. "Every single elder abuse case I do is about staffing. It's either not enough staff, [or] not enough qualified staff. It's either the training or the [staff] numbers or both." It's also about high turnover, which is not uncommon for the assisted living and skilled nursing industries. High turnover is endemic, in fact, according to advocates who say larger assisted living companies can have as much as 200 to 300 percent staff turnover in a single year.

When Flores ran her own care homes, she said she paid higher wages than competitors, offered better benefits, and treated staff with kindness to retain them. "It's not an assembly line," she said. "Better paying jobs will attract staff. Treating them well is just as important," because staff departures upset residents who thrive on consistency. "I think it's incredibly traumatic when they lose a caregiver they have clicked with," she said.

Even when caregivers remain committed to the role, advocates say companies do not always train them effectively for the inevitable emergencies that arise. When Monique Dixon worked at Brookdale Chanate, she said she would never expect night-shift employees to attend training during the day, which was the case at Villa Capri. "You don't expect your day shift to come in at 2 a.m. to do training. Why would you expect your NOC shift to come in at 2 p.m.?" she said. Dixon also described what often passes as accepted training in California for caregivers who tend the most vulnerable: "Here's the handout; you're trained."

However, Dixon was quick to cut Villa Capri's executive director—and all executive directors—some slack. "We put a huge amount of expectation on our EDs to wear all these hats," she said. "We expect them to be educators, [but] an educator goes to school to learn how to teach." Dixon said it's unfair to expect them to understand teaching methodologies that would ensure effective adoption of the skills taught.

Emergency preparedness consultant Bo Mitchell, who was deposed on behalf of the plaintiffs in Kathryn Stebner's lawsuit, is familiar with this approach. "Great plans are a smart thing, and training is everything," he said, but "if we don't get the words off paper and into people's heads, then it doesn't matter what assisted living has put on paper." Mitchell, a former Connecticut police commissioner and founder of 911 Consulting, went a step further. "If it hasn't been trained in the last 364 days, then [companies] are not compliant with the law," he said, but even then, once a year is not enough. That's why detailed emergency plans and repeated practical training are paramount for resident safety. "All your employees are the first responders," he said, and they need to be trained as such, not by online modules or handouts, but routine practice.

Yet staffing ratios, training requirements, and the education level of those staff members are inconsistent across state lines because there are no federal regulations for residential care homes for the elderly. Utah distinguishes two levels of assisted living based on whether residents can exit buildings on their own in an emergency. If they are incapable of securing their own safety, the facility has to assign one staff member to assist each resident. This is not the case in California. This disparity is an example of how a state-dependent patchwork of regulations manifests itself across the industry and affects emergency evacuations.

The lack of consistent oversight is also a byproduct of powerful lobbying from the assisted living industry, according to Lee. "[Assisted living] is a multi-billion-dollar industry. They have a lot of money," he said. Two large national organizations, Argentum and the National Center for Assisted Living, partner with state lobbying groups to represent for-profit assisted living companies. Argentum says it works "to ensure state rules and regulations are aligned with the senior living community's best interests." It also lobbies against federal oversight. On the trade association's website, Argentum states, "The pandemic has put a spotlight on all senior living and long-term care communities, and the threat of intrusive federal oversight is upon our industry.... Join us in our fight for federal resources and in combating onerous and crippling federal regulation." In California, Argentum's partner is CALA, the California Assisted Living Association. Oakmont Management Group's CEO and president, Courtney Siegel sits on its board of directors, along with executives from other large California elder care providers.

Harrington, who ran the California Department of Health Licensing and Certification Program for hospitals and nursing homes in the late 1970s, said state regulators sometimes forget who they are meant to serve. "[Regulators] consider these providers to be their clients. They don't consider the residents to be their clients" because the industry and its lobbyists are "where the money is," she said. "They have their big associations with attorneys, dozens and dozens of paid lobbyists. These are huge powerful industry organizations. And all we have [in California] to counter that is one small advocacy group called CANHR. There's no one else out there who cares."

The companies donate to more than just the lobbyists. "They give money to the state legislators. They give money to the governor and to the attorney general. They contribute [to] every election," Harrington said. Legislators, in turn, are mindful of the industry, especially one valued at $23.4 billion in state and local tax revenue nationwide, according to Argentum's economic impact analysis. "Every legislator has nursing homes and assisted living in their district, and they do not want to upset them," Harrington said. She gave the example of how she recently spoke to legislative staff about regulatory changes they hoped to see made. "They said 'Have you talked to the nursing home industry about it? You have to get them to agree.' Are you kidding me? It's insane."

For example, S.B. 1207, a California bill that would have required all skilled nursing facilities in California to have an alternative source of power for 96 hours during a power outage, had nearly unanimous bipartisan support in the state Legislature in 2020 and received a critical endorsement from the AARP. But Governor Newsom ultimately vetoed the bill, saying it relied "on an unclear federal standard as justification" and that the timeline for implementation was "unfeasible given the need for significant renovations that facilities would need to complete to comply."

"It is beyond our comprehension how the governor could veto this vital bill in the midst of the pandemic and the worst wildfire season in California's history," McGinnis said at the time, noting that the California nursing home industry was the only vocal opponent to S.B. 1207. "Residents desperately need him to help protect their lives right now, not the financial interests of nursing home lobbyists."

In Florida in September 2017, 12 elderly skilled nursing facility residents ranging in age from 57 to 99 died due to sweltering conditions left in the wake of a power outage from Hurricane Irma. Some of the residents who perished had body temperatures of nearly 110 degrees. The tragedy prompted lawmakers to pass new state laws requiring every nursing home and assisted living facility in Florida to have a backup generator and power sources that can regulate temperature for at least 96 hours. But it took strong pressure from state regulators over the course of a couple years to bring most nursing homes and skilled nursing facilities into compliance.

That's the concern CANHR's McGinnis has if similar legislation is enacted in California. It's not enough to just pass laws. "You've got to get the state to enforce the law," McGinnis said. "If they're not enforced, they are just paper tigers. They are useless." Multiple advocates said enforcement of existing laws is weak in California because state regulators take a consultative instead of disciplinary approach to violations. Industry attorneys "are consistently in touch every single day with the regulators trying to get them to back off," Harrington said. According to an investigation conducted by KQED, San Francisco's NPR affiliate, "auditors found deficiencies in the majority of skilled nursing homes in California during the two years after the devastating 2017 fires." Public records KQED requested showed "the California Department of Public Health caught 78 percent of nursing homes violating fire safety and emergency planning standards over a two-year period." Despite those findings, the investigation also uncovered that "regulators rarely penalized assisted living homes over inadequate emergency planning." In 2019 state inspectors cited just 3 percent of the long-term care facilities statewide. Chris Murphy, who directs the watchdog group Consumer Advocates for RCFE Reform, told KQED the Department of Social Services will rarely come down on the side of the consumer. She said the department is functioning as "a provider protection agency, not a consumer protection agency."

But protection is what seniors need, and the reason why many of them choose to move into a place on the senior living continuum, be it independent living complexes such as Varenna, assisted living like Villa Capri or its Traditions Memory Care center, or a federally regulated nursing home or skilled nursing facility. Experts say all types of senior living communities face the same challenges: staffing, training, corporatization, insufficient regulation, and weak enforcement. And while those threats reside within the building's footprint, others threaten from the outside.

The KQED investigation, for example, found wildfire is a significant hazard at 35 percent of California's roughly 10,000 senior living facilities because they were built in the wildland-urban interface, in state-designated fire-hazard severity zones, or both. And many, like Villa Capri and Varenna, were knowingly built within burn scars. Outside of California, senior communities often exist in flood plains and on waterfront property in regions vulnerable to sea level rise. "There have been horror stories with all the hurricanes and nursing home deaths in Florida and Texas and Louisiana. It happens over and over again," Harrington said.

The risk is not only from disasters familiar to each region; the last few years have shown that unexpected catastrophic events can strike just about anywhere. Such phenomena require new ways of thinking.

"People see problems as happening to somebody else. We don't see ourselves in nursing facilities or as assisted living residents," Justice in Aging's Carlson said. "People need to kick and scream and raise hell sometimes on these issues."

It's a cultural problem that will require a cultural solution, according to emergency preparedness consultant Mitchell. "This is America. People are stubborn about masks, about planning…. In Europe and Russia and Japan, they don't have this problem. Everybody gets it. They have laws that say 'You'd better get your act together or we're coming after you,'" Mitchell said. "But you're supposed to have your act together. The threats are on the front page every day."

As climate change brings an increasing frequency and intensity of firestorms, floods, freezes, heat waves, hurricanes, and tornadoes, and as Baby Boomers move at a record pace into senior living communities run by a burgeoning for-profit industry, the potential is high for replays of the neglect and abandonment that occurred at Villa Capri and Varenna. The unsettling question is how many communities will need to count on people like Kathy and Mark Allen, Melissa Langhals, Joey Horsman, and R.J. and Steffany Kisling to prevent the next calamity from becoming an unspeakable tragedy.

EPILOGUE

Among the countless goals that accompanied her quest for investigations, legislation, and above all else, accountability, Beth Eurotas-Steffy had one more: to bring together in one place all who were involved in the rescues at Villa Capri, as well as family members with whom she had shared countless tears and trials. On a sunny spring afternoon in April 2019, we helped her do exactly that, inviting rescuers, family members, and one former Oakmont employee for a Sunday brunch at Beth's single-story bungalow in central Santa Rosa.

For the two of us authors, it was a chance to bring clarity to the jumble of facts and experiences we had pulled together from documents, depositions, and personal interviews. More to the point, it was an opportunity to build consensus on the sequence of events that night, plug gaps in timelines, and add details that could only be recovered through the kind of organic interactions that occur among people bonded by a traumatic event. But the gathering proved to be more than we had hoped for. It was as poignant as it was revelatory, a roller coaster ride of emotion punctuated by moments of laughter, outrage, and for those reliving the fire, catharsis. For some, it was the first time they had met face-to-face. For others, it was their first encounter since the early hours of the Tubbs Fire, a chance to affirm that what they or their loved ones experienced that night was not a bad dream.

***

Melissa gave a nervous chuckle when Kathy first walked through the door of Beth's home.

"Hello," Kathy said, hugging her partner in the Villa Capri rescue. "It's good to officially meet you."

Melissa held the embrace for an extra moment. "It's good to officially meet you too," she said.

Kathy admitted she wasn't sure she was going to recognize Melissa in the daylight. It had been nearly 18 months, after all.

"I know, right?" Melissa said, shifting to embrace Mark.

The three of them arrived an hour before the others so we could talk with them more directly about the events of that night. After settling in with some refreshments and getting them mic'd up for a video recording, we had them tackle some basic questions, such as who arrived first at Villa Capri. Mark pointed at Melissa, while Melissa pointed at Mark.

"I thought you were there first," said Mark, sitting in a deep armchair and steadying a mug of coffee on his blue jeans. "No," Melissa said with a quizzical look, seated in a dining room chair next to him. Kathy then helped clarify that she and Mark got there at 2 a.m. while Melissa arrived shortly thereafter.

"I had assumed you already had been working with them and kind of knew what was going on," said Mark.

Melissa shook her head. "No, I had no idea." she said. "We were just winging it."

From there, they worked through a timeline of the night, pointing out on a map where and when specific events took place. They marveled at certain aspects of the night, including how Joey Horsman's patrol car managed to survive despite being parked just feet from the incinerated Villa Capri. They shared in more detail the stressful moments and even some humorous ones, such as when Henrietta barked at Mark for leaving her closet door open when he went to retrieve her shoes.

"She still has those shoes," chimed in Elizabeth Bruno, the former Villa Capri activities director who had since arrived with others. "She said, 'I'm never getting rid of those.'"

"When you look back on that night, what do you think about?" we asked at one point.

"It never should have happened," Melissa said. "I'm just happy that you guys were there," she said, turning to Mark and Kathy, "and we were able to do something about it." She paused for a moment. "I mean, yeah, it was traumatic," she continued.

"But it was more traumatic after, than when we were there," offered Mark.

"Yes," Melissa said. "Because there you've got all the adrenaline going."

"And you're just doing what you need to do to get things taken care of," added Mark, motioning with his hand as if moving invisible chess pieces. "And you're thinking, 'What's the next step?'"

"Exactly," Melissa said.

"But afterward, you think about it," said Mark. "I mean what if we hadn't showed up?" he said motioning toward Melissa. "We would have lost, what, 25 to 30 people, easily."

"I get upset when I think about it," Kathy added.

Kathy then looked toward Melissa. "I remember telling you a couple of times, 'Go ahead and go,' and you said, 'No, I'm not going to leave you by yourself.' And I really appreciate that."

Mark and Melissa's eyes glistened as they nodded in agreement.

"I don't know what I would have done if you hadn't been there," Kathy said.

We asked whether anyone from Oakmont had ever reached out to thank them. Mark chuckled. No one from OSL or OMG had ever asked to interview them, thank them, or to offer counseling support, he said. Sons and daughters of residents, however, did track down the Allens, but that was difficult for Kathy. "They all want to go out to lunch and relive it," she said. "It's embarrassing. I don't like to be the center of attention."

The rest of the morning offered similar exchanges of stories, hugs, and tears. Dawn Ross told the group her mom passed in December 2017 and her father died six months later. "I definitely think they both died sooner because of the fire," she said.

Ruthie Kurpinsky shared how her mother, Ruth Callen, who used to sing and was full of life—"in her head, she danced,"—had declined significantly right after the fire. She had become more fragile and had fallen at one point and broken her femur. "I don't want to do this anymore," she told Ruthie. By then, Ruthie felt she had already lost her mother because of the fires. "We don't count these deaths for some reason," she said of the Tubbs Fire's formal fatality count.

During the group conversation, Elizabeth turned to Melissa with a realization. "You're the one," Elizabeth said, her voice elevated. She realized it was Melissa whom she had met in front of the Veterans Memorial Building as she helped Henrietta and other Villa Capri residents. "It was *you*," Elizabeth said. "You looked at me, you took my hands, and you said, 'They just left them.'"

"Yeah, that was me," Melissa confirmed.

"Oh my God, I've been trying to find out who that person was all this time," Elizabeth said, noting that for the past year, Henrietta had repeatedly asked her, "Who was that woman who was driving that SUV?" Elizabeth was excited to tell her she'd met Melissa in person.

Elizabeth still visited Henrietta once a month at her Brookdale assisted living home. "The nightmares are still there," Elizabeth said, "so, everybody went downhill." A week before the reunion, Henrietta told Elizabeth that Villa Capri representatives had called her to ask her to move into the rebuilt facility.

"So you going?" Elizabeth asked her.

"Are you?" Henrietta retorted.

"No," Elizabeth said.

Later, in a sweet moment as Elizabeth was leaving Brookdale, Henrietta said, "I'd go back to Villa Capri if you were there."

"Well then, we're never going to be back," Elizabeth said.

Melissa told the group how her mother was moved at least five times—from shelters to temporary care—after the fire. Each change of location was difficult on the bedridden Virginia, especially the stint at Belmont Village, where she rolled off an air mattress and spent a night in the hospital. She declined rapidly in the days that followed. "I'm just amazed that everybody's doing so much about this to try to make it right because it was wrong," said Melissa looking around the room. "And we really need to do something to make sure it doesn't happen again."

When it was Beth's turn to talk, she explained how her involvement began soon after she realized that Oakmont was not telling the real story. The truth "needs to be told," she said. "And not just because I want some justice for the victims, most of which are no longer with us, but I want change to happen." All heads in the room nodded. "I want to have some ammunition when I'm talking to [legislators] and want to be able to say, 'Look at this story. This is why you can't brush me off....' There's strength in numbers." Beth then made one final promise to all who were there: "I'm never going to stop fighting."

***

In October 2022, as Santa Rosa reached the fifth anniversary of the Wine Country Fires, the community's scars were still visible, though they were getting harder to see. Of the 1,600 homes the Tubbs Fire destroyed in Fountaingrove, roughly 75 percent had been rebuilt or were under construction. In Coffey Park, more than 95 percent of the 1,422 homes burned had been replaced. But the reconstruction of lives was a much slower process. For some, it never really got started.

Ruth Callen died just days after the 2019 reunion. Frank Perez, the runner whose efforts to stomp out the flames at the patio door of his North Building apartment may have saved Varenna from greater destruction, did not return to his badly damaged unit until May 2018. The only thing he was able to recover was a pair of Nike running shoes, which he washed extensively to lessen the smell of smoke. Never having fully recovered from the lung damage he suffered the night of the fire, Frank died in December 2020. He was 93.

Frank's good friends and upstairs neighbors, Bob Mitton and Mimi Vandermolen, moved back into their apartment at the same time as Frank. The trio had lunch together that first day and compared notes on the night. But the challenges of being back in the area and the daily reminders of all that they went through proved too powerful for Bob. When he tried to resume his daily three-mile walk around Fountaingrove, it was too hard. "I was walking through an area that had virtually no houses left," he said. "And it was one of the factors that emotionally struck me the hardest because I thought, 'What happened to all these people? What happened to the pets?'"

Within three months of returning to Varenna, Bob and Mimi moved back to Vancouver, Canada, full-time. Bob remained friends with SRPD Officer "Constable" Dave Pederson, and the two made good on their promise to share a beer, although they opted instead for an afternoon coffee. They sat well past the dinner hour and replayed the night's events. "I enjoy him," Bob said later. "He's an old-fashioned policeman with a tremendous amount of integrity and a real commitment to the people of Santa Rosa. They should have a hundred more like him." The new friends continued to check on one another by email until Bob's sudden death at age 76 in April 2021. "Some people think that the fire also had a lot to do with his early death, but who knows," Mimi said by email from Vancouver.

Michael Kulwiec reported that the time his father resided at Villa Capri from 2015 until the fire was "one of the happiest periods of his life." Len Kulwiec loved living there and spending time with his many friends. But after the fire, he was not the same. "The PTSD from the fire and his aging took its toll on his spirit," he said. "Nonetheless, he made people smile every day, till the very end of his life." Len died in March 2020.

Though Nell and John Magnuson had sued Oakmont, they still considered moving back into Villa Capri once it was rebuilt. But when they visited a trailer near the demolished site to ask for a brochure, they were denied. Somebody apparently recognized their names as two of the litigants. "You have to talk to your lawyer," they were told, according to Nell. She walked away. "I'm not going to beg for a brochure," she said. Instead, the couple moved into another senior living community until John's death in April 2019. "He didn't do well at all after the fire," Nell said. "It was bad for him." From there, Nell moved into a friend's window-laced house, one overlooking the Fountaingrove Country Club where she could still be near friends from Villa Capri.

Many residents and family members continue to hold resentment toward Oakmont Senior Living for what happened. "Oh my God, you have no idea," said Vivian Flowers, who eventually got her mother, Viola Sodini, settled in a private, 13-bed memory care home where her dementia only worsened. "I'm angry with [Gallaher], and I'm angry with Sonoma County that they didn't make him more accountable for his actions and the fact that nothing happened and he was able to rebuild."

Family members still grapple with the trauma too. Mark is haunted by his decision not to return to Villa Capri for Kathy. R.J. Kisling had occasional nightmares about leaving someone behind as he went door-to-door, trying to clear out a smoke-filled building. Beth cringes at the memory of telling her sister in the early morning hours of October 9 that she was sure Oakmont had safely taken all residents off the hill hours before the fire approached. "I told [Gloria] that, and I still feel sick that a company responsible for the safety and well-being of my mom, and all the other residents, let them all down in such a profound way," Beth said.

Former Varenna maintenance worker Andre Blakely is still weighed down by the memory of dumping Edel Burton out of her wheelchair as they fled down Varenna's steep driveway. Andre found a measure of comfort a couple of months after the fire when he met with Edel. She had recovered from her injuries, but "I couldn't apologize to her enough," he said. She would have none of it.

"I'm OK," she told him after hugging him. "I'm just glad you came back for me." Edel then took his hands. "Andre. Why did you come back?" she asked. "I mean I'm glad that you did, but why did you come back?"

Andre said he never had any intention of leaving her. He was determined to get her off that hill or perish in the attempt.

"You know, they left us to die," she said to him. Andre thought about that conversation many times over the weeks and months that followed.

"That was true," he said. "They left us to die."

All three Villa Capri caregivers also still wrestle with the emotional aftermath, especially during fire season. Anett Rivas continued to work 60-hour weeks as a night-shift caregiver so she could spend her days with her two children. In the summer of 2022, Cynthia Arroyo was raising 3-year-old twin girls and working as a vet tech assistant for an animal hospital. Both young women spoke with us on multiple occasions, bravely and tearfully sharing their recollections and eager to get their side of the story told.

It took more than a year for Elizabeth Lopez to trust us with her story. She was still getting through it, she told us, and it was too painful to revisit. She knew the truth of what happened, and she was inclined to leave it in the past. But three years after the fire, in October 2020, Elizabeth was ready. It was easier for her to answer dozens of questions than provide a narrative, but bit by bit, her story emerged. She told of driving some of her favorite residents, Bill and Wanda Lee and Viola Sodini to safety that night. But it came at a cost of not staying and helping Kathy and Melissa get back inside the burning building. Elizabeth had intended to return, she said, and she agonized for days that someone had been left behind.

We shared with Dawn Ross a video that Elizabeth's then-boyfriend had taken as they left Villa Capri, and a backseat passenger can be heard saying, "Buildings are burning like mad over there."

Dawn could tell who it was. "It was clearly my dad's voice," she said. She asked for Elizabeth's contact information and sent her an email thanking her for "helping to save my parents from the fire. I have been trying to piece together how they were saved that night, but no one seemed to know," Dawn wrote.

She asked to meet with her so she could express her gratitude in person and give Elizabeth a monetary gift. Elizabeth never responded. She and her husband, daughter, and baby have since moved to the Midwest, where Elizabeth continues to work as a caregiver.

Of the Oakmont employees who assisted with the evacuations, few are still with the company. And no one, including Andre and Michael, was ever interviewed by Oakmont managers about what transpired during the fire.

Three of the five Oakmont employees who DSS accused of either failing residents or making false claims have continued in leadership positions within Oakmont companies. Pouya Ansari, the regional maintenance director who told DSS investigators that he had driven several residents to safety and that he didn't find anyone left behind at Varenna, was promoted to executive director of another Oakmont property. And Debie Smith, the former Villa Capri executive director state regulators initially sought to ban for life from working at state-licensed care homes, was serving as Varenna's assistant executive director as of spring 2023.

Nathan Condie continued as Varenna's executive director until mid-2021, when he left to work for a different senior living company. If he had to do it all over again, "I would have done everything differently," he acknowledged in the fall of 2021. Before he left, he said he made sure Varenna was better prepared for the next emergency, though state and local officials mandated many of the changes he implemented. Varenna now has stair chairs, a contract with a bus company, and designated evacuation zones with different assembly areas, he said. Each resident receives a go-bag to pack with essentials in case of an emergency evacuation. And because Varenna residents had trouble getting their cars out of the parking garage to flee, Nathan purchased portable generators that could open the metal doors in a power outage. Varenna staff also now hold two full evacuation drills each year, but it's difficult to convince residents to participate, Nathan said.

While he didn't suffer fire-related trauma, Nathan said it took a long time to recover from "having my name dragged through the mud, my reputation tarnished" with accusations of abandoning residents. "That's the biggest insult and character attack," he said. He noted he could have easily switched careers after the fire, but he loves working with seniors. "I love what I do so much, I'm going to keep doing it."

Not wanting all the work she did in 2018 to go to waste, attorney Kathryn Stebner took on two more cases involving the fire, one on behalf of Varenna residents. Those cases also settled out of court for undisclosed sums, as did the class action lawsuit against all Oakmont communities Stebner had filed before the fire. As part of that settlement, Oakmont had to make changes to its assessment and billing systems at its California assisted living communities.

Meanwhile, Bill Gallaher's OSL/OMG empire has continued to expand. In 2020, Argentum—the national trade organization for senior living communities—listed Oakmont as No. 53 among the nation's largest senior living providers. By 2022, OSL had jumped to No. 27 with 49 retirement complexes in California and Nevada.

However, Gallaher never found success in his 15-year battle with the City of Santa Rosa for approval of his 676-unit Elnoka Villa project. Neighbors steadfastly opposed the project, primarily because of the dense development's potential impact on evacuation routes. Ultimately, in December 2022, Gallaher sold the property, which he had purchased for $15 million, to a nonprofit developer of affordable housing for $3 million. "I think we were just sort of done," Gallaher told the *Press Democrat* in a rare interview. That same year, the county successfully auctioned off the old Sonoma County Hospital site off Chanate Road, which Gallaher had sought to redevelop for $11.5 million. The sales price to a new developer was $15 million.

Gallaher's legal and political battles have continued in other areas as well. In 2019, Gallaher sued the town of Windsor when the community joined a growing list of cities requiring most new homes to use electric instead of gas appliances. When Santa Rosa did the same thing in the fall of 2019, as part of its goal to reduce its carbon footprint to net zero by 2030, Gallaher sued that city as well. Then, in August 2021, a Gallaher company agreed to a $500,000 settlement in response to a whistleblower lawsuit filed by a former employee who claimed she was fired after uncovering extensive affordable housing fraud at a 232-unit apartment complex that Gallaher developed north of Santa Rosa. In the lawsuit, a former property manager accused the apartment complex of leasing rent-restricted apartments to Gallaher family members and friends despite the fact these residents made too much money to qualify for low-income units. In the end, a 2022 Sonoma County Grand Jury report called on the county to beef up its "inconsistent and inadequate" oversight of developers with affordable housing agreements that include public funding.

In the end, the Gallaher family's interactions with the Sonoma County District Attorney's Office weren't over either. Just two days after the rejection of the district attorney recall effort in September 2021, authorities announced the arrest of one of Gallaher's sons for allegedly stealing from Gallaher's bank. Santa Rosa police had arrested Marco Gallaher, a Poppy Bank shareholder, and his girlfriend, Rachele Eschenburg, on July 22, 2021, on suspicion of making "unauthorized purchases and payments" totaling $102,000. Marco Gallaher told the *Press Democrat* the allegations were based on "a misunderstanding" between him and his estranged family. "I've been trying to distance myself from my family for a while," he said.

The Sonoma County District Attorney's Office was investigating the case at the same time the Gallaher-funded campaign was sending out mailers to have the district attorney recalled. But Ravitch removed herself from any involvement in the case and never brought it up during the campaign. Two months later, on January 6, 2022, the district attorney's office filed grand theft charges against Marco and Rachele.

All the while, Beth's push for legislative reform has continued, this time with a refined focus on mandating permanent, on-site emergency power generators for assisted living facilities, similar to what's required in Florida. Although she has continued to meet with state lawmakers, as of the fifth anniversary of the Tubbs Fire, no such law exists in California.

On October 18, 2017, Sonoma County fire officials reported the number of fatalities from the Tubbs Fire at 22 and never increased it. The tally does not include the four Villa Capri residents—Louise Johnson, Bess Budow, Virginia Gunn, and Wanda Lee—who died within 10 weeks of the fire. Their families continue to contend the deaths were a direct result of the injuries or trauma each experienced that night.

SOURCES

Our reporting in *Inflamed* comes from interviews, depositions, legal documents, news archives, 911 dispatch transcripts, reports, books, and other sources. In instances of conflicts between a source's interview and deposition, we chose the earlier record, usually the deposition, unless the source wrote a narrative shortly after the fire. These notes will hopefully clarify the primary sources used in each chapter. Repeated requests to interview the Gallahers and managers with Oakmont Management Group and Oakmont Senior Living were either denied or went unanswered. We relied on depositions for key managers' testimonies and the recollections of others who interacted with them.

PROLOGUE

Interviews

Kathy Allen and Mark Allen, daughter-in-law and son of Helen Allen; R.J. Kisling and Steffany Kisling, grandson and granddaughter of John Hurford; Melissa Langhals, daughter of Virginia Gunn.

Legal Documents and Depositions

Accusation for license revocation against Varenna, LLC et al., filed September 4, 2018, State of California Department of Social Services, CDSS No. 7218241101, obtained via public records request.

Budow et al. v. Oakmont Senior Living, LLC et al., filed November 20, 2017, Superior Court of California County of Sonoma, Case No. SCV-261552, available on Sonoma Superior Court portal, https://sonoma.courts.ca.gov/online-services/case-portal.

Kathy Allen, June 7, 2018, in *Budow et al. v. Oakmont Senior Living, LLC et al.*

Mark Allen, June 7, 2018, in *Budow et al. v. Oakmont Senior Living, LLC et al.*
Melissa Langhals, June 6, 2018, in *Budow et al. v. Oakmont Senior Living, LLC et al.*

PART I: FOOTPRINTS
CHAPTER 1: HANLEY

Published Material and Other Sources

Bill Van Niekerken, "Wine Country fire of 1964: Eerie similarities to this
     week's tragedy," *San Francisco Chronicle*, October 10, 2017, https://www.
     sfchronicle.com/chronicle_vault/article/Wine-Country-fire-of-1964-Eerie-
     similarities-to-12267643.php?utm_source=marketing&utm_medium=-
     google&utm_campaign=content_acquisition&utm_content=core_local&g-
     clid=Cj0KCQiApb2bBhDYARIsAChHC9syjM2azl2nQA3V6ECRx-
     kj11jAKtGQGwp1v48gPXWZt0AimfV91ElMaAs0mEALw_wcB.
Gaye LeBaron, "Tubbs fire revives memory of a blaze that now haunts Santa Rosa,"
     Press Democrat, October 14, 2017, https://www.pressdemocrat.com/article/news/
     gaye-lebaron-tubbs-fire-revives-memory-of-a-blaze-that-now-haunts-santa-ro/.
Jeff Elliot, "The 1964 Hanly Fire," *Santa Rosa History* (blog), September 11, 2019,
     http://santarosahistory.com/wordpress/2019/09/the-1964-hanly-fire/.
John Olney, "Alfred Loving Tubbs and the birth of Chateau Montelena," *St.
     Helena Star*, August 3, 2006, https://napavalleyregister.com/community/
     star/lifestyles/alfred-loving-tubbs-and-the-birth-of-chateau-montelena/arti-
     cle_ede31320-6e12-5747-a204-6522c565bdc9.html.
Sandi Funke and Michelle Halbur, "Fire Ecology for Non-Scientists:
     The Fire Triangle & Fire Behavior," *Pepperwood Preserve: Field Notes*,
     September 4, 2020, https://www.pepperwoodpreserve.org/2020/09/04/
     fire-ecology-for-non-scientists-the-fire-triangle-fire-behavior/.
"Winemaking in Calistoga, Pt.1," Napa County Historical Society, March 3,
     2015, https://napahistory.org/winemaking-in-calistoga-pt-1/.

CHAPTER 2: UTOPIA

Published Material and Other Sources

"Áegis Assisted Living at No. 3," *INC 5000*, February 28, 2003, https://www.inc.
     com/profile/aegis-assisted-living-%5Baccent-egu-over-a%5D.
Áegis Living Corporate Fact Sheet, https://paperzz.com/doc/6892617/
     corporate-fact-sheet.

Andrew Warfield, "New upscale senior living communities riding the gray wave," *Business Observer*, November 18, 2018, https://www.businessobserverfl.com/news/2018/nov/09/new-upscale-senior-living-communities-riding-the-gray-wave/.

Bob Schmidt, "Why Build a Castle?" *Press Democrat*, Letters to the Editor, March 10, 2007, https://www.pressdemocrat.com/article/news/why-build-a-castle/.

Champaign Williams, "Building Boom: The Future of Senior Housing Screams Luxury," BisNow, July 11, 2016, https://www.bisnow.com/national/news/senior-housing/building-boom-the-future-of-senior-housing-screams-luxury-62422.

Danielle Garduno, "Kanaye Nagasawa: The Wine King of California," *Multicultural Roots Project* (blog), City of Santa Rosa, August 30, 2021, https://www.srcity.org/Blog.aspx?IID=64.

Editorial, "Ridge Housing: Protecting Santa Rosa's Hilltops Must be City's First Priority," *Press Democrat*, February 11, 2005, https://www.pressdemocrat.com/article/news/ridge-housingprotecting-santa-rosas-hilltops-must-be-citys-first-priorit/.

"Facts & Figures," American Health Care Association/National Center for Assisted Living, September 26, 2020, https://www.ahcancal.org/Assisted-Living/Facts-and-Figures/Pages/default.aspx.

Gaye LeBaron, "Fountaingrove's strange history reads like fiction," *Press Democrat*, July 18, 1993, https://library.sonoma.edu/about/gallery/digital-exhibits/lebaron/fountaingrove.

Gaye LeBaron and Bart Casey, *The Wonder Seekers of Fountaingrove* (Historia II, 2018).

Gaye LeBaron, "Santa Rosa ignored nature's warning," *Washington Post*, October 18, 2017, https://www.washingtonpost.com/opinions/santa-rosa-ignored-natures-warning/2017/10/18/54240560-b425-11e7-be94-fabb0f1e9ffb_story.html.

Gaye LeBaron, "Serpent in Eden: The Final Utopia of Thomas Lake Harris and What Happened There," *Markham Review*, no. 4 (February 1969): 14-24, https://northbaydigital.sonoma.edu/digital/collection/Lebaron/id/1204.

Gaye LeBaron, "Tubbs fire revives memory of a blaze that now haunts Santa Rosa," *Press Democrat*, October 14, 2017, https://www.pressdemocrat.com/article/news/gaye-lebaron-tubbs-fire-revives-memory-of-a-blaze-that-now-haunts-santa-ro/.

Maria L. La Ganga, "Paying in gold for the golden years," *Los Angeles Times*, June 12, 2008, https://www.latimes.com/archives/la-xpm-2008-jun-12-me-luxury12-story.html.

Mike McCoy, "Fountain Grove Traffic Plan Emerges: Suggested fixes for deadly
hillside parkway include elimination of left turns, adding signals," *Press
Democrat*, November 25, 2007, https://www.pressdemocrat.com/article/news/
fountain-grove-traffic-plan-emergessuggested-fixes-for-deadly-hillside-par/.

Mike McCoy, "Planners cite senior housing need as reason to
approve controversial project in Fountaingrove," *Press Democrat*,
May 27, 2005, https://www.pressdemocrat.com/article/news/
planners-cite-senior-housing-need-as-reason-to-approve-controversial-projec/.

Neil Howe, "The Graying of Wealth," *Forbes*, March 16, 2018, https://www.forbes.com/
sites/neilhowe/2018/03/16/the-graying-of-wealth/?sh=3665aa31302d.

"Our History," Áegis Living website, accessed March 4, 2023, https://www.aegis-
living.com/about/history/.

Scott James, "Boomers Create a Surge in Luxury Care Communities," *New York
Times*, December 4, 2018, https://www.nytimes.com/2018/12/04/business/
retirement/continuing-care-retirement-communities-baby-boomers.html.

Staff, "What HP saw in Santa Rosa 40 years ago," *North Bay Business Journal*,
January 22, 2013, https://www.northbaybusinessjournal.com/article/
industry-news/what-hp-saw-in-santa-rosa-40-years-ago/.

Wendy Patterson, "Entrance fees range from $300,000 to over $1 million," *Press
Democrat*, July 14, 2004, https://www.pressdemocrat.com/article/news/
entrance-fees-range-from-300000-to-over-1-million/.

CHAPTER 3: HALCYON DAYS

Interviews

Elizabeth Bruno; six anonymous former Oakmont Senior Living or Oakmont
Management Group employees, including three high-level managers and one
former executive director; Tim Delaney, son of Mary Lou Delaney; Henrietta
Hillman and son Corky Cramer and daughter Margie Cramer; Len Kulwiec
and son Michael Kulwiec.

Legal Documents and Depositions

Leonard Kulwiec, June 29, 2018, in *Budow et al. v. Oakmont Senior Living, LLC
et al.*

Published Material and Other Sources

Oakmont Senior Living, LLC website, versions from April 2011 through January
2019, accessed via the Internet Archive Wayback Machine.

CHAPTER 4: LIFEGUARD

Interviews

R.J. Kisling and Betty Kisling, grandson and granddaughter-in-law of John Hurford.

CHAPTER 5: CASTLE

Interviews

Jonell Jel-Enedra, Eric Johnson, and Craig Johnson, children of Louise Johnson; Kathy Allen and Mark Allen, daughter-in-law and son of Helen Allen; Eric Carlson, director, Long-Term Services and Supports Advocacy, Justice in Aging; Ruth Callen and daughters Liz Schopfer and Ruthie Kurpinsky; Dawn Ross, daughter of Bill and Wanda Lee; Len Kulwiec and son Michael Kulwiec; Alice Eurotas and daughters Beth Eurotas-Steffy and Gloria Eurotas; Bob Mitton and Mimi Vandermolen.

Legal Documents and Depositions

Declaration of Dawn Ross to State of California Department of Social Services for its investigation into Villa Capri, CDSS No. 7218241101, August 24, 2018, courtesy Dawn Ross.

Kathy Allen, June 7, 2018, in *Budow et al. v. Oakmont Senior Living, LLC et al.*

Leonard Kulwiec, June 29, 2018, in *Budow et al. v. Oakmont Senior Living, LLC et al.*

Mark Allen, June 7, 2018, in *Budow et al. v. Oakmont Senior Living, LLC et al.*

Ruth Callen, June 7, 2018, in *Budow et al. v. Oakmont Senior Living, LLC et al.*

Published Material and Other Sources

"Best Senior Care Providers of 2017," SeniorAdvisor.com, accessed March 4, 2023, https://www.senioradvisor.com/about/best-senior-care-providers-2017.

"Gourmet. Every. Day.," Oakmont Senior Living, LLC website, posted from January 14 through October 6, 2017, accessed via the Internet Archive Wayback Machine.

"Milestones: Louise W. Johnson," *The Cloverdale Reveille*, December 28, 2017.

National Weather Service Bay Area (@NWSBayArea), "A wind advisory…," Twitter, October 6, 2017, 1:16 p.m., https://twitter.com/NWSBayArea/status/916396823841001472.

National Weather Service Bay Area (@NWSBayArea), "An early look at...,"
Twitter, October 8, 2017, 8:59 a.m., https://twitter.com/NWSBayArea/
status/917056924218265601.

National Weather Service Bay Area (@NWSBayArea), "Chilly morning temperatures...," Twitter, October 4, 2017, 7:29 a.m., https://twitter.com/
NWSBayArea/status/915584683395764224.

National Weather Service Bay Area (@NWSBayArea), "Fire Weather Watch...,"
Twitter, October 5, 2017, 11:12 a.m., https://twitter.com/NWSBayArea/
status/916003286255263744.

National Weather Service Bay Area (@NWSBayArea), "Graph 1: Long period...,"
Twitter, October 6, 2017, 12:23 p.m., https://twitter.com/NWSBayArea/
status/916383321176838144.

National Weather Service Bay Area (@NWSBayArea), "Heads Up! Gusty
winds...," Twitter, October 6, 2017, 6:30 a.m., https://twitter.com/
NWSBayArea/status/916294671332192256.

National Weather Service Bay Area (@NWSBayArea), "Hold onto your hats...,"
Twitter, October 8, 2017, 7:18 a.m., https://twitter.com/NWSBayArea/
status/917031326481559555.

National Weather Service Bay Area (@NWSBayArea), "Looks for a warm-
ing trend...," Twitter, October 4, 2017, 5:35 a.m., https://twitter.com/
NWSBayArea/status/915555863972253696.

National Weather Service Bay Area (@NWSBayArea), "Red Flag Warning
issued...," Twitter, October 6, 2017, 10:33 a.m., https://twitter.com/
NWSBayArea/status/916355692524658688.

National Weather Service Bay Area (@NWSBayArea), "Reminder that a Wind
Advisory," Twitter, October 7, 2017, 4:26 p.m., https://twitter.com/
NWSBayArea/status/916806970761412613.

National Weather Service Bay Area (@NWSBayArea), "Reminder we are still...,"
Twitter, October 8, 2017, 3:45 p.m., https://twitter.com/NWSBayArea/
status/917159121496965120.

National Weather Service Bay Area (@NWSBayArea), "The calendar may say...,"
Twitter, October 7, 2017, 6:52 a.m., https://twitter.com/NWSBayArea/
status/916662448656134144.

National Weather Service Bay Area (@NWSBayArea), "Very High Fire
Danger...," Twitter, October 5, 2017, 7:40 p.m., https://twitter.com/
NWSBayArea/status/916130950945345542.

National Weather Service Bay Area (@NWSBayArea), "Windy conditions are expected…," Twitter, October 8, 2017, 5:51 a.m., https://twitter.com/NWSBayArea/status/917009618655694848.

"October 2017 Weather in Santa Rosa," Time and Date AS, accessed March 4, 2023, https://www.timeanddate.com/weather/usa/santa-rosa/historic?month=10&year=2017.

"October 2017 North Bay Fires," National Oceanic and Atmospheric Administration, National Weather Service, San Francisco Bay Area Weather Forecast Office, July 3, 2020, https://noaa.maps.arcgis.com/apps/Cascade/index.html?appid=790ba363d4e74c77a94d861a7dd533fe.

Robert Digitale, "Retirement home for gays and lesbians debuts in Fountaingrove," *Press Democrat*, June 15, 2011, https://www.pressdemocrat.com/article/news/retirement-home-for-gays-and-lesbians-debuts-in-fountaingrove/.

PART II: FIRE
CHAPTER 6: SPARK

Interviews

Daniel Swain, Ph.D, climate scientist with the UCLA Institute of the Environment and Sustainability, research fellow in the Capacity Center for Climate and Weather Extremes at the National Center for Atmospheric Research, California Climate Fellow at The Nature Conservancy, and author of *Weather West* blog; Mountain Volunteer firefighters Caroline Upton and Tony Albright; Elizabeth Lopez; Anett Rivas; Cynthia Arroyo; Andre Blakely; Michael Rodriguez; Bob Mitton and Mimi Vandermolen; Carole Williams; Jessica Kilcullen, granddaughter of Sally Tilbury.

Legal Documents and Depositions

Anett Rivas, June 20, 2018, in *Budow et al. v. Oakmont Senior Living, LLC et al.*

Cynthia Arroyo, June 14, 2018, in *Budow et al. v. Oakmont Senior Living, LLC et al.*

Elizabeth Lopez, July 26, 2018, in *Budow et al. v. Oakmont Senior Living, LLC et al.*

Marie So, June 12, 2018, in *Budow et al. v. Oakmont Senior Living, LLC et al.*

Published Material and Other Sources

911 call transcripts, California Department of Forestry and Fire Protection Sonoma-Lake-Napa Unit, from October 8, 2017, at 9:28 p.m. through October 9, 2017, at 5:24 a.m., obtained via public records request.

California Department of Forestry and Fire Protection, "CAL FIRE Investigators Determine the Cause of the Tubbs Fire," Cal Fire press release, January 24, 2019, http://s1.q4cdn.com/880135780/files/doc_downloads/wildfire_ updates/January-24-2019-%E2%80%93-CAL-FIRE-Press-Release.pdf.

California Department of Forestry and Fire Protection, Sonoma-Lake-Napa Unit, Tubbs Fire Investigation Report, July 2011, https://www.documentcloud.org/ documents/5693976-Cal-Fire-Tubbs-Fire-Investigation-Report-20190124.

PG&E customer letter in response to authors' request, noting outage began at "23:10" and was out for "110 minutes," August 10, 2021, signed Jeffrey Jung, PG&E Electric Distribution Engineer.

Sonoma County Sheriff's Office, "Multiple fires reported around Sonoma County," Nixle Advisory, October 8, 2017, 10:51 p.m., SoCo Data, http:// local.nixle.com/alert/6197177/.

CHAPTER 7: SMOKE

Interviews
Cynthia Arroyo; Anett Rivas; Elizabeth Lopez; Capt. Mike Stornetta.

Legal Documents and Depositions

Anett Rivas, June 20, 2018, in *Budow et al. v. Oakmont Senior Living, LLC et al.*

Cynthia Arroyo, June 14, 2018, in *Budow et al. v. Oakmont Senior Living, LLC et al.*

Deborah Smith, June 14, 2018, in *Budow et al. v. Oakmont Senior Living, LLC et al.*

Elizabeth Lopez, July 26, 2018, in *Budow et al. v. Oakmont Senior Living, LLC et al.*

Marie So, June 12, 2018, in *Budow et al. v. Oakmont Senior Living, LLC et al.*

Published Material and Other Sources

Diane M. Smith, "Sustainability and Wildland Fire: The Origins of Forest Service Wildland Fire Research," May 2017, *U.S. Department of Agriculture, Missoula Fire Sciences Laboratory, Rocky Mountain Research Station*, https://www. fs.usda.gov/sites/default/files/fs_media/fs_document/sustainability-wildland-fire-508.pdf.

Editorial, "The warnings that never came," *Press Democrat*, October 13, 2017, https://www.pressdemocrat.com/article/opinion/ pd-editorial-the-warnings-that-never-came/?sba=AAS.

Frank K. Lake, "Trails, Fires and Tribulations: Historical and Cultural Fires, Tribal Management, and Research Issue in Northern California," *Occasion* 5, (February 2013): https://arcade.stanford.edu/occasion/

historical-and-cultural-fires-tribal-management-and-research-issue-north-ern-california.

"Hurricane Irma Local Report/Summary," National Weather Service, July 23, 2018, https://www.weather.gov/mfl/hurricaneirma.

"Hurricane Irma Recovery," Monroe County Florida, accessed March 4, 2023, https://monroecounty-fl.gov/726/Hurricane-Irma-Recovery.

J.D. Morris, "'You failed us:' Records show how Sonoma County reacted to warning shortfall in October fires," *Press Democrat*, July 13, 2018, https://www.pressdemocrat.com/article/news/you-failed-us-records-show-how-sonoma-county-reacted-to-warning-shortfal/.

"Major Hurricane Harvey—August 25-29, 2017," National Weather Service, August 26, 2022, https://www.weather.gov/crp/hurricane_harvey.

Nick Rahaim, "Sonoma County's emergency alerts face scrutiny in wake of deadly wildfires," *Press Democrat*, October 13, 2017, https://www.pressdemocrat.com/article/news/sonoma-countys-emergency-alerts-face-scrutiny-in-wake-of-deadly-wildfires/.

"Nixle Alert Data," SoCo Data, https://data.sonomacounty.ca.gov/Government/Nixle-Alert-Data/t8rm-jkfw/data.

Sandi Funke and Michelle Halbur, "Fire Ecology for Non-Scientists: Fire Followers," *Pepperwood Preserve: Field Notes*, February 14, 2018, https://www.pepperwoodpreserve.org/2018/02/14/fire-ecology-for-non-scientists-fire-followers/.

Sonoma County Sheriff's Office, "Evacuations Ordered near Calistoga...," Nixle Advisory, October 8, 2017, 11:14 p.m., SoCo Data, http://local.nixle.com/alert/6197193/.

Sonoma County Sheriff's Office, "Mandatory evacuation ordered...," Nixle Alert, October 8, 2017, 11:03 p.m., SoCo Data, http://local.nixle.com/alert/6197185/.

Sonoma County Sheriff's Office, "How the Sonoma County Sheriff's Office uses Nixle," Nixle Community Message, August 26, 2021, https://nixle.us/D2REN?_ga=2.235149185.1079489554.1641251941-796286503.1641072699.

"Wireless Emergency Alerts (WEA)," Federal Communication Commission, accessed August 29, 2022, https://www.fcc.gov/consumers/guides/wireless-emergency-alerts-wea.

CHAPTER 8: FIREBALL

Interviews

Daniel Swain, Ph.D; Elizabeth Bruno; three former employees who requested
anonymity; Noella "Nell" Magnuson; Henrietta Hillman; Cynthia Arroyo;
Elizabeth Lopez; Anett Rivas; Bess Budow's daughter Sherry Minson, granddaughter Sarah Minson, and caregiver Maritza (last name withheld upon
request); *Press Democrat* photographer Kent Porter; former *Press Democrat*
managing editor Ted Appel.

Legal Documents and Depositions

Deborah Smith, June 14, 2018, *in Budow et al. v. Oakmont Senior Living, LLC
et al.*

Marie So, June 12, 2018, in *Budow et al. v. Oakmont Senior Living, LLC et al.*

William P. Gallaher, July 12 and 20, 2018, in *Budow et al. v. Oakmont Senior
Living, LLC et al.*

Published Material and Other Sources

Chris Smith, "He was the first to die in the 2017 Tubbs Fire, and his family was forever
changed," *Press Democrat*, October 8, 2022, https://www.pressdemocrat.com/article/
news/he-was-the-first-to-die-in-the-2017-tubbs-fire-and-his-family-was-forever/.

Christi Warren, "2017 is Santa Rosa's hottest summer ever," *Press Democrat*,
September 9, 2017, https://www.pressdemocrat.com/article/
news/2017-is-santa-rosas-hottest-summer-ever/.

"Diablo Winds," Fire Safe Marin, https://firesafemarin.org/prepare-yourself/
red-flag-warnings/diablo-winds/.

Jeff Elliot, "Not Our Wettest Year, Not Even Close," *Santa Rosa History*
(blog), March 4, 2017, http://santarosahistory.com/wordpress/2017/03/
not-our-wettest-year-not-even-close/.

"Precipitation Data for Sonoma, CA 95476," Rain Harvest Calculator, http://
www.rainharvestcalculator.com/Rainfall/CA/Sonoma/95476.

Press Democrat Staff, "Firestorm Nightmare: How we covered the early hours
of California's most destructive fire," Pulitzer Prize Entry: Breaking News,
Submission for 2018 award consideration, https://www.pulitzer.org/cms/
sites/default/files/content/01pressdemocrat-breakingnews-2.pdf.

"Sonoma County Hazard Mitigation Plan, Appendix D: Climate Change," Permit
Sonoma, April 2017, https://permitsonoma.org/Microsites/Permit%20

Sonoma/Documents/Pre-2022/Department%20Information/Cannabis%20
Program/_Documents/17_Appendix-D-Climate-Change_APA.pdf.
"South Napa Earthquake," United States Geological Survey,
August 15, 2015, https://www.usgs.gov/news/featured-story/
south-napa-earthquake-one-year-later.
"Staff Training," California Assisted Living Association, https://caassistedliving.
org/provider-resources/laws-regulations/staff-training/.
Tom Di Liberto, "Very wet 2017 water year ends in California," October
10, 2017, https://www.climate.gov/news-features/featured-images/
very-wet-2017-water-year-ends-California.

CHAPTER 9: CHAOS

Interviews

Capt. Mike Stornetta; Elizabeth Lopez; Melissa Langhals, daughter of Virginia
Gunn, and Melissa's partner, Roxanne Campbell; Dick and Nancy
Lemmerding; Andre Blakely; Michael Rodriguez; Nathan Condie; Gena
Jacob; seven former employees who requested anonymity; Len Kulwiec;
Vivian Flowers, daughter of Viola Sodini; Cynthia Arroyo; Anett Rivas;
Kathy Allen and Mark Allen, daughter-in-law and son of Helen Allen.

Legal Documents and Depositions

Anett Rivas, June 20, 2018, in *Budow et al. v. Oakmont Senior Living, LLC et al.*
Cynthia Arroyo, June 14, 2018, in *Budow et al. v. Oakmont Senior Living, LLC et al.*
Elizabeth Lopez, July 26, 2018, in *Budow et al. v. Oakmont Senior Living, LLC et al.*
Kathy Allen, June 7, 2018, in *Budow et al. v. Oakmont Senior Living, LLC et al.*
Marie So, June 12, 2018, in *Budow et al. v. Oakmont Senior Living, LLC et al.*
Mark Allen, June 7, 2018, in *Budow et al. v. Oakmont Senior Living, LLC et al.*
Melissa Langhals, June 6, 2018, in *Budow et al. v. Oakmont Senior Living, LLC et al.*
Nathan Condie, June 28 and July 20, 2018, in *Budow et al. v. Oakmont Senior
Living, LLC et al.*
Tammy Moratto, July 6, 2018, in *Budow et al. v. Oakmont Senior Living, LLC et al.*

Published Material and Other Sources

Colin Atagi, "During a wildfire, here's how Sonoma County dispatchers alert residents and firefighters," *Press Democrat*, October

19, 2021, https://www.pressdemocrat.com/.article/news/
during-a-wildfire-heres-how-sonoma-county-dispatchers-alert-residents-and/.

Erin Allday, "Wine Country wildfires: Huddled in pool amid blaze, wife
dies in husband's arms," SFGate, October 12, 2017, https://www.sfgate.
com/bayarea/article/Forced-by-Wine-Country-fire-into-a-swimming-
pool-12274789.php.

Julie Johnson, Nick Rahaim, Randi Rossmann, and Christi Warren, "911 recordings
released for Sonoma County fires," *Press Democrat*, December 5, 2017, https://www.
pressdemocrat. com/article/news/911-recordings-released-for-sonoma-county-fires/.

Julie Johnson, "The Tubbs fire: How its deadly march from Calistoga to Santa Rosa
unfolded," *Press Democrat*, October 14, 2017, https://www.pressdemocrat.com/article/
news/the-tubbs-fire-how-its-deadly-march-from-calistoga-to-santa-rosa-unfolded/.

Kathy Allen, Contemporaneous notes and timeline, prepared October 10, 2017,
courtesy Kathy Allen.

PG&E customer letter in response to authors' request, noting outage began at
"23:10" and was out for "110 minutes," August 10, 2021, signed Jeffrey
Jung, PG&E Electric Distribution Engineer.

Sonoma County Sheriff's Office, "Santa Rosa fire spreading quickly," Nixle
Advisory, October 8, 2017, 1:22 a.m., SoCo Data, http://local.nixle.com/
alert/6197295.

CHAPTER 10: VELOCITY

Interviews

Janice Laskoski; Elizabeth Bruno; five former employees who requested anonym-
ity; Henrietta Hillman and son Corky Cramer; Len Kulwiec; Gena Jacob;
Kathy Allen and Mark Allen, daughter-in-law and son of Helen Allen;
Michael Allen and Julie Allen, grandchildren of Helen Allen; Alice Eurotas;
Ruth Callen; Melissa Langhals, daughter of Virginia Gunn; Nathan Condie;
Michael Rodriguez; Chris DeMott; Mika Alcasabas; Cynthia Arroyo; Norma
Porter; Anett Rivas; Elizabeth Lopez; Dawn Ross, daughter of Bill and Wanda
Lee.

Legal Documents and Depositions

Anett Rivas, June 20, 2018, in *Budow et al. v. Oakmont Senior Living, LLC et al.*
Barbara Lawler, June 13, 2018, in *Budow et al. v. Oakmont Senior Living, LLC et al.*
Cynthia Arroyo, June 14, 2018, in *Budow et al. v. Oakmont Senior Living, LLC et al.*
Deborah Smith, June 14, 2018, in *Budow et al. v. Oakmont Senior Living, LLC et al.*

Declaration of Dawn Ross to State of California Department of Social Services for its investigation into Villa Capri, CDSS No. 7218241101, August 24, 2018, courtesy Dawn Ross.

Elizabeth Lopez, July 26, 2018, in *Budow et al. v. Oakmont Senior Living, LLC et al.*

Joel Ruiz, June 20, 2018, in *Budow et al. v. Oakmont Senior Living, LLC et al.*

Joseph Horsman, June 5, 2018, in *Budow et al. v. Oakmont Senior Living, LLC et al.*

Kathy Allen, June 7, 2018, in *Budow et al. v. Oakmont Senior Living, LLC et al.*

Mark Allen, June 7, 2018, in *Budow et al. v. Oakmont Senior Living, LLC et al.*

Pouya Ansari, June 29, 2018, in *Budow et al. v. Oakmont Senior Living, LLC et al.*

Tammy Moratto, July 6, 2018, in *Budow et al. v. Oakmont Senior Living, LLC et al.*

Published Material and Other Sources

911 call from Deborah Smith, Sonoma County Sheriff's Office, October 9, 2017, 2:24 a.m., obtained via public records request.

Mike McCoy, "Fountaingrove neighbors oppose proposed fire station," *Press Democrat*, April 11, 2010, https://www.pressdemocrat.com/article/news/fountaingrove-neighbors-oppose-proposed-fire-station/.

Rancho Adobe Firefighters, Facebook post, October 26, 2017, https://www.facebook.com/profile/100063699923968/search/?q=Engine%209161.

Sonoma County Sheriff's Office, "Fire Update," Nixle Alert, October 8, 2017, 2:09 p.m., http://local.nixle.com/alert/6197337/.

Staff, "These are some of the victims of the Northern California firestorm," *Los Angeles Times*, October 27, 2017, https://www.latimes.com/local/lanow/la-me-northern-california-fire-victims-20171016-htmlstory.html.

Will Schmitt, "Santa Rosa officials admit former Fountaingrove fire station too small, placed in 'dangerous' site for fire," *Press Democrat*, March 20, 2019, https://www.pressdemocrat.com/article/news/santa-rosa-officials-admit-former-fountaingrove-fire-station-too-small-pla/.

CHAPTER 11: SAMARITANS

Interviews

Kent Porter, photojournalist, the *Press Democrat*; Kathy Allen and Mark Allen, daughter-in-law and son of Helen Allen; Elizabeth Lopez; Anett Rivas; Cynthia Arroyo; Carole Williams; Andre Blakely; Nathan Condie; R.J. Kisling and Steffany Kisling, grandchildren of John Hurford; Betty Kisling, wife of R.J. Kisling; Gena Jacob, daughter of Arlen Jacob; Susie Pritchett and daughter Cindy Lee; Michael Rodriguez; B.M., relative of Edel Burton; Bob Mitton and Mimi Vandermolen; Frank Perez; Vivian Flowers, daughter of

Viola Sodini; Melissa Langhals, daughter of Virginia Gunn; Noella "Nell" Magnuson; Ruth Callen; Norma Porter; Liz Schopfer, daughter of Ruth Callen; Tim Callen, son of Ruth Allen.

Legal Documents and Depositions

Anett Rivas, June 20, 2018, in *Budow et al. v. Oakmont Senior Living, LLC et al.*

Cynthia Arroyo, June 14, 2018, in *Budow et al. v. Oakmont Senior Living, LLC et al.*

Elizabeth Lopez, July 26, 2018, in *Budow et al. v. Oakmont Senior Living, LLC et al.*

Jane Torres, RN, June 12, 2018, in *Budow et al. v. Oakmont Senior Living, LLC et al.*

Joel Ruiz, June 20, 2018, in *Budow et al. v. Oakmont Senior Living, LLC et al.*

Joseph Horsman, June 5, 2018, in *Budow et al. v. Oakmont Senior Living, LLC et al.*

Kathy Allen, June 7, 2018, in *Budow et al. v. Oakmont Senior Living, LLC et al.*

Kenneth H. Garnett Jr., July 5, 2018, in *Budow et al. v. Oakmont Senior Living, LLC et al.*

Marie So, June 12, 2018, in *Budow et al. v. Oakmont Senior Living, LLC et al.*

Mark Allen, June 7, 2018, in *Budow et al. v. Oakmont Senior Living, LLC et al.*

Melissa Langhals, June 6, 2018, in *Budow et al. v. Oakmont Senior Living, LLC et al.*

Nathan Condie, June 28 and July 20, 2018, in *Budow et al. v. Oakmont Senior Living, LLC et al.*

Pouya Ansari, June 29, 2018, in *Budow et al. v. Oakmont Senior Living, LLC et al.*

Ruth Callen, June 7, 2018, in *Budow et al. v. Oakmont Senior Living, LLC et al.*

Tammy Moratto, July 6, 2018, in *Budow et al. v. Oakmont Senior Living, LLC et al.*

Published Material and Other Sources

Chris Smith, "Fire survivors from Santa Rosa's Journey's End feel 'like we've been abandoned,'" *Press Democrat*, October 2, 2018, https://www.pressdemocrat.com/article/news/fire-survivors-from-santa-rosas-journeys-end-feel-like-weve-been-abando/.x

Gaye LeBaron, "Santa Rosa's Fountaingrove Round Barn won't be rebuilt, but the memory endures," *Press Democrat*, September 29, 2019, https://www.pressdemocrat.com/article/news/gaye-lebaron-santa-rosas-fountaingrove-round-barn-wont-be-rebuilt-but-t/.

Juan Carlos Gonzalez, Facebook Post, October 10, 2017, https://www.facebook.com/chalesdj.gonzalez/photos?lst=201600349%3A100013872391096%3A155760357.

Lorraine Boissoneault, "As Wildfires Rage Across California Wine Country, a Historical Structure Turns to Ash," *Smithsonian*, October 11, 2017, https://www.smithsonianmag.com/history/wildfires-rage-across-northern-califor-nia-historical-structures-turn-ash-180965227/.

Richard Webb Porter Obituary, Legacy.com., July 30, 2004,
    https://www.legacy.com/obituaries/pressdemocrat/obituary.
    aspx?n=richard-webb-porter&pid=2468335.
Staff, "Lost Landmarks: Remembering Iconic Places Burned in Sonoma County
    Fires," *Sonoma Magazine*, January 2018, https://www.sonomamag.com/
    lost-landmarks-remembering-iconic-places-burned-in-sonoma-county-fires/.

CHAPTER 12: SOULS

Interviews
Capt. Mike Stornetta; R.J Kisling and Steffany Kisling, grandchildren of John
    Hurford; Betty Kisling, wife of R.J. Kisling; Mountain Volunteer Fire Capt.
    Tony Riedell and firefighters Caroline Upton and Tony Albright; Bob Mitton
    and Mimi Vandermolen; Melissa Langhals, daughter of Virginia Gunn;
    Mark and Kathy Allen, son and daughter-in-law of Helen Allen; Gena Jacob,
    daughter of Arlyn Jacob; Alice Eurotas and daughters Beth Eurotas-Steffy and
    Gloria Eurotas; Carole Williams; Santa Rosa Police Officer Orlando Macias;
    Elizabeth Bruno; Henrietta Hillman and daughter Margie Cramer; CityBus
    driver Gary Basile; Ruthie Kurpinsky, daughter of Ruth Callen

Legal Documents and Depositions
Detective James Vickers, June 27, 2018, in *Budow et al. v. Oakmont Senior Living,
    LLC et al.*
Kathy Allen, June 7, 2018, in *Budow et al. v. Oakmont Senior Living, LLC et al.*
Mark Allen, June 7, 2018, in *Budow et al. v. Oakmont Senior Living, LLC et al.*
Melissa Langhals, June 6, 2018, in *Budow et al. v. Oakmont Senior Living, LLC et al.*
Officer Andrew Adams, June 27, 2018, in *Budow et al. v. Oakmont Senior Living,
    LLC et al.*
Officer David Pedersen, June 27, 2018, in *Budow et al. v. Oakmont Senior Living,
    LLC et al.*
Sergeant Steven Pehlke, June 27, 2018, in *Budow et al. v. Oakmont Senior Living,
    LLC et al.*

Published Material and Other Sources
911 call transcripts, California Department of Forestry and Fire Protection
    Sonoma-Lake-Napa Unit, from October 8, 2017, at 9:28 p.m. through
    October 9, 2017, at 5:24 a.m., obtained via public records request.

Amy Graff, "130 patients evacuated from Kaiser hospital in Santa Rosa," SFGate, Oct. 9, 2017, https://www.sfgate.com/bayarea/article/Kaiser-Santa-Rosa-fire-patients-evacuated-Tubbs-12264180.php.

"Atlas Fire (Southern LNU Complex)," California Department of Forestry and Fire Protection, last updated October 24, 2022, https://www.fire.ca.gov/incidents/2017/10/9/atlas-fire-southern-lnu-complex.

Background event chronology, Santa Rosa Police, Event No. SR172820144, October 9, 2017, obtained via public records request.

California Department of Forestry and Fire Protection, Sonoma-Lake-Napa Unit, Tubbs Fire Investigation Report, July 2011, https://www.documentcloud.org/documents/5693976-Cal-Fire-Tubbs-Fire-Investigation-Report-20190124.

Claire Hao, "It's been five years since the catastrophic Tubbs Fire. Survivors are still tending to the scars," *San Francisco Chronicle*, October 8, 2022, https://www.sfchronicle.com/california-wildfires/article/It-s-been-five-years-since-the-catastrophic-17496357.php.

Derek Watkins, Troy Griggs, Jasmine C. Lee, Haeyoun Park, Anjali Singhvi, Tim Wallace, and Joe Ward, "How California's Most Destructive Wildfire Spread, Hour by Hour," *New York Times*, October 21, 2017, https://www.nytimes.com/interactive/2017/10/21/us/california-fire-damage-map.html.

Jill Tucker, "Wine Country fires: Karen Aycock, 54, dead in Tubbs Fire," *San Francisco Chronicle*, October 15, 2017, https://www.sfchronicle.com/bayarea/article/California-wildfires-Karen-Aycock-54-dead-in-12280011.php#photo-14325375.

"October 2017 North Bay Fires," National Oceanic and Atmospheric Administration, National Weather Service, San Francisco Bay Area Weather Forecast Office, July 3, 2020, https://noaa.maps.arcgis.com/apps/Cascade/index.html?appid=790ba363d4e74c77a94d861a7dd533fe.

Police body camera footage, Santa Rosa Police, October 9, 2017, obtained via public records request.

Police dispatch recordings, Santa Rosa Police Channels 1 and 2, October 8 to October 19, 2017, obtained via public records request.

Police dispatch transcripts, Santa Rosa Police Channels 1 and 2, from October 8 to October 19, 2017, obtained via public records request.

Police incident/investigation reports including officer narratives, Santa Rosa Police, Case No. 17-0014043, obtained via public records request.

Press Democrat collection of Tubbs Fire coverage, YouTube channel, October 9 through November 2, 2017, https://www.youtube.com/watch?v=bhTGQL_tyZA&list=PLJTpo1qsFtOt9_EiNN76-Ma2gUs0bKEbS&index=23.

"The Last Stand: Evacuating a Hospital in the Middle of a Wildfire," U.S.
Department of Health and Human Services Administration for Strategic
Preparedness and Response, Technical Resources, Assistance Center, and
Information Exchange (TRACIE), 2019, https://files.asprtracie.hhs.gov/
documents/aspr-tracie-the-last-stand-evacuating-a-hospital-in-the-middle-of-
a-wildfire.pdf.
Tim Carl, "Vineyards as Firebreaks," *North Bay Biz*, June 28, 2018, https://www.
northbaybiz.com/2018/06/28/vineyards-as-firebreaks/.

CHAPTER 13: RESCUE

Interviews

Elizabeth Lopez; Mark and Kathy Allen, son and daughter-in-law of Helen
Allen; Anett Rivas; Bob Mitton and Mimi Vandermolen; Carole Williams;
Katheryn Mann; Frank Perez; Mountain Volunteer Capt. Tony Riedell and
firefighters Caroline Upton and Tony Albright; Santa Rosa Police Officer
Orlando Macias; R.J. Kisling and Steffany Kisling, grandchildren of John
Hurford; Windsor Fire Protection District Capt. Mike Stornetta; Anett Rivas;
Elizabeth Lopez.

Legal Documents and Depositions

Anett Rivas, June 20, 2018, in *Budow et al. v. Oakmont Senior Living, LLC et al.*
Elizabeth Lopez, July 26, 2018, in *Budow et al. v. Oakmont Senior Living, LLC et al.*
Jane Torres, RN, June 12, 2018, in *Budow et al. v. Oakmont Senior Living, LLC et al.*
Joel Ruiz, June 20, 2018, in *Budow et al. v. Oakmont Senior Living, LLC et al.*
Joseph Horsman, June 5, 2018, in *Budow et al. v. Oakmont Senior Living, LLC et al.*
Marie So, June 12, 2018, in *Budow et al. v. Oakmont Senior Living, LLC et al.*
Officer David "Dave" Pedersen, June 27, 2018, in *Budow et al. v. Oakmont Senior
Living, LLC et al.*

Published Material and Other Sources

Angeli Singhvi and Derek Watkins, "Satellite Images Show 1,800 Buildings
Destroyed by Fire in Santa Rosa," *New York Times*, October 12, 2017, https://
www.nytimes.com/interactive/2017/10/12/us/santa-rosa-california-fires-dam-
age.html.
Background event chronology, Santa Rosa Police, Event No. SR172820144,
October 9, 2017, obtained via public records request.

Berkeley Fire Department, "Firefighter perspective—Tubbs Fire Santa Rosa," *KTVU Fox San Francisco*, YouTube channel, October 15, 2017, https://www.youtube.com/watch?v=HCNSDk7fyYE.

California Department of Forestry and Fire Protection, Sonoma-Lake-Napa Unit, Tubbs Fire Investigation Report, July 2011, https://www.documentcloud.org/documents/5693976-Cal-Fire-Tubbs-Fire-Investigation-Report-20190124.

Derek Watkins, Troy Griggs, Jasmine C. Lee, Haeyoun Park, Anjali Singhvi, Tim Wallace, and Joe Ward, "How California's Most Destructive Wildfire Spread, Hour by Hour," *New York Times*, October 21, 2017, https://www.nytimes.com/interactive/2017/10/21/us/california-fire-damage-map.html.

Kevin Fixler, "Police body-camera footage from Sonoma County wildfires shows harrowing escapes," *Press Democrat*, October 3, 2022, https://www.pressdemocrat.com/article/news/police-body-camera-footage-from-sonoma-county-wildfires-shows-harrowing-esc/.

Police body camera footage, Santa Rosa Police, October 9, 2017, obtained via public records request.

Police dispatch recordings, Santa Rosa Police Channels 1 and 2, October 8 to October 19, 2017, obtained via public records request.

Police incident/investigation reports including officer narratives, Santa Rosa Police, Case No. 17-0014043, obtained via public records request.

Will Schmitt, "'Limbo for the next couple of years': Uphill path to rebuilding Santa Rosa's Fountaingrove neighborhood," *North Bay Business Journal*, January 27, 2020, https://www.northbaybusinessjournal.com/article/article/limbo-for-the-next-couple-of-years-uphill-path-to-rebuilding-santa-rosa/.

CHAPTER 14: EXODUS

Interviews

Monique Dixon, senior living industry expert, former executive director and operations specialist at Brookdale Senior Living, and former director of senior living at Avalon Senior Living; Kathy Allen and Mark Allen, daughter-in-law and son of Helen Allen; Vivian Flowers, daughter of Viola Sodini; Cynthia Arroyo; Ruthie Kurpinsky and Liz Schopfer, daughters of Ruth Callen; Carole Williams; R.J. and Steffany Kisling, grandchildren of John Hurford; Windsor Fire Protection District Capt. Mike Stornetta.

Legal Documents and Depositions

Cynthia Arroyo, June 14, 2018, in *Budow et al. v. Oakmont Senior Living, LLC et al.*

Joel Ruiz, June 20, 2018, in *Budow et al. v. Oakmont Senior Living, LLC et al.*
Kathy Allen, June 7, 2018, in Budow et al. v. Oakmont Senior Living, *LLC et al.*
Mark Allen, June 7, 2018, in *Budow et al. v. Oakmont Senior Living, LLC et al.*
Pouya Ansari, June 29, 2018, in *Budow et al. v. Oakmont Senior Living, LLC et al.*
Ruth Callen, June 7, 2018, in *Budow et al. v. Oakmont Senior Living, LLC, et al.*

Published Material and Other Sources

B.M., relative of Edel Burton, Contemporaneous notes and timeline, prepared October 10, 2017, courtesy B.M.
Staff, "California fires coverage: Crews gain upper hand on deadliest blazes as search and recovery efforts continue," *Los Angeles Times*, last updated October 16, 2017, https://www.latimes.com/local/california/la-northern-california-fires-live-coverage-hundreds-evacuated-blazes-ravage-napa-sonoma-20171009-htmlstory.html.
Steffany Kisling, Personal video posted as a comment on Betty Kisling's post, Facebook, October 9, 2017, https://www.facebook.com/betty.kisling/posts/pfbid02K9aFxbyugK3VVtaGH733eFpA15CtcjSzh6djHwNpY6pQgBm-w1ZybRK9UAprG7i8hl.

CHAPTER 15: EXHAUSTED

Interviews

Anne Reynolds, division disaster director for state of California, Red Cross; Melissa Langhals, daughter of Virginia Gunn; Len Kulwiec and son Michael Kulwiec; Susie Pritchett; R.J. Kisling and Steffany Kisling, grandchildren of John Hurford; Betty Kisling, wife of R.J. Kisling; Terry Van Pelt, daughter-in-law of Sheila Van Pelt; Mary Tilbury and Jessica Kilcullen, daughter and granddaughter of Sally Tilbury; Mark and Kathy Allen, son and daughter-in-law of Helen Allen; Dawn Ross, daughter of Bill and Wanda Lee; Noella "Nell" Magnuson; Ruth Callen and daughters Ruthie Kurpinsky and Liz Schopfer; Bess Budow's daughter Sherry Minson, granddaughter Sarah Minson, and caregiver Maritza (last name withheld upon request); B.M., relative of Edel Burton; Alice Eurotas and daughters, Beth Eurotas-Steffy and Gloria Eurotas.

Legal Documents and Depositions

Declaration of Dawn Ross to State of California Department of Social Services for its investigation into Villa Capri, CDSS No. 7218241101, August 24, 2018, courtesy Dawn Ross.

Kathy Allen, June 7, 2018, in *Budow et al. v. Oakmont Senior Living, LLC et al.*

Leonard Kulwiec, June 29, 2018, in *Budow et al. v. Oakmont Senior Living, LLC et al.*

Mark Allen, June 7, 2018, in *Budow et al. v. Oakmont Senior Living, LLC et al.*

Melissa Langhals, June 6, 2018, in *Budow et al. v. Oakmont Senior Living, LLC et al.*

Tammy Moratto, July 6, 2018, in *Budow et al. v. Oakmont Senior Living, LLC et al.*

Published Material and Other Sources

Cara Strickland, Amy B. Wang, and Lea Donosky, "'A hell-storm of smoke and ash': Deadly wine-country wildfires force thousands to flee," *Washington Post*, October 10, 2018, https://www.washingtonpost.com/news/post-nation/wp/2017/10/10/a-hell-storm-of-smoke-and-ash-wine-country-wildfires-force-thousands-to-flee/.

Laura J. Nelson, "Firefighters make significant progress Monday, but face challenges in Oakmont," *Los Angeles Times*, October, 16, 2017, https://www.latimes.com/local/california/la-northern-california-fires-live-coverage-hundreds-evacuated-blazes-ravage-napa-sonoma-20171009-htmlstory.html.

Paresh Dave, "Searchers pick through burned-out California homes for bodies," Reuters, October 11, 2017, https://www.reuters.com/article/us-california-fire-idUKKBN1CG124.

Peter Fimrite, "'Like a blowtorch': Powerful winds fueled tornadoes of flame in Tubbs Fire," SFGate, October 18, 2017, https://www.sfgate.com/bayarea/article/Tubbs-Fire-unleashed-fiery-tornadoes-that-12289228.php#photo-14375640.

Randi Rossmann, "Firefighters from across nation lend welcome hand battling Sonoma County fires," *Press Democrat*, October 18, 2017, https://www.pressdemocrat.com/article/news/firefighters-from-across-nation-lend-welcome-hand-battling-sonoma-county-fi/?ref=related.

Stolen vehicle report, Santa Rosa Police, Call ID 172820144, October 9, 2017, obtained via public records request.

PART III: FALLOUT
CHAPTER 16: OUTRAGE

Interviews

Alice Eurotas and daughters, Beth Eurotas-Steffy and Gloria Eurotas; Vivian
Flowers, daughter of Viola Sodini; Ruthie Kurpinsky, daughter of Ruth
Callen; Dawn Ross, daughter of Bill and Wanda Lee; Kimberly Lange,
Oakmont regional health services manager; Elizabeth Lopez; Frank Perez;
Michael Rodriguez; Bob Mitton and Mimi Vandermolen; Noella "Nell"
Magnuson; Norma Porter; Betty Kisling, wife of R.J. Kisling; R.J. Kisling
and Steffany Kisling, grandchildren of John Hurford; Kathryn Stebner,
attorney; Bess Budow's daughter Sherry Minson, granddaughter Sarah
Minson, and caregiver Maritza (last name withheld upon request); Jonell
Jel-Enedra, Eric Johnson, Craig Johnson, children of Louise Johnson; Kathy
Allen and Mark Allen, daughter-in-law and son of Helen Allen; Anett Rivas;
Henrietta Hillman and son Corky Cramer and daughter Margie Cramer;
Jessica Kilcullen, granddaughter of Sally Tilbury; Melissa Langhals, daughter
of Virginia Gunn; Michael Allen and Julie Allen, son and daughter of Kathy
and Mark Allen; Gena Jacob, daughter of Arlen Jacob; Cynthia Arroyo;
Michael Rodriguez; Andre Blakley; B.M., relative of Edel Burton; Chris
DeMott; Mika Alcasabas.

Legal Documents and Depositions

Budow et al. v. Oakmont Senior Living, LLC et al.

Christian Holland, July 11, 2018, in *Budow et al. v. Oakmont Senior Living, LLC
et al.*

David Hunter, June 26, 2018, in *Budow et al. v. Oakmont Senior Living, LLC et al.*

Joseph Horsman, June 5, 2018, in *Budow et al. v. Oakmont Senior Living, LLC et al.*

Kathy Allen, June 7, 2018, in *Budow et al. v. Oakmont Senior Living, LLC et al.*

Mark Allen, June 7, 2018, in *Budow et al. v. Oakmont Senior Living, LLC et al.*

Published Material and Other Sources

Alice Eurotas, Video of her retelling her own story, October 28, 2017, courtesy
Beth Eurotas-Steffy.

Anh Do, "Lawsuit accuses Santa Rosa senior home of abandoning residents as
wildfire approached," *Los Angeles Times*, https://www.latimes.com/local/
lanow/La-me-ln-fire-evacuation-lawsuit-20171121-story.html.

Annie Sciacca and Sam Richards, "Concord, Albany centers take in evacuated seniors from Santa Rosa," *East Bay Times*, October 10, 2017, https://www.eastbaytimes.com/2017/10/10/concord-albany-centers-take-in-evacuated-seniors-from-santa-rosa/.

Beth Eurotas-Steffy, Contemporaneous notes, October 2017 through January 2021, courtesy Beth Eurotas-Steffy.

Beth Eurotas-Steffy, Post to Santa Rosa Firestorm Update group, Facebook, October, 27, 2017, https://www.facebook.com/groups/586292148428439/permalink/619479518443035/.

Betty Kisling, Facebook post, October 10, 2017, https://www.facebook.com/betty.kisling/posts/pfbid02K9aFxbyugK3VVtaGH733eFpA15CtcjSzh6d-jHwNpY6pQgBmw1ZybRK9UAprG7i8hl.

Bill Swindell, "4 residents sue Oakmont Senior Living, alleging they were abandoned during wildfires," *Press Democrat*, November 20, 2017, https://www.pressdemocrat.com/article/news/4-residents-sue-oakmont-senior-living-alleging-they-were-abandoned-during/.

California Department of Forestry and Fire Protection, Sonoma-Lake-Napa Unit, Tubbs Fire Investigation Report, July 2011, https://www.documentcloud.org/documents/5693976-Cal-Fire-Tubbs-Fire-Investigation-Report-20190124.

Casey Tolan, Tatiana Sanchez, Marisa Kendall, and Aaron Davis, "Death toll spikes to 35 as firefighters gain ground in long fight," *Mercury News*, October 14, 2017, https://www.mercurynews.com/2017/10/13/containment-increases-but-winds-returning-as-california-wildfires-become-the-states-deadliest/.

Claire Hao, "It's been five years since the catastrophic Tubbs Fire. Survivors are still tending to the scars," *San Francisco Chronicle*, October 8, 2022, https://www.sfchronicle.com/california-wildfires/article/It-s-been-five-years-since-the-catastrophic-17496357.php.

Complaint Investigation Report, California Department of Social Services Community Care Licensing Division, Complaint Control Number 21-SC-20171016155019, September 6, 2017, obtained via public records request.

Complaint Investigation Report, California Department of Social Services Community Care Licensing Division, Complaint Control Number 21-SC-20171010143819, September 6, 2018, obtained via public records request.

Declaration of Dawn Ross to State of California Department of Social Services for its investigation into Villa Capri, CDSS No. 7218241101, August 24, 2018, courtesy Dawn Ross.

Email from Bob Mitton to Officer Dave Pedersen, October 11, 2017, and Officer Pedersen's reply, October 12, 2017, both courtesy public records request.

Emails between Construction Director David Hunter, Oakmont Senior Living, and Division Chief Fire Marshall Scott Moon, Santa Rosa Fire Department, Thursday, October 19, 2017, obtained via public records request.

Emails from Oakmont of Villa Capri to "Friends and Families," October 9 and 10, 2017, "Friday Updates: Containment Improves On Fires As Confirmed Death Toll Rises To 35, UPDATE 11:50 a.m.," *Capital Public Radio*, December 13, 2017, https://www.capradio.org/articles/2017/10/13/friday-updates-california-wildfires-containment-lines-improve-fires-still-active/, courtesy Villa Capri residents' family members.

Guy Kovner, " Lawsuit alleges fraud, elder financial abuse at Oakmont Senior Living," *Press Democrat*, September 14, 2017, https://www.pressdemocrat.com/article/news/lawsuit-alleges-fraud-elder-financial-abuse-at-oakmont-senior-living/.

J.D. Morris and Randi Rossmann, "Settlement reached on eve of trial over evacuations at Villa Capri senior care facility during October wildfires," *Press Democrat*, August 17, 2019, https://www.pressdemocrat.com/article/news/settlement-reached-on-eve-of-trial-over-evacuations-at-villa-capri-senior-c/.

J.D. Morris, "State investigation launched into fire evacuation at Oakmont Senior Living complex in Santa Rosa," *Press Democrat*, October 17, 2017, https://www.pressdemocrat.com/article/news/state-investigation-launched-into-fire-evacuation-at-oakmont-senior-living/.

Kevin McCallum, "Gov. Brown in Santa Rosa: Fires 'a horror no one could have imagined,'" *Press Democrat*, October 14, 2017, https://www.pressdemocrat.com/article/news/gov-brown-in-santa-rosa-fires-a-horror-no-one-could-have-imagined/.

Laura J. Nelson, Sonali Kohli, Paige St. John, Dakota Smith, Nina Agrawal, "Death toll from Northern California fires jumps to at least 34; 5,700 structures destroyed," *Los Angeles Times*, October 13, 2017, https://www.latimes.com/local/lanow/la-me-ln-fires-20171013-story.html.

Letter from Jennifer Lyle, Sonoma County Local Enforcement Agency, Sonoma County Department of Health Services, to Dustin Abbott, Vice President, M&M Services, granting emergency waiver for debris removal, October 10, 2017, obtained via public records request.

Martin Espinoza, "Residents return to rubble and recount escape from Santa Rosa's Fountaingrove neighborhood," *Press Democrat*, October 10, 2017, https://www.pressdemocrat.com/article/news/residents-return-to-rubble-and-recount-escape-from-santa-rosas-fountaingro/.

Martin Espinoza, "Varenna at Fountaingrove, retirement community," *Press Democrat* Facebook Live, October 10, 2017, https://fb.watch/ipsvekDDwD/.

Martin Espinoza, "Varenna on Fountaingrove Pkwy," October 10, 2017, *Press Democrat* Facebook Live, October 10, 2017, https://fb.watch/ipsDwTofIr/.

Melanie Woodrow, "Attorney says understaffing at Oakmont Senior Living may have played a role in evacuation," *ABC7 News Bay Area*, October 19, 2017, https://abc7news.com/an-attorney-is-looking-into-whether-understaffing-played-a-role-in-the-evacuation-at-oakmont-senior-living-santa-rosa-depart-ment-of-social-services-has-two-open-investigations-evacuations-from-varen-na-fountaingrove-also-known-as-main-building-and-villa-capri/2552194/.

Melanie Woodrow, "Dozens of senior citizens may have been left by staff at burning Varenna Oakmont Senior Living Community," *ABC7 News Bay Area*, October 12, 2017, https://abc7news.com/north-bay-fires-in-the-firefighters-deadly/2526856/.

Melanie Woodrow, "Family, employee who helped evacuate assisted living facility question if fire evacuation plan existed," *ABC7 News Bay Area*, October 16, 2017, https://abc7news.com/north-bay-fires-in-the-firefighters-deadly/2541421/.

Melanie Woodrow (@MelanieWoodrow), "JUST IN: Dept of Social Services investigating…," Twitter, October 13, 2017, 4:48 p.m., https://twitter.com/MelanieWoodrow/status/918986719935963138.

Melanie Woodrow (@MelanieWoodrow), "#Oakmont followers—looking to speak with…", Twitter, October 12, 2017, 1:15 p.m., https://twitter.com/MelanieWoodrow/status/918570936650960896.

Melanie Woodrow (@MelanieWoodrow), "Which is it?…," Twitter, October 17, 2017, 9:53 p.m. https://twitter.com/MelanieWoodrow/status/920150791490375680?s=20&t=bEkdHT6uKC5mV_d9tRQE3w.

Melanie Woodrow, "Officials: Oakmont Senior Living removed fire debris without permit or US EPA sweep," *ABC7 News Bay Area*, October 25, 2017, https://abc7news.com/oakmont-senior-living-north-bay-fires-evacuation/2568263/.

Melanie Woodrow, "SF attorney files lawsuit accusing Oakmont Senior Living of elder abuse and negligence," *ABC7 News Bay Area*, November 20, 2017, https://abc7news.com/santa-rosa-assisted-living-facility-north-bay-fires-oak-mont-senior-elder-abuse-at/2676181/.

Oakmont Senior Living, LLC website, versions from April 2011 through January 2019, accessed via the Internet Archive Wayback Machine.

Obituary, Edward W. Ellwanger, https://www.legacy.com/us/obituaries/pressdemocrat/name/edward-ellwanger-obituary?id=15376836.

Officer Michael C. Heiser, Incident/Investigation Report, Supplement Narrative, Santa Rosa Police Department, Case Number 17-0014043, December 18, 2017, obtained via public records request.

Officer Michael J. Lazzarini, Incident/Investigation Report, Supplement Narrative, Santa Rosa Police Department, Case Number 17-0014043, October 26, 2017, obtained via public records request.

Paresh Dave, "California wildfire evacuees allowed home as crews search for bodies," Reuters, October 17, 2017, https://www.reuters.com/article/uk-california-fire-idAFKBN1CM0X0.

Paul Payne, "Santa Rosa brothers face jail for going to mom's burned home after the Tubbs fire," *Press Democrat*, January 10, 2018, https://www.pressdemocrat.com/article/news/santa-rosa-brothers-face-jail-for-going-to-moms-burned-home-after-the-tubb/.

Press Democrat Staff, "A salute to Sonoma County wildfire first responders," *Press Democrat*, October 26, 2017, https://www.pressdemocrat.com/article/lifestyle/a-salute-to-sonoma-county-wildfire-first-responders/.

Randi Rossmann and J.D. Morris, "Oakmont Senior Living under new investigation following Santa Rosa fire," *Press Democrat*, October 25, 2017, https://www.pressdemocrat.com/article/news/oakmont-senior-living-under-new-investigation-following-santa-rosa-fire/?artslide=2.

Randi Rossmann and Julie Johnson, "Sonoma County death toll from fires climbs to 11," *Press Democrat*, October 10, 2017, https://www.pressdemocrat.com/article/news/sonoma-county-death-toll-from-fires-climbs-to-11/.

Randi Rossmann, "Santa Rosa investigation: No permit issued for initial Villa Capri fire debris work," *Press Democrat*, May 13, 2008, https://www.pressdemocrat.com/article/news/santa-rosa-investigation-no-permit-issued-for-initial-villa-capri-fire-deb/.

Sherry Minson, Video of her at her mother Bess Budow's bedside at Petaluma Valley Hospital, October 23, 2017, courtesy Sarah Minson.

Sergeant Josh D. Ludtke, Incident/Investigation Report, Supplement Narrative, Santa Rosa Police Department, Case Number 17-0014043, November 1, 2017, obtained via public records request.

CHAPTER 17: DICHOTOMY

Interviews

Anonymous former business associate of Bill Gallaher; Doug Bosco, former member, U.S. House of Representatives and California State Assembly; anonymous elected official; anonymous former county Department of Health official.

Legal Documents and Depositions

Gallaher et al. v. Sonoma Media Investments, LLC [DBA The Press Democrat], filed December 21, 2016, Superior Court of California County of Sonoma, Case No. SCV-259927, available on Sonoma County Superior Court portal, https://sonoma.courts.ca.gov/online-services/case-portal.

William P. Gallaher, July 12 and 20, 2018, in *Budow et al. v. Oakmont Senior Living, LLC et al.*

Published Material and Other Sources

Austin Murphy, "Proposed Elnoka project would add 676 living units near Oakmont in Santa Rosa," *Press Democrat*, June 5, 2021, https://www.pressdemocrat.com/article/news/proposed-elnoka-project-would-add-676-living-units-near-oakmont-in-santa-ro/.

"Bill Gallaher," Gallaher Companies website, https://www.gallahercompanies.com/Bill-gallaher-bio.

Bleys W. Rose, "Unions Funding Zane, Furch: Labor Groups Pouring Money into 3rd, 5th District Supervisor Races," *Press Democrat*, October 24, 2008, https://www.pressdemocrat.com/article/news/unions-funding-zane-furch-labor-groups-pouring-money-into-3rd-5th-distri/.

Campaign contributions sourced from Public Portal for Campaign Finance Disclosure, https://public.netfile.com/Pub2/AllFilingsByDate.aspx.

Doug Bosco, "INTERVIEW: Former North Coast Congressman Praises Oakmont Senior Living Center Staff," *KSRO*, September 20, 2018, https://www.ksro.com/2018/09/10/interview-former-north-coast-congressman-praises-oakmont-senior-living-center-staff/.

Elaine Holz, "The Rainbow Connection," *North Bay Biz*, January 25, 2012, https://www.northbaybiz.com/2012/01/25/the-rainbow-connection/.

Heather Irwin, "Downtown SR watering hole Upper Fourth closes its doors," *Press Democrat*, September 23, 2009, https://www.pressdemocrat.com/article/news/downtown-sr-watering-hole-upper-fourth-closes-its-doors/.

Jane Hodges Young, "A tale of three cities," *North Bay Biz*, November 20, 2009, https://www.northbaybiz.com/2009/11/20/a-tale-of-three-cities/.

J.D. Morris, "Sonoma County's Chanate Road ex-hospital site could become 800-unit housing development," *Press Democrat*, Feb. 7, 2017, https://www.pressdemocrat.com/article/news/sonoma-countys-chanate-road-ex-hospital-site-could-become-800-unit-housing/.

Jeffrey Steele, "Changing the World," Multi-Housing News, March 2015, https://www.bluetoad.com/publication/?m=35510&i=247490&p=24&ver=html5.

John Beck, "Upstairs and upscale" A new cocktail lounge coming to Old Courthouse Square is after the well-heeled crowd," *Press Democrat*, August 18, 2006, https://www.pressdemocrat.com/article/news/upstairs-and-upscale-a-new-cocktail-lounge-coming-to-old-courthouse-square/.

Kerry Benefield, "Wood shop program saved by developer," *Press Democrat*, April 28, 2009, https://www.pressdemocrat.com/article/news/wood-shop-program-saved-by-developer/.

Kevin King, "Our South Korean Sister: Jeju and the Dol Hareubang Statues," *Multicultural Roots Project* (blog), City of Santa Rosa, December 16, 2020, https://www.srcity.org/Blog.aspx?IID=12#:~:text=Jeju%20and%20Santa%20Rosa%20have,better%20world%20to%20thrive%20in.

Kevin McCallum, "Fundraising lopsided so far on Santa Rosa cellphone tax measure," *Press Democrat*, October 24, 2014, https://www.pressdemocrat.com/article/news/fundraising-lopsided-so-far-on-santa-rosa-cellphone-tax-measure/.

Kevin McCallum, "Santa Rosa City Council candidates benefit from unprecedented spending," *Press Democrat*, October 28, 2016, https://www.pressdemocrat.com/article/news/santa-rosa-city-council-candidates-benefit-from-unprecedented-spending/.

Kevin McCallum, "Santa Rosa City Council race taken by newcomers Jack Tibbetts and Chris Rogers, incumbents Julie Combs and Ernesto Olivares," *Press Democrat*, November 8, 2016, https://www.pressdemocrat.com/article/news/santa-rosa-city-council-race-taken-by-newcomers-jack-tibbetts-and-chris-rog/.

Kevin McCallum, "Santa Rosa to take up shifting of Oakmont ridgeline," *Press Democrat*, December 18, 2014, https://www.pressdemocrat.com/article/news/santa-rosa-to-take-up-shifting-of-oakmont-ridgeline/.

"Komron Shahhosseini," LinkedIn profile, accessed March 15, 2023, https://www.linkedin.com/in/komron-shahhosseini-a410588/details/experience/.

Martha Drum, "Ringside Chat: Zume Gallaher Gets Candid About First Grand Prix Wins, Adoption And Inclusion," *Chronicle of the Horse*, July 29, 2020, https://www.chronofhorse.com/article/ringside-chat-zume-gallaher-gets-candid-about-first-grand-prix-wins-adoption-and-inclusion?fbclid=IwAR1aAppbq3H-aVW0Id_8R7-OHqRxh4GNyUIi3lLsSwop3Sub14YdVP1_9lc.

Mary Fricker, "Inspired by Trione family, William Gallaher set sights on founding a bank," *Press Democrat*, June 20, 2004, https://www.pressdemocrat.com/article/news/inspired-by-trione-family-william-gallaher-set-sights-on-founding-a-bank/.

Nancy Johnson, "A Place for Us," *North Bay Biz*, April 28, 2014,https://www. northbaybiz.com/2014/04/28/a-place-for-us/.

Oakmont Senior Living, "Oakmont Senior Living & The Tubbs Fire: Family Member Testimonial," Oakmont Senior Living press release, August 18, 2018, https://markets.businessinsider.com/news/stocks/oakmont-senior-living-the-tubbs-fire-family-member-testimonial-1027468477.

Obituary, Edward W. Ellwanger, https://www.legacy.com/us/obituaries/ pressdemocrat/name/edward-ellwanger-obituary?id=15376836.

Paul Payne, "Former Oakmont Senior Living lawyer accuses William Gallaher of reimbursing employees' campaign donations," *Press Democrat*, November 15, 2017, https://www.pressdemocrat.com/article/news/ former-oakmont-senior-living-lawyer-accuses-william-gallaher-of-reimbursing/.

Paul Payne, "Press Democrat sued for libel over coverage of campaign spending," *Press Democrat*, January 24, 2017, https://www.pressdemocrat.com/article/ news/press-democrat-sued-for-libel-over-coverage-of-campaign-spending/.

Randi Rossmann and J.D. Morris, "Oakmont Senior Living under new investigation following Santa Rosa fire," *Press Democrat*, October 25, 2017, https:// www.pressdemocrat.com/article/news/oakmont-senior-living-under-new-investigation-following-santa-rosa-fire/?artslide=2.

Shirlee Zane, "Let's Build Affordable Housing Now," *North Bay Biz*, April 20, 2017, https://www.northbaybiz.com/2017/04/20/ lets-build-affordable-housing-now/.

Terkel, "Bill Gallagher—Real Estate Developer," *Pursue the Passion* (blog), August 13, 2007, https://pursuethepassion.com/nutured-risk/.

CHAPTER 18: INVESTIGATION

Interviews

Kathryn Stebner; Melissa Langhals, daughter of Virginia Gunn; Sherry Minson and Sarah Minson, daughter and granddaughter or Bess Budow; Ruthie Kurpinsky, daughter of Ruth Callen; Len Kulwiec and son Michael Kulwiec; Noella "Nell" Magnuson; Elizabeth Lopez; Dawn Ross, daughter of Bill and Wanda Lee; Vivian Flowers, daughter of Viola Sodini; Henrietta Hillman and son Corky Cramer and daughter Margie Cramer; Tim Delaney, son of Mary Lou Delaney; Jessica Kilcullen, granddaughter of Sally Tilbury; Beth Eurotas-Steffy, daughter of Alice Eurotas; Kathy Allen and Mark Allen, daughter-in-law and son of Helen Allen; Cynthia Arroyo; Bo Mitchell, founder and president, 911 Consulting; Eric Carlson, director, Long-Term Services and

Supports Advocacy, Justice in Aging; Pat McGinnis, executive director, California Advocates for Nursing Home Reform; anonymous executive-level California Department of Social Services employee; Terry Van Pelt, daughter-in-law of Sheila Van Pelt; Mary Tilbury and Jessica Kilcullen, daughter and granddaughter of Sally Tilbury; Mike Connors, advocate, California Advocates for Nursing Home Reform.

Legal Documents and Depositions
Accusation for license revocation against Varenna, LLC et al., filed September 4, 2018, State of California Department of Social Services, CDSS No. 7218241101, obtained via public records request.
Barbara Lawler, June 13, 2018, in *Budow et al. v. Oakmont Senior Living, LLC et al.*
Budow et al. v. Oakmont Senior Living, LLC et al., filed November 20, 2017, Superior Court of California County of Sonoma, Case No. SCV-261552, available on Sonoma Superior Court portal, https://sonoma.courts.ca.gov/online-services/case-portal.
Christine Anne Kasulka, July 12, 2018, in *Budow et al. v. Oakmont Senior Living, LLC et al.*
Christian Holland, July 11, 2018, in *Budow et al. v. Oakmont Senior Living, LLC et al.*
Complaint Investigation Report, California Department of Social Services Community Care Licensing Division, Complaint Control No. 21-SC-20171016155019, filed September 6, 2017, courtesy Beth Eurotas-Steffy.
Cynthia Arroyo, June 14, 2018, in *Budow et al. v. Oakmont Senior Living, LLC et al.*
David Hunter, June 26, 2018, in *Budow et al. v. Oakmont Senior Living, LLC et al.*
Deborah Smith, June 14, 2018, in *Budow et al. v. Oakmont Senior Living, LLC et al.*
Declaration of Dawn Ross to State of California Department of Social Services for its investigation into Villa Capri, CDSS No. 7218241101, August 24, 2018, courtesy Dawn Ross.
Defendants' trial brief, filed August 16, 2018, Superior Court of California County of Sonoma, Case No. SCV-261552, obtained via public records request.
Elizabeth Lopez, July 26, 2018, in *Budow et al. v. Oakmont Senior Living, LLC et al.*
Jane Torres, RN, June 12, 2018, in *Budow et al. v. Oakmont Senior Living, LLC et al.*
Joel Ruiz, June 20, 2018, in *Budow et al. v. Oakmont Senior Living, LLC et al.*
José Antonio Moreno Herrera, June 13, 2018, in *Budow et al. v. Oakmont Senior Living, LLC et al.*

Joseph Horsman, June 5, 2018, in *Budow et al. v. Oakmont Senior Living, LLC et al.*

Karen Ellis, June 26, 2018, in *Budow et al. v. Oakmont Senior Living, LLC et al.*

Kenneth H. Garnett Jr., July 5, 2018, in *Budow et al. v. Oakmont Senior Living, LLC et al.*

Leonard Kulwiec, June 29, 2018, in *Budow et al. v. Oakmont Senior Living, LLC et al.*

Marie So, June 12, 2018, in *Budow et al. v. Oakmont Senior Living, LLC et al.*

Nathan Condie, June 28 and July 20, 2018, in *Budow et al. v. Oakmont Senior Living, LLC et al.*

Officer Andrew Adams, June 27, 2018, in *Budow et al. v. Oakmont Senior Living, LLC et al.*

Plaintiffs' trial brief, filed August 16, 2018, Superior Court of California County of Sonoma, Case No. SCV-261552, obtained via public records request.

Pouya Ansari, June 29, 2018, in *Budow et al. v. Oakmont Senior Living, LLC et al.*

Ruth Callen, June 7, 2018, in *Budow et al. v. Oakmont Senior Living, LLC et al.*

Ruth Kurpinksy, June 7, 2018, in *Budow et al. v. Oakmont Senior Living, LLC et al.*

Sergeant Daniel Marincik, June 27, 2018, in *Budow et al. v. Oakmont Senior Living, LLC et al.*

Sergeant Steven Pehlke, June 27, 2018, in *Budow et al. v. Oakmont Senior Living, LLC et al.*

Stipulation, waiver and order, California Department of Social Services, Case No. 7218241101-F and Office of Administrative Hearings No. 2018091018, filed September 4, 2018, obtained via public records request.

Sue McPherson, July 5, 2018, in *Budow et al. v. Oakmont Senior Living, LLC et al.*

Tammy Moratto, July 6, 2018, in *Budow et al. v. Oakmont Senior Living, LLC et al.*

Tony Ruiz, June 20, 2018, in *Budow et al. v. Oakmont Senior Living, LLC et al.*

William P. Gallaher, July 12 and 20, 2018, in *Budow et al. v. Oakmont Senior Living, LLC et al.*

Published Material and Other Sources

Campaign contributions sourced from California Secretary of State independent expenditures and campaign finance databases, https://powersearch.sos.ca.gov/.

"Christian Holland, General Counsel," Oakmont Senior Living website, https://oakmontseniorliving.com/christian-holland/.

Dori Coleman, "Friday's Letters to the Editor: Elders abandoned," *Press Democrat*, March 23, 2018, https://www.pressdemocrat.com/article/opinion/fridays-letters-to-the-editor-150/.

Email from Ruth Callen to her attorney at Stebner & Associates transcribed by Ruthie Kurpinsky, April 18, 2018, courtesy Ruthie Kurpinksy.

Giovanniello Law Group website, https://giolawgroup.com/.

J.D. Morris and Randi Rossmann, "Settlement reached on eve of trial over evacuations at Villa Capri senior care facility during October wildfires," *Press Democrat*, August 17, 2019, https://www.pressdemocrat.com/article/news/settlement-reached-on-eve-of-trial-over-evacuations-at-villa-capri-senior-c/.

J.D. Morris, "Judge cancels Sonoma County's sale of Santa Rosa site for proposed housing development," *Press Democrat*, July 26, 2018, https://www.pressdemocrat.com/article/news/judge-cancels-sonoma-countys-sale-of-santa-rosa-site-for-proposed-housing/.

J.D. Morris, "Proposed 867-unit Chanate Road housing project gets critical reception at Santa Rosa neighborhood meeting," *Press Democrat*, June 25, 2018, https://www.pressdemocrat.com/article/news/proposed-867-unit-chanate-road-housing-project-gets-critical-reception-at-s/.

J.D. Morris, "Sonoma County cancels real estate deal intended to produce 867 housing units in Santa Rosa," *Press Democrat*, October 9, 2018, https://www.pressdemocrat.com/article/news/sonoma-county-cancels-real-estate-deal-intended-to-produce-867-housing-unit/.

Joseph V. Schaeffer, "The Apex Deposition: Practice Tips and Standards," American Bar Association, April 29, 2018, https://www.americanbar.org/groups/litigation/committees/pretrial-practice-discovery/practice/2018/the-apex-deposition-practice-tips-and-standards/.

Letter to Varenna "residents and responsible parties" from Nathan Condie, September 12, 2018, courtesy Beth Eurotas-Steffy.

Melanie Woodrow, "Exclusive: Lawsuit against Oakmont Management Group amended to include 'wrongful death,'" *ABC7 News Bay Area*, January 18, 2018, https://abc7news.com/santa-rosa-assisted-living-facility-north-bay-fires-oakmont-senior-elder-abuse-at/2965608/.

Melanie Woodrow, "Family, employee who helped evacuate assisted living facility question if fire evacuation plan existed," *ABC7 News Bay Area*, October 16, 2017, https://abc7news.com/north-bay-fires-in-the-firefighters-deadly/2541421/.

Paul Gullixson, "Were the bedridden residents of Villa Capri really at fault?" *Press Democrat*, March 17, 2018, https://www.pressdemocrat.com/article/opinion/gullixson-were-the-bedridden-residents-of-villa-capri-really-at-fault/.

Paul Payne, "Lawsuit over fire evacuation alleges Oakmont Senior Living offered employees money for silence," *Press Democrat*,

January 20, 2018, https://www.pressdemocrat.com/article/news/
lawsuit-over-fire-evacuation-alleges-oakmont-senior-living-offered-employee/.

Randi Rossmann, "Santa Rosa investigation: No permit issued
for initial Villa Capri fire debris work," *Press Democrat*, May
13, 2008, https://www.pressdemocrat.com/article/news/
santa-rosa-investigation-no-permit-issued-for-initial-villa-capri-fire-deb/.

Tim Mullaney, "Oakmont Launches Website to Explain, Defend
Its Actions During Wildfire," *Senior Housing News*, July
26, 2018, https://seniorhousingnews.com/2018/07/26/
oakmont-launches-website-explain-defend-actions-wildfire/.

CHAPTER 19: UNSETTLED

Interviews

Michael Rodriguez; Cynthia Arroyo; Anett Rivas; Michael Fiumara; Noreen
Evans; Eric Johnson, son of Louise Johnson; Beth Eurotas-Steffy, daughter
of Alice Eurotas; Pat McGinnis, executive director, California Advocates for
Nursing Home Reform; Michael Connors, advocate, California Advocates for
Nursing Home Reform.

Legal Documents and Depositions

Blakely et al. v. Varenna Assisted Living et al., filed April 2, 2019, Superior Court
of California County of Sonoma, Case No. SCV-264208, available on
Sonoma Superior Court portal, https://sonoma.courts.ca.gov/online-services/
case-portal.

Published Material and Other Sources

Andrew Beale, "Gov. Gavin Newsom signs bill inspired by abandonment of
seniors during 2017 wildfires," *Press Democrat*, June 27, 2019, https://www.
pressdemocrat.com/article/news/gov-gavin-newsom-signs-bill-inspired-by-
abandonment-of-seniors-during-2017/.

Business registration information sourced from California Secretary of State, "biz-
file Online" database, https://bizfileonline.sos.ca.gov/.

California Assembly Bill 3098, effective January 1, 2019, accessed via
California Legislative Information, https://leginfo.legislature.
ca.gov/faces/codes_displaySection.xhtml?lawCode=HSC&section-
Num=1569.695.&article=6.&highlight=true&keyword=AB%20
3098.

Campaign contributions sourced from California Secretary of State independent expenditures and campaign finance databases, https://powersearch.sos. ca.gov/.

Editorial, "Getting seniors protection they deserve," *Press Democrat*, July 5, 2019, https://www.pressdemocrat.com/article/opinion/ pd-editorial-getting-seniors-protection-they-deserve/.

Elder Abuse and Dependent Adult Civil Protection Act, Cal. Welf. & Inst. Code § 15657 (1991), *amended by* SB 314 (2019), https://leginfo.legislature.ca.gov/ faces/codes_displaySection. xhtml?sectionNum=15657&lawCode=WIC.

Julie Johnson and Randi Rossmann, "Operator of Santa Rosa care homes admits staff abandoned seniors in Tubbs fire," *Press Democrat*, November 20, 2018, https://www.pressdemocrat.com/article/news/operator-of-santa-rosa-care-homes-admits-staff-abandoned-seniors-in-tubbs-f/.

Julie Johnson, "Defamation lawsuit by Bill Gallaher and Scott Flater against The Press Democrat dismissed by appellate court," *Press Democrat*, https://www.pressdemocrat.com/article/news/ defamation-lawsuit-by-bill-gallaher-and-scott-flater-against-the-press-demo/.

Melanie Woodrow, "Oakmont Senior Living caregiver speaks out about Tubbs Fire evacuation," *ABC7 News Bay Area*, April 4, 2019, https://abc7news. com/tubbs-fire-oakmont-senior-living-center-villa-capri-north-bay-wild-fires/5234797/.

Melanie Woodrow, "Varenna Oakmont Senior Living in Santa Rosa reaches settlement after deadly North Bay Fires," *ABC7 News Bay Area*, November 21, 2018, https:// abc7news.com/oakmont-senior-living-santa-rosa-north-bay-fire-settlement/4727697/.

"North Bay Fire Relief Fund," Redwood Credit Union Community Fund website, https://www.rcucommunityfund.org/north-bay-fire-relief.

Provider Information Notice, "2018 Chaptered Legislation Affecting Residential Care Facilities for the Elderly and Continuing Care Retirement Communities," California Department of Social Services, December 13, 2018, https://caassistedliving.org/pdf/implementationplans/18implementa-tionplans.pdf.

Residential Care Facilities for the Elderly: Emergency and Disaster Plans, Cal. Health & Safety Code § 1569 (1985), *amended by* AB 3098 (2018), https:// legiscan.com/CA/text/AB3098/2017.

"The Real Story Regarding Oakmont Senior Living & The Tubbs Fire," Oakmont Senior Living History website, available July 26, 2018.

Will Schmidt, "Oakmont Senior Living revives Emerald Isle project in Fountaingrove as age-restricted apartment complex," *Press Democrat*,

January 3, 2019, https://www.pressdemocrat.com/article/news/
oakmont-senior-living-revives-emerald-isle-project-in-fountaingrove-as-age/.

CHAPTER 20: REVENGE

Interviews

Jill Ravitch, Sonoma County District Attorney; David Kim, Sonoma County
    Deputy District Attorney; Beth Eurotas-Steffy, daughter of Alice Eurotas;
    Maddy Hirschfield, political director, North Bay Labor Council; Amanda
    Roze; Leo Buc, Reject Revenge campaign consultant; Doug Bosco, former
    member, U.S. House of Representatives and California State Assembly.

Published Material and Other Sources

Emma Murphy and Lori A. Carter, "New pro-recall ads single out Sonoma County
    lawmakers allied with DA Jill Ravitch," *Press Democrat*, September 10, 2021,
    https://www.pressdemocrat.com/article/news/new-pro-recall-ads-single-out-
    sonoma-county-lawmakers-allied-with-district/?artslide=3.

Emma Murphy and Lori A. Carter, "Sonoma County district attor-
    ney recall fails as voters back keeping Jill Ravitch," *Press Democrat*,
    September 14, 2021, https://www.pressdemocrat.com/article/news/
    sonoma-county-district-attorney-recall-losing-as-voters-back-keeping-ravitc/.

Emma Murphy, "Bill Gallaher funnels more money into Ravitch recall effort,"
    Press Democrat, August 18, 2021, https://www.pressdemocrat.com/article/
    news/bill-gallaher-funnels-more-money-into-ravitch-recall-effort/.

Emma Murphy, "Drive to recall Ravitch holds big fundrais-
    ing edge, latest filings show," *Press Democrat*," August
    10, 2021, https://www.pressdemocrat.com/article/news/
    drive-to-recall-ravitch-holds-big-fundraising-edge-latest-filings-show/.

Emma Murphy, "Jill Ravitch supporters say recall is about one man's revenge,"
    Press Democrat, July 28, 2021, https://www.pressdemocrat.com/article/news/
    jill-ravitch-supporters-say-recall-is-about-one-mans-revenge/.

Emma Murphy, "Push to recall DA Ravitch gets another financial boost from
    Gallaher," *Press Democrat*, August 26, 2021, https://www.pressdemocrat.com/
    article/news/push-to-recall-da-ravitch-gets-another-financial-boost/.

Julie Johnson, "Oakmont Senior Living to pay $500,000 to settle state, county inves-
    tigation into abandonment of seniors during 2017 wildfires," *Press Democrat*,
    September 3, 2019, https://www.northbaybusinessjournal.com/article/news/
    oakmont-senior-living-to-pay-500000-to-settle-state-county-investigation/.

Julie Johnson, "Sonoma County developer Bill Gallaher launches recall campaign against District Attorney Jill Ravitch," *Press Democrat*, October 25, 2020, https://www.pressdemocrat.com/article/news/sonoma-county-developer-bill-gallaher-launches-recall-campaign-against-dist/.

Notice of Intention to Circulate Recall Petition Seeking the Recall of District Attorney Jill Ravitch, filed October 23, 2020, Sonoma County Registrar of Voters, https://srp-prod-public-pdfs.s3-us-west-2.amazonaws.com/iNvZNO-amv5-WarY8_DJCO2ITCLI.pdf.

Paul Payne, "Ravitch Wins: In ousting Passalacqua, veteran prosecutor becomes county's first female district attorney," *Press Democrat*, June 9, 2010, https://www.pressdemocrat.com/article/news/ravitch-wins-in-ousting-passalacqua-veteran-prosecutor-becomes-countys-f/.

Rebecca Smith, "Sonoma County District Attorney Jill Ravitch Squashes Recall Bid," KQED, September 14, 2021, https://www.kqed.org/news/11888512/sonoma-county-District-attorney-on-track-to-beat-recall.

Recall Ravitch Campaign, "Statement from the Recall Ravitch Campaign," Recall Ravitch Campaign press release on Election Night loss, September 14, 2021.

"Reject Revenge" election night event at Teamsters Local 665 North union hall, September 14, 2021, attended by authors.

"Reject the Recall" event at Sally Tomatoes with speeches by Rohnert Park Mayor Gerard Giudice, District Attorney Jill Ravitch, Mark Allen, and State Senator Mark McGuire; attended by author Paul Gullixson and contributing editor Lauren A. Spates.

Robert Digitale, "Families, workers in Sonoma County on edge as rental market tightens after fires," *Press Democrat*, November 11, 2017, https://www.pressdemocrat.com/article/news/families-workers-in-sonoma-county-on-edge-as-rental-market-tightens-after/.

Sonoma County Office of the District Attorney, "Owners and Operators of Varenna and Villa Capri Settle Law Enforcement Action Related to 2017 Tubbs Fire," District Attorney press release, September 3, 2020, https://da.sonomacounty.ca.gov/varenna-and-villa-capri-settle-law-enforcement-action.

Superior Court of the State of California, Stipulation for Entry of Stipulated Injunction and Final Judgment, Case No. SCV-267007, September 3, 2019, obtained via public records request.

CHAPTER 21: A WARNING

Interviews

Daniel Swain, Ph.D; Monique Dixon, senior living industry expert; Brian Lee, executive director, Families for Better Care; Eric Carlson, director, Long-Term

Services and Supports Advocacy, Justice in Aging; Charlene Harrington, Ph.D, RN, FAAN, professor emeritus, University of California San Francisco School of Nursing; Pat McGinnis, executive director, California Advocates for Nursing Home Reform; Christina Flores, Ph.D, RN, founder and principal, Elder Care Advocacy Bay Area; Bo Mitchell, founder and president, 911 Consulting.

Published Material and Other Sources

"2020 Census Will Help Policymakers Prepare for the Incoming Wave of Aging Boomers," U.S. Census Bureau, *America Counts*, December 10, 2019, https://www.census.gov/library/stories/2019/12/by-2030-all-baby-boomers-will-be-age-65-or-older.html.

Adam B. Smith, "2017 U.S. billion-dollar weather and climate disasters: a historic year in context," *Beyond the Data* (blog), National Oceanic and Atmospheric Administration, January 8, 2018, https://www.climate.gov/disasters-2017.

Andrea Januta, "Pacific Northwest heat wave 'virtually impossible' without climate change," Reuters, July 8, 2021, https://www.reuters.com/business/environment/heat-wave-pacific-northwest-could-soon-repeat-due-climate-change-research-2021-07-07/.

Andrew Weber, "Texas Winter Storm Death Toll Goes Up To 210, Including 43 Deaths In Harris Ardeshir Tabrizian, "Oregon's heat wave death toll grows to 116," *Oregonian*, December 1, 2021, https://www.oregonlive.com/data/2021/07/oregons-heat-wave-death-toll-grows-to-116.html.

"Argentum Advocates," Argentum, https://www.argentum.org/advocacy/argentum-advocates/.

"Assisted Living Facility Type I & II Resident Assessment," Utah Department of Health and Human Services, February 2017, https://health.utah.gov/hflcra/forms/ALASSESSMENT.pdf.

County," *Houston Public Media*, July 14, 2021, https://www.houstonpublicmedia.org./articles/news/energy-environment/2021/07/14/403191/texas-winter-storm-death-toll-goes-up-to-210-including-43-deaths-in-harris-county/.

Carol Marbin Miller and Mary Ellen Klas, "After Wilma, bills were pushed to ensure nursing homes had emergency AC. They were killed," *Miami Herald*, September 14, 2017, https://www.miamiherald.com/news/local/community/broward/article173365916.html.

Carol Marbin Miller and Mary Ellen Klas, "Florida's lax oversight of nursing homes spills over from one deadly crisis to the next," *Miami Herald*, Mary 8,

2020, https://www.miamiherald.com/news/health-care/article242595251. html.

Charlene Harrington, Joshua M. Wiener, Leslie Ross, and MaryBeth Musumeci, "Key Issues in Long-Term Services and Supports Quality," Henry J. Kaiser Family Foundation, October 2017, https://www.kff.org/medicaid/issue-brief/key-issues-in-long-term-services-and-supports-quality/.

"Charlene Harrington, RN, Ph.D, FAAN," University of California San Francisco website, https://profiles.ucsf.edu/charlene.harrington.

Christine Sexton, "Many nursing homes, assisted living facilities still can't meet Florida's mandate for backup power," *South Florida Sun Sentinel*, April 17, 2019, https://www.sun-sentinel.com/news/florida/fl-ne-nsf-nursing-home-generators-20190417-story.html.

"Climate Change: A Defining Challenge of the 21st Century," U.S. Geological Survey, accessed December 2021, https://www.usgs.gov/science/science-explorer/climate.

"Economic Impact: The Senior Living Effect," Argentum, July 2019, https://www.argentum.org/wp-content/uploads/2019/07/Senior-Impact-WhitePaper-Final.pdf.

Elder Abuse and Dependent Adult Civil Protection Act, Cal. Welf. & Inst. Code § 15657 (1991), *amended by* SB 314 (2019), https://leginfo.legislature.ca.gov/faces/codes_displaySection.xhtml?sectionNum=15657&lawCode=WIC.

Elizabeth Chuck, "How climate change primed Colorado for a rare December wildfire," CNBC, January 1, 2022, https://www.cnbc.com/2022/01/01/how-climate-change-primed-colorado-for-a-rare-december-wildfire.html.

Elizabeth Koh, "After Irma deaths, 60% of nursing homes still don't have 4 days of backup power for AC," *Miami Herald*, August 30, 2019, https://www.miamiherald.com/news/weather/hurricane/article234502422.html.

EM-DAT: The International Disaster Database, Center for Research on the Epidemiology of Disasters, Université Catholique de Louvain, School of Public Health, Brussels.

"Facts & Figures," American Health Care Association/National Center for Assisted Living, https://www.ahcancal.org/Assisted-Living/Facts-and-Figures/Pages/default.aspx.

"February 2021 Winter Storm-Related Deaths—Texas," Texas Department of Health and Human Services, Medical Operations Center's Disaster Mortality Surveillance Unit, December 31, 2021, https://www.dshs.texas.gov/sites/default/files/news/updates/SMOC_FebWinterStorm_MortalitySurvReport_12-30-21.pdf.

Gillian Flaccus, "Oregon heat wave victims older, lived alone, had no AC," Associated Press, July 13, 2021, https://apnews.com/article/canada-environment-and-nature-oregon-heat-waves-76bb82bebd17c6bef7fd8af97c311984.

Governor Gavin Newsom statement after vetoing Senate Bill 1207, September 25, 2020, https://www.gov.ca.gov/wp-content/uploads/2020/09/SB-1207.pdf.

Howard Gleckman, "What We Don't Know—But Should—About Assisted Living Facilities," *Forbes*, February 5, 2018, https://www.forbes.com/sites/howardgleckman/2018/02/05/what-we-dont-know-but-should-about-assisted-living-facilities/?sh=77326678e043.

John Ryan, "2021 heat wave is now the deadliest weather-related event in Washington history," *KUOW Radio*, July 19, 2021, https://www.kuow.org/stories/heat-wave-death-toll-in-washington-state-jumps-to-112-people.

Jorge L. Ortiz, "'Absolute nightmare': 4 former Florida nursing home staffers charged in 12 Hurricane Irma deaths," *USA Today*, August 27, 2019, https://www.usatoday.com/story/news/nation/2019/08/27/florida-nursing-home-hurricane-irma-4-charged-12-deaths/2136076001/.

Martin Espinoza, "Legislature passes bill inspired by abandoned seniors during 2017 wildfires," *Press Democrat*, June 10, 2019, https://www.pressdemocrat.com/article/news/legislature-passes-bill-inspired-by-abandoned-seniors-during-2017-wildfires/?sba=AAS.

Mary Ellen Klas, "Nursing-home industry agrees to install generators, but wants more time," *Miami Herald*, September 22, 2017, https://www.miamiherald.com/news/weather/hurricane/article174814631.html.

Molly Peterson, Lisa Pickoff-White, April Dembosky, and Danielle Venton, "Even After Care Homes Abandoned Residents, California Still Isn't Ready for Wildfires," KQED, August 10, 2020, https://www.kqed.org/science/1968076/even-after-care-homes-abandoned-Residents-california-still-isnt-ready-for-wildfires.

Nadja Popovich and Winston Choi-Schagrin, "Hidden Toll of the Northwest Heat Wave: Hundreds of Extra Deaths," *New York Times*, August 11, 2021, https://www.nytimes.com/interactive/2021/08/11/climate/deaths-pacific-northwest-heat-wave.html.

Patrick Svitek, "Texas puts final estimate of winter storm death toll at 246," *Texas Tribune*, January 2, 2022, https://www.texastribune.org/2022/01/02/texas-winter-storm-final-death-toll-246/.

Residential Care Facilities for the Elderly: Emergency and Disaster Plans, Cal. Health & Safety Code § 1569 (1985), *amended by* AB 3098 (2018), https://legiscan.com/CA/text/AB3098/2017.

Staff, "14th Person Dies After Nursing Home Lost Power In Irma," *CBS News Miami*, October 9, 2017, https://www.cbsnews.com/miami/news/nursing-home-hurricane-irma-hollywood-florida/.

Star Harvey, "The 2021 Texas Freeze: A timeline of events," *CW39 News*, February 16, 2022, https://cw39.com/news/local/the-2021-texas-freeze-a-timeline-of-events/.

"State Partners," Argentum, https://www.argentum.org/about-argentum/state-partners/.

Stephanie Pappas, "Quad-State Tornado May Be Longest-Lasting Ever," *Scientific American*, December 14, 2021, https://www.scientificamerican.com/article/quad-state-tornado-may-be-longest-lasting-ever/.

Tom Di Liberto, "Astounding heat obliterates all-time records across the Pacific Northwest and Western Canada in June 2021," National Oceanic and Atmospheric Administration, June 30, 2021, https://www.climate.gov/news-features/event-tracker/astounding-heat-obliterates-all-time-records-across-pacific-northwest.

Western Regional Climate Center, Monthly Climate Summary for Boulder, Colorado, for period August 1, 1948, to December 31, 2005, https://wrcc.dri.edu/cgi-bin/cliMAIN.pl?coboul.

Washington State Department of Health, "Heat Wave 2021: Data Tables," https://doh.wa.gov/emergencies/be-prepared-be-safe/severe-weather-and-natural-disasters/hot-weather-safety/heat-wave-2021#heading88458.

EPILOGUE

Interviews

Beth Eurotas-Steffy, daughter of Alice Eurotas; Melissa Langhals, daughter of Virginia Gunn; Kathy Allen and Mark Allen, daughter-in-law and son of Helen Allen; Ruthie Kurpinsky, daughter of Ruth Callen; Dawn Ross, daughter of Bill and Wanda Lee; Sarah Minson and Sherry Minson, granddaughter and daughter of Bess Budow; Elizabeth Bruno; Bob Mitton and Mimi Vandermolen; Michael Kulwiec, son of Len Kulwiec; Noella "Nell" Magnuson; R.J. Kisling, grandson of John Hurford; Andre Blakely; Michael Rodriguez; Nathan Condie.

Published Material and Other Sources

Andrew Graham and Ethan Varian, "Gallaher companies to pay $500,000 to settle claim from whistleblower who alleged affordable housing fraud," *Press*

Democrat, August 21, 2021, https://www.pressdemocrat.com/article/news/
gallaher-companies-to-pay-500000-to-settle-claim-from-whistleblower-
who-a/.

Andrew Graham and Ethan Varian, "Sonoma County Civil Grand Jury
calls for stronger oversight of affordable housing compliance," *Press
Democrat*, June 28, 2022, https://www.pressdemocrat.com/article/news/
sonoma-county-civil-grand-jury-calls-for-stronger-oversight-of-affordable-h/.

Andrew Graham, "Bill Gallaher's son arrested on suspicion of
grand theft from Poppy Bank," *Press Democrat*, September
17, 2021, https://www.pressdemocrat.com/article/news/
bill-gallahers-son-arrested-on-suspicion-of-grand-theft-from-poppy-bank/.

Andrew Graham, "Bill Gallaher's son charged with felony theft for
allegedly stealing from Poppy Bank," *Press Democrat*, January
10, 2022, https://www.pressdemocrat.com/article/news/
developers-son-charged-with-felony-theft-for-allegedly-stealing-from-poppy.

Will Schmitt, "Developer Bill Gallaher sues Santa Rosa over natural gas ban as city doubles down on climate goal," *Press Democrat*,
January 17, 2020, https://www.pressdemocrat.com/article/news/
developer-bill-gallaher-sues-santa-rosa-over-natural-gas-ban-as-city-double/.

ACKNOWLEDGMENTS

First and foremost, we would like to thank our spouses, Mason Belden and Tamara Gullixson, and our children, Asher and Wyatt Belden, and Christopher and Clara Gullixson, for holding down our forts, listening to new revelations, and excusing all the evenings, weekends, and holidays that we disappeared into "the book."

For their assistance at various stages in the book process, we'd like to thank Jeremy Hay, Robert Eversz, William Rohrs, Mark Fernquest, Melody Karpinski, Tyra Benoit, Margot Nassau, Mark Thiessen Oxford and Amie Glass. We owe a debt of gratitude to Ted Appel, Kent Porter, Martin Espinoza, and the staff and editors of the *Press Democrat*, whose Pulitzer Prize-winning reporting on the 2017 fires laid the foundation for much of our story. A special thanks to *Press Democrat* photographer John Burgess for the telling photo he shot on October 17, 2017, that became our book cover. Additional thanks to Donald Laird for the expert drone photos, Roberta MacIntyre for videotaping the reunion, Dennis Bolt for our maps, and our attorney, Thomas Burke of Davis Wright Tremaine, LLP in San Francisco, for his careful and pain-staking review of our manuscript.

We greatly appreciate the support of our agent, Jill Marr, and publisher, Jacob Hoye, who believed in this project from the start and graciously granted us the time to do it right, as we juggled day jobs, the pandemic, more catastrophic Sonoma County fires, and our own challenges with caring for aging parents.

We especially want to thank our contributing editor, Lauren A. Spates, along with her accommodating husband, Dan, and daughter, Beatrice, for all the time, insight, and expertise she provided this project. We appreciate how she always managed to keep the big picture in mind, even when she had to pull us out of the weeds to see it.

Finally, we realize this book wouldn't exist without the residents, rescuers, caregivers, family members, former employees, and others who entrusted us to chronicle this story—your story. We know that many of you set aside your own trauma to do so, and we sincerely hope *Inflamed* will provide what many of you have desired from the start: truth, accountability, and reforms to make sure history doesn't repeat itself. Thank you for helping us piece it all together and, to the best of our ability, tell it like it happened.

ABOUT THE AUTHORS

Anne E. Belden runs the journalism program and advises the newsroom at Santa Rosa Junior College. During the 2017 Wine Country fires, she drove students into devastated fire zones to report on the disaster. Their work won numerous state and national awards and saw global syndication; Anne now instructs on how to cover wildfires. Before teaching, she spent eighteen years as a journalist, working as a reporter and editor on the *San Francisco Peninsula* where her news, feature, and investigative articles were recognized by the California Newspaper Publishers Association, San Francisco Peninsula Press Club, and Parenting Publications of America. Anne holds a bachelor's degree in mass communication from UCLA and a master's degree in media studies from Stanford University. She lives with her family on a Sebastopol ridgeline, from where she's had clear view of six past fires and has only had to evacuate once.

***

Paul Gullixson is communications manager for Sonoma County. He previously worked for thirty-seven years as a journalist, including as editorial director for *The Press Democrat* in Santa Rosa, where he played key roles in several team awards, including the 2018 Pulitzer Prize awarded to *The Press Democrat* for coverage of the October 2017 fires. He has also received numerous individual awards from the California Newspaper Publishers Association and the San

Francisco Peninsula Press Club and is a past recipient of the *New York Times* Co. Chairman's Award for editorial writing. Paul taught journalism for five years at Sonoma State University, serving as faculty adviser for the student newspaper, and later worked as associate vice president of strategic communications for the university. He lives with his family in east Santa Rosa where they have been repeatedly evacuated due to wildfires...but is thankful that their home has been spared so far.

***

Lauren A. Spates is a Sonoma County journalist with a degree from the University of Maryland Philip Merrill College of Journalism. A recent California Humanities fellow with work recognized by the California Newspaper Publishers Association, Lauren cowrote and produced *Chronic Catastrophe*, an NPR-syndicated podcast examining the toll of unrelenting natural disasters on Sonoma County residents' minds, bodies, and spirit. Lauren splits her time working both for Santa Rosa Junior College's journalism department where she supports the student news media operation, and from home where she cares for her lively, bicycle-loving preschooler. Lauren is a native New Yorker who lives in western Sonoma County's densely forested redwoods with her husband, their 4-year-old daughter, and their 11-year-old spaniel. 2021 was the first year in the previous four that they did not have to evacuate their home multiple times under the threat of wildfire.